I0031840

The Akan People

Volume II

THE AKAN PEOPLE

Volume I
A Documentary History

Edited by Kwasi Konadu

This first-of-its-kind collection
features a new array of primary sources
that provide fresh and nuanced perspectives
on the histories of the Akan peoples.

ISBN 978-1-55876-579-5

Akan Peoples
in Africa
and the Diaspora

A Historical Reader

Edited by

Kwasi Konadu

Markus Wiener Publishers
Princeton

Copyright © 2015 by Kwasi Konadu

Cover illustration: Ashanti yam ceremony, 1817. Reprinted from *Mission from Cape Coast Castle to Ashantee* (London, 1819; reprinted by Frank Cass, 1966), between pages 274 and 275.

All rights reserved. No part of this book may be reproduced or transmitted in any form or by any means, whether electronic or mechanical—including photocopying or recording—or through any information storage or retrieval system, without permission of the copyright owners.

For information, write to: Markus Wiener Publishers
231 Nassau Street
Princeton, NJ 08542
www.markuswiener.com

Library of Congress Cataloging-in-Publication Data

Akan Peoples in Africa and the diaspora : a historical reader /
edited by Kwasi Konadu.
    Volumes cm
 Includes bibliographical references and index.
 A two-volume anthology.
 ISBN 978-1-55876-586-3 (hardcover : alk. paper)
 ISBN 978-1-55876-587-0 (paperback : alk. paper)
 1. Akan (African people)—History—Sources. 2. Akan (African people)—
Social conditions—Sources. 3. Akan (African people)—Social life and
customs—Sources. 4. Africa, West—Social life and customs—Sources.
5. African diaspora—Sources. I. Konadu, Kwasi, editor of compilation.
 DT510.43.A53A46 2013
 305.8963385--dc23
                2013025434

Markus Wiener Publishers books are printed in the United States of America on acid-free paper and meet the guidelines for permanence and durability of the Committee on Production Guidelines for Book Longevity of the Council on Library Resources.

Contents

Preface

The Akan are among the most well known and most studied of all African societies—on the continent of Africa and in the diasporas spawned by transatlantic slavery and, in recent times, by choice. Their cultures, histories, and peoples fill the pages of over five thousand books and an even greater number of scholarly articles, in fields as varied as history, anthropology, archaeology, linguistics, agronomy, and the biomedical sciences. The Akan, a composite group of 25 million, are found predominantly in central and southern Ghana, and to a lesser extent in Ivory Coast (Côte d'Ivoire) and Togo, and its constituent members include Adanse, Ahanta, Akwamu, Akwapem, Akyem, Anyi, Aowin, Asante, Assin, Baule, Bono, Denkyira, Gyaman, Fante, Nzema, Twifo, and Wassa peoples. The Ghanaian homeland of these peoples lies at the intersection of the equator and the prime meridian, bordering Burkina Faso to the north, Togo to the east, Ivory Coast to the west, and the Gulf of Guinea to the south.

The archaeological evidence places the Akan (or proto-Akan) in the forest—at a latitude between 8.0 and 4.5 degrees north—for at least the past two millennia, and most foundational Akan societies self-identify as autochthonous throughout the forest and its peripheries. Cartographical evidence from European sources strengthens such claims for most of these societies. This is particularly so for those societies between the Tano and Volta rivers and from the coast to the forest fringe, which exhibited great historical continuity within those spatial parameters between the sixteenth and nineteenth centuries, notwithstanding migration, displacement, and shifts in polities. The foregoing suggests that Akan societies, and their historic forms of social (matrilineal) and political organization, developed in the distant past and have since shaped patterns of human activity in those societies.

Indeed, both within and on the periphery of the tropical forest heartland, the Akan are defined by a shared or composite culture. *Akan* is therefore used in this volume to mean the composite culture created by West African forest settlers (whoever they might have ultimately been) between the Bandama and Volta rivers from the southern coast to the northerly edge of the forest. It is defined by a distinctiveness in culture and spirituality reflecting a shared language, ethos, calendrical system, sociopolitical order, and traditions of origin, as well as a high degree of ideological conformity.

From at least the fourth century CE, the Akan created numerous states and confederations based largely on gold production, an agrarian culture, and local and regional commerce linked to Sudanic Africa and the Mediterranean world. Attracted by its gold, Europeans established their West African bases in the region they called the Gold Coast and built commercial relations with indigenous settlements along the Atlantic coast and in inland states such as Denkyira in the west, Asante in the central forest, and Akwamu in the east. As these states gained wealth from regional and European commerce, gold was surpassed in importance as a commodity by the trafficking in African captives to be used in the overseas European colonies in the Americas. Europeans established over 40 trading forts along 341 miles of the Akan-dominated coastline, thereby underscoring the importance of the region. The lessons learned from the rise and fall of numerous Akan states ultimately led to the development and expansion of the best-known Akan empire, the Asante Empire. Throughout their histories, the Akan have been innovators of sophisticated sociopolitical organizations and of material culture (e.g., Adinkra symbols, *kente* cloth), and have also produced notable figures such as the Pan-Africanist—and Ghana's first president—Kwame Nkrumah and Sub-Saharan Africa's first U.N. Secretary-General, Kofi Annan.

This first-of-its-kind collection provides fresh and nuanced perspectives on the histories of the Akan peoples and their engagement with the West African region and the broader world of Atlantic Africa.

A Note on Style (Asɛm bi)

This two-volume anthology contains works from many different historical periods, authors, and perspectives. I have tried to keep my editing and abridgment to a minimum in the interest of preserving tone and reflecting the historical context in which each work was written. In doing the translations and transcriptions for this volume, I have attempted as much as possible to remain true to both the flavor and meaning of the original text. I have tried to choose English words that are as close as possible to the Twi (Akan) or European language counterparts. In instances where it seemed essential to provide some further explanation or clarification, I have used brief and unobtrusive brackets. A number of the selections were substantially abridged due to space considerations, and most of the parenthetical references and all the footnotes were removed. Interested readers can find at the end of each volume the full citations of the original articles or the sources used.

Those familiar with the changing history of Twi (Akan) orthography will notice variations in the spelling of commonly (and not-so-commonly) used words—among others, *okomfo* and *ɔkɔmfoɔ, oman* and *ɔman, kese* and *kɛseɛ*, Ashanti and Asante, and Brong and Bono. With respect to proper names and Twi (Akan) language orthography, I have made a practice of rendering these as they appeared in the original texts and in all the essays by the contributors. Some Twi terms have different spellings, but because the contributors, and the sources herein, did follow a prescribed or consistent orthography, I hope readers will bear with us.

Introduction

In a talk given at a joint meeting with the Royal Commonwealth Society in 1966, and published as "A New Look at the History of Ghana" in *African Affairs*, Adu Boahen noted with pride a departure from the perspectives and history writing that characterized the period before the 1960s:

> My colleagues and I are now looking at [the history of Ghana] from the inside, that is, from the African standpoint. [My colleagues and I] . . . are now using sources which the earlier historians never used or even had access to. The three historians in questions [i.e., W. W. Claridge, W. E. F. Ward, and J. D. Fage] used only published sources mainly in English and some oral tradition. Now besides these, we have been exploiting unpublished documentary material not only in English but also in Dutch, Danish and Portuguese. Secondly, we are also now relying very heavily on Arabic sources written mainly in northern Ghana by Ghanaians themselves. This particular source whose richness is now becoming obvious has been hitherto virtually ignored, and it is this neglect that accounts not only for the fact that northern Ghana has received only scant attention in existing history books but also for the erroneous but widely held view that literacy was first introduced into Ghana by European missionaries. In addition to these documentary sources, we are also using evidence provided by such disparate disciplines as archaeology, linguistics, ethnography, and even ethno-musicology, all of which had hardly got off the ground in Ghana even by the time of Fage [in 1961].[1]

---

[1] Adu Boahen, "A New Look at the History of Ghana," *African Affairs* 65, no. 260 (1966): 213.

The 1960s and early 1970s was, indeed, an important period of African historical research in Ghana and elsewhere, and there was new value placed on sources and on the origins of West African peoples, especially from historians within African societies. In Ghana, Adu Boahen was at the forefront of this moment and his access to the new crop of sources made him one of the first historians of the period to interrogate those sources, hoping they would disclose insights into Akan origins. The first five essays in this collection deal with this question of Akan origins and the problems posed by it from documentary, linguistic, archaeological, oral-historical, and anthropological perspectives.

Adu Boahen, in "The Origins of the Akan," traces the question of Akan origins to Thomas E. Bowdich, a member of the 1817 British mission to Kumase who concluded that the Akan migrated or that their primary cultural traits were derived from ancient Egypt. Though dismissed by Boahen, the mythology which Bowdich insinuated has stubbornly persisted into the present, so much so that it was the topic of a recent essay by T. C. McCaskie entitled "Asante Origins, Egypt, and the Near East: An Idea and Its History."[2] Unlike Bowdich, however, Boahen placed the origins of the Akan "somewhere in the Benue-Chad region." As Kenya Shujaa has already noted in the first volume, Boahen was to later revise this hypothesis, a move occasioned, in part, by a range of new archaeological evidence becoming available. In the context of the archaeological record, the late Kwaku Effah-Gyamfi not only classified the corpus of oral narratives that place the Akan between the forest fringe and the coast as autochthones rather than as migrants but also postulated two main centers where the vast majority of the Akan would have originated, while concluding that many of the traditions of origin concerning holes and caves do point to authentic ancient settlement sites that require further archaeological investigation. Indeed, as James Anquandah argued some time ago, archaeology has become a vital recourse for the reconstruction of the history and culture development of the Akan; archaeology, however, can only provide a partial picture of

2. See T. C. McCaskie, "Asante Origins, Egypt, and the Near East: An Idea and Its History," in Derek R. Peterson and Giacomo Macola, eds., *Recasting the Past: History Writing and Political Work in Modern Africa* (Athens: Ohio University Press, 2009), 125–48.

the past, and as such, concerns about matters of origins and "ethnic" or linguistic nomenclature continue unabated. The late archaeologist David Kiyaga-Mulindwa takes up this matter in "The 'Akan' Problem," and in that essay argues that the generally accepted definitions of "Akan" confound our historical understanding of the region they inhabited before 1400 CE, and that our failure to recognize shifts in usage and meaning of the term "Akan" has contributed much to this confusion. In the end, according to Kiyaga-Mulindwa, the term "Akan" obscures the processes through which various groups that came to be called "Akan" have reworked diverse cultural forms toward more general patterns.

In the debate about Akan origins, there are no last words on the topic. Only recently has the debate been revived in a lively and important exchange between anthropologist A. Norman Klein and historian Ivor Wilks. Using the medium of a review essay, A. Norman Klein's "Slavery and Akan Origins?" focuses on the first three chapters of Ivor Wilks's *Forest of Gold*. These chapters outline Wilks's reconstruction of Akan origins and state formation, as well as a reconstruction that, according to Klein, has attained the status of "universal acceptance" or "academic myth." Klein further argues that important scholars "are among the numerous students of Ghanaian history and prehistory who have uncritically repeated Wilks's argument that foreign slaves generated a food-producing revolution and a population explosion in the fifteenth through seventeenth centuries, resulting in the formation of the Asante state at the close of the seventeenth century." For Wilks's part, his response boils down to Klein's "major misunderstandings" and his "highly insecure" grasp of Wilks's thesis. In the end, Wilks remained unconvinced of Klein's reading of his thesis and the evidence used, and "only wish[ed] he [Klein] had read what I [Wilks] have written a little more carefully." The last exchange between the two saw a very brief response from Klein where he accused Wilks of "hiding behind a semantic fog" and that Wilks's "wordplay" and clouding of the "issues" would be addressed in an essay subsequently published in the journal *Africa* (London). Wilks's last words on the matter—essentially, a reaffirmation of his thesis—appeared in print in 2003 and again in 2005.[3] Though neither hypotheses nor informed speculations will resolve the vexed question of Akan origins, scholars who have combined a range of sources and disciplines in their work have produced some of the most substantial interpretations of early Akan societies, conceding, at least implicitly, that the ultimate origins of the Akan is as obscure as most peoples' temporal origins.

Antecedent Histories and Akan Historiography

The next set of essays leaves the matter of origins and takes up the task of explicating the socio-economic and political histories of early Akan societies in a rather vague era most historians call "pre-colonial." Sam Spiers's "From European Contact to the Komenda Wars: The Eguafo Kingdom during the Height of the Gold Trade" offers readers a detailed account of Eguafo's rise to prominence at the height of the sixteenth century gold trade and its eventual marginalization by the eighteenth century. In that account, Spiers, an archaeologist, uses a range of non-archaeological sources to chart the social, economic, and political history of the Eguafo Kingdom from the late fifteenth century to the close of the seventeenth century. Like Eguafo, the Akani profited from the burgeoning gold trade in the seventeenth century and came to exercise great influence as a result. In the next essay, "Zones of Exchange and World History: Akani Captaincies on the Seventeenth Century West Afrcican Gold Coast," Ray A. Kea places the seventeenth century Akani

---

3. For Klein's essay in Africa, see A. Norman Klein, "Toward a New Understanding of Akan Origins," *Africa* 66, no. 2 (1996): 248–73. On Wilks's most recent statements, see Adu Boahen et al., eds., *"The History of Ashanti Kings and the Whole Country Itself" and Other Writings by Otumfuo Nana Agyeman Prempeh I* (New York: Oxford University Press, 2003), 85; and Ivor Wilks, "The Forest and the Twis," *Journal des Africanistes* 75, no. 1 (2005): 19–75, and online at http://africanistes.revues.org/188. Recent critiques of Wilks's Akan origins thesis can be found in Gérard L. Chouin, "The 'Big Bang' Theory Reconsidered: Framing Early Ghanaian History," *Transactions of the Historical Society of Ghana, New Series*, 14 (2012): 13-40; Kwasi Konadu, *The Akan Diaspora in the Americas* (New York: Oxford University Press, 2010), chap. 2, esp. 27–30; and Gérard L. Chouin and Christopher R. DeCorse, "Prelude to the Atlantic Trade: New Perspectives on Southern Ghana's Pre-Atlantic History (800-1500)," *The Journal of African History* 51 (2010): 123-145.

gold trade and its organization within a world history context. The attention given to Eguafo and the Akani are justly deserved—the histories of these societies have not been probed sufficiently, or in the context of world and so-called Atlantic world history.

Staying in the seventeenth and eighteenth century, the next three essays focus on the neglected histories of Sefwi, the expansionist history of the Fante, and disconcerting issues that still plague Akan historiography. Very little has been written about the "pre-colonial" history of Sefwi, and equally little attention has been devoted to the historical study of the region. In "A Precolonial Political History of the Sefwi Wiawso *Oman*," Sefano Boni notes the lack of documentation for the Sefwi area, but is able to skillfully map the early history of Wiawso— the largest of the three Sefwi polities—through an assortment of documented and oral historical sources. As a bonus, Boni offers a reflection on his archival and field research over the years in the Sefwi area. Though somewhat reflective, Pierluigi Valsecchi's "State Formation and Intercommunal Alliances in the Gold Coast" examines some of the crucial issues that have characterized historical research into the Akan region. Therein, Valsecchi argues that the historiography of Akan societies needs to go beyond the confines of restricted political and historical entities or specific "ethnic" realities, and focus on the networks of relationships operating across the entire region. Whereas Valsecchi makes the case against an "historiography dominated by Asante," James Sanders, in "The Expansion of the Fante and Emergence of Asante in the Eighteenth Century," assesses the relative importance of Asante influence in the consolidation of the Fante in the eighteenth century and suggests that Fante conquest of its coastal neighbors and its trade dominance were not the result of Asante activities on the coast, but rather were linked with the presence of the English, who supplied firearms to the Fante. Indeed, the Fante polities were capable of acting on common interests and forging local political alliances, though constrained to maintain good relations with Asante because they were determined to be the exclusive middlemen for the enslaved captives that came down from Asante and beyond.

Empire State and the Colonial Context

The next set of essays takes us into the nineteenth and twentieth centuries, with each essay attempting to tackle a set of thematic issues in
Asante and other Akan societies in the context of Gold Coast ("colonial") history. Ivor Wilks's "Asante at the End of the Nineteenth Century: Setting the Record Straight" addresses the received versions of
Asante's passage from independent nation to colonial dependency and
argues that these accounts are in need of very significant revision, since
Asante was brought into the British Empire by political intrigue rather
than military conquest, and the supposed Anglo-Asante war of 1900
(the "Yaa Asanetewa War") was in fact an Anglo-Kumase war, as Asante divisions beyond Kumase remained for the most part uninvolved.
By 1901, Asante and other Akan societies were under British colonial
rule and, though international and domestic enslavement had been abolished, the latter persisted as "the meaning of people and land ... shifted
to economic resources in the twentieth-century."[4] It is in this context
that Kwabena Opare Akurang-Parry's "Slavery and Abolition in the
Gold Coast: Colonial Modes of Emancipation and African Initiatives"
may be appreciated, for it reevaluates the British-Indian model and other
modes of emancipation, discussing how some of those modes became
vehicles of freedom and why others paled into insignificance. Akurang-
Parry offers a detailed analysis of slave and pawn desertions and the alteration in the British-Indian model, and, more importantly, pays
specific attention to African responses and initiatives in the emancipatory process.

   Though matters of domestic slavery and emancipation were important in shaping nineteenth and twentieth century Akan societies, key
concepts related to ritual and family life also remained central. The concept of *mmobomme* is the focus of Adam Jones's "'My Arse for Okou':
A Wartime Ritual of Women on the Nineteenth-Century Gold Coast."
In it, Jones discusses a ritual called *mmobomme* that was practiced in
times of war among Akan women in southern Ghana and eastern Côte

---

4. Konadu, *The Akan Diaspora*, 89.

d'Ivoire. Though most of the features of *mmobomme* can be currently observed, the function and meaning of these phenomena have probably changed over time, given the difficulty interpreting what is written of this ritual in nineteenth century documents.

Documents have always posed their own specific challenges, but they often, in spite of their limitations, provide the only fragments or clues the historian has. While sifting through archival documents, Jean Allman was struck by the term *ntamoba*, a concept seemingly central to a "web of obligations, responsibilities and rights which bound a matrilineage (*abusua*) to the husbands/fathers of its members." In "Archival Fragments: *Ntamoba* and the Political Economy of Child-Rearing in Asante," Allman notes that if *ntamoba* had been central to defining and mediating the economy of childrearing in "pre-colonial" Asante, its disappearance in the late nineteenth and early twentieth century provides important clues to the ways in which family economy in Asante was transformed over the past century.

Nexus: Akan and African Diasporas

In the last four essays, the past and the future in Akan studies are central. In the late Susan Benson's "Connecting with the Past, Building the Future: African Americans and Chieftaincy in Southern Ghana," the author grapples with the effects of a deliberate and explicit innovation in Ghanaian traditions of chieftaincy: the incorporation of non-Ghanaians, especially African Americans, into Akan institutions of chieftaincy. Benson notes that many such individuals have been enstooled as *nkosohene* ("progress" or "development" chiefs)—a title initiated in 1985 by Asantehene Opoku Ware I and adopted widely—and though public opinion in Ghana is sharply divided on the usefulness of this involvement, the broader question of building effective, collaborative relationships between diasporic Africans and those on the continent remains an integral part of such innovations and the debates occasioned by them. The themes of diaspora and "development" also form the axes around which the next essay by Lynda R. Day revolves. In 2000, the centenary commemoration of the anti-colonial war led by Yaa Asantewa in 1900 was launched both to honor her memory and to boost the tourist industry in the Ashanti Region. In "What's Tourism Got to Do With It? The Yaa Asantewa Legacy and Development in Asanteman," Day asserts that while the tourist-development effort initiated new configurations of local cultural maps, the future success of tourist development will require the elaboration of new global cultural linkages connecting the people of the Ashanti Region and the diasporic Africans, who compose a growing percentage of visiting tourists.

The issues about which both Benson and Day speak are part of a process one might call "diaspora discourses." In the next essay, Konadu's "Diaspora Discourses" looks thematically at cultural and diasporic issues in the Akan experience in North America and at the uneven dialogue between diasporic Africans and Akan people from Ghana. The claims that both diasporic Africans and Akan people make to culture and diaspora constitute the crux of that internal dialogue. At a crossroads where diasporic Africans are adopting Akan cultural and spiritual practices and seeking the right to an ancestral adobe, Akan persons in Ghana are increasingly undergoing Christianization and are leaving for North America and parts of Europe. These phenomena associated with the Akan diaspora, Konadu argues, suggest that the study of a composite African diaspora must be one of ongoing movement—viewed as histories without closure—but at a new level of internal dialogue amongst Africa-based and diasporic African communities.

In T. C. McCaskie's "Asante History: A Personal Impression of Forty Years," he focuses on his forty years of involvement with Asante history, reflecting on the past and future of Akan history/studies as well as on a people, place, and past that have dominated his entire career as a historian. In this mode, McCaskie's own experience is central and, justifiably, it is used as a basis for broader commentary that has implications for the future of Akan and African history.

Together, these essays provide new and nuanced perspectives on an African people, their pasts, and on a present that is increasingly being shaped by interactions between Africa and its diasporas. This collection of critical essays, and its preceding volume of primary sources, resoundingly says that Akan history in particular and studies on the Akan in Africa or the diaspora are still very much relevant. Indeed, in the two-volume collection of sources and perspectives from the historians who use them, much of Carl C. Reindorf's historical vision is redeemed. Students of Akan studies will find an invaluable resource, and Akan and Ghanaian peoples may be encouraged, like Reindorf, to also think "it is most desirable that a history [or histories] of [Ghana] and its peoples should be written by [those] who [have] not only studied [their own history], but [have] had the privilege of initiation [via their culture] into [that] history."[5] To be sure, much work remains for the Akan and those who study them, but the reader who has come this far can be justifiably assured that this collection places the student, scholar, or interested reader on a solid footing.

---

5. Carl Christian Reindorf, *The History of the Gold Coast and Ashanti* (1895, 1966), iv.

The Origins of the Akan

A. ADU BOAHEN

The late A. Adu Boahen was one of Ghana's and Africa's pre-mier historians of the twentieth century. He was professor of history at the University of Ghana at Legon and the author of Britain, the Sahara, and the Western Sudan, 1788-1861 *(1964),* Topics in West African History *(1969), and* African Perspectives on Colonialism *(1989), and the editor of* UN-ESCO's General History of Africa, vol. 7: Africa under Colonial Domination, 1880-1935 *(1990). In the essay below, originally published in 1966, Adu Boahen argues that the proto-Akan peoples originated somewhere in the Benue-Chad region and migrated to their present location in the dense, forested area of what is now southern Ghana.*

The Akan are in many ways, the most interesting of the peoples of modern Ghana. Ethnically, they constitute well over forty percent of the entire population of the country. Geographically, they dominate about two-thirds of the area of Ghana, and occupy the areas between the Black Volta and the Guinea coast. Culturally, they are also the dominant group. The colorful Kente cloth, which is Ghana's trademark in the outside world, is Akan and if ever Ghana is to have her own *lingua franca*, it will almost certainly be Twi, the language of the Akan. Who then are the Akan and where did they originate?

The Akan are those groups of peoples in Ghana among whom a number of identical or virtually identical cultural traits and institutions are found. The first of these unique traits is linguistic. All the Akan groups speak the Twi language, or dialect of the same that are mutually intelligible. This language belongs to the Kwa sub-family of Niger-Congo, a sub-family to which Ewe, Ga-Adangbe, Fon, Yoruba, Nupe, Edo and Ijo belong. The second common trait is institutional. All the Akan groups have a common calendar, common religious beliefs, naming ceremonies, and marriage institutions and matrilineal systems of inheritance. They also have a monarchical system of government.

In many ways, the most interesting of these common institutions are their identical exogamous matrilineal and patrilineal clans. Each genuine Akan group is divided into eight principal matrilineal and eight patrilineal clans. The former and their moieties are Ekoona and Asokore, Oyoko (Anona in Fante) and Dako, Asona and Toa, Bretuo (Twidan in Fante) and Tena, Asakyiri and Amoakaade, and Aduana and Atwea and Aberade. The principal patrilineal groups are Bosommuru, Bosompra, Bosomtwe, Bosommaram, Nketia, Poakwa, Afram and Abankwaade. Not only do the same clans exist among all the Akan groups wherever they are found, but also what is more interesting, members of the same clan consider themselves as brothers and sisters irrespective of where they hail from. An Akyem who belongs to the Asona clan considers an Asante or Denkyera or Fante of the same clan as his or her brother, observes the same taboos with him, looks on the same animal as their totemic animal, shares funeral expenses with him, and cannot marry him or her. "And often," writes Mensah Sarbah, "doth the way lost weary sojourners in a most unexpected place through this relationship become the recipient of free hospitality." This practice whereby a Fante of the Aduana clan receives ready hospitality in an obscure village in Asante or Ahafo in the house of a fellow clan member is observed to this day. In other words, clan membership, affiliations and loyalties cut across [cultural] and political boundaries. The other fascinating thing about this Akan clan structure is that it gives a very important clue to the origins of the Akan states. All the Akan states that emerged in modern Asante—Twifo, Adansi, Denkyira, Fante etc—were, in the final analysis, the result of the imposition of the power of a lineage or a family belonging to one of these matrilineal groups, through either force or diplomacy, on the pre-existing peoples or states. Twifo, Akwamu and Saltpond were the creation of a lineage or family of the Aduana or Aberade clan, Denkyira that of the Agona, Mampong that of the Bretuo, Mankessim and Ejisu that of Asona, and the Asante Empire that of the Oyoko.

According to these linguistic and cultural criteria, it seems to me that the Akan are today the Asante, the Akyem, the Kwahu, the Akuapem, the Wassa, the Twifo, the Assin, the Fante and the Gomoa. The Guan, the Brong, the Sefwi, the Aowin, the Nzima, the Anyi and the Baule are not pure Akan for though their languages are very closely related to Twi they are not intelligible to the Akan except that of the Brong. Moreover, the patrilineal and matrilineal divisions as outlined above are not found among them. As I will show, the ancestors of all these peoples as well as those of the Akan are ethnically the same and must have lived together at one time in the same place. This accounts for the closeness of the present languages of their descendants that are considered by linguists as in fact branches of the Akan or Guan languages. However, is seems the ancestors of the Akan broke away from this group before their characteristic traits referred to earlier were evolved.

Where did these Akan originate? This question, it is interesting to note, has haunted scholars and historians since the beginning of the nineteenth century if not earlier, and different answers have been given to it. The first person to consider this question, as far as I know, is Thomas E. Bowdich, a member of the British mission sent to Kumasi in 1817. After comparing "the laws and customs of the Abyssinians, Ashantees, and ancient Egyptians," he concluded in a rather justifiably little known pamphlet published in Paris in 1821 that "most of the higher classes (of Ashantees) are descended from eastern Ethiopians who had been improved by an intercourse with the Egyptian emigrants and colonists." Dupuis who visited Kumasi three years later at the head of another British mission, on the other hand, traced the Akan to only northern Ghana from where they were driven southwards "by the believers in the early age of Islam." He considered Asante as "contrary to what may have been represented, the parent country, and the stock from which the early generations of Fantes and Dinkras sprung."

It is interesting to note that until 1925, none of the scholars who considered this question ever associated the Akan with ancient Ghana. They either supported Bowdich or Dupuis or hit on a third answer that the Asante originated from the Nile-Chad region. Both Beechman and Cruickshank who wrote their accounts in 1841 and 1853 respectively sided with Dupuis. Vice Admiral John Hay, who took part in the Sargrenti War, traced the Akan to "The banks of the mysterious Quorra or Niger." MacDonald, at one time Director of Education in the Gold Coast Colony, and, Reindorf both said in the 1880s and 1890s that the Asante were chased down south by "the advancing Mohamedan tribes or Moors." Finally, Claridge, Rattray and Buell after exhaustive research confirmed the northern origin of the Akan. Claridge traced them to "the open country beyond the forest belt and farther north than Salaga." In a letter to J. J. Williams, the author of *Hebrewisms in West Africa*, in October 1925, Rattray wrote, "All I can say so far about the origin of the Ashantis is that I feel sure they came from the North or North-West. They do not know this themselves, because all their myths record their origin as being from Ashanti proper." In the book referred to, J. J. Williams himself favored the Abyssinian origin of the Akan.

During the first three decades of this century when American and British anthropologists and ethnologists joined in this quest for the origin of the Akan, they tended to move the cradle eastwards, though not as far as Abyssinia. Using mainly linguistic evidence, Sir Harry Johnston concluded, "the Ashanti groups of Negroes once came from the Niger north of Yorubaland, in the Borgu country." Relying mainly on cephalic and nasal indexes as well as stature, a method very much in vogue in the early decades of this century, Dixon and Pittard, both American anthropologists, traced the Asante, in 1923, to the northeast, the region between the Chad and the Nile.

Three years later, however, a hypothesis was advanced for the first time by W. T. Balmer, a former headmaster of Mfantsipim School, which with varying modifications, has dominated the field ever since. "It is very probable," he tentatively suggested, "that the Fanti, Ashanti, Ahanta and Akan people in general formed originally part of this ancient Negro Kingdom (Ghana) dwelling in districts more or less remote from the central city of government, Walata." Since this was published, there have emerged three schools of thought on this question of the connection between the ancient Ghanaian Empire and the Akan. There is the school that subscribes to the hypothesis that the Akan came from Ghana though its members talk in terms of a migration from ancient Ghana to modern Ghana rather than of modern Ghana being part of the ancient Empire. This school includes J. C. de Graft-Johnson and J. D. Fage.

The former asserts quite categorically "There is little doubt that the Akan people migrated from somewhere in the Ghana Empire." Though Fage, in an excessively critical review of de Graft-Johnson's book in 1955, rejected this view partly because "Traditions of migration among the Akan-speaking peoples hardly point further to the north than the Niger Bend," he seems to have had second thoughts on the subject. In an article in the *Transactions of the Historical Society of Ghana* two years later, he virtually eats up his own words. In this article, he admits that there is "evidence of historical tradition which is extremely relevant to the idea of a migratory movement linking the Akan states with ancient Ghana," and concludes that the movement from ancient Ghana referred to by Delafosse of "pagan and Negro elements towards the south-east to Djenne" and the earlier movement referred to by Mauny from Djenne further to the south-east "in point of time ... could well be one, or at least in some way associated."

There is the second school of thought that admits the Akan-Ghana connection but traces the Akan even further northeastwards or eastwards. The two protagonists of this school are Eva Meyerowitz and the late J. B. Danquah. In a series of four books published between 1952 and 1961 Meyerowitz has concluded that Akan culture is not "Negro African in origin but could be classed on the whole as Libyo-Berber, more precisely perhaps as Libyo-Phoenician or Carthaginian, a civilization which owed almost everything to the Near East and Egypt." She is convinced that the ancestors of "the present Akan aristocracy were the descendants of Dia or Za (who originally came from Abyssinia or southern Arabia), Libyan Berbers and the Gara (originally of Kushite Stock) of the oasis of Djado in the Tibesti region who emigrated when the Arabs conquered North Africa and founded the Dia Kingdom on the Niger between Djenne and Timbuctu." From this kingdom, part of them conquered and ruled ancient Ghana while the rest of them moved south after Dia was conquered by the Islamized Berbers in 1009-10 and founded Bono and Kumbu. Both of these kingdoms were later destroyed and from Bono migrated the Fante, the Aguafo, and the Afutu, while from the latter emerged the Akan of today—Asante, Denkyira, Akyem etc.

Dr Danquah, on the other hand, traces the Akan not to eastern Sahara or Egypt or even Abyssinia, but further east still, to the valley of Tigris and Euphrates, the home of the Turanian people. In a radio talk given on March 7, 1957, he pointed out that the Akan as well as the Ewe, Ga, the Gonja and the Bantu are part of the Turanian people of Sumer and Akkad, and that their culture was Turanian. He went on to say that the immigration of the people of Ghana to Africa took place before 750 BCE, that they settled first at a place south of Libya where their name was Akane, that they left that place as a result of the Assyrian conquest of Egypt in 650 BCE and moved across the Sahara and established a kingdom between the Niger and South-Western Sahara in about 500 BCE, the kingdom which the Arabs named Ghana, "a semitic rendering of Akane." When the Almoravids conquered Ghana in 1076 the Akan and the other Negroes moved south again to "the golden land between the Comoe and the Volta Rivers." From there they began to move south in different waves. The first wave, he maintains, were the Nta people, some part of which call themselves Guan; the second wave were the Fante and the third the Asante, Denkyira, etc. In a series of seven articles and radio talks collected together by Danquah himself under the title "The Quest for Ghana," he advanced arguments to support his conclusions.

It seems then that though Danquah starts much further away, he ultimately catches up with Meyerowitz in the oasis of Djado and in double harness they cross the Niger together and break the tape together with Dupuis and his associates in the basin of the Ofin and the Pra. We should not, however, forget that there is a point where Danquah and Meyerowitz go out of step. According to the former, it was the Akan who founded Ghana, while the latter maintains, "there are no traditions which suggest that any group among the Akan came originally from Ghana" but rather that "there is a possibility that the founders of Ghana and the founders of the Akan kingdoms had a common origin."

A third school of thought is exceedingly critical of the claim that the Akan originated from the valleys of the Niger, or the Nile or the Tigris and Euphrates though its members do not advance any alternative hypothesis themselves. Exponents of this school include Ward, Tait, Goody, Mauny and Irwin. Ward was the first historian to challenge this Akan claim to origin from Ghana. After reviewing the evidence, he concluded, "There can be no question with our present knowledge of ruling out the Ghana possibility entirely; but I think the evidence is against it."

Ward was followed in 1953 by the late Tait who, in his review of Meyerowitz's *Akan Traditions of Origins*, found her argument "most unconvincing." In a similar review of Meyerowitz books and some of Danquah's articles, Professor Irwin concluded: "No dispassionate historian (or book reviewer) can do other than admit regretfully that, so far as the origins of the Akans are concerned, we are not out of the wood yet, that hypothesis has not yet given place to coherent theory, much less to certainty, and that the verdict on Mrs. Meyerowitz's latest book, as indeed on its predecessors must be: Not proven." The most outspoken critics of Balmer, Meyerowitz and Danquah, have, however, been R. Mauny and J. R. Goody. The former did not consider "these assertions of a connection between the Akan and, Ghana as being worthy of serious consideration," though he admits that the Akan tradition of ancient relations with Dia, is worth consideration, and that it is in that direction that "one must look for possible connexions between the Empire of Ghana and the Gold Coast." Goody's conclusions were equally critical though no less negative—"I do not wish to imply," he wrote "that there have been no connexions between the present state of Ghana and the medieval kingdom of the same name, even with North Africa and the Near East. There certainly have. However, to interpret the Akan peoples in terms of a wholesale migration from one place to the other is to disregard three basic facts: (1) that the Akan language is placed by all authorities among the languages spoken over the greater part of the forest belt of West Africa; (2) that the culture of the Akan speaking peoples has never been regarded by trained observers as being 'non-Negro,' indeed the religious institutions as described by Rattray, Busia and others have many parallels among the inhabitants ·of other parts of Africa south of the Sahara; and (3) that their physical characteristics are not noticeably different from other forest dwellers."

Now then the protagonists (whom I will hereafter refer to as the migrationists) of the theory that the Akan originated from either ancient Ghana, or the ancient Dia kingdom, or the oasis of Djado in Eastern Sahara, or Abyssinia or Babylonia based their contentions on three main grounds: oral traditions, linguistic similarities and cultural identities between the Akan and the people or region to which they happen to take fancy. Meyerowitz says she was told in Bono that their ancestors came from the Sahara; she contends that there is some similarity between the names of the Kormantse on the coast and the Garamantes of Herodotus, between Gonja which she insists is Guan-Dia, Guan being the same as Agwas or Gwa or Gua the name given to the Oasis of Djado by the Tuaregs of Air and Dia being the name of the ancient kingdom on the Niger as well as the name of one of the founders of the Zaga kingdom in the Oasis of Djado. Balmer claims that there is the similarity between the name Ghana and Akan, and that the coastal peoples told the Portuguese who arrived there in the fifteenth century that their ruler lived in Walata. Danquah also maintains that Akan was derived from Akkad and Ghana from Akan, that Su in the Sumerian language has the same meaning as the Akan *su* or *nsu* meaning "water" or "river," that *tu* means power in Sumerian language as in Twi, that like Turkish or Suomi, and Turanian, the Akan Language is agglutinative and that the suffixes *tu* or *ta* or *ti* commonly met with in the names of Akan and Bantu peoples are the same as *Tu* of the Turanian race. All the migrationists also harp on the cultural identities between the Akan and their own chosen people. Meyerowitz makes capital out of the divine kingship, identical belief concerning immortality, the influence of ancestors in human affairs, similar rules and ceremonies in connection with death, burial and transfiguration found among the ancient Egyptians and the Akan. Bowdich draws attention to the fact that human sacrifice, priesthood, the sacredness of the white color, drunkenness during festivals, pouring of libation, funeral customs, matrilineal succession, licentious conduct of women of the upper class, sandals and architecture are identical among the ancient Egyptians and the Akan. He sees the practice of the king speaking only through a linguist, kings attended by judges or civil authorities in war, the importance of provincial governors or kings, festivals such as the Yam Festival and the Markal, swearing on the kings head, the beginning of the year, as being identical among the Abyssinians and the Akan. Danquah on the other hand insists that most of these practices as well as Kwaku Ananse, the hero of Akan folk-tales, the Akan Planetary Forty-day Calendar and the Akan Adinkra symbols are all Turanian, and that the Akan did not borrow or copy or imitate them but they were part of the people who originated them, and carried them "to another clime and country."

The critics of the protagonists of this migration school base their stand on the fact that the oral traditions on which the migrationists hinge their conclusions are not confirmed among the pure Akan, that verbal similarities are a notorious trap, and that lexical comparisons can be regarded as satisfactory evidence of linguistic affinity only if they are truly mass correspondences, and finally that cultural likenesses could be interpreted at least in three ways only one of which is considered by the migrationists. They may be the result of diffusion either through migration or simply through contact in the course of trade or other modes of intercourse they may be the result of independent invention or as Dixon puts it "the inevitable outcome of ordinary human experience" and "the similarity might be due merely to chance and the basic unity of the human mind which confronted with similar conditions reacted to them in a similar way," or they may be due to the fact that both have a common cultural ancestor.

Overall, I side with the Tait-Mauny-Goody school of thought. Like them, I found the arguments of the migrationists unconvincing and their conclusions illogical. The very fact that all the earlier authorities, Bowdich, Dupuis and above all Rattray and Claridge never heard of or referred to the Akan-Ghana connection, that linguistically the Akan language is totally different from the Sarakole or Soninke language, that the Akan are true negroes and could therefore not have originated from the valley of the Tigris and historical times, that there is nothing like a "ruling aristocracy or higher classes" among the Asante or Akan and that the clan that constitute the ruling aristocracy in one Akan state might be a subject clan in the next state—all these considerations leave me in no doubt whatsoever about the emptiness of the claim that the Akan originated from Sumeria or Libya or Abyssinia or ancient Ghana.

Where then did they originate? The evidence of geography, as well as oral traditions, linguistics, serology and botany suggests four separate cradles for the ancestors of the Akan people: the Chad-Benue region, the area between the lower Volta and the middle Niger, the region between the Comoe and the Black Volta, and finally the basin of the Pra and the Ofin. It seems to me that the Akan like most of the West Africans and the Bantu began their evolution most probably in the region between the Chad and the Benue. From there the ancestors of the present

West Africans broke off and moved westwards across the Niger and settled in the area known to Geographers as the Dahomey gap, the area
between the middle Niger and the lower Volta. Another dispersion occurred from this center and some peoples moved across the Niger to
become the ancestors of the modern Ibo and Nupe; the ancestors of the
Yoruba migrated eastwards settling first in the savannah region to the
north and later moving into the forest regions of the modem Western
Region of Nigeria; a third group moved south-westwards leading to the
evolution of the Kwa-speaking peoples of the Ivory Coast and Liberia;
a fourth group moved south and south-eastwards to become the Fon,
the Ewe and the Ga-Adangbe; another group migrated westwards up
the valley of the Afram, skirted the forest region, and settled ultimately
in the region between the Black Volta and Comoe River, the region of
modem Tekyiman, Banda and Gyaman. In addition, the branch hived
off from this group and moved south into the forest region to settle in
the area of the confluence of the Pra and the Olin that developed into
the Akan of today. As I will show presently, it was in this region that
they developed the distinctively Akan institutions and culture, the Twi
language, the Akan Forty-Day Calendar, and the matrilineal and patrilineal clans already referred.

Now let us consider the evidence for this hypothesis beginning with
language since, as Kroeber said, language is the only part of man's culture in which regularities have been found. It is generally agreed among
linguists that the Twi language of the Akan belong to the Volta-Comoe
group, which in turn belongs to the Kwa sub-family of Greenberg's
Niger-Congo family. Since all these groups of languages are said to be
genetically related, it means that the ancestors of the original speakers
of each of these branches must at one time have lived together in one
region before dispersing. In other words, one should postulate a nuclear
people who spoke the Niger-Congo language from which the Bantu languages and peoples as well as the West Atlantic, Mande, Gur and Kwa
languages and their original speakers in West Africa evolved, another
nuclear Kwa-speaking people, which broke off from the first, and a third
nuclear Akan-Guan group and its descendant, a nuclear Twi speaking
group from which the Akan evolved. Where then did these various nuclear peoples live? Greenberg placed the nucleus from which the Bantu

languages evolved in the Central Benue River Valley, while Guthrie placed it in Central Africa. To reconcile the two views one could postulate a movement from West Africa so remote in time that it ought to be called pre-Bantu and not proto-Bantu, and that "a speculative hypothesis would be that the pre-Bantu were one group in the Lake Chad region." It seems then that one may place the original home of the speakers of the nuclear Niger-Congo language in the Chad-Benue region.

From archaeological and geographical evidence, it is clear that the ecological and environmental conditions of the region between the Chad and the valley of the Nile down to the middle of the third millennium BCE were the same and that there were considerable contacts between the peoples living in the areas. Indeed, according to Frankfurt, they all shared a common material culture, the Amratian culture, which "extended well into Libya and reached the Red Sea in the East," and he adds further "Pharaonic civilization arose upon this North-east African Hamitic substratum." It is not at all unlikely then that what Bowdich, Meyerowitz and Danquah classified as borrowings from ancient Egypt and Abyssinia as well as what Oliver and Fage describe as the basic elements of "Sudanic civilization," might well be due to this common substratum on which all these cultures were based. Since the art of writing was unknown among both the Eastern and Western Negroes, it is not unlikely that they began to disperse from this cradle south-eastwards and south-westwards before the invention of writing, and the dispersion might well have been due to the steady desiccation of the Sahara during the third and second millennia B[CE].

Clues to the possible cradle of the Kwa sub-family are provided by geographical and linguistic data. To the south of the savannah belt in which the cradle of the Niger-Congo nuclear peoples has been placed, the thick tropical forest stretches from the Gambia to the Congo. Most authorities are agreed that before the introduction of iron working and/or better yielding tropical crops from South-East Asia, at about the beginning of the Christian era the Negroes could not fully exploit the tropical rain forest. However, between Western Nigeria and Western Ghana, there is a gap in which, as Allison has pointed out, "the normal coastal belt of forest gives place to a wide corridor of savannah country which connects the coast with the savannah of the interior." This gap is not only the centre of the Kwa languages, but the home of what is supposed to be the oldest of that language group, the Togo Remnant languages. The Kwa languages are, moreover, in no way related to the languages dominant in Northern Nigeria, the Hausa and the Chadic languages that belong respectively to the Afro-Asiatic and central Saharan families. From all these considerations, it seems to me that the cradle of the speakers of the nuclear Kwa languages should be placed in the Dahomey gap.

That the Akan belong to the nuclear speakers of this group is borne out not only by the fact that their language is a member of the group, but also by two important traits common to nearly all the speakers of the Kwa languages. The first is the fact that with the exception of the speakers of the Kru and Lagoon languages in Ivory Coast and Liberia, all the others have, as Livingstone has shown, very high frequencies of sickle cell trait. Secondly, all the Kwa speakers, again with the exception of the Lagoon and Kru peoples, have yam, particularly the *Dioscorea Cayenensis*, either as their staple food or, where it has now ceased to be so, as a food with which certain rituals are attached. The Odwira of the Asante and the Akwapim and the Ohum of the Akyem are all connected with the harvesting of yam, while it is that foodstuff which is used when any Akan wants to "purify" his soul or "feed" his ancestors. Yam is of the same ritual importance among say the Kpe of the Cameroons. Furthermore, the major cultivation of yam is limited to the Kwa speakers. The traditional western limit of yam cultivation and the beginning of rice cultivation is the Bandama River in the Ivory Coast. This river, described by Christopher Fyfe as "a food frontier," is also the boundary between the low frequency and high-frequency occurrence of that sickle-cell trait common to many Kwa-speakers. If Livingstone's conclusions on the distribution of the sickle cell are acceptable, then the nuclear Kwa speakers must have lived in the "Dahomey Gap" for a very long time, for over two millennia. Since their dispersion was consequent on the coming of iron as well as the introduction or domestication of more food crops one could hazard the guess, first that the subsequent dispersion of the Kwa-speaking peoples must have been due to population explosion, and that this dispersion occurred not too long after these two new revolutions.

Where then did these Akan-Guan ancestors settle prior to their final dispersion? First, oral traditions among all the Akan and the Guan are virtually unanimous, as the earlier writers from Dupuis to Meyerowtz have shown, on the claim that the Akan came from the area to the north of forest zone, specifically from the Bono-Takyiman-Gyaman regions. Had the ancestors of the Akan of today entered the forest and coastal regions of modern Ghana directly, their language would most probably be closely related to Ga-Ewe-Fon cluster. On the contrary, Twi belongs to the sub-branch of the Kwa sub-family which includes Baule, Anyi, Brisa, Sanwi, Sefwi, Brong and Guan, most of which are (or used to be found) in the north. We do know from documentary sources, for instance, that the Baule and the Anyi moved southwards only during the seventeenth century. From oral tradition as well as from the linguistic situation, one may reasonably conclude that the ancestors of the speakers of the Akan-Guan languages skirted the forest regions westwards into the region of the Comoe River and the Black Volta and it is there that the characteristics peculiar to their present cluster of languages developed. Many historians now think that from this region, the new arrivals established not only commercial but also cultural contacts with the peoples who later founded the medieval Empires of Western Sudan, namely, Ghana and Mali. The cultural similarities that some observers have noticed between ancient and modern Ghanaian peoples may well be the result either of these contacts or the fact, already adverted to, that the cultures of the two peoples sprang from a common substratum at some very remote period.

The final southward move of the ancestors of the Akan into the forest region more than three thousand years ago may well have been the outcome of political upheavals in the region of the Niger bend, population pressure or greater economic possibilities. That it was in the forest region, in the region of the confluence of the Pra and the Ofin that the Akan as we know them today did finally emerge is borne out by a number of considerations. In the first place, Twi must have crystallized into its present form only after the migration of the ancestors of its present native speakers from the north. The second piece of evidence is the clan divisions already described. Meyerowitz's view of the presence of the clan divisions among the Brong is open to serious doubt. Rattray, a far

more reliable authority, stated in the 1920s that "Both Ashanti and Fanti
are generally considered to have immigrated from a common centre in
Northern Ashanti near Tekyiman, where the Brong, who are generally
thought to be of the same stock, still reside. I was surprised, therefore,
to discover that the pure Brong are apparently wholly ignorant of these
Ashanti and Fanti clan names, and that exogamous divisions seem based
upon an entirely different model.... There, such exogamous divisions
as appear to exist apparently take their names from the streets or quarters in the towns." This practice is found among the Guan to this day.
My own admittedly limited research has so far confirmed Rattray's
view. Rattray did consider this a problem but he was "unable satisfac-
torily" to solve it and therefore commended it to other students of Gold
Coast history. My own solution to this problem is that the Akan developed this clan system only after their arrival in the forest regions. There
are three grounds for this conclusion. First, most of the clans trace their
origins to the present Amanse, Adanse and Denkyira region, that is, the
basin of the Ofin and Pra Rivers and the heart of the Asante Empire.
The Ekoona say they hail from Adwafo in Adansi; the Bretuo say they
descended from the sky by a silver chain at Ahensan in Adansi, the Ase-
nee maintain that they descended from a bead called Berewua in Adansi,
while the Oyoko are fully convinced that they came from a hole in
Asumenya Asantemanso near Kumasi, and the Agona say they came
from Denkyira. While all these juicy details should be ignored, the significant fact is that all the places mentioned are found in Asante. Secondly, the names of the patrilineal groups that I have been able to
identify so far are names of rivers or lakes in Asante or Akyem. Bosomtwe is the lake about eighteen miles from Kumasi, Bosompra is derived from the River Pra that rises in Asante, Afram from the River
Afram that has its source in Asante, and Bosummuru, according to Rattray, is "a river in Akyem." Neither the Tano nor any of the rivers in the
north—the Volta, the Oti, the Comoe or the Bia—appear in the names
of the patrilineal clans. Thirdly, the totemic animals of the matrilineal
groups are either exclusively forest animals such as the grey parrot, or
animals that can live both in the forest and in the open savannah such
as the bat, the dog, the buffalo, the bush crow, the vulture, and the black
kite. Since some of these totemic animals are exclusively of the forest

region while there is none exclusively of the savannah region, one could suppose that the forest and not the savannah was the region in which they were collected.

The third unique possession of the modern Akan is their forty-day calendar with its weekdays named, according to Danquah, after the planets. Since this is not found among any of the Kwa or Niger-Congo peoples, I find it hard to accept Danquah's contention that the Akan brought it with them from Turania. Either they may have invented it independently or they may have borrowed it, like the Hausa, from the Arabs and adapted it to suit their festivals, systems of worship and seasons.

To conclude, it seems to me that the Akan are an integral part of the [Africans] of West Africa, that their ancestors originated somewhere in the Benue-Chad region and moved south-westwards, westwards and finally southwards into the region of Asante where they developed those institutions and cultural traits with which they are now so exclusively identified.

The "Akan" Problem

DAVID KIYAGA-MULINDWA

The late David Kiyaga-Mulindwa was former president of the Pan-African Archaeological Association and founder of the Archaeology program at the University of Botswana. He published important archaeological studies of the Birim Valley in Ghana.

Referring to the 19th-century travelers' accounts on Africa, [J. D.] Clark (1970) saw the diverse customs and economies of the African herdsmen, cultivators, and hunters these accounts recorded as providing an essential link between the prehistoric past and the new, independent Africa. Such a view recommends Africa as an archaeologist's paradise, with living examples of continuity, variation, and change in culture. It may, however, oversimplify the complexity of Africa. In the Birim Valley of eastern Ghana, for instance, one of the problems one identifies in considering the oral data and matching these data to the archaeological record is the identification of ethnic, political, and linguistic groups in the region's past. As this is considered further, it can be seen as a problem not merely in the interpretation of the Birim Valley data, but also in the reconstruction of the general patterns of settlement and cultural change in the region now occupied by the Twi-speaking peoples. When attention is given to the logic of discernment of various cultural groups denoted in traditions and in the literature, it becomes clear that considerable contribution could be made to the comprehension of the West African past through clarifying and rationalizing the terminology for cultural groups in the area. In attempting this rationalization, it becomes necessary to reconsider the terminology that has developed over time.

To someone familiar with the historiography of Ghana, the question

"Who are the Akan?" must seem overworked. It has been asked so often, and so many answers have been given, over a period of some 50 years of scholarship that a resurrection of the debate may seem an unrewarding exercise. Certainly, the majority of students of "the Akan" would agree that the discourse has reached a point where it is "your answer or mine." Nevertheless, one can still make a few comments, particularly in light of the fact that some of the generally accepted definitions of "Akan" confound our understanding of the history of the region in the period before 1400 CE.

The origin of the term "Akan" is obscure. The term has been appearing in print for over 400 years, and its usage has changed with time. Failure to recognize these shifts in usage and meaning has contributed much to the confusion that envelops the pre-15th-century history of the peopling of Ghana. The term "Akan," as it is generally used today, groups together large numbers of people who may now appear relatively undifferentiated but whose forebears—certainly before the 15th century—were of diverse origins and different cultures. The term "Akan" therefore obscures the processes through which various groups have reworked varied cultural forms toward more general patterns. Observers of Ghanaian peoples since the 15th century have contributed to this generalized usage of the term "Akan" by discarding, for the sake of coherence, any data reflecting variations. For example, Balmer says that his aim "has been to give the story in as connected a narrative as possible. . . . What has been *omitted of deliberate intent* is matter that, if preserved, would make African history a mere 'chronique scandalense.' Such stuff were best dropped clean out of mind." The general tendency in studies on the "Akan" has therefore been to emphasize similarities among peoples so designated with a view to proving their common origin. This has not only masked the structures of the pre-"Akan" communities—upon which later communities developed—but also disguised the process of change that these forest communities have experienced outside the more recent and analytical category of "Akan."

Diverse and often flawed concepts of "Akan" have infiltrated studies in history, anthropology, linguistics, and even geography. While there has been considerable discussion of "Akan" origins, arising particularly from critiques of the works of Meyerowitz, the debate has focused on the origins of the "Akan" as if everyone knew who they were. As a result, no voice has been raised questioning the application of the term "Akan." A consideration of the varying usages of the term therefore seems appropriate. The term "Akan" has, at different times, been used to denote *(a)* a race or "stock," *(b)* a language group or a people speaking those languages, and *(c)* a state, nation, or "tribe." Problems arise from this multiple usage of the term particularly when it is found in a single work. Herskovits warned against the confusion of physical form with cultural and linguistic usage, pointing out: There is, perhaps, no word that has been more loosely used in writings on Africa than the word "race." It has been used to designate tribal—that is, politico-cultural—groupings, as in the "Bemileke race" or the "Shona race." It is most notable misuse, perhaps, is found in the appellation "Bantu race," used to name a vast number of peoples who differ in physical type and culture, but speak languages that have certain features in common.

It is along these lines that a certain group of people has been defined, under the collective name of "Akan," as a race or "stock." [J. B.] Danquah for instance, says that "the Akim Abuakwa belong to the Akan racial stock." "This race," he maintains, "includes the Ashanti, Fanti, Akim, Akwapim, Assin and several of the present (Twi-speaking) 'races' of the Gold Coast and Ivory Coast." Elsewhere, Danquah (1928) suggests that Kotoko might have been the collective name of both the "Akan" and the "Fante" before they separated—the distinction between "Akan" and "Fante" being unclear. (One can only presume that he meant to distinguish the "Asante" from the "Fante.") Yet, in another place, he says, "Akan" means "the first race." Balmer also speaks of the various "tribes" of the "Akan race" occupying the lands of the west coast of Africa.

It is difficult to decide what was intended to be conveyed by the term "stock," but there is certainly no proof that the people called "Akan" today are in any physical sense a distinct race or even a discernible branch thereof, as both Danquah and Balmer would have us believe. The population of the region in no way differs, in physical terms, from other populations in West Africa. Any racial specification seems to arise solely from careless selection of descriptive terminology. Danquah's use of the word "race," as in "several of the present (Twi-speaking) 'races,'" brings this out quite clearly. One would think that the more appropriate term in this context would have been "ethnic group." (Probably this is what [Raymond] Mauny [(1954)] means by "ethnic stock.") "Tribe," freed from its derogatory connotations, might have been another suitable term, but now this term would be unusable in Ghanaian contexts. In any event, to use "tribe" for this broader category of population would cause analytical problems, for "tribe" has been used in the literature on Ghana to denote a particular polity—Akim Abuakwa, Denkyira Ashanti, Assin, Fante, Akim Kotoku, and so forth. The point here, however, is that the present-day population of southern Ghana does not constitute a distinct racial type within the family of man, nor, obviously, does any segment of this population constitute a "race."

One way people may refer to themselves or be referred to by others is by the language or dialect they speak. There has been a shift here, too, as far as usage of the term "Akan" is concerned. Sarbah (1968) talks of the "Akan language" as the parent language of Fante and the dialects spoken by the Wassa, Assin, Denkyira, and Akim. Linguistically, according to Westermann and Bryan (1970), "Akan" refers to a language group that is part of the Kwa subfamily of the Niger-Congo family of languages. In their scheme, the "Akan language group" consists of a Twi-Fante dialect cluster, an Anyi-Baule dialect cluster, and a Guang dialect cluster. They point out that "Akan was originally a collective name used to cover the inhabitants of Akwapem, Akem, Asante (Ashanti), Akwamu, and some other territories, but is now used by Europeans to denote the whole group of people speaking languages of this group, also known as 'the Akan-speaking peoples.'" They further remark that the name of this language, according to native speakers, is not "Akan" but *Twi kasa* (Twi language). While making this concession, they do not explain why they call the linguistic group "Akan." (They do offer such an explanation in the case of what they see as the larger linguistic family, Kwa, to which they say Twi belongs.)

This linguistic categorization implies that all these dialects or languages have a common origin and that their speakers are ethnically related. However, no writer has so far lent support to [John] Sarbah (1968) in considering "Akan" the ancestral language. [Akin] Mobogunje (1972), describing the Asante, presents them as "typical in every respect of the Akan-speaking peoples." [J. G.] Christaller (1881) saw "Akan" not only as a country or nation, but also as a language, though he used "Akan" in a very different manner from Mobogunje. While Christaller was meticulously consistent in using the term "Twi-speaking," where others might have used "Akan-speaking," he was of the opinion that "Akan" was a dialect of "Twi." [J. P.?] Brown (1929) seems to have supported Christaller here when he argued that "Akan" dialects are prevalent in Wassa, Mfantsi, and Akim and that "Akan," in its purest form, is spoken only in Akim country. All this is in contradiction to Westermann and Bryan's stand, which treats "Akan" as a much larger linguistic family containing within it dialect clusters of which the Twi-Fante cluster is just one.

Yet another group of writers has used "Twi" and "Akan" interchangeably. While most writers recognize "Twi" as a name of a language, Danquah remarked, "Twi is the ancient, almost forgotten, name of the Akan race or of a race originally wider . . . of which the Akan formed part." Danquah (1944) has argued that "Akan" comes from the word *okanniba*, which means "son of Akan," that "Akan" means "foremost" or "genuine," and that its root is *kan*, meaning "first," with a suffix *ni* meaning "person." (The language examined here is presumably Twi; Danquah does not say.) For this interpretation, he appears to have relied on Christaller. One suspects, however, that imaginative conjecture, as opposed to concrete historical or linguistic evidence, may have been employed here. Christaller (1881) defined *e-Kan* as "the first, foremost." He also defined *okanni* as "a man of Akan descent," a man speaking "the Akan or Tshi [Twi] language," and as a "nice, refined, well-mannered man." While Christaller was wrong in regarding "Akan" and "Twi" as synonymous in his first definition of *okanni,* his second definition of *okanni* as "a well-mannered man" may be quite acceptable. However, the interpretation that Danquah imposed on it seems far-fetched. According to field observations, Twi-speaking peoples, particularly the Akimfo and the Asantefo, still use the word *okanni* or *okanniba* in situations where a breach of morals and personal honor are concerned. They say, almost swearing, *"Me ye okanni,"* meaning "Look here, I am *okanni,"*—i.e., a genuine native as opposed to a stranger (*opoto-ni*) who does not know how to behave. The implication is "I am a native of this place, knowing all the morals and values of my people, and therefore not one to be suspected of unbecoming behavior." Thus, in Christaller's example, *okanni* is being used to distinguish a native, judging him by his behavior according to the accepted norms, from a stranger *(ohohoo)* or a slave *(odonko)*. It seems quite possible that the word *okanni* gained common usage with the increased appearance of strangers, possibly slaves, among the Twi-speaking peoples. What is implied here is the emergence of a new social category in a particular social and economic setting rather than a preservation of an ancient ethnic or family name of the sort of Adamic character that Danquah attaches to "Akan." But perhaps the real flaw in Danquah's etymology is his simply and uncritically considering the terms "Akan" and *okanni* as having the same root.

At a conference held in 1974 in Bondoku, Ivory Coast, the delegates reached consensus with regard to who should be called "Akan" and who should not. What they came up with was a definition, not for the term "Akan," but for a contemporary cultural group which they called "Akan." The strategy of definition focused on a list of cultural traits; if a significant number of these traits were noted for a particular group, that group qualified to be called "Akan." According to this analysis, the distribution of this cultural group covers most of the forest region of Ghana, about half of that of the neighboring Ivory Coast and some areas of the derived savanna zone to the north of the forest in both Ghana and Ivory Coast. Even if this distributional analysis were valid for the present-day situation (and, indeed, the strategy appears to be flawed by a certain circularity in trait selection), it would tell us nothing about the composition of the population of southern Ghana in the past. I feel that, with regard to the analytical logic and consistency of an internally derived "Akan," we have not advanced very far beyond Danquah and Sarbah.

The literature on the region also denotes "Akan" as a society. The records indicate that by the beginning of the 16th century there was a "tribe" called "Akan" settled in the interior of the Gold Coast. The term first appears in Pacheco Pereira's description of the various groups of people from the interior that frequented the coast to trade with the European seamen. Pacheco Pereira recorded that gold was "bartered from the negro who bring it thither from distant lands. These merchants belong to various tribes; the Bremus, Atis, Heccanys, Boroes, Mandinguas, Cacres, Andese or Souzoa and others which I omit." In this context, then, the Heccanys (Akans) were apparently one of the several distinct inland groups. Several of the groups that Pacheco Pereira mentions with the "Heccanys" would in today's usage be folded into "Akan" without further comment. Portuguese, Dutch, and English documents from the 15th, 16th, and 17th centuries make frequent mention of "Arcanny," "Akan," "Accanny," "Hecanny," "Heccany," or "Arcania" and also refer to the "Accanists" as a people—often as merchants. A 1502 war between Atis and "Akan" is mentioned, as are negotiations and the inauguration of trade between the Portuguese and "Akan" in 1517. Messengers from the "King of Akan" are reported as visiting the coast in 1519; presents were sent to the rulers of "Akan" in 1520, and a civil war among the "Akanis" was recorded in 1548. There is, however, an unexplained disappearance of "Akan" from the records, a gap which Boahen has noted, from the 18th century onward.

Several inland polities are denoted on the celebrated 1629 map of the Gold Coast, and accompanying notes indicate the distinguishing characteristics of the countries and their inhabitants. Among the peoples or states indicated are "Akanij," "Great Akanij," and "Akan." This, along with the clear distinctions made by the early Europeans between "Akan" and other peoples that are now also regarded as "Akan," points to the strong possibility that the application of the term was then strictly limited to specific groups. Historians have, of course, tried to identify the countries indicated on the 1629 map, but in the case of "Akan" there has been rather little agreement. Boahen (1973) has amplified the work of [Kwame] Daaku (1966) and brought in other evidence to conclude that Great Akanij, Akanij (elsewhere rendered as Akan *petit,* "Little Akan"), and Akan may be identified as Akim Abuakwa, Assin, and Akim Kotoku. At the same time he asserts that, while Great Akanij and Akan were kingdoms, Little Akan was not a kingdom, but a geographical region north of the Pra-Ofin confluence and south of the Kwisa Hills, and that it was this area that eventually came to be occupied by the Assin states of Atandanso and Ansa (now Apemanim).

Indeed, Great Akanij was also identified as Akim on the map. Quoting Heerman Abramsz's report of 1679, in which mention is made of "Akimse Akkanists," Boahen (1973) identifies this with the present-day state of Akim Abuakwa. He also refers to an oral tradition that Akim Abuakwa was emerging east of the Pra-Ofin confluence at that time, but he does not indicate which tradition. To identify Akim on the 1629 map, in a political sense, with Akim Abuakwa as we know it today would be to ignore the existing reconstructions of historical sequence. The oral tradition of the Akim Abuakwa ruling family of the Asona clan is very specific about the family's origins. It is said that they migrated from Adanse Kokobiate after the defeat of Adanse by Denkyira. They crossed the river Pra and settled in Akim. The story about their settling in Akim is supported by both the Asamankese and Akwamu traditions. Their leader was found by an Asamankese hunter, who led him to his chief. The chief, in turn, directed the newcomer to the Akwamuhene at Nyanaoase to ask for permission to settle. It would appear from these stories that the Akwamuhene was already well established in Nyanaoase, which is an indication that he was no longer vassal to the Ga Manche of Accra. Hence, there is good reason to place the entry of the Akim Abuakwa Asona paramount-stool family into Akim country in the period after 1680, certainly after the Abramsz report of 1679. The evidence at hand seems to negate the suggestion that Great Akanij of 1629 was the same as Akim Abuakwa, though Akim Abuakwa may have succeeded it.

Boahen's identification of "Akan" as Akim Kotoku also leaves much to be desired. He first equates Abramsz's "Cocoriteese Akan" with the present-day Akim Kotoku:

This is evident not only from the similarity between 'Kotoku' and 'Cocoriteese,' but also from the fact that though Akyem Kotoku is now situated south of Akyem Abuakwa with the modern town of Akyem Oda as its capital, it is quite clear from their oral traditions that in the sixteenth and seventeenth centuries Akyem Kotoku was rather in the area of modern Asante Akyem, that is, to the north of Akyem Abuakwa or Great Akani, with its capital town in the region of modern towns of Agogo and Bompata. According to Daaku, while they were there the Akyem Kotoku were known as 'Kwadukro' which sounds nearer to Cocoriteese than even Kotoku.

What Boahen implies here is that Abramsz, on hearing "Kotoku," or, even worse, "Kwadukro," wrote down "Cocoriteese." He therefore concludes, "There cannot be a shred of doubt, then, that Akan, shown north of Great Akan on the 1629 map and referred to as Cocoriteese, was Akyem Kotoku." It is difficult, first, to see any similarity between "Cocoriteese" and "Kotoku," "Cocoriteese" and "Kwadukro" (pronounced Kwad[j]ukro in Kotoku), or "Kotoku" and "Kwadukro." Two phrases—"which later became corrupted into" and "which came to be rendered by early European writers as"—have been used uncritically and unsparingly in Ghanaian historiography whenever people have been unable to explain the source or meaning of a certain place name or other term. Even to the most casual observer, however, such claims are obviously unwarranted by any of the possible linguistic shifts in Twi. One is reminded of similar linguistic inferences made by Danquah and Meyerowitz, of which [Jack] Goody (1959) has given historians sharp warning.

Second, to infer that the "Akan" shown north of "Great Akanij" on the 1629 map is the same as present-day Akim Kotoku is also questionable. The present location of Akim Kotoku is as recent as ca. 1865, and we now know that the stay of the early founders of Akim Kotoku at Gyadam in Akim Abuakwa was very short. Although Boahen is possibly correct in estimating the geographical position of "Akan" on the 1629 map to be equivalent to the area of present-day Asante Akyem, the Kotoku appear to have moved to Asante Akyem much later, during the mid-18th century, under an Asante order. In fact, present-day Akim Kotoku did not become known as such until its leader, then fugitive from Denkyira, "bought" the Kotoku lands from the people of Obuohie Kwai. This transaction appears to have been effected after the battle of Feyase (ca. 1699), which was also long after the 1629 map was made and after Abramsz's 1679 report. What Boahen's analysis misses is the complex intervening history of population movements and political geography in the region before the middle of the 19th century. The interpretation that "Akanij" was not a state, but a geographical region, while "Akan" and "Great Akanij" were polities is also untenable. This interpretation by both Boahen and Daaku (1966) appears to have been because there are no direct indications of any early state in this area before the arrival of the people of Assin from Adanse ca. 1659. What is either forgotten or deliberately overlooked in this interpretation is that there were several Etsi settlements in this area at the time of the Assin immigration and settlement. It is also overlooked that this area was between "Great Akanij" and Denkyira to the west. The several conflicts between these two peoples—for example, the war between "Akan" and Denkyira and another war between "Asante" and Denkyira in which some 3,000 "Akim" were killed (Bosman 1967)—may have been fought in this area, thus causing displacement of peoples and the disappearance of any states that might have been there earlier.

It is evident, therefore, that the term "Akan" has eluded precision of definition. Increasingly, it appears, the term has been used consensually, that is, on the assumption that the readers of a particular article or monograph know what is meant by the term even if no specific definition is provided. From the foregoing it is clear that more is implied by this term than is revealed. It is unfortunate that, over the years, the use of the term "Akan" has obscured the complexity of the social and cultural composition of the region in the ages or periods that preceded the more recent processes of regional unification.

In the absence of a recognition of the extent of influences or forces pressing toward cultural unity during the past two or three centuries, it is quite unlikely that clear and useful identifications and interpretations can be made of the physical remains left by peoples of an earlier time. Such identifications must rest on a specific and consistent terminology. This article is intended to unveil the complexity that has been folded into and lost within the loose concept of "Akan." It is also intended to provoke comments and suggestions that may stimulate research on the nature, if not the identity, of the societies that may have inhabited this forest region of southern Ghana prior to the 15th century.

Slavery and Akan Origins?

A. NORMAN KLEIN

After completing a dissertation at the University of Michigan in 1980 on the meanings of slavery and social servitude in Asante, A. Norman Klein taught in the Department of Sociology and Anthropology at Concordia University in Montreal for twenty-five years. In his review essay of Ivor Wilks's Forests of Gold *below, Klein argues that slavery was the "unifying idea" that informed Wilks's thinking on Akan origins and the Asante polity. According to Klein's reading of Wilks's "unifying idea," enslaved persons were imported (in exchange for gold) to clear the forest, and this led to a population boom, a "new class formation" led by "slave-owning entrepreneurs," and an agricultural revolution that initiated the formation of southerly Akan states. For Klein, this is an "academic myth" that has uncritically received wide acceptance. The backbone of Wilks's myth, according to Klein, is anachronism in that Wilks used nineteenth-century data, chiefly oral histories, to make fifteenth- and sixteenth-century interpretations; that is, Wilks "project[ed] well-known historical conditions into an unknown past."*

Ivor Wilks is the dean of scholars writing about the Asante of Ghana. His massive *Asante in the Nineteenth Century* (1975) has become the standard work. In a new book, *Forests of Gold: Essays on the Akan and the Kingdom of Asante*, Wilks updates and combines in a single volume expanded and revised versions of his most important papers on the Akan since 1975. The new collection covers a wide range of topics about Akan history. The first three chapters deal with the origins of the Akan of southern Ghana and the emergence of Akan states, up to the appearance of Asante at the close of the seventeenth century. Chapters 4 through 10 discuss mostly nineteenth-century Asante political culture, including a study of the symbolism of Asante wealth, social stratification, and power (chap. 4); an analysis of political conflict in late-nineteenth-century Asante (chap. 5); an original, imaginative essay explaining the Asante cognitive strategies of their own territorial and chronological reckoning (chap. 6); Wilks's contribution to a debate he initiated in 1975 on the meaning of human "sacrifice" in Asante, in which he ventures into what is for him new territory—Asante religious beliefs and the consequences of European missionaries' visits to Asante (chap. 7); and three studies of important military and political figures in nineteenth-century Asante that offer an updated view of Wilks's account of Asante political organization since 1975 (chaps. 8-10). The last essay is about a remarkable Asante woman, Akyaawa Yikwa[n], who was the principal negotiator, on the Asante side, of the Anglo-Asante Treaty of 1831.

I shall focus on the first three chapters, comprising more than one-third of the new book, because only Wilks's reconstruction of Akan origins and state formation has attained the status of universal acceptance, or academic myth. Wilks's willingness to republish his interpretation essentially intact, despite his claim to have "virtually rewritten" it, along with the fact that almost all of the data, with no substantive additions, have been available for sixteen years, testifies to his confidence in its reception. Such confidence is justified. Ray Kea, T. C. McCaskie, and Ann Stahl are among the numerous students of Ghanaian history and prehistory who have uncritically repeated Wilks's argument that foreign slaves generated a food-producing revolution and a population explosion in the fifteenth through seventeenth centuries, resulting in the formation of the Asante state in the late seventeenth century. In fact, by omitting any reference to Wilks's myth about Akan origins in the most severe and widest ranging attack on Wilks's work in print, McCaskie (1992) tacitly acknowledges its entrenchment.

The outlines of Wilks's narrative are well known to students of West Africa. For readers... who are not Africanists, however, the following is a review of his reconstruction. Slavery informs Wilks's interpretation of all questions relating to Akan origins and the origins of Akan states. It provides the unifying idea that allows him to conflate different questions and yet construct a forceful and novel argument. After he establishes a rising "world market for bullion" in the fifteenth and sixteenth centuries as the prime mover, his story unfolds. First, he identifies the early Akan with invaders who came from the north and occupied their present home in the gold-bearing forest of southern Ghana during the fifteenth and sixteenth centuries. Second—and this is Wilks's major premise so far as the origins of Akan economy and society are concerned—he presumes that these invaders, faced with "the chronic shortage of labor in the forest country," imported slaves for the heavy work of forest clearance. They exchanged their gold for these slaves, who rewarded their Akan masters by creating an "agricultural revolution" during the fifteenth and sixteenth centuries. Third, these foreign slaves contributed significantly to a "population explosion" in the forest during the sixteenth and seventeenth centuries. Fourth, he argues that the fifteenth-century slave trade in the forest activated new class formations among the Akan, leading to a new class of "entrepreneurs." Slavery and class formation develop together in Wilks's interpretation of the origins of the southern Akan and their states. He concludes by crediting individualistic, slave-owning entrepreneurs with sequentially generating an agricultural revolution and then initiating the formation of Akan states, all within a scant two to three centuries—a "big bang."

Though widely accepted, Wilks's myth is beset by many problems. The most pervasive is the anachronistic use of data, which supports the assumption that a mode of production based on large-scale slave labor could exist among hunters-becoming-agriculturalists. How were they able to extract backbreaking labor from their chattels in a new, difficult, and dangerous environment? How were these small communities, bands of foragers, able to prevent slaves from simply running off or even seizing power? Moreover, these hunter-early agriculturalists would seem to have been in an especially weak position to control slaves, since the heavy work of clearing was likely left to able-bodied men. Hunters, even those who have initiated food production, are regularly away from their campsites to hunt for game, leaving behind infants, young children, and the elderly. Who watched over the slaves at such times?

According to Wilks, Akan kinship and marriage, rather than the policing power of Akan military units, provided the instruments that effectively "controlled" and "administered" this large immigrant, alien labor force while its members or, more correctly, their descendants were being assimilated as free men and women into Akan societies. The need to socially control slave labor combined with the well-known openness of matrilineal descent groups to generate a "socioeconomic revolution" during the era of great clearances in the Akan forest. Wilks follows up on a lead from Terray, proposing that in the fifteenth and sixteenth centuries a "new form of social organization ... [the Akan matriclan] ... appeared at the time of the clearances":

> The matriclan functioned to facilitate the assimilation of strangers and, to the point, of the unfree labor being drawn into the forest country... the level of social organization represented by the matriclan was commensurate with the level of the control and management of labor in the era of the great clearances and the level of social organization represented by the lineage was commensurate with the level of control and management of labor in the succeeding periods of regular food crop production.

The socioeconomic revolution seems to have continued after a new agrarian regime, which had replaced the social and economic dominance of the Akan matriclans of the era of the great clearances, stabilized in the forest. Stabilization and maintenance required a different scale and organization of labor than clearing. According to Wilks, a forest agricultural regime entailed the reproduction, so far as possible, of free laborers, or freeborn members of the new Akan forest communities. The lineage, the smaller descent group, then replaced the matriclan as the functional unit of administration and regulation of labor supply. "With the agrarian order firmly established in the forest lands by the sixteenth or early seventeenth century, the size of the production community became more restricted, the demand for immigrant [that is, slave] labor consequently dropped to lower levels, and the social relations of production were 'realized' in the lineage rather than the matriclan."

The revolution in the social economy was interwoven with a parallel revolution in the political economy of Akan communities as early Akan states developed in the forest during the sixteenth and seventeenth centuries. In the fifteenth and sixteenth centuries, "a foraging mode of production gave way to an agricultural one." "In the course of this transformation the forest people reorganized themselves in such a way that the bands appropriate to the older mode of production were replaced by the matriclans appropriate to the newer." The transformation from bands to matriclans "also engendered the emergence of political structures of a new kind: the *aman.*" The emergence of these *aman* (states or polities) brings us back to Wilks's ideas about the genesis and development of classes in the Akan forest. Wilks's "entrepreneurs" (proto-bourgeoisie?), the *aberempon* ("big men"), or land "developers" (ibid.: 97), were those who controlled the production of gold, which they exchanged for slaves who cleared the forest and established the arable bases for the earliest forest settlements. These aberempon-created "estates" ("*berempon-doms*") were the venues in which band members became matrikin as the principle of descent (which structured the Akan matriclans) replaced previous band social organization. Wilks thus links descent and property through slavery, a la Engels, to the origin of classes in the Akan forest.

But unlike Marx and Engels, who would have sought out the source of the force behind the master-slave relation, Wilks is proposing that intermarriage between free Akan and slaves provided an assimilating mechanism that allowed the children of slaves, or perhaps their grandchildren or great-grandchildren, to slip invisibly—at least invisibly to those who did not belong to their free parent's lineage segment—into the protective enclosure of Akan matriliny. Marriage, childrearing, and finally descent replace force as the critical social mechanism controlling the behavior of slaves in Wilks's myth. In matrilineal Asante the children of a free woman by a slave man were automatically free lineage members. The more common union (at least in the nineteenth and early twentieth centuries) between a free Asante man and his slave wife allowed their children, grandchildren, and so forth to fictionalize a descent line from their free father's mother to whose lineage they finally "belonged." "The view has been expressed to the writer on many occasions, that 'in the old days' women married at a young age and men at a relatively advanced one; that a male slave might even become the third, fourth or even fifth husband of a (by them elderly) free woman, so that any children she bore by him would be free; and that female slaves were often married by free men and their children immediately adopted into the father's lineage" (ibid.: 81).

To analyze and to resolve the problems of a slave mode of production among foragers and the issue of force we must confront the problem besetting Wilks's entire myth: anachronism. His interpretation of fifteenth- and sixteenth-century marriage rules in the "proto-Akan" forest is drawn from an early-nineteenth-century source and late-twentieth-century informants. But the society of proto-Akan hunters in the process of becoming food producers cannot simply be assumed to replicate the social situation in the nineteenth-century Asante described in Wilks's source. Moreover, Wilks misquotes, takes out of context, and distorts a comment in Bowdich, who reports that "infants are [as] frequently wedded by adults and elderly men." Wilks has confused a nineteenth-century Akan strategy for entrapping adulterers into paying fines with what he seems to think was a general Akan marriage rule.

In anachronistically transporting observations made during the early nineteenth century in Kumase back into the fifteenth and sixteenth centuries, Wilks uncritically adapts them to his own purpose: to demonstrate the role of intermarriage between free men and women and slaves in transforming an exploitative proto-Akan slavery into an assimilative one. As a consequence, he misinterprets a nineteenth-century Asante arrangement whereby an adult husband-to-be of a child or infant Asante bride contracts with her household or lineage segment head to unite their two families, or to extort adultery payments from naive men who so much as gave the child a gift or touched it affectionately, or both. The whole paragraph, in which the phrase Wilks cites appears in the opening sentence, consists of an account told to Bowdich in 1817 by an eminent Asante statesman, Opoku Frefre. He explained how a man could profit from being cuckolded:

Infants are frequently married to infants, for the connection of families; and *infants are as frequently wedded by adults*

and elderly men.... [Opoku Frefre then described the Asante
marriage ceremony.] Apokoo told me it was a good plan for
a man to adopt who wished to get gold, for as the circumstance was seldom generally known, the most innocent freedom when the girl became ten or eleven years old, grounded
a palaver against the individual, though he might consider he
was fondling a child and be wholly ignorant of her marriage.
I afterwards understood from several others that this view
was the leading motive.

It is questionable whether these arrangements between parents of young
girls, even infants, and well-to-do Asante men—in the Asante capital
in the early nineteenth century—are relevant to Wilks's anachronistic
assumptions about marriages between free Asante and slaves during the
formative pre- and early historic period of Akan society. Can we assume
that norms for intermarriage between free Akan and slaves from the fifteenth to the seventeenth centuries corresponded to a specific nineteenth-century Asante marriage arrangement that was designed to extort
adultery fees from unsuspecting men? And can we even assume that
the ease with which slaves were invisibly assimilated via the kinship
idiom into nineteenth- and early-twentieth-century Asante society was
true in the fifteenth through seventeenth centuries? Might not such an
assimilating strategy have been strengthened as a mechanism of social
control after the appearance of Akan states, warfare, and slave raiding,
all of which multiplied the number of slaves in Akan societies and all
of which intensified in the wake of the Atlantic trade?

The difference between domestic slaves and state slaves and between
captives and their descendants inside the contexts of the Asante state
and Akan matriliny is critical. Although Wilks recognizes the significance of generational differences between captives and their offspring
in Asante society (1975: 86), he has chosen either to pass over the difference between domestic and state slaves or else to relegate domestic
slavery to insignificance in his focus on the Asante state. The key differences between these Akan-Asante slaveries are related to the rights
of slave owners to the product of their chattel's labor and to the different
communities in which each type was situated during the nineteenth cen-

tury, when reliable information first became available.

Owners of domestic slaves had no legal right to the product of their chattel's labor or any other property the slave acquired by his or her efforts. Domestic slaves and their matrilineal descendants were distinguished from free men and women by their obligation to perform such unpleasant tasks as latrine duty for their masters and by the rule that they could not wear gold or be buried in the family burial ground with other members of their owner's family. Although domestic slaves were burdened with onerous tasks and symbolic humiliations, there were no limits on their accumulation of wealth and property. Some slaves even grew richer than their masters, an achievement that was impossible for state slaves. The Asante state, for example, in the person of the Asantehene, or the powerful men of nineteenth-century Kumase who also controlled entire villages of state slaves, had definite rights to the product of their chattel's labor. The difference in the property rights between domestic and state slaves is vital, since the well-documented rights of domestics to their self-acquired property blocked their effective incorporation into a mode of production based on slave labor. Alternatively, the rights of owners of state slaves to a share of their chattel's productivity in nineteenth-century Asante reflected their interest in an active mode of production based on slave labor.

Domestic slaves also lived in a different social and legal relationship to their owners than did state slaves in Bowdich's time, or certainly in the living memory of Wilks's informants. Nineteenth- and early-twentieth century domestics "enjoyed" an individual relation to a free master or mistress in a community whose characteristic members were other free men, women, and children. State slaves, on the other hand, often peopled entire villages whose populations were subjected to servitude as groups as well as individually. Furthermore, entire communities of state slaves were apparently assimilated into Asante en bloc. The contrasting isolation of domestic slaves from one another—especially foreign captives—and from free men and women in their communities was a defining feature of domestic slavery. The kinlessness, isolation, and enforced residence rule that compelled the domestic slave to live in his, or more usually her, owner's house were further barriers to the creation in local Akan settings of a mode of production based on the labor of groups of slaves above the level of domestic economy, even in nine-teenth-century Asante.

But even in communities of Asante state slaves, whose labor was un-deniably essential to a mode of production on which the state relied, Wilks is still plagued by anachronism. The key phrase in his statement about the integration of "communities of unfree background" into As-ante society is "within a generation or two." Wilks has shown how the Asante law forbidding inquiry into another's origins served to assimilate the descendants of slave women into Akan lineages. But let us now leave the nineteenth century (from which his examples are drawn) and turn back to the fifteenth and sixteenth centuries. We are no longer speaking of people of unfree background, that is, two, three, or more generations away from their captive ancestors. We are now speaking about the captives themselves: the successive groups of able-bodied captives presumably brought into the Akan forest during the two or more centuries of forest clearing and increasing reliance on food pro-duction, who later contributed to a presumed "population explosion" in the sixteenth and seventeenth centuries.

Wilks's analysis contains a conceptual as well as a generational gap, between the alien forced laborer and the kinsman, between the com-modity and the clan member. As Wilks knows, when he defined the ge-nealogical space between them ("within a generation or two"), it is essential to distinguish the captive from the descendants when speaking of their status inside Akan matriliny. Because his examples are drawn from a later period—where the force available to the Asante state was an ever-present, if not always immediately visible, reality—and trans-posed whole onto an earlier one, Wilks is, of necessity, implicitly retro-jecting Asante state power into a period before it existed. Nowhere does he suggest any realistic strategies by which forced labor could have been converted into willing subordination (inside a marriage to a free Asante spouse?) within the everyday situations of a single lifetime. Nor does Wilks suggest any mechanisms whereby Akan lineages or other pre-state organizations could have controlled a captive labor force of significant size over at least two centuries.

It is important, when speaking of the control of slave labor, to avoid taking the distinction between "domestic" and "state" slaveries too literally or extending the specifics of our discussion outside the Akan context. Akan domestic and state slaveries represent opposite ends of an arc of possible forms of social domination or subordination. Just as it would probably have been difficult to locate domestic slaves in Akan households who were entirely free of economic exploitation despite traditional law, so the reproductive-assimilative function of the villages of nineteenth-century Asante state slaves seems at times to have been as important as, if not more important than, their capacity as producers. Certainly, in the broader West African context, there were domestic varieties of slavery that were unambiguously organized as modes of production whose slave-owning groups developed explicit instruments of coercion to control their slaves. However, the control was always in the context of developed states. What relation then does the distinction between nineteenth-century Akan domestic and Asante state slavery have to fifteenth- and sixteenth-century Akan hunters-becoming-agriculturalists? If we begin by recognizing that we are dealing with analogies—evocative comparisons, not literal truths—two kinds of comparison generate suggestive leads. The first employs what we know about slavery among hunter-gatherers and early agricultural societies to guide our tentative reconstruction of an unknown past. The second compares domestic and state slaveries in nineteenth-century Asante and other Akan societies with the slaveries that developed among contemporary nineteenth-century West African peoples. Such a comparison may provide hints about the balance between coercion and consent that regulated master-slave relations in precolonial Asante.

Slavery was widespread among the Indians of North America. Not including the developed state societies of Mexico, Driver, in his extensive survey of Amerindian cultures (1969), refers to slavery no fewer than thirty times. Slavery appeared among such diverse culture areas as the Arctic, the Sub-Arctic, California, the East, the Northeast, the Northwest Coast, the Plateau, the Southeast, and the Southwest. The peoples of the Arctic, the Sub-Arctic, California, the Northwest Coast, and the Plateau were hunters; the rest were at least partially dependent on agriculture. In each case the slavery described by Driver was of the domestic variety. Nowhere north of the pre-Columbian states of Mexico is there any hint of large numbers of forced laborers engaged in anything on the scale of labor required by Wilks for the relatively rapid clearing of the Akan forest. Even among the peoples of the Northwest Coast, whose rich environment provided them with a higher standard of living than many agriculturalists and whose "social classes and hereditary slavery set it off sharply from other non-farming culture areas of the continent," Driver is only able to report a domestic variety of slavery. By the same criteria, so far as I know, there are no African band or segmentary societies that employed slave labor on the scale Wilks, basing himself on a late-seventeenth-century source, suggests. "Some impression of the nature of the task forces employed in clearing land, in this case on the Gold Coast and not heavily forested, may be obtained from Eich's account of the three hundred slaves divided into two or three work teams or companies, who prepared the site of the Danish trading post at Fetu in the seventeenth century." It is hardly surprising that seventeenth-century representatives of Danish state power, experienced with class rule and firearms, and their African allies could control such a workforce. On the other hand, I think it would have been truly remarkable if fifteenth- and sixteenth-century stateless Akan forest communities could have accomplished such a feat.

In comparing nineteenth-century Akan slavery and other contemporary West African slaveries, Horton's reconstruction of how the New Calabar (Owame) society in the eastern Niger Delta responded to the Atlantic slave trade presents an instructive analysis of how force and the threat of force operated in tandem with the consensual mechanisms of marriage and the kinship idiom to control and assimilate significant numbers of slaves (1971). Horton describes an inner group, *koronogbo,* of the association of headhunters. "The main object of the association ... [had been since pre-state times] ... the catching and killing of men." But the *koronogbo* appears to have had a unique function:

> Older informants say that its members came out on certain appointed nights and challenged everyone they met. If those challenged gave their names with a good Kalabari accent, they were allowed to go their way. But, if they gave their names with an accent belonging to Ibo or Ibibio origin, they were promptly seized and killed. My own [that is, Horton's]

feeling is that *koronogbo* was probably more important in threat than in execution. It may well have been an instrument for terrorizing the poorly acculturated and for encouraging them to hurry up and learn the Kalabari language.

The *koronogbo* represents an extreme case of how the rulers-slave owners of New Calabar adapted an earlier institution, the association of the headhunters, to pressure slaves into submission to the norms of their masters' society and to deter any impulse to flee from or to resist their unfree status.

There were real similarities between nineteenth-century Akan domestic slavery and slavery in New Calabari society. Both were demographically decentralized, and significant numbers of slaves were isolated among individual owners in both cases. While the social isolation was threatening to the slave, it also allowed talented slaves to achieve great personal power and wealth in each society—the carrot as well as the stick. More importantly, both forms of slavery existed in the milieus of developed states. But there is no parallel institution to the *koronogbo*, or even the headhunters' associations, among the Akan beneath the state level. A parallel exists, however, in the threat to use state-backed terror, between the *koronogbo* and the public executions in nineteenth-century Kumase. Employed as mechanisms of social control, each represented the ultimate threat of death to subordinate groups as the penalty for deviance. Wilks has previously described how the conformist function of terror inherent in the public performance of these executions was explicitly recognized by the Asante rulers who staged them. He now extends and develops his interpretation of "human sacrifice" in Asante in the light of current controversy.

Force is a concrete issue where slaves are concerned. If the "established order" of a developed nineteenth-century Asante state needed "legal terror and violence" to control its free citizens as well as its unfree, what did the changing societies of Akan pioneers who were moving into the forest in the fifteenth through the sixteenth centuries use to control their unfree labor force? The only instruments of coercion that surface in Wilks's works are inseparable from Asante state power. But his agencies of consensual assimilation—slave-free intermarriage and absorption of its descendants into Akan matrilineages via the kinship idiom—are well documented in slavery among stateless peoples. Following this line of thought, our two comparisons suggest that first, as in stateless Amerindian societies, the slavery that developed in early Akan (or proto-Akan) societies corresponds to what we know of later forms of domestic slavery. Its decentralized character would have hindered effective control and regulation of large numbers of laborers. Second, as in New Calabar, Asante state slavery, and in large measure even the profuse domestic slavery found within nineteenth-century Akan societies, was largely a consequence of Akan state formation and not the reverse, as Wilks argues. Wilks has not analytically separated the features of the pre-state societies of early Akan hunters from those of a nineteenth-century Asante state society, nor has he accounted for the balance between coercion and consent that was necessary to the stability of any society where large numbers of slaves lived among their masters.

The analytic separation of Akan domestic slavery from Asante state slavery is essential to an understanding of how the latter contributed to the political economy of Asante state power. Not only must Wilks explain how an earlier, presumably domestic form of slavery (which he describes when he uses nineteenth-century sources to explain intermarriage between slave and free in Asante) provided the economic base for the division of classes in early Akan states, he must also explain how and why the property rights of domestic slaves to the product of their own labor was restored—thus undercutting any mode of production based on slave labor—after the Asante state appeared. Unlike the domestic forms of slavery in New Calabar and in Sudanic states, Akan domestic slavery could not have provided the economic substance for "class" divisions of the sort Wilks describes and, by implication, could not have contributed significantly to the political economy of Asante state power.

Wilks's myth is also pervaded by anachronisms of a different kind than those that project well-known historical conditions into an unknown past. I am referring to the way Wilks has set the oral histories of Akan, especially Asante, in real historical time. Although this is not the place to develop even an outline critique of his use of oral materials in the construction of a chronology of Akan origins, I should point out that such vividly "remembered" mythologized events as the Akan arrival in the forest may have occurred millennia ago, as did some of the most dramatically rendered events in the Old Testament. The chronology of the arrival and settlement of the early Akan in the forest is still veiled in uncertainty.

The oversimplified, anachronistic reconstruction of an Akan past has led Wilks to neglect two complex demographic issues: the improbability of foraging bands subsisting in the forest and the different gender requirements of clearing and fertility. First, the authors of a global ethnographic and archaeological survey were unable to find evidence of "hunters and gatherers who lived in and drew subsistence solely from the tropical rain forest." But Wilks's interpretation of Asante oral tradition requires him to depict the original Akan as immigrant hunters who invented an agricultural regime in their new forest environment by using slaves to clear their earliest settlements. How did they survive in the forest during the interval before they arrived in their current location and were able to buy slaves with gold?

Wilks's second demographic problem stems from the fact that forest clearing and fertility require different sexes. We know, for example, that "young males between the ages of twelve and fifteen without illness or blemish of any sort commanded the highest prices from black Mina traders." Along with Vogt, I assume that this preference reflected the need for porters who could be profitably resold on northern markets. Moreover, the preference for young able-bodied males ran counter to the general West African tendency to value a woman's fertility more highly than a man's economic productivity during the period between the mid-fifteenth and the opening of the eighteenth century. For example, Fage notes that "the reason why only one in three of the slaves offered to Europeans" by West Africans were women in their reproductive years "seems to be that child-bearing female slaves were appreciably more valuable [to West Africans] than male slaves."

But Wilks contends that a market favoring healthy young males was evidence that "unfree labour was being drawn into the forestlands from both north and south" for the arduous labor of clearing land and for producing children. Changing the sex ratio of a population by adding males cannot raise its birthrate, however. On the contrary, changing the sex ratio of relatively small groups of forest settlers in the fifteenth and sixteenth centuries would almost certainly have had an opposite effect. Adding men would lead to a significant rise in the food-energy cost per capita but would have no effect on the absolute population growth potential of early forest Akan groups. Yet these were the groups whom Wilks assumes were multiplying rapidly enough to generate a "population explosion, marked by extensive clearances and settlement" in the sixteenth and seventeenth centuries. As any cattle breeder knows, adding more females increases herd size, since one stud bull can service a large number of cows. The same is true of humans: a harem is a better model for population growth than a chain gang.

Wilks's third major problem is his ideological biases, which distort the data in ways that support his anachronistic reasoning. His first bias is rooted in the widespread view among historians of West Africa that there "must have been" slave markets in the Akan forest in the fifteenth and sixteenth centuries. By accepting and reinforcing this view, Wilks blinds himself to more empirical, Akan-based alternatives. His second bias is theoretical. Wilks's particular use of Marxist theory leads him to assume social classes among fifteenth- and sixteenth-century proto-Akan hunters-becoming-agriculturalists. When we consider these biases in connection with his anachronistic use of data, we are questioning the major empirical and theoretical premises of his overall interpretation. To argue against an overall interpretation of a critical period in Akan history ultimately requires an alternative interpretation. Since I have done this elsewhere, I shall limit myself to presenting some details in the historical record that cast doubt on Wilks's empirical assumption of significant and sustained slave markets in the Akan forest during the fifteenth and sixteenth centuries and on his misuse of the notion of class. I shall also mention the almost ad hoc way in which the concepts of an "Atlantic economy" and "world system" seem tacked onto Wilks's myth.

Although Wilks creates the impression that the use of slave labor as well as slave markets were established facts in the Akan forest during the fifteenth and sixteenth centuries, the claim cannot withstand scrutiny of the available evidence. Part of his certitude comes from a consensus

among historians of West Africa that inland slave markets and even societies depending on slave labor existed as early as the fifteenth century.
But their conclusions are based on known conditions in Islamized Sudanic and savanna states and perhaps other areas in the West African
forest. Social, political, and economic conditions in the Akan forest during these same two hundred years were apparently quite different. True,
the earliest suggestion of slave trading by the Akan in the forest implies
early contact with Mande-speaking Wangara merchants, who had a long
experience of productive slavery and slave trading in their savanna
homeland. By the fifteenth century Wangara traders had established
connections with the peoples of the forest as they pressed southward in
search of gold, kola, ivory, and slaves. It is also possible that these
traders purchased porters from the Akan to carry forest kola and ivory
to northern markets. Akan chiefs were in a position to sell local crimi-
nals and foreign captives to these Wangara merchants who "were already in the Elmina area when the Portuguese arrived there in 1471."
But the presence of slave traders does not make a slave society, at least
not one that, as Wilks assumes, was dependent on slave labor for clearing the fifteenth-century forest. If the Akan bought slaves, which is
likely, they probably preferred women who were valued as reproducers
rather than men who were valued for the heavy labor of clearing. That
would certainly have been consistent with other fifteenth-century data,
as we have seen. There is even evidence of an intra-African coastal
slave trade in the south that antedated the arrival of Europeans. The Portuguese found a maritime trade, carried on by Wangara middlemen, between what they would shortly call the Gold Coast and Benin. And
Wilks was insightful when he pointed out that Akan gold miners in the
forest were a key link between European markets and those on Africa's
west coast. By regularly supplying gold, first to the Wangara and then
to the Portuguese, the Akan gave incentive to both. Active Akan cooperation was essential to the entire enterprise.

Another important element in the late-fifteenth [to] early-sixteenth-
century trading relationship between Elmina, Benin, and Portugal was
the steady demand for slaves at the Elmina end. This demand has been
scrutinized carefully by Vogt (1979). His recovery of the Portuguese
data on the Sao Tome-Elmina trade raises serious questions about the

existence, much less the extent, of a forest Akan market for slaves during the fifteenth and sixteenth centuries. In his readiness to accept as given the existence of significant and sustained slave markets in the Akan forest during the fifteenth and sixteenth centuries, Wilks has overlooked the implications of a well-documented episode in a source he cites elsewhere. Vogt has carefully examined the demand for slaves at Elmina during the period in question. The results of his research raise serious questions about the existence of a forest Akan market for slaves. If there was a real market for slaves in the fifteenth- and sixteenth-century Akan forest, as Wilks assumes, how are we to interpret an extraordinary trip by a large party of Akan merchants to Mina in December 1529? Until then, Portuguese efforts to lure Akan to Elmina seem to have been unsuccessful. Only once before, in 1502, was there any "direct evidence of inland traders at Sao Jorge." Then, several merchants accompanied the "son of an Akan ruler" to the fort (ibid.). Otherwise, despite Portuguese awe at the quality of Akan gold, only the occasional Akan merchant visited the fort (ibid.). So the 1519 trading expedition to the fort, like that of 1502, was a singular, memorable event for the Portuguese. Yet, despite the Akans' eagerness to buy "varying quantities of almost every item in the post storehouses," despite the "vast quantities of goods" that they purchased, which left the "warehouses at Sao Jorge ... so depleted ... in December that further trade had to await the arrival of a supply caravel," they bought no slaves!

The greatest quantity of any single item these Akan bought was 19,155 brass bracelets (*manilhas*). So much brass needed carriers. But they bought none, which is consistent with Daaku's report that "ordinary citizens vied with each other to carry the chief's commodities." If there was a market for able-bodied male slaves in the forest, as Wilks asserts, transport costs could have been written off by selling the porters. Moreover, the years 1519-31 represent the most complete records available for the Mina trade. We may be certain that no slaves were purchased from individual soldiers or officers at the fort. The Portuguese did not even sell one of the more than sixteen captives used by them as porters and manual laborers, despite the relative ease with which they could have been replaced from Sao Tome in 1519-30. There is, in fact, no direct trace in the Portuguese archives or in the archaeological record of a major forest Akan market for slaves in the fifteenth and sixteenth centuries. Nor is there any evidence of Wangara sales to forest peoples or of the location of slave markets in the forest during these two hundred years. And this event took place at the beginning of the second quarter of the sixteenth century, a full century after Wilks's putative forest clearings by slaves had already begun and when the demand for slave labor would presumably have been at its height.

This is not to deny that the Akan bought slaves or that they used slave labor. It is rather to question the place and scale of slavery, indeed of classes, in fifteenth- and sixteenth-century Akan societies. On the basis of late-sixteenth-century Dutch sources, Wilks would have us believe that such early Akan groups were already "class" societies based on a distinction between "an appropriating class and a producing class." In the appropriating class Wilks sees "a class of Akan entrepreneurs emerging: a class of those able to use the strength of the world bullion market and the availability of [slave] labor locally (whether through Wangara or Portuguese suppliers), in such a way as to create a new agrarian system."

But all this elaboration of a fifteenth- and sixteenth-century "entrepreneurial class" is based on a late-sixteenth-century Dutch source who "implicitly postulates the existence of an appropriating class and a producing class." It is just at this point, at Wilks's reading of the Dutch source as "implicitly" postulating classes, that we must pause. Such "implicit postulates" are at the root of Wilks's anachronistic and prejudgmental misappropriation of class concepts. For example, the statements into which he reads the "implicit postulate" of classes in a late-sixteenth-century Dutch document are open to another reading. The citations that refer to, but do not describe, gold mining in the interior and potential Portuguese arrangements for African miners in the event they found gold, may have omitted explicit references to class relations because no such phenomenon was present—either to African informants or to Dutch reporters.

And we know that using detailed late-sixteenth-century Dutch sources to reconstruct "postulated" conditions described only vaguely at Elmina in the fifteenth and early sixteenth century is misleading. For example, Garrard "has convincingly argued that, over several centuries, annual output from the interior gold mines most probably averaged about one ton (1016 kg) and employed about 30,000 miners." Were these miners slaves, however? Seventeenth-century Dutch sources and nineteenth-century English sources contain many references to slave miners in Akan states. But Hair explicitly warns us against the anachronistic problem inherent in using later Dutch documents to explain earlier Portuguese ones. He cautions us not "to interpret the fragmentary Portuguese evidence beginning in the 1480s in the light of the fuller Dutch evidence beginning in the 1600s [as is done, for instance, in Garrard 1980: 48-59]. This may be dangerous ... I deliberately leave the Portuguese evidence to stand on its own and ignore the later Dutch reports."

Although the pages criticized in Garrard's book do not correspond to those on which he speaks of "30,000 miners," the message is clear. The relevance to Wilks's reading of the "implicit postulate" of classes in fifteenth- and sixteenth-century forest Akan societies is also clear. Mota and Hair also translate a Portuguese document from Mina in the mid-fifteenth century, in which an African informant spoke of gold and gold mining in the interior. The African's account does not mention that the miners were slaves. He or she reported "that when a black man or woman went to extract gold, normally twelve *pesos* would be extracted in one day," which suggests that free men and women were individually prospecting for profit, rather than gangs of slaves in the mines. It is possible that only free Akan men and women prospected for gold or that both slave and free mined gold in the fifteenth century—we simply do not know.

When we combine these data about the Akan visit to the Portuguese fort and about the difficulties in the sources with Wilks's acknowledgment that "there is no precise information ... on the destination of the slaves sold by the Portuguese at Elmina" during the period in question, we can only wonder how many slaves sold to Africans at Elmina ended up with Akan owners. Even if we discount the needs of the Wangara and other African traders for porters and accept the most unlikely scenario in which the Akan took all of the highest estimate of slaves landed at Elmina, the numbers still seem inadequate to account for Wilks's dramatic "explosion" in Akan population during the sixteenth and seventeenth centuries. Between 1482 and 1500, no more than three hundred slaves per year were delivered to Elmina; between 1500 and 1540 the average doubled, declining rapidly after 1536 and diminishing to insignificance after 1540. The Elmina-Benin trade was active from the 1470s while the Sao Tome-Elmina connection, which increased the numbers delivered to Mina, became important after 1500. Around that time Sao Tome had become a collection point from which slaves were transshipped to the Atlantic islands (Madeira and the Azores) and to Europe as well as to Elmina.

At this point numbers would help. Unfortunately, we know nothing about the size and density of fifteenth- and sixteenth-century forest populations, still less about the numbers of slaves they imported. In short, we know nothing about the numbers of slaves sold to people in the Akan forest during this crucial period in Wilks's myth. But from what we do know about the numbers of slaves imported by the Portuguese to Elmina and Sao Tome and finally shipped to Europe itself, a different and more specific picture of an Atlantic economy than the one vaguely hinted at in Wilks emerges. Tracking the known numbers of slaves imported into these areas permits us to see clearly the increasing domination of European economic development during these two centuries. But when we compare the numbers of slaves imported into Elmina with those imported into Sao Tome, Elmina begins to sink into insignificance as an importer of slaves, at least in an Atlantic economy context.

The total economic dependence of Sao Tome on slavery—commodity slavery as well as productive slavery—can be gauged by the 62,600 slaves imported onto this island of only 372 square miles between 1501 and 1551. This number gives an average of 1,252 slaves per year for fifty years during the half century immediately prior to the establishment of the Atlantic slave trade to the New World. That is more than double the yearly average optimally imported into Elmina during the high import years from 1500 to 1536. Even though such high levels were not maintained for the twenty-five years between 1526 and 1550—the period just before the Atlantic slave trade was firmly established—Sao Tome was nevertheless the "largest single exporter of slaves." Curtin conservatively estimates an annual average of 750 slaves per year imported into Sao Tome during this period.

When we compare demand at Elmina to that at Sao Tome, the number of slaves (possibly) purchased by Akan at Mina, plus those that might have been resold to Akan in the forest by African middlemen, does not support Wilks's assumptions about the significance of Akan slavery in the setting of an Atlantic economy, much less a world system. In the context of the development and spread of European capital, of which the thriving plantation economy and slave warehouses on Sao Tome were an extension, there was no economically significant demand for slaves in the Akan forest from the fourteenth through the sixteenth centuries. Although the fertility of female slaves may have helped make up for losses from European diseases, slave raiding, and wars that followed the opening of the Atlantic trade, these numbers, especially if they were mostly able-bodied men, cannot account for a regional "population explosion" of the sort Wilks describes.

Neither Akan matriliny nor Asante state formation was the main economic beneficiary of slavery during the critical period of the fifteenth and sixteenth centuries. It was rather a young, energetic, and expanding European capitalism that benefited the most from African slaves during this period. A steep rise in demand for slaves occurred in Portugal between 1460 and 1590, peaking in 1552 when prices rose to roughly ten times those of 1460. The price rise was reflected in the numbers of African slaves imported into Portugal. By 1551 African slaves amounted to almost 10 percent of the one hundred thousand inhabitants of Lisbon. The volume of European demand for slaves dwarfed that at Elmina and even at Sao Tome. "Slaves originating from the region between Arguin and Sierra Leone, who entered Lisbon and the ports of the Algarve between 1441 and 1505, totaled between one hundred and forty and one hundred and seventy thousand. In the sixteenth century total exports from West Africa to Portugal numbered some three hundred thousand slaves."

It was during this period—between 1489 and 1539—that the Portuguese crown was rewarded "with the greatest gold treasure Europe has ever known." Portuguese individuals as well as the Crown made fortunes on the slave market at Elmina. The gold from Elmina returned to Portugal. Returns from the productivity of the slaves from Arguin to Sierra Leone and later from Kongo and Angola also returned to Portugal, whatever their final destination. Many of these slaves were transshipped to Spain, Italy, and other European countries and later in the sixteenth century to the New World. As Wilks applies them, the concepts "Atlantic economy" and "world system" deflect our attention from the rise to dominance of Europe, first in its relation to West Africa and then, after the opening of the Atlantic slave trade in the seventeenth century, in its relation to the New World.

Compared with what we know of the contributions of African slaves to the development of early capitalism in Europe and its extensions in Sao Tome, the Atlantic islands, and later the Americas, the possible contribution in labor and reproductively of slaves to the Akan during the fifteenth and sixteenth centuries seems minuscule. If Wilks chooses to follow through on his recent alignment with "historical materialism in the Marxist tradition," as well as his "Atlantic economy" and "world system" contexts, he ought to consider spelling out the implications of Asante state formation for European capitalist development as well as for the maritime slave trade. The reorientation of his focus would be a productive alternative to anachronistic worries about "classes" in a fifteenth- and sixteenth-century Akan forest with its nineteenth-century marriage rules. The notions of an Atlantic economy and world system can be useful tools in examining fifteenth- and sixteenth-century events binding West Africa to Europe, so long as they focus on the most important process of that period: the development of European capital. Wilks's myth deflects and blurs our vision.

The evidence requires the following conclusions. First, the scale of early forest slave markets and even their sustained existence are questionable. Second, the relation of the forest Akan to coastal and northern slave markets from the fifteenth through the sixteenth centuries is still shrouded in too many unknowns. For example, the readiness to sell women and children on the Grain Coast and the high demand for them on the Gold Coast in the late fifteenth-century hint that there was an established coastal pattern of slave trading between these areas. But there is no hint of a strong, sustained market for able-bodied males in the forest. Nor does the fact that the Gold Coast was a net importer of slaves "until about the middle of the seventeenth century" automatically lend support to a hypothesis about a strong forest Akan market. Strong coastal as well as savanna and Sudanic markets are well documented, in addition to a high European demand for African slaves, especially during the fifteenth and sixteenth centuries. During those two centuries

Elmina operated as an entrepot from which gold and slaves were shipped to Europe. But the empirical evidence for an important, more or less continuous, slave market in the Akan forest from the fifteenth through the seventeenth centuries still eludes us.

Nevertheless, a sustained market for slaves in the forest from the fifteenth through the sixteenth centuries is the cornerstone of Wilks's "big bang" myth. Slave labor animates the whole story—beginning with invaders from the north in the fifteenth century who, together with their captives, clear the forest, develop agriculture, and expand their presence sufficiently to generate a "population explosion" during the sixteenth and seventeenth centuries and organize themselves finally into states; during which interval they, proto-Akan, become Akan and then Asante. Wilks has given us a radical interpretation of Akan prehistory and early history. Perhaps his myth perseveres because of its daring and the simplicity with which it encompasses complex questions about Akan origins, the origins of forest agriculture, and the origins of slavery in Akan society. But any scrutiny will reveal that Wilks's myth suffers from an over dose of anachronistic detail that only averts our eyes from the fact that we do not possess the information to compose a precise story of Akan origins.

We may just have to accept that we may never know the whole story. For whatever reasons, Wilks's story about slavery and Akan origins has become a myth among students of West African history since he first published it in 1977. Enough new material, in several fields, has accumulated since. It is time for a new interpretation. Apart from the problems discussed here, Wilks's myth suffers from another serious problem of omission. Nowhere has Wilks considered the biomedical history of Akan—indeed West African—populations since they have settled into the forest zone. Malaria, dysentery, and other infectious diseases have inflicted terrible infant and childhood mortalities on these populations while they have also debilitated adults, depriving the communities of full productivity. Enough is known, and still more can be inferred, to sketch the barest outlines of a much longer and different Akan life in the forest than Wilks envisages. Small, early forest populations had different, more urgent worries than the problems of controlling a hypothetical slave labor force. In fact, I think that slave labor was irrelevant to the origins of the Akan.

"Slavery and Akan Origins?" A Reply

IVOR WILKS

Ivor Wilks is Professor Emeritus of History at Northwestern University and a specialist on the history of Asante and of Islam in northern Ghana. He lived in Ghana from 1953 to 1966, where he made extensive collections of Asante oral histories and archival research, culminating in his classic work, Asante in the Nineteenth Century, *published originally in 1975. Below, readers will find his response to A. Norman Klein's review of his collection of essays,* Forests of Gold. *In this response and in the end, Wilks remained unconvinced by Klein's argument and by archaeological research that continued to cast doubt on his chronology for the emergence of southerly Akan polities in the forest, and that pointed to a much earlier (proto-)Akan presence.*

A new Stormin' Norman has appeared, but the action has shifted from the Persian Gulf to the Gulf of Guinea and from the sands of the Arabs to the forests of the Akan. Stormin' Norman Klein sets out to destroy not missile sites but rather an "academic myth." It is one that I supposedly created two decades ago and recently republished, "essentially intact," in *Forests of Gold* (hereafter cited as *FG*). In the interim, I have apparently fooled a number of excellent scholars (Klein names Kea, McCaskie, and Stahl) into "uncritically" accepting the myth. Well, well!

I shall not bore the reader with speculations about just what Klein means by "myth." Suffice to say that my problematic was the transition from foraging to agriculture in the Akan country between the Pra and Offin Rivers, and that my procedure was to work with an imagined scenario on the one hand and the available evidence (written records, orally transmitted texts, archaeological findings, and so forth) on the other, to secure as close a fit as possible between scenario and sources. If such is the stuff of "myth," so be it. Klein, we may note, several times remarks that in 1995 he will publish a new "interpretation" that will supplant my "myth." On this matter judgment must be reserved, for we are given few hints of its substance.

In attempting to respond usefully to Klein's review, I face the problem that his grasp of my thesis—may we drop "myth" at this stage?—is highly insecure. In the space available, I am obviously unable to address his points one by one. I shall therefore ignore the more trivial matters and focus on the major misunderstandings. "First," writes Klein, "he [Wilks] identifies the early Akan with invaders who came from the north and occupied their present home in the gold-bearing forest of southern Ghana during the fifteenth and sixteenth centuries." It so happens that I make no reference whatsoever to any such "invaders," though they crop up time and time again in Klein's review. His reading of my text is an utter travesty of anything I have ever thought or, I hope, written. It is true that I do refer to the existence of Akan traditions of migration from more northerly locations, but I specifically comment that the veracity of such traditions is of no concern to my inquiry (*FG,* 69). If indeed a southerly movement of people from the grasslands did occur (and I suppose it must have, since humans did not originate in the West African forests), then I think of this as taking place in remote antiquity and certainly not in the fifteenth and sixteenth centuries! (In the mid-1960s there were moves to have me deported from Ghana precisely because I opposed the view that the Akan were migrants, in the historic period, from the western Sudan or beyond. Fortunately for me, wiser counsels prevailed, but this is not a story I should tell here.) The whole thrust of my argument is, in fact, that it was forest foragers who transformed themselves into cultivators. Thus I wrote of "a major transformation in the system of production such that an economy with a primary dependence upon hunting and gathering gave way to one with a primary dependence upon the cultivation of food crops," adding that "the social relations of production of the forest peoples were accordingly modified by the creation of the great exogamous matriclans and the redistribution of communities between them" (*FG,* 71). Klein's fanciful introduction of "invaders" into the process makes nonsense of many of his subsequent points, and I have difficulty in knowing how to reply to them.

Klein clearly has problems in dealing with hunters and gatherers. In one curious passage he suggests the "improbability of foraging bands subsisting in the forest" and cites authors who were apparently unable to find evidence of "hunters and gatherers who lived in and drew subsistence solely from the tropical rain forest." It so happens that the Akan with whom I am concerned lived, as I hope I made clear, in moist semi-deciduous forest (*FG,* 42-43). But that is by the way. There is, owing in no small measure to the surveys of Oliver Davies (1972), unquestionable evidence of neolithic cultures scattered throughout the Akan forestlands. The mode of production, or the "mode of exploitation of the land," of those who made the ground and flaked stone tools must surely have been a foraging one, though I recognize that a vegecultural component may well have developed within the subsistence system, involving perhaps most notably the cultivation of yams and some management of such oleaginous trees as the oil palm (*FG,* 64). I should stress again, however, that my concern is not with the origins of cultivation as such, but with the emergence of a fully formed agrarian order.

To the best of my knowledge, no one has attempted to model the subsistence strategies of hunting and gathering bands in the relevant regional context, though considerable pertinent literature exists for comparative purposes. I recognize that my thesis on the development of an (Akan) agricultural mode of production requires a much fuller consideration of the earlier ("proto-Akan," shall we say?) foraging mode. I can do no more here than briefly indicate the lines along which such an inquiry might proceed. We have, I think, to envisage the forestlands between the Pra and Offin as comprising several subsistence territories. Each was hunted by bands bound together by ties the nature of which we can only guess at, and each had as its focus a camp where women, children, and the elderly remained while the able-bodied men undertook prolonged seasonal hunts. Food was stored in such camps, the occupants of which might also combine foraging for wild crops with an increasing involvement in vegeculture. Five such camps may, I suggest, be identified. They are the places I refer to as the "cradles of the

Akan," known to the Akan themselves as the *akanman piesie nnum,* "the five first-born Akan towns": Adansemanso, Abuakwa Atwumamanso, Asantemanso, Asenmanso, and Abankeseso (*FG,* 91).

Excavations have been carried out at Asantemanso and Adansemanso by Peter Shinnie in collaboration with Brian Vivian. At the former and more extensively investigated site, calibrated radiocarbon dates indicate continuous occupation perhaps from the later part of the first millennium CE, and certainly from the thirteenth century, to the middle of the seventeenth. The area of settlement shifted slightly over time, but at no place on the extensive site was evidence of occupation found deeper than two meters. Nor, I believe, did any clear evidence emerge to show that the people of Asantemanso engaged in agriculture, though this may well have been the case in the later phases of settlement. I am greatly indebted to the excavators for many personal communications on the progress of their work. Shinnie has suggested that the evidence from Asantemanso casts doubt upon the chronology I adopt for the transition from foraging to cultivation in the forest: it is too recent. But there is, he adds, "nothing to suggest that the mechanism by which agriculture and the subsequent political and social developments of the proto-Asante was other than that which he [Wilks] proposes in his important papers" (Shinnie forthcoming). I treat this comment very seriously indeed, but I remain unconvinced. Asantemanso was, I continue to think, an old hunting camp that became something more like a town as a shift from residential mobility to sedentism took place. It was progressively abandoned as its hunters moved out to become cultivators on the new arable land, a process I have treated in some detail (*FG,* 65-66, 97-98, 101).

Sedentism based upon agriculture seems to have been developing in the savanna hinterlands of the Akan forests perhaps as early as the middle of the second millennium BCE. Ann Stahl has recently reviewed the state of knowledge of the so-called Kintampo culture (1986). It is, then, an implication of my thesis that foraging remained the subsistence base of communities in the forest for two to three millennia after cultivation had become that of communities in the savanna. Is such a scenario possible? Susan Gregg has explored a comparable situation in a prehistoric Central European context, in which (mesolithic) foragers and (neolithic) farmers coexisted over an extended period of time (1988). Gregg's model of change, however, is one that envisages forms of mutualistic interaction ultimately permitting penetration of the hunting grounds by cultivators. Can it be argued that savanna farmers "penetrated" the Akan hunting grounds; that, in other words, agriculture was introduced into the forest from the savanna?

That bearers of the Kintampo culture made inroads into the forest is witnessed by the appearance of characteristic artifacts in the Kumase area, thirty to forty miles south of the (present) forest limits. But if, and this is a big "if," the intruders were farmers, they seem not to have been successful ones. The major site, Boyasi Hill, lies in an area of savanna vegetation. Newton and Woodell suggest that this may be a relic of a distant time "when the whole area was much drier." My guess is that the intruders, lacking the techniques of forest cultivation, clear felled land, whereupon excessive isolation, and soil erosion resulting from the heavy rainfalls, terminated any attempts at farming they may have made—and so allowed a savanna vegetation climax to establish itself (*FG*, 64).

The case of Boyasi Hill, then, does not encourage the application of Gregg's model of "penetration" to the case of the Akan. In general terms I would argue that the ecological divide between savanna and forest was such that methods of food crop production within the former were neither adoptable nor adaptable within the latter. Rainfall and soils, labor requirements, farm size and fallow management, crops and crop rotation, and so forth: all varied greatly between the two environments. The evolution of forest agriculture, I have argued, "involved the acquisition on the part of the [Akan] cultivators, over time, of a sensitive awareness of the restraints imposed upon the exploitation of the soil by the nature of the bioclimatic system" (*FG*, 44). In short, the Akan had to pioneer the techniques of forest farming; there was no one to borrow them from! To this comment I add a rider. I now believe that the full and decisive transformation to food crop cultivation in the Akan country probably had to await the adoption of high yielding plants of American origin: of the maize, cassava, and cocoyams that came to be principal staples of the Akan farmer. That their introduction preceded the European appearance on the coast in the later fifteenth century seems unlikely in the extreme. We are in need of further relevant botanical studies, but the work of H. G. Baker on the weed complex of the forest country is also suggestive of the late development of agriculture there.

I have argued that increasing sedentism, associated with an increasing reliance on domestic rather than wild resources, "led ultimately to population growth and the consequent search for more land to cultivate" (*FG,* 72). Klein has me referring to a "population explosion," though at that point I was in fact summarizing the views of Oliver Davies (*FG,* 64). But never mind. I certainly do think that considerable population growth in the forest country resulted from the transition to cultivation. The fifteenth through seventeenth centuries saw the creation of numerous villages, and by the end of the period a new agrarian landscape had taken shape. The archaeological record, fragmentary though it is, attests to this. I am thinking, for example, of Davies' excavation at Mamponten, those of Davies and David Calvocoressi at Ahinsan, and those of Shinnie and Vivian at Esiease and Anyinam, of which Vivian remarks, "In every one of these examples ... the occupations identified were found to span 300-400 years at the most." But I am thinking more of the numerous orally transmitted accounts of Asante village origins, those important and much valued foundation "charters," the chronologies of which seem consistently to refer to the same period (*FG,* 64-66, 96-97).

Klein seems to have trouble with all of this. Early in his review he has me attributing to "foreign slaves" a "significant contribution" to population growth. A glance at the passage he cites (*FG,* 64) will show that I do no such thing. I am in fact cautious about the volume of unfree labor that was absorbed into Akan society in the early agricultural period (*FG,* 76). Klein does not let the matter rest there, however. He again takes up the matter of a "population explosion" in the following argument. First, the unfree labor imported into the forest country was male. Second, this male labor would have no effect on the absolute population growth potential of early Akan groups. "As any cattle breeder knows," he points out, "adding more females increases herd size, since one stud bull can service a large number of cows." (Fancy that, Norm!) Therefore, concludes Klein, the unfree labor could not have generated a "population explosion." Since I have never argued this anyway, and since I do not necessarily share Klein's assumption that the unfree labor was exclusively male, we may perhaps pass on to what I do think.

I accept the conventional wisdom that population growth usually results from the transition from foraging to cultivating. But why? Considerable literature exists on this topic. The key lies in the matter of birth-spacing. The hunting territories I have posited for the Akan (or proto-Akan) were extensive, and had to be so, since the faunal resources of the forest country were probably relatively meager and certainly relatively inaccessible, with much of the game inhabiting the canopies. Hunting bands were therefore likely to be away from camp for prolonged periods, thus increasing birth-spacing among their women. The paucity of food may have generated taboos designed to achieve the same end—taboos, for example, on postpartum sexual intercourse for specified periods of time (of which traces remain in contemporary Akan society). With increased sedentism, and a lessening dependence on wild resources for subsistence, birth-spacing decreased. Men were in camp for longer periods. Improved supplies of food, moreover, presumably lowered the incidence of miscarriage, and the period of lactation probably shortened. This is not the place to argue these points in detail. Studies of the effects of sedentization in other contexts have shown populations doubling in a quarter of a century. We do not need to postulate anything like so high a rate of increase in the Akan country to be able to speak even (yes!) of a "population explosion."

I return to the issue of slavery that, Klein asserts, "informs Wilks's interpretation of all questions relating to Akan origins and the origins of Akan states. It provides the unifying idea that allows him to conflate different questions and yet construct a forceful and novel argument." Despite the compliment, however, I do not think I saw, or see, slavery as playing anything like a central role in my argument. In fact I seldom speak of "slaves" other than in my discussion (and, by and large, rejection) of the views of Rattray and Potekhin (*FG*, 92-94). I do, however, refer to "unfree labor." The distinction is not mere sophistry. It was the acquisition of labor over and above family labor that was essential to the development of agriculture. That the additional labor acquired was unfree resulted from the particular historical conjunctures of the fifteenth and sixteenth centuries. The world bullion market was such that there was a strong demand for gold, first in the Wangara trading posts north of the forest and later in those of the European traders on the coast to the south. The subsistence strategies of the Akan, I argue, had a flexibility that enabled them to extend their exploitation of forest resources to include foraging for gold. "Those who controlled the production and sale of gold were those able to procure a supply of unfree labor," I wrote, and "those who procured unfree labor were those able to create arable within the forest" (*FG,* 96). In different historical circumstances the additional labor might just as well have been that of free immigrants attracted by pecuniary rewards, grants of land, or whatever. Thus when Klein says that I argue "that foreign slaves generated a food-producing revolution," he parodies my views. I think that Akan entrepreneurs, those who arranged the marketing of gold and the procurement of labor, *generated* the transformation. The laborers, unfree as it happens, *facilitated* it.

I find Klein's lengthy discussion of what he calls "state" and "domestic" slavery of little relevance to my theme. Indeed, as he says, the evidence that leads him to make this (to my mind, dubious) distinction is drawn from the nineteenth century, "when reliable information first became available." Klein has difficulty in understanding how early Akan farmers might control their unfree labor. How, he asks, were they "able to prevent slaves from simply running off?" Throughout most of the nineteenth century "slaves" might indeed run off, to seek refuge in the British Protected Territory (and later Colony) of the Gold Coast. But in the fifteenth and sixteenth centuries, where might they go? Perhaps a few did take off into the depths of the forest. If so, their survival would seem highly unlikely. To use an expression much favored by Klein, we have here an "anachronistic use of data." I note in passing that Klein repeatedly rather shrilly accuses me of this sin, but justifies his own use of data from later periods (and indeed other societies) as "dealing with analogies—evocative comparisons, not literal truths."

Klein is much exercised by another closely related question. It has to do with the instruments of coercion available to the early Akan not yet organized into states. What, he asks, was to prevent laborers imported into the forest from "seizing power?" I agree that my scenario does not accommodate the possibility. I envisage small groups of imported laborers, working side by side with (to use Klein's expression)

"Akan hunters-becoming-agriculturalists" at scattered locations in the forest, to clear land for planting. That such groups might maintain communication with each other, and plot rebellion, is (to me at least) just not in the cards.

I do not know how to deal with this matter succinctly. It has to do not so much with relations of reproduction—specifically, intermarriage between free and unfree, as Klein thinks—but rather with relations of production—specifically, the manner in which the labor of the unfree was appropriated by the free. Did the unfree acquire the usufruct of a proportion of the land cleared (and a third would be a very "Akanish" share)? Was this usufruct conditional upon their continuing to render tributes and services to the landowners? We are in the realm of speculation, but it is speculation controlled, I think, by one major consideration: Any model we develop has to explain the existence of the *gyaasefo* within Akan society, constituting one of its essential components (*FG*, 99-100). I have worked with those of this peculiarly servile yet nonetheless peculiarly powerful status over many years, but in my writings have yet to afford them the attention they deserve. Klein ignores them completely. Throughout the Akan country there are families in which any of the men may be called upon, by ancient custom, to serve in their chief's household *(ahenkwaa),* and any of the women, by ancient custom, to become one of his wives *(ayete)* (for a special case, see *FG*, 333-34). I incline to look for the origins of this arrangement in the relationship between the early Akan landowners and their unfree subjects. I may be wrong, but had Klein paid some heed to this matter he might have spared us his lengthy but largely irrelevant discussion of marriage and adultery.

I might take up Klein's remark on my "particular use of Marxist theory," and his suggestion that this leads me "to assume social classes among fifteenth- and sixteenth-century proto-Akan hunters-becoming agriculturalists." On reflection, however, I doubt whether this would be particularly useful, since I nowhere argue for the existence of "classes," in anything like Marx's sense, in the period in question. I am grateful to Norman Klein for devoting so many pages to a scrutiny of my thesis about the development of the Akan agrarian order. This effort is in a tradition of scholarship that, these days, is to be cherished. I only wish he had read what I have written a little more carefully.

Reply to Wilks's Commentary on "Slavery and Akan Origins?"

A. NORMAN KLEIN

Offering a counter-narrative to Wilks's, Klein has argued in-stead (based upon archaeological and biomedical data) that for millennia the Akan forest was inhabited by agricultural-ists, who responded to later Eurasian diseases and slave raiding by clustering into denser populations. This placed a greater emphasis on fertility (especially that of imported women) as a weapon against social dislocation, slavery, and disease in the late fifteenth to early eighteenth centuries. For more of Klein's counter-argument, readers should consult the following article and the partial response to it by Wilks: A. Norman Klein, "Toward a New Understanding of Akan Ori-gins," Africa 66, no. 2 (1996): 248-73; Ivor Wilks, "The For-est and the Twis," Journal des Africanistes 75, no. 1 (2005): 19-75 (http://africanistes.revues.org/188).

Much of Ivor Wilks's reply to my arguments in "Slavery and Akan Ori-gins?" is made up of examples of my alleged misreading of his text. In fact, he is hiding behind a semantic fog. Three examples of Wilks's wordplay will suffice to illustrate how his reply misrepresents what I say and clouds the issues. First, Wilks objects that my reference to "in-vaders" from the north into the Akan forest misreads his position. In-stead he speaks of "traditions of migration" and "intruders." Well, perhaps "invaders" was too strong a word. I'll settle for "intruding mi-grants." Second, Wilks objects to my use of the word "slavery" and speaks instead of "unfree," "imported" labor that was "additional" to the labor required for subsistence farming. Sorry, but in the context of clearing the West African forest in the sixteenth century these "imported laborers" sound like old-fashioned slaves to me. Third, Wilks concludes that my remark about his "particular use of Marxist theory" is relatively meaningless, "since I nowhere argue for the existence of 'classes,' in anything like Marx's sense, in the period in question." But read Wilks's own words in the book being reviewed:

> The Portuguese 'blueprint' of 1572 associates gold mining, forest clearing, and food production, and *implicitly postulates the existence of an appropriating and a producing class.* It is, I suggest, mutatis mutandis, a paradigm of sorts for the early Akan state. Those who controlled the production and sale of gold were those able to procure a supply of unfree labor. Those who procured unfree labor were those able to create arable within the forest. Those who created the arable land were those who founded the numerous Akan polities. *We see, in other words, a class of those able to use the world bullion market, and the availability of labor locally (whether through Wangara or Portuguese suppliers), in such a way as to create the new agrarian system. These entrepreneurs were known as the aberempon (sing. oberempon), literally "big men" but correctly glossed in an early European source as "a superior rich man."* (*Forests of Gold*, 95-96; emphasis added)

Are not these "entrepreneurs" what Marxists would call "an indigenous bourgeoisie"? And are they not, as Wilks's Portuguese source implies, and as Wilks himself spells out, "an appropriating class" extracting a surplus product from their slaves? All of Wilks's word magic cannot dispel his identification of two classes: of slave-owning "entrepreneurs" and their "unfree labor." And if this is not an example of a "particular use of Marxist theory," then I have no other name for it.

When I used the word "myth," against which Wilks protests, to describe his entrenched interpretation, I was using "myth" in a perfectly normal way. This needs to be stressed. When an interpretation becomes so widely accepted that it resembles an unquestioned truth, we call it a myth. I argue against Wilks's entrenched interpretation of the verifiable data, not against those data themselves. After all, no one is more familiar with the scholarship on the Akan than Wilks. In an article to be published next year in *Africa* I present an alternative approach to the questions Wilks has raised and at the same time offer an alternative interpretation of his verifiable data, in terms of which slave labor is irrelevant. My interpretation of Akan origins employs a different, earlier chronology than Wilks's and is based not only on specific archaeological data, which I interpret differently than Wilks, but also on biomedical data that Wilks has not even considered. Let future work in archaeology and the biomedical sciences decide which of our interpretations is the more useful.

From European Contact to the Komenda Wars: The Eguafo Kingdom during the Height of the Gold Trade

SAM SPIERS

Sam Spiers teaches in the Archaeology Program at La Trobe University, Australia. This essay is drawn from his 2007 dissertation entitled "The Eguafo Kingdom: Investigating Complexity in Southern Ghana" and is part of the ongoing Central Region Project, headed by Christopher DeCorse at Syracuse University. Interested readers can consult either the dissertation or the author on the archaeological, documentary, and oral sources used herein.

In early December 1686, a chief factor of the Royal African Company of England, based at their factory in Komenda, made a rare visit to the hinterland town of Eguafo, the capital of the Kingdom of the same name. The purpose of this mission was to get permission from the King of Eguafo in order to finalize plans for the construction of the British fort on the western side of the Susu lagoon. This encounter, occurring some years before both a period of civil unrest in Eguafo and the beginning of the Komenda Wars, tells us much about the expectations of both this British trading company and the Eguafo elite, and hints at the political structure of the Kingdom. The British traders were keen to keep the roads to Komenda open, while the King wanted compensation for the trade passing through his borders, including both a monthly payment and an annual festival payment. The negotiations took place in the presence of the King, his younger brother and a royal official suggesting what historian Kwame Arhin called a diffuse political authority. But who were the Eguafo, and what role did they play in the formation of the Atlantic world? Was the Kingdom that the Royal African Company were trading with in late seventeenth century the same as that which the Portuguese first traded with along the Mina coast in the late fifteenth century?

This essay attempts to chart the social, economic and political history of the Eguafo Kingdom during the height of the gold trade, largely from the beginning of European contact along the former Gold Coast to the close of the seventeenth century. Though this end date may seem somewhat arbitrary, it does relate to certain changes in African and European trading patterns on the coast; as by the end of the seventeenth century the trade in gold had been largely overshadowed by the consolidation of the transatlantic slave trade, which reached its apogee in the eighteenth century. Further, it reflects changes in the political landscape: the rise of the increasingly powerful merchants on the coast and the emergence of centralized hinterland states such as Asante and Akwamu, which while ceasing to raid within their own territories, would readily invade and raid other areas and take control of trading networks to the south. The Eguafo Kingdom rose to prominence in the sixteenth century during the height of the gold trade, but by the eighteenth century, it had become increasingly marginalized.

Introducing the Eguafo Kingdom

The contemporary town and archaeological site of Eguafo is situated in the immediate coastal hinterland of the Central Region of Ghana. The landscape consists of gently rolling hills, with intruding granite batholiths typical of the Birrimian system that underlies the surface soils in this region. On the eastern and western borders of the traditional Kingdom, there are major drainages with mangrove swamps in the lowlying areas where the rivers meet the ocean. The soil is mostly forest ochrosols, which are easily tilled and hence suitable for agriculture. When cleared it can be prone to erosion, and with the removal of the forest canopy, drought.

Today, the people of Eguafo are largely subsistence and plantation farmers. Natural plant and animal resources have long been exploited, leading to the decimation of some wild species and the deforestation of much of the landscape in the area. Where stands of protected forest remain, it is often because they are considered sacred groves, though some logging has occurred within them, and some groves have physically disappeared in the wake of urban development. Mineral resources include clay, which is still used in house construction and hearth building, though the manufacture of pottery ceased in the twentieth century. Further, the laterite soil is rich in iron and alluvial gold, the latter of which is still sought after by local gold miners, known as *galamsey*.

The people of Eguafo are Fante speakers, and more broadly are considered to be members of the coastal Akan. The Akan group of the Volta-Comoé languages of Ghana includes dialects such as Akuapem, Asante, Fante, Wasa, Agona, Akyem, Bron/Abron, Kwahu and Gomua. The term Twi usually refers to all non-Fante dialects of the Akan group (Asante, Akuapem, Akyem and Kwahu) while Fante has a number of sub-dialects of its own, including Anomabo Fante, Abura Fante, Agona and Gomua. Within the Central Region, however, Twi (Asante) and Fante are mutually intelligible.

It must be remembered that this is a linguistic classification, though today the Akan also share broadly similar, cultural practices. Social organization, including descent and inheritance are primarily (though not exclusively on the coast) organized on lines of an exogamous matriclans or *mmusua* (singular: *abusua*), where title and land is vested in the community, although its absolute ownership is vested in the stool of the matrilineage, the symbol of political authority. The head of the matrilineage, or *abusua panin*, represents the family on the local council of elders. He acts as an intermediary between the spirit world of the ancestors and the physical world; he administers family property; acts as the custodian of family tradition; and acts as the arbitrator in family disputes. Though membership to the matrilineage is accorded at birth, adoption into the clan, formerly in the case of the enslaved or estranged, can also occur. This matrilineal organization is further cross-cut with several patrilineal affiliations, such as *ntoro*, an essence or "spirit" which people are born with defining consanguinity in patrilineal terms.

More specifically, the coastal Fante have patrilineal organizations, notably the *asafo* companies which have led some anthropologists to suggest a system of double descent. Among the Eguafo, the Asante, and the Fante, residence is patrilocal or avunculocal, usually based on the *asafo bron* or ward where members of the same company reside together within the village.

Oral traditions recorded in the twentieth century discuss the origins of the Eguafo people and the Eguafo Kingdom. Though there is limited consensus between them, they generally claim that the Eguafo people were the first settlers, and that the Eguafo Kingdom is the oldest polity, in the area. It is often extremely difficult to anchor oral traditions in time and space, and the nature and context of their production makes it problematic to map them uncritically backwards through time. Often several historic figures become condensed into one mythic figure, or events that may have happened over several decades become conflated into one event. Further, there is the problem of "feedback," where more contemporary recorded traditions become reworked into contemporary myths of origin. For example, in the recorded "History of Eguafu and Possessions" of 1922, Kofi Atta suggested that while some believe the origin of the people of Eguafo came from the Dumpow mountain, it was suggested that they also migrated from Egypt. Therefore, while these traditions must be treated with some caution several threads suggest a tie with the Dumpow, a prominent forested hill and important sacred grove, and what we know to be the earliest archaeological settlement in present day Eguafo.

Early lists of vocabulary collected by traders and travelers (for example by Eustache de la Fosse), though limited in nature, would suggest that "Akan" (Twi-Fante) was spoken on the coast earlier than the last quarter of the fifteenth century, and probably prior to European contact. It is important to note, however, that this only demonstrates that "Akan" had become the main language of communication and trade on the coast, and does not rule out that other communities may have other language components. For example, Kropp Dakubu has questioned Fynn's appellation of the Kingdom of Efutu, which borders Eguafo to the east, as an Eastern Fante State, as a Guang language (Awutu/Afutu) is spoken there. What is important to remember is that this ethno-linguistic ap pellation of 'Akan' is not the way the Portuguese described the coastal peoples, nor (going by European sources) was it the way in which they described themselves, but does suggest a more broadly shared set of cultural traits.

What we may conclude from this is that Akan speakers were probably on the coast prior to European contact. More significantly, based on recent archaeological work, there appears to be a strong continuity over the past thousand years, in ceramic production and settlement pattern to circa CE 1700. It seems that people lived in small, mobile farming communities that still relied heavily on hunting and fishing, and made use of natural features in the landscape for defense.

The early European documentary sources are somewhat lacking when it comes to specifically describing the Eguafo Kingdom and the socio-cultural organization of its people. It is ambiguous as to whether the Portuguese began trading with a complex chiefdom, kingdom or state. The documentary evidence provides some oblique references to persons of authority. For example, Rui de Pina was probably collecting material on the Gold Coast during the 1490s for his manuscript that he began in the early sixteenth century. He described a dispute or war between two men who lived near Elmina in 1490. It has been suggested that they represented the two different Kingdoms of Eguafo and Efutu that bordered the town of Elmina. One King had fooled the other into thinking that he had the support of the Portuguese. The other, thinking that he was now out-numbered, retreated from the battle to the detriment of his army. By 1503, we have a more concrete reference to a person of authority: the "Xeryfe," who had become King of Eguafo who marched toward Elmina to ensure trade routes to the Portuguese castle were clear; and a further reference to the King of Efutu, indicating the anxiety on the part of the Portuguese to keep trade open throughout both polities. Vogt has argued that one of Governor Fernão Lopes Correa's last actions at Elmina in 1519 was to try to broker a peace between the rulers of Eguafo and Efutu.

We have a clearer sense of the political boundaries of these two Kingdoms in the early seventeenth century. De Marees' 1602 publication described the relationship between Komenda and the town of Eguafo, where the King lived, which he stated was located on a mountain in the

interior. In 1629, an anonymous Dutch map illustrated the relative positions of forty-three coastal and hinterland polities, trading groups and
markets. On this map Eguafo is depicted as being bordered to the west
by Yabiw and Ahanta, to the north-west by Adom (and later Wassa), to
the north by Abrem, and to the east by Efutu. Komenda is listed as the
Kingdom's principle port, and suggests that Elmina is to some degree
independent from Eguafo. The relative positioning of all these polities
holds good for most of the seventeenth century. One of the things that
linked these polities, together with the European posts along the coast,
was obviously trade, and while the early sources may not speak to the
socio-political organization of such polities in great detail, they do provide a clearer picture of the impact of the competition for coastal trade.
This commercial aspect is reflected in European concerns over taxation,
trade routes and trade goods.

Eguafo was not one of the major gold producing kingdoms, so apart
from provisioning, its main source of revenue seems to have been from
imposing fines or taxes on African traders making their way to the
coastal ports of Komenda and Elmina through Eguafo lands, or to fine
or tax European companies in order to build forts and trading posts, and
to keep the terrestrial trade routes into the hinterland open. Seventeenth-
century sources suggest that tax collectors seemed to live either close
to the trade routes or in the ports themselves, though it is not clear how
far back we can map this practice. African gold traders who were being
taxed as they passed through the Kingdom were generally referred by
the Europeans as the Akanists, though it remains unclear as to whether
these traders came from a single kingdom or constituted a trade confederacy. It has been suggested that the trade network must have pre-
dated 1600, and further that in the seventeenth century, the Dutch would
often refer to them as *Akannisten*, which translates as "professional
Akans" rather than people from a place of the same name.

At its height, the Eguafo Kingdom stretched from the Sweet River
in the east to the Pra River in the west, and provided access to two significant coastal ports located within its territory: Elmina and Komenda.
While the Kingdom did not have significant resources in gold, it was
able to collect revenue in the form of fines or taxes levied against other
traders (both African and European) who passed through, or traded on,

its borders. It would appear that the King resided in the town of Eguafo, some twelve kilometers north-east of Elmina, though the origin of the institution of kingship, or the extent of his powers, is unclear prior to the seventeenth century. It would seem that during the seventeenth century the King's power was circumscribed by the royal family and other office holders.

Living in the Town of Eguafo: Housing and Subsistence

Detailed descriptions of the town of Eguafo are rare for the period under discussion. In the latter part of the sixteenth century both Eguafo and Efutu were described as being small villages consisting of less than a hundred buildings. This would suggest that hinterland towns were considerably smaller than those immediately on the coast such as Shama or Elmina at this time, which may reflect the initial migrations of people, and the consequent depopulation of the "country," for the growing urban settlements on the coast. Accounts in the seventeenth century place the town of Eguafo on a mountain, which continued into the eighteenth century, where a 1729 map, by d'Anville shows Eguafo on a hill, as does a 1750 French map "Carte Particulier de la Coste d'Or." Archaeological excavations in the Dumpow, an important sacred grove of the Eguafo Traditional Area, uncovered evidence of this earlier settlement indicating that the hill-top was probably abandoned during the seventeenth century.

We have no record of the specific village layout or types of houses which were built at Eguafo during the height of the gold trade. The town was also said to be divided into three quarters at least in the mid-seventeenth century and some have argued further that such divisions were a common feature during the seventeenth century, and that this may reflect the divisions into wards for manceroes, or young men. Such organization may reflect early precedents of the asafo system mentioned above. General observations by Europeans on the coast, however, are instructive, and given the archaeological evidence for housing and subsistence (such as the presence of daub, the use of red-slipping on hearths, and faunal remains), are probably of a similar nature to those at Eguafo at this time. There are several early references to housing in the wattle and daub style on the Guinea coast. Martin Frobisher, who was imprisoned by the Portuguese at Shama and taken to Elmina in 1555, recounts in a report dated 27 May 1562, that the African houses about the castle were made of "canes and reedes." Kitchens were usually separate from living quarters, and of a more open construction which remains a common practice in Eguafo. De Marees describes how the floors were of compact clay, which had been smoothed and then slipped with reddish clay. This is also still practiced in Eguafo, especially in the treatment of the doorways, kitchen floors and cooking hearths, and is associated with cleanliness.

In the coastal region, subsistence was chiefly agricultural, supplemented with hunting, gathering, husbandry, and fishing. Indigenous crops included sorghum, pearl millet, African rice, fonio, pepper, malaguetta pepper, Guinea pepper and various varieties of yam. Palm oil was manufactured and consumed locally, though this item was not significant in the trade with the Europeans until the second quarter of the nineteenth century. Agricultural products introduced from Europe included figs, melons, pomegranate, sugar cane, citrus fruits, eggplants, chickpeas, onions, garlic, tiger nuts, cucumber, and other kitchen garden plants. These crops, though it is difficult to say with certainty, were probably introduced to the coast in the Portuguese period.

Asian cultigens which were probably introduced by Portuguese traders included bananas and plantains, Asian rice, Asian yams, coconuts, ginger, cinnamon, cloves, cardamom, turmeric, tamarinds, and pigeon peas. American crops introduced by the Portuguese include maize, cassava (slightly later than maize), peanuts, sweet potatoes, common beans, lima beans, capsicum peppers, pumpkins, squash, pineapples, papayas, guavas, cashew nuts, and tobacco. Tomatoes may be a later introduction, possibly in the nineteenth century.

Such introduced species were probably adopted fairly quickly on the coast. For example, the use of maize was documented by the mid-sixteenth century when Eden related how corn was ground between two stones to form a meal, then water added to form dough which was then fermented in the heat of the sun. The planting season was often marked with some ceremony. For example, William Cross wrote in 1687 that he "send up Nuna to the King of Aguaffo; with an anchor of rum, as custome upon putting his corn in the ground ... but [the King] told him rum was a liquor the people there did not much care for, and desired an anchor of brandy more." An anonymous Dutch manuscript, probably written between 1642 and 1655, describes the planting season on the Gold Coast, stating that "milie" (either maize or millet) is planted in February and March, and if it is to be eaten fresh it is picked in July, and if it is to be used in making "bread" (possibly *kenkey*), then it is left until August. July was the season for yams, and September for beans, and a second season of large "milie" (possibly maize) is planted. The manufacture of palm wine was also early documented early on, for example, when Eden related how palms were tapped, and the sap collected in gourds hanging from the tree or on the ground under the tree, and then left to ferment over night.

The common domesticated fauna include sheep, goats, dwarf shorthorn, chickens, pigs, guinea fowl (which is indigenous to West Africa), ducks, pigeons, dogs, and cats. Oxen or cows were historically much rarer. Hunted or trapped species indigenous to Ghana included the grasscutter and various species of deer, buffalo, antelope, primates including chimpanzee, leopards, civet cats, warthogs, wild pig, jackal, hares, porcupine, elephant, pangolin, land snails, snakes, lizards, crocodiles and tortoises. From the archaeological deposits relating to the later period of settlement at Eguafo, the largest percentage of identifiable mammal remains were from the bovids (including sheep, goats, pigs and cows).

The socio-cultural impact of new crops and animals in the hinterland region is poorly understood. For an example from much further east, Guyer has argued that the introduction of New World staples such as cassava and maize, which were seen to be completely female farming activities in southern Cameroon, would have important implications for the distribution of these crops, the production of which differed from other traditional, shared farm labour. Historically, with regard to Efutu, Wilhelm Johann Müller wrote in the second half of the seventeenth century that, apart from the men who sold palm-wine and sugar cane, only women "stand in public markets to trade." Change in the type of crop grown, for example maize, during the early European trade period may have also influenced the frequency of trading in Eguafo, with the establishment of more daily markets and may have also supported greater populations. The King reportedly established a number of large, subsidiary villages for farming in the Eguafo polity during 1630 to 1640s, which Kea hypothesized employed enslaved labour.

Gateways of Trade: The Coastal Ports of the Eguafo Kingdom

The coastal ports of the Eguafo Kingdom were chiefly Komenda and Elmina. European activities at these two ports provide valuable sources of documentation about the Eguafo Kingdom, both in terms of its politics and economy, as several European powers had trading posts at the ports, including the Portuguese, the Dutch, the English and the French; not to mention those nations who simply traded from their ships. From these sources, we can get very clear picture of the types of goods in demand in the coastal hinterland, and glean some information regarding the political makeup of the Eguafo Kingdom and its relation to the towns along the coast.

Trade routes to the interior of the Gold Coast varied, but it is likely that at least three major ones existed in the early contact period, connecting inland entrepôts such as Begho with the coast. Wilks' outlined one from Elmina to Twifo, Twifo to Ahafo to Dormaa and then Begho; another from Cape Coast through Assin, Adansi, Tafo (later Kumasi) and Wenchi; and a third which connected Accra through the Afram plains. The earliest and most important port for the Kingdom of Eguafo was Elmina. Elmina became politically independent from both Eguafo and Efutu early on in the Portuguese period, forming what was later described as a "republic" or a "kind of Corporation under the subjection of the Castle, and hath several superior Officers of their own." Certainly, by the late seventeenth century Jean Barbot could describe Elmina as a form of small republic.

At the time of the Dutch conquest in 1637, the town of Elmina was described as being between the sea and the Benya Lagoon, with the only potable water source being located at the Sweet River to the east. The townsfolk were mostly fishermen and traders, and bartered for their supply of foodstuffs from surrounding towns in both Eguafo and Efutu, though some made a living from craft production, for example polishing coral for beads. The provisioning trade also seems significant through-out the coast. This is probably the result of Akan farming populations migrating to the coastal areas to make use of available land and intro-duced species. For example, a letter from 1709 by Dalby Thomas to the Royal African Company back in London described the relationship be-tween those living in the immediate hinterland who bartered palm wine, corn, yam, fruits and sugar cane with those on the coast, in return for fish. In the case of gold, however, it would appear that those living in the coastal towns acted as brokers for their country neighbors.

The Portuguese, trading first at Shama, and then from Elmina, early found that the most popular items for trade included cloth, brass, beads and a growing market for slaves. Slaves were brought from Benin until the mid 1530s, and beyond Benin and farther south in the Congo, by the Portuguese, through São Tomé to Elmina for gold. The Dutch con-tinued to import slaves into the seventeenth century, though more for their own use rather than to trade inland. Slaves were often used as porters in the gold trade. Such long distance trade routes may have been in existence before the Portuguese started trading in the late1470s, where the early demand for slaves at Elmina has led some to suggest that routes pre-date Portuguese trade. In his 1555 publication, Eden re-counts John Windham's voyage to Guinea in 1553 mentioning the im-portance of both pepper and gold to the early English trade. Lok's journey of 1554-1555 also managed to sell cloth at Elmina and got gold at Shama, which was later known to be rich in gold. Lok describes the traders as being very careful, and using weights and measures to ensure the amounts were correct. William Towerson was apprenticed to the trader Miles Mording, who was principally a cloth exporter at the time of Towerson's voyages. His account of three voyages to Guinea in the mid-sixteenth century suggest that at this time, the trade in gold had al-ready begun to decline at Elmina, though this may have been the result of other interlopers. By the late seventeenth century, the most popular imported trade items can still be grouped into beads, cloth and metal wares. Brandy and firearms (such as "snap pans") were also much de-sired commodities, the latter especially for ceremonies.

The other major port associated with the Eguafo Kingdom was

Komenda, located almost halfway between Shama and Elmina, which became prominent in the seventeenth century. In 1602 de Marees wrote that Komenda was a good place to trade, as the people there had little power, and many hinterland states traded there. Further, in the early seventeenth century it was popular with several European nations as there were initially no permanent European trading posts to monopolize trade as at Elmina. The village attracted traders from Ahanta, Adom, Wassa, and Eguafo, especially to purchase Venetian beads, copper basins, iron, mirrors and cloth. Some traders, however, lamented the fact that though there were many African traders, they only bought small amounts with them to trade. Gold was often melted down and cut into smaller pieces, and thus it was easy to cut the gold with brass to defraud European sellers. Traders from Abrem and Akani located to the north of Eguafo were important sources of gold. The Abrem traders had to pass through Eguafo to trade at either Komenda or Elmina, and through Efutu to trade at Mouri. While the coastal port of Komenda was significant in the gold trade, it was also used, particularly by the British in the seventeenth century to provision other ships or factories along the coast with corn. For example in 1608 Pieter van den Broecke wrote of provisioning his ship there, and between 1681/82 there are several references to the British having bought chests of corn to send back to Cape Coast, and further in 1686/87 a reference to purchasing "three or four hundered chests of corn" to send to Cape Coast.

In order to make the most of this trade through Komenda, in the mid-to-late-seventeenth century the competition between the French, English, Dutch and Brandenburgers became increasingly fierce. The Dutch West India Company had erected a lodge at "Little Commany" in 1638. Also from 1638 the French had established trade there, but had not been able to establish a more secure lodge or fort until 1687. William Cross wrote from the British lodge at Komenda in 1686 that the French "went to give the king a visit at Great Comendo... for they have a design to settle either here or at Ampena and build a ffortification and went in order to gett the kings leave, which tis said by great presents they have obteyn'd," though later in the month he stated that the King of Eguafo had declined permission. Robert Ewles, who replaced Cross at Komenda, wrote in 1687 that "the Dutch have been supplied with a great many Negroe soldiers from the Mina, likewise at Ampeny the same, imagining the French may settle either here or at Ampeny," and indeed the French began building a wattle and daub post in Komenda in 1687, "about a pistoll shott from the Dutch" fort, and had contracted with the King of Eguafo to build a stronger fort in about a years time. A plan of Komenda dating to circa 1687 shows the relationship between the English Fort on the west bank of the Susu Lagoon, and the French post and Dutch Fort on the east side of the Lagoon. A Dutch slave apparently set fire to the French post in January in 1688.

Up until that time, the Dutch had the majority of trade with the Eguafo state through Komenda. The destruction of the French trading house, however, led to a civil war within the Eguafo Kingdom between pro-French and pro-Dutch factions, for example the then King favored the Dutch, and tried to expel the French from Komenda, though he then allowed them to return a month later. The Eguafo King felt that the French had not lived up to their original agreements of constructing a strong fort—which the Dutch then promptly promised to do prior to the attack, providing the English lodge was not attacked. In 1681, the Dutch post was burnt down by the Komenda, and the company planned to rebuild it in 1682. Even though they had plans to fortify their lodge around 1686-1687, by 1689 the Dutch also had plans to "drop Commany and to take away whatever men there may be at present." The Dutch post, however, called Vredenburgh, was fortified in 1689 on the east bank of the Susu Lagoon.

The Dutch position in Komenda was seriously disadvantaged, however, by their breakdown in relations with John Kabes, a powerful trader who also had varying relations with the English, and who was purportedly feared by local rulers as well. It was reported in 1687 that the Dutch intended to make war on Eguafo, using troops from Adom and Twifo. Also in this year many skirmishes were reported between Twifo and neighboring states of Abrem, Efutu and Eguafo. In 1688, the English factor at Komenda wrote that "the Great Fatera [of Eguafo] is defeated, and by its means it is thought Aguaffo will be worsted, though as yet wee have no ill news from the King, but that he has fought stoutly. It is reported the Litle Fatera has routed the Cuferas [Twifo]. The enemies have taken and burnt all the upper croomes [villages], but as yet have not attempted our parts here." The Eguafo troops were completely routed, and the King and several of the "Grandees" or noblemen of the Kingdom were killed. Taking advantage of their weakened position, the Dutch were then able to enter into a much more binding agreement with the Eguafo, which divested the control of Komenda (and indeed the shoreline between the Pra and the Benya Rivers) from the Kingdom, though this was very difficult to enforce.

In part, these tensions lead to the Komenda Wars, which began circa 1694, from an incident where some of the Dutch company employees mining gold at a nearby source were attacked. It was suggested later that the attack was instigated by John Kabes, who had previously invited the Dutch to mine at Sika Burgh without the consent of the King of Eguafo, though Daaku suggests that the Dutch may have acted intentionally in order to precipitate such a war. The Komenda Wars have a complicated history, and involve several attempts on the part of the Dutch to establish peace and keep their trade routes open. They managed to negotiate one peace in 1696 that was favorable to them, but this was sabotaged by the British. Hostilities began again and lasted until circa1700 and another negotiation, which again was frustrated by British interests and "their assassination of the Commany King." The English then entered into hostility with Eguafo, and tried to get support from the Fante; and when that failed, the Dutch. The Dutch suggested they could enlist the help of Tekki Ankan, the younger brother of the King, who had also been involved in the King's murder.

After the hostilities, and when Tekki Ankan had become the new King of Eguafo, the Dutch tried a second treaty in August 1702, which had similar clauses as the treaty of 1696, including exclusive trading rights (shared with the English Royal African Company) to the beaches in Eguafo, Efutu and Asebu, and threats of war to keep the trade routes open, and the inland traders safe. Tekki Ankan and the principal members of his court co-signed a further treaty that sold all coastal lands between Shama and British Komenda, and between Dutch Komenda and Elmina in 1703, including Sika Burgh, or the contentious "Gold Hill," where past events had sparked the Komenda Wars, to the Dutch. Though note that when confronted by the English, Tekki Ankan denied signing any such treaty. Tekki Ankan's death in August 1704, and the succession of his brother Tekki Addico to the stool, instituted a new treaty between the Dutch and Eguafo. For the British, trade through Komenda consisted primarily of gold at this time, with very few references to slaves. The factory also supplied provisions to Cape Coast Castle and other ships, as discussed above. In part, this cycle of abandonment by the Dutch, English and French at Komenda in the latter part of the seventeenth century, was due to poor trade, but also the political instability within the Eguafo Kingdom and in neighboring Abrem. After the Komenda Wars, Dutch and British Komenda, as the two portions on either side of the river came to be known, became independent from the Eguafo Kingdom. It would seem that the powerful trader John Kabes managed to found the paramount stool for British Komenda around this time.

The above discussion of Elmina and Komenda clearly shows the complex nature of interactions between the coast and the hinterland, and the European companies who had a vested interested in keeping trade routes open, and maximizing their own share in the profits. In some regard, this jockeying for position shown by European companies in the coast towns and ports, matched that of rival kingdoms in the hinterland. It is this relationship I now wish to briefly focus on, in particular Eguafo's relations with its nearest neighbors: Efutu to the east, and Adom and Yabiw in the west.

Eguafo and the Neighboring Kingdoms of Efutu, Yabiw, and Adom

If we look at Eguafo in relation to its nearest hinterland neighbors, the Kingdoms of Efutu, Yabiw, and Adom, we can see a similar pattern of initial benefit from the increase in trade along the coast. This included the migration of hinterland groups to the coast, the consolidation of heterarchical forms of government, the growing taxation of trade and an increased access to European trade goods. This relationship also suggests a growing competition for the European trade, especially with the emergence of larger states in the hinterland at the end of the seventeenth century. This, coupled with the shift in the focus of trade from gold to slaves, lead to the eventual inability of the coastal hinterland kingdoms to maintain control over their trade routes, ports and political boundaries. What is important to point out, however, is while there are transformations in the economic and political spheres, there is continuity in social identity.

The Kingdom of Efutu borders Eguafo to the east. We have two detailed descriptions of this Kingdom dating roughly to the middle of the seventeenth century: one by Nicolas Villault, the other by Wilhelm Müller which was first published in 1673 and detailed his time as Lutheran pastor for the Danish African Company at Fort Frederiksborg between 1662 and 1669. While Müller drew on some previously published sources, he also provided a detailed description of the government of Efutu in the seventeenth century. He described the King as having limited absolute power and the government being run more by a form of aristocracy, where a council of elders and other "most important of the people" must approve of any decisions that affected the Kingdom. As other commentators had discussed, the King's house was separated from other dwellings, around their own courtyard, but with no other mark of distinction obvious to him. He described the King's retinue in some detail, particularly his steward or linguist who acted as interpreter and was the administrator of the court and royal household; and his *marini*, or tax-collectors, who were based at Cape Coast and Frederiksborg, at Amanful, where the Danish had a small trading fort. Within the court there was also an administrative position known as the *day*, which Müller described as being a "stadtholder" and treasurer. The position of court linguist was a common feature of coastal Fante societies, while the *day* appears to be peculiar to the Kingdom of Efutu and the Fante state.

To the west of Eguafo, on the Pra River, are the Yabiw and Adom Kingdoms. David Henige has stated that these two Kingdoms are not referred to in the extant records of the Portuguese traders during the fifteenth, sixteenth or seventeenth centuries. While the coastal town of Shama is frequently mentioned, it is unclear as to whether this coastal town is part of a Kingdom (initially like Komenda was to Eguafo) or an independent settlement (as Elmina became). Shama was used by the Portuguese as a provisioning station for other ports. By the mid-seventeenth century, it has been suggested that there were kings in both Yabiw and Shama, though Henige has argued that it was more likely that there were only "Caboceros" in Shama, a situation similar to that between Eguafo and Komenda. It would appear that Shama was politically dependent on Yabiw at this time, though this may have been reversed by the eighteenth century. In the late nineteenth century, the Yabiw King was considered a divisional military chief of Shama.

On the Dutch map of 1629, Yabiw is described as being a small country with a single town on the river. By the second half of the seventeenth century, Yabiw was able to impede trade on the western borders of Eguafo, but with the rise of more powerful, centralized states in the area the political territory significantly changed the earlier alignment of kingdoms in this area, and Yabiw ceased to be a dominant player. Bosman stated that the Kingdom was inconsequential at the beginning of the eighteenth century, and while good in marketing millet, their more powerful neighbors to the north, Adom, would continually "fleece and keep them under." The Kingdom of Adom bordered the states of Yabiw to the south, Eguafo and Abrem to the East, and Wassa and Denkyera to the northwest, and Ahanta to the southwest. The Kingdom had rich gold resources, and controlled a large portion of the trade along the Pra and Ankobra rivers, acting as conduits for European traders based at the coastal ports of Butre, Axim, Sekondi and Shama. What is significant about the Kingdom of Adom is that its political structure in the late seventeenth century was organized around several important noblemen rather than a single king. Shortly after this, a sizeable reduction of the political territory of the state may have occurred in the face of the expanding Wassa and Denkyira States. This may have caused a retreat to a more defensible position on an island in the Pra; protecting Adom trade routes along one of the main rivers bordering their Kingdom. As with Yabiw, our knowledge of the organization of the Kingdom prior to this, however, is scant, especially since it did not border the coast.

Conclusion

Before the Portuguese began trading along the Gold Coast, quickly followed by other European companies, the coastal hinterland population of central Ghana probably lived in small farming communities, which were fairly mobile and still relied on hunting and fishing as well. Some of these settlements were defensive in nature, for example on hilltops such as the Dumpow, or surrounded by earthworks such as those in the Birim Valley, or near Abrem Berase. Others, such as the coastal sites of Coconut Grove, Brenu Akyinim, and large sites around the Benya and Aborobeano Lagoons, however, were not defensive settlements. In the early contact period there is reference to persons of importance within the coastal communities, such as Caramansa at Elmina, but it is not until the early sixteenth century that we see the distinction between "kings," "xeryfe" and "noblemen" for inland polities, though the use of these terms is somewhat unclear. In the early seventeenth century, the borders of the Eguafo Kingdom stretched from Elmina and Efutu on the east, to the Pra River on the west, and were to remain stable until the early eighteenth century, though by this time the coastal ports had become independent of the Eguafo Kingdom. The political organization of the Kingdom during its early history remains unclear, but it seems probable that it was not governed by a rigid hierarchy, but more a heterarchical structure where power was shared between lineage heads, ritual specialists and, increasingly, those involved in trade. The main source of revenue for the Kingdom came through the taxation of trade, predominantly from the so-called "Akani" who had to travel through territories such as Eguafo to reach the coastal markets.

Zones of Exchange and World History: Akani Captaincies on the Seventeenth Century West African Gold Coast

RAY A. KEA

Ray A. Kea is Professor of History at the University of California (UC) at Riverside. After teaching African history for eight years at The Johns Hopkins University, Kea joined the UC-Riverside Department of History in 1991. He is the author of the classic work Settlement, Trade, and Polities in the Seventeenth Century Gold Coast. *The following essay is a revised paper presented at the All-University of California Economic and All-University of California History Groups Research Conference, November 2006, UC-San Diego. Interested readers can contact the author about the sources used herein.*

Introduction

Scholarly investigations of Ghanaian history have shown how questions surrounding state formation, urbanization, cultural politics and production, networks of trade, migration, communication, governance, cultural-religious articulations, idioms, connectivities, and the complexity of identity strategies and markers were prominent throughout the region's "pre-colonial" history. Historical scholarship has demonstrated how a range of groups contributed to shaping legal, political, social, and cultural contours of the region and to initiating new forms of me-

79

diation, dialogue, and understanding. One such group can be identified as "Akani" merchant-brokers. For much of the seventeenth century they dominated a great deal of the Gold Coast's import-export trade through their captaincy organization. In this study the "captaincy" is treated as a fundamental category through which Akani culture and commercial practices may be observed and theorized.

Anthropologist Michel-Rolph Trouillot's perceptive study of "global transformations" provides a framework for understanding the relationships between the agency and localized practices of Akani merchant-broker organization, globalization (i.e., global flows), and world history (i.e., interconnections). He writes,

> Culturally, the world we inherit today is the product of global flows that started in the late fifteenth century and continue to affect human populations today. Yet the history of the world is rarely told in those terms. Indeed, the particularity of the dominant narratives of globalization is a massive silencing of the past on a world scale, the systematic erasure of continuous and deep encounters that have marked human history throughout the globe.... After all, [facts about global flows] were always part of the available record. That they were rarely accorded the significance they deserve suggests the existence and deployment of mechanisms of silence that make them appear less relevant than they are, even when they are known.... Thus, a theoretical task parallel to the documentation of these flows is to assess the terms of the dominant narratives of world history—the words used, the concepts deployed, the setting of the plots and subplots, the depiction of the characters and the connections made or ignored between all of the above. (Trouillot 2003, 34–35)

Advocating a decolonization strategy in historical construction of the past, Trouillot regards with suspicion and skepticism "universalizing" words such as "modernity," "progress," "development," and "globalization." These categories are formulated in dominant meta-narratives, which register the temporality of modernist ideology and the orientations of mainstream world history. Trouillot's objection to this position is that these categories project the North Atlantic experience on a universal scale, which they themselves helped to create; the universals do not describe the world but offer visions of it, and in the process silence their own history. In his view, it is incumbent on historical scholarship to unearth the silences, including those conceptual and theoretical missing links that make the universals so attractive.

Following Trouillot's guidelines, the present study deploys categories, sets, plots, and subplots, and depicts characters in order to unearth silences pertaining to a West African agency in the early modern world economy. The focus is on the commercial activity of seventeenth century Akani merchant-brokers and their Gold Coast-based captaincies. In the seventeenth century, Akani merchant-brokers were highly esteemed in Gold Coast ports as wealthy and honest gold traders and they were particularly obvious in those coastal towns where European trading companies maintained castles, forts, and factories. The captaincy organization may be seen as an institutional complex with a capacity to manage a socio-commercial environment of wealth and capital accumulation. The present study hypothesizes that its genesis is traceable to the Pra-Ofin-Birim basin. The Akani commercial formation with its trade routes, markets, caravans, merchants and merchant-brokers, and social and cultural networks may be understood on theoretical grounds as a distinctive phase in the *longue durée* of the Pra-Ofin-Birim basin's modes of production and systemic accumulation cycles. Unearthing the Akani captaincy organization and its social-economic and cultural preconditions bring attention to an early modern agency characterized by long-distance commercial connections and participation in global flows of gold bullion. (Historian Sanjay Subrahmanyam argues that "the 'early modern' in Eurasia and Africa ... extend from the middle of the fourteenth to the middle of the eighteenth century")

Akani commercial transactions entailed an ensemble of relations that belongs to what Felicity Nussbaum calls, in another context, "prehistories of globalization" and what C. A. Bayly refers to as "archaic globalization." The point to be made is that, historically speaking, there were different kinds of globalization and global shifts. From the fifteenth century onwards Gold Coast ports were privileged commercial sites which involved an expanding maritime-based mercantile capitalist system, operating out of a northwestern European regional world-system, on the one hand, and an expanding land-based Akani trading organization, which operated on the southern edge of a vast transcontinental system of exchange, on the other. In the ports were to be found the requisite mechanisms (contracts and treaties), social groups (artisans, brokers, officials, militias, etc.), and infrastructures (warehouses and markets) that facilitated commercial exchange and capital accumulation. Based on existing evidence, it may be proposed that the organizational and wealth accumulating capacities of the Akani captaincies reached their peak in the seventeenth century. The captaincy helped bring about new forms of interaction and commercial exchange and new agendas for political and social collaboration. The captaincy's modes of interaction define what little is known about Akani associational or public life in the coastal towns. One aspect of captaincy associational life embraced the market and the exchange of trade goods; another involved the captaincy in public ceremonialism and ritualized celebration.

In its analysis and interpretation of the Akani commercial phenomenon, the present study carries several underlying premises. The Akani system was a privileged site of commerce and exchange within the larger West African world-region. It was the subject and agent of a specific historical praxis, a praxis that was tied to long-term cultural, political, social, and material reconfigurations in the Pra-Ofin-Birim basin. A further premise is that the Akani commercial formation can be linked, conceptually and empirically, to early modern processes of globalization (or "global flows") across the Afro-Eurasian *oikumene* through long-distance commercial interconnections and the "universal development of productive forces," or, phrased in another way, "expanding technological capacity." The various discourses of the socio-historical world called "Akanland" arose out of what I term the historical processes of globalization and the development of productive forces. The discourses have been interpreted in different ways by historians but they are representative of what Castoriadis calls in another context "the imaginary dimension of society." With regard to the historical growth of productive forces and the expansion of Akani commercial organization, the relevant time period is the fifteenth and sixteenth centuries and the locus of transformative change was the Pra-Ofin-Birim basin. What did the development of the productive forces in the basin entail? Archaeological and historical studies indicate that this process included the establishment of new trade routes, new markets, and technical changes in mining, metalworking, and the expansion of agricultural production through land clearance. Another consideration relates to the cognitive and conceptual mapping of Akani commercial networks, principally prestige goods networks, and the growth of productive forces in the Pra-Ofin-Birim basin. A dynamic relationship existed between the expanding geography of Akani commerce—that is, its material and social capital as institutionalized in the captaincy organization—and the expanding geography of Akani ideas, knowledge, and cultural-symbolic expressions as represented in ceramic traditions, terracotta sculptures, the cult of the dead, and gold weight iconography, which generated cultural imagery of an emergent "Akanland" world. Within this complex matrix, social, cultural, and symbolic connections were shaped and re-shaped, engendering new forms of political collaboration, new social alliances, new cultural imaginaries, and new definitions of the citizen and the political actor.

Akani merchant-brokers left no documented account of their operations and organization. What, then, is the historian's source of information about them? How is a history of Akani captaincies to be narrated and presented? A particularly rich source of information can be found in the seventeenth century archival records of European trading companies (for two studies of Akani commercial life based largely on trading company records see van Dantzig 1990; Kea 1982, chapter 7). In their totality these records, which are of varying quality, constitute the preserved knowledge systems and institutional memories of chartered mercantile organizations. Since they are primarily concerned with situational conditions and specific events, as these related directly or indirectly to trade, they do not tell the story of Akani trade, nor do they define Akani merchant-brokers as a subject of historical inquiry, but they do provide the historian with the necessary data for a construction of certain features pertaining to the organization and activity of Akani captaincies. The data comprise letters, daybooks, diaries, trade journals, debtors' lists, accounts books, legal cases, inventories, treaties and con-

tracts, and reports and registers of different kinds. Published texts from
the period in Danish, Dutch, English, German, French, Portuguese,
Latin, Swedish, and Italian are also informative sources as long as one
is able to define the ideological space of mercantilist thinking within
the political frame of European chartered companies. Through an in-
terdisciplinary methodology, a conceptual framework, and a critical historical analysis of the companies' records, these archival and published
source materials can yield important information notwithstanding their
Eurocentric vantage point. Among the companies were the Old West
Indies and New West Indies Companies (Dutch), the Guinea, East Indies, and Royal African Companies (English), the African and West Indies and Guinea Companies (Danish). The Swedish African Company
was active in the Gold Coast trade from 1649 until 1663 and the Brandenburg Company from the 1680s until the early 1720s. Other seventeenth century companies like the "Company of Adventurers of London
Trading to Gynney and Bynney" and the "Company of Merchants Trading to Guinea" had short commercial life spans in West Africa. With
the exception of the Brandenburg Company, whose trading establishments were ill-positioned to benefit from the activities of Akani merchant-brokers, the other companies spared no effort in attracting them
to the coastal towns where they maintained trading stations. For obvious
reasons, trading company records focus on the commercial transactions
of the captaincy organization's associational life and considerably less
on social, ceremonial, and ritual practices, cultural production, and symbolic value and capital associated with Akani captaincies.

Archival and published sources are clearly not enough in the historical construction of Akani captaincies or for that matter the genesis and
expansion of the Akani trading formation. This is evident if historical
construction and analysis are formulated with reference to multiple temporalities. Archival and published documents provide information relating to a range of situated events and circumstances—that is, one kind
of temporality—but they do not give explicit data concerning conjunctures and long durations. Nor do they furnish information about the preconditions and social possibility of seventeenth century Akani
mercantile culture. Archaeology, on the other hand, furnishes the kind
of information that enables the historian to postulate conjunctures and

long durations in the construction of an Akani commercial past, and at the same time, contributes to an understanding of the material, cultural, and social preconditions that made this past possible. In addition, Arabic and Ajami manuscripts, oral histories, art history, metrology, and historical geography represent other bodies of evidence with different temporalities, ranging from single events to long-term perspectives. At the same time, these data throw light on material culture, social and cultural networks, and symbolic reservoirs. The present study is to be understood as a preliminary theoretical and empirical investigation of the Akani captaincy organization from the perspective of events, praxis, and the *longue durée*. It draws attention to the need for a fuller and more systematic examination of Akani commercial life in the early modern period.

Historicizing the Akani Commercial Formation

How do we set the boundaries and agency of the Akani commercial formation over time and space? Historical evidence clearly indicates that in the medieval and early modern periods (1450-1700), West African gold played a key role in the world economy. Gold production in the Pra-Ofin-Birim basin was a major contributor to West Africa's gold export trade in this period. A number of studies attest to the global significance of West African gold. One study relates that "by the late thirteenth and fourteenth centuries, Genoa was receiving 'enormous quantities of gold' from West Africa and during the whole of the fifteenth century 'the gold of Ghana' still reached Italy mainly through the port of Genoa," and the Republic of Genoa maintained far-flung commercial and financial networks and competed for access to the "gold of Ghana" (a reference to West African gold). Of particular significance is the fact that some scholars locate the origins of world capitalism in the Italian city-states of the thirteenth and fourteenth centuries, especially Genoa. Appropriately, William Martin has noted, "world-systems analysis, like the capitalist world-economy, has deep African roots." Summing up the pivotal importance of African gold in the medieval period, another writer comments, "there is every indication that the central and western half of the Medieval world economy (that part west of the Straits of Malacca and evidently extending all the way to the Caribbean) was based on African gold." And according to yet one more work,

> the gold of [West] Africa, for sheer quantity, had no real rival in the medieval world [and] access to [West] African gold helped assure the economic primacy of the Muslim shores of the Mediterranean over Iraq, Iran or Byzantium and, after 1200, it helped the economic success of the Christian shores of the Mediterranean and the decisive dominance of the Italians and the Catalans. (Postan 1987, 470)

The medieval world-economy represents then a temporal and spatial boundary and a benchmark in the trans-regional history of the Akani commercial formation.

The spatial and temporal scale of West African gold bullion circulation is detailed in another innovative study. In his multi-volume work on the history of mining, metallurgy, and the minting of silver and gold in the Mediterranean basin from the decline of the Roman Empire until 1575, economic historian Ian Blanchard reconstructs long bullion cycles of Afro-European supremacy in gold and silver production from 1125 to 1475 and the transfer of supremacy from Europe and Africa to the Americas from 1475 to 1575. According to Blanchard, West African gold production increased substantially from the tenth century onward and continued to grow through the fifteenth and sixteenth centuries. The flows of gold and silver between Europe and northern Africa contributed to the emergence of a single Afro-European bullion market in the Mediterranean basin in the twelfth century, a market characterized by "the long term stable distribution of gold and silver, as well as by falling prices which increased consumption, fuelling a new international economy which lasted for a further three centuries." The primacy of the West African world-region as a leading source of gold in the early and high medieval world-economy can be attributed in part to the expansion of the gold extractive industry in the Pra-Ofin-Birim basin in the late first millennium CE. Here is another temporal and spatial marker of a trans-regional Akani commercial system. The West African moment in the production and distribution of gold represents, in Blanchard's study, a global shift in bullion production from Central Asia to West Africa. It is likely though not firmly established empirically that in this period a new center of gravity of West African commercial and productive activity took shape in the Pra-Ofin-Birim basin. In other words, the proposition is that the genealogy of historical capitalism and the "modern" world-system is tied to technological and other changes in West Africa, including the Pra-Ofin-Birim basin. The question to be raised concerning the data on the globality of West African and specifically Pra-Ofin-Birim gold must be "what are the implications and how might they relate to the construction of a world historiography"? However, the *longue durée* of the basin's historical development has yet to be written.

The continued dominance of African gold in the world-economy in more recent centuries has been pointed out in a recent work on the early modern Indian Ocean world. In his conclusion, the author observes that in the seventeenth century the principal commodities Europe exchanged in Asia were American silver and African gold. There is other compelling evidence. Two economic historians, Dennis O. Flynn and Arturo Giráldez, comment on the global role of African gold in the sixteenth and seventeenth centuries. "So Italy stood at the crossroads where the south–north axis maintained by Spanish policy and the Genoese *asientos* met the east–west axis running to the Levant and the Far East, where the golden road from Genoa to Antwerp met the silver road to the east." The Spanish Crown needed European financiers to transfer gold to soldiers in Flanders, who always demanded at least part of their pay in gold. American silver was therefore exchanged for African gold in Italy, "whereupon American silver headed off to China and African gold was forwarded to the Low Countries." This is a period which economic historians call the "first global age." At the heart of these early modern developments was, as Trouillot phrases it, "the continuous centrality of the Atlantic as the revolving door of major global flows." The sixteenth and seventeenth centuries compose another temporal and spatial boundary in the history of the Akani commercial formation and the commodity chain networks that this formation articulated. In this framework, we can situate the well-documented Akani captaincy organization.

By the second half of the seventeenth century European chartered companies (Dutch, Danish, English, Swedish, and Brandenburg) had set up trading stations—castles, forts, and lodges or factories—in the port towns along the Gold Coast seaboard. Since the late fifteenth century the primary attraction of European merchant capital to the Gold Coast was the availability of an abundance of fine quality gold. The total West African gold exports between 1471 and 1500 amounted to an estimated seventeen tons and a substantial share very likely came from mines in the Pra-Ofin-Birim basin. This gold helped the Portuguese Crown to finance its most expensive venture, namely the opening up of a Cape route to the Asian trade. The Portuguese were buying an unknown portion of gold from the "Acanes" (van Dantzig 1990). Later, in the second half of the seventeenth century, Gold Coast gold exports were again subsidizing European commercial operations in South Asia and East Asia. At this time, according to Dutch reports, Akani captaincies were annually supplying European trading stations with two-thirds of the gold exported from the Gold Coast. By 1700 gold and various luxury and bulk goods products from the Americas, Asia, Europe, and Africa were integrated into a single global circuit of pricing and commodity flows. From the fifteenth century through the end of the seventeenth Akani captaincies were crucial actors in movement of gold bullion in the world economy.

The Akani captaincy system was very likely a product of interactions within the basin between economic networks and power relations that date from the late first millennium CE ("medieval" period) and were continuous through the sixteenth century and up to the late seventeenth century ("early modern" period). The interactions probably materialized initially in large towns like Asantemanso (phases one and two, 800-1500) and Adansemanso (abandoned by the late sixteenth century) and in some of the numerous earthwork sites in the Birim River Valley. At what point during this lengthy period the captaincy organization was created remains an open question. One may hypothesize that over time the Akani commercial formation passed through different phases of material expansion and adjustment, and that over time the captaincy organization emerged as an instrument of commercial exchange that eventually became the dominant structure of exchange. It promoted commercial and cultural integration throughout much of the greater Gold Coast region.

Who were the Akani? From the fifteenth to the early eighteenth century Akani merchants and merchant-brokers are referred to in European trading company records under varied designations, e.g., "Acane," "Acanes," "Acanij," "Akanists," "Accanisten," "Akanisten," "Arcani," "Arcania," "Arcanies," "Arcanians," and "Hacanys." The term "Akan" means "first," eminent, or "foremost," and apparently signifies an achieved elite (or noble) status. Seventeenth century Akani merchant-brokers were known throughout the towns and polities of the Gold Coast littoral as *abirempon* (singular, *obirempon*)—that is, rich, great, and powerful men (and, in some instances, women). Historian Albert van Dantzig identifies the "Akani" in the following way:

> The Akanists seem to have had in common a language, Akan, and a profession, gold trading, but they apparently did not constitute a single state.... They may have constituted something coming quite close to the late medieval Hansas of Europe. Like the founders of the Hansas, the original Akanists were probably of diverse ethnic origins, but adopted a kind of *lingua franca*, Akan in this case, and formed associations of individual itinerant traders, who may have adopted or continued to some extent the Mande caravan traditions. Later they organized the arteries of communication linking them. In the process of consolidating their economic and political power they also left their socio-cultural mark, 'akanizing' a large part of the West African forest zone just like the Hansa Germanized the Baltic area of Europe. (van Dantzig 1990)

Van Danzig defines the Akani ("Akanists") as gold merchants engaged in long-distance trading systems, which included Muslim merchants. The processes, events, and developments that he describes occurred in the inland Pra-Ofin-Birim basin, which was not only a center of gold production but also a cultural and political homeland of the "Akanists." As was stated above, the basin's socio-economic complex was an active contributor to West Africa's medieval and early modern gold bullion exports—from the Mediterranean world to India. I would suggest that in this global context, land clearance—that is, agrarian expansion—was articulated in the fifteenth and sixteenth centuries as a political-administrative act, either by a single polity or a federation of polities, and as a form of (Akani?) merchant capital investment. This development marked a particular phase in the material expansion of the productive forces in the Pra-Ofin-Birim basin and did not signify the beginning of agriculture in the rain forest. The organizational viability of the Akani captaincy system presupposes certain preconditions: new types of centralized power, an expansion of property and asset use, surplus wealth accumulation, the arrangement of credit and other financial instruments, and the creation of ritual-cultural complexes linking heterogeneous social groups into material and symbolic (that is, moral and spiritual) networks of interaction.

Becoming an "Akani"—a person of achieved or ascribed high status—would have meant privileged access to material, cultural, and ritual and ceremonial resources as well as favored access to exchanges of goods and services. The ranks of the Akani were, in theory, open to anyone of talent and ambition. Van Danzig defines the Akani ("Akanists") as gold merchants engaged in long-distance trading systems, which included Muslim merchants, and he suggests that they may also be identified as powerful "brokers" of cultural, social, and symbolic capital. The consolidation of their economic and political power produced an instrument that was necessary for the implementation of commercial relations, contracts, and policies. The complex local and global conjunctures that enabled these phenomena have yet to be examined.

Identity formation is a complex process. Identities take shape over a period of time for varied ends and through varied means. Because they are historically derived, sociologically presented, and discursively constituted, it is necessary to locate the contexts of identity formation across cultural, linguistic, social, political, and economic spaces in order to understand what identities are and how they are constituted. To comprehend what Akani identities were and how they were constituted means constructing the varied spaces in which identity formation processes occurred. Over the centuries the "Hansa-like" Akani merchants achieved commercial and cultural ascendancy in these spaces, which to some extent archaeological investigations have already revealed. These investigations also provide necessary and broader temporal and material contexts, although they do not push their interpretations into world-spanning trajectories.

The Captaincy Organization

It can be said that in its emergent and "mature" state the space-economy of the Akani commercial system had an extensive dimension—that is, an expanding geographical range—as well as an intensive dimension—that is, a network of nodal or urban centers. The evidence for this is perhaps to be found in a 1629 annotated Dutch map which depicts "the [coastal and inland] regions of the Gold Coast in Guinea." For the purposes of this study the map represents an early-seventeenth-century commercial and political geography of the Akani commercial formation. Within the formation, Gold Coast towns provided an organizational framework as knowledge-rich matrixes of marketing and exchange strategies, credit-debt relations, caravan formation, and trading agents. They were integral parts of commodity and trading capital circulation, and were sites where circulation was organized and where decisions about the use of commodities and capital were made.

A published Dutch source of 1601 provides a relevant account concerning the coastal and sub-coastal urban geography of the Gold Coast.

> The towns which lie towards the interior of the country [i.e., 5-15 miles from the coast] are richer in goods and gold than the [coastal] towns, and have more houses and are more populous than the seaside towns; they also have wealthier merchants who conduct more trade than those in the coastal towns whose inhabitants are the interpreters, boatmen, pilots, officials, fishermen, and slaves of the inhabitants of the interior towns.... The inland towns are extremely large compared to the coastal towns ... but I have learned from the Blacks that further inland still are larger towns containing multitudes of people. (Pieter de Marees [1601] quoted in Kea 1982, p.

23; for a long-duration view of the Gold Coast littoral and its
hinterland see Cook and Spiers 2004)

Archaeological surveys and excavations have confirmed this description. In the course of the seventeenth century, the coastal and sub-coastal
towns became sites where Akani captaincies and caravans engaged in
commercial exchanges with local merchants, stool-holders, and European factors. (Archaeological fieldwork has yet to identify distinctive
Akani quarters in any former coastal and sub-coastal town sites.)

In 1601 there was, as far as is known, only one captaincy on the
Gold Coast. It was located in the coastal town of Elmina, the largest of
the Gold Coast ports. In the 1620s and 1630s there is evidence that captaincies were being set up in several ports along the Fante coast, east of
Elmina, but there is no precise information about the names of the captains or their assistants. In the 1610s there are specific references to captaincies in four unnamed sub-coastal towns. In this period, most of the
captaincies were to be found in sub-coastal towns such as the capitals
of the coastal polities—Eguafo, Afutu, Fante, and so on. By 1650, there
were six coastal captaincies and by the 1660s there were between nine
and fifteen. In the 1640s and 1650s, captaincies were established in the
coastal towns where the English and Swedish trading companies located
their trading stations. From the 1670s to 1700 there were ten permanent
coastal captaincies and another five to ten temporary ones, the latter included captaincies that were located in towns for only one to five years.
During the same period the number of captaincies in the sub-coastal
towns is uncertain but is likely to have ranged from five to ten. It should
be noted that for most of the seventeenth century the Akani captaincies
kept no boats, although in the second half of the century there were exceptions. If they needed to travel by sea, they tended to rely on European
factors at the trading stations or local dignitaries from whom they would
rent the use of boats and crews.

The captaincies were guild-like with respect to their internal organization and occupied distinct quarters either within coastal and sub-
coastal towns or on the outskirts. A captaincy was headed by a "captain"
and his assistant, or "lieutenant." They had under their authority senior
and junior merchant-brokers who included younger brothers and sons.

There are no references to Akani women serving as captains, but Dutch records refer to senior merchant-brokers in the captaincies who were the wives, sisters, and widows of captains and senior merchant-brokers. The captain can be characterized as a master merchant-broker who supervised senior, junior, and apprentice merchant-brokers. The number of senior and junior merchant-brokers attached to a captaincy ranged from fewer than ten at a small port to more than fifty at a large one. In addition, there were servants and slaves who performed services and other functions. Merchant-brokers and their families were mobile. It was not unusual for a senior merchant-broker to be assigned (by his political superiors in "Akanland") to several different ports over a period of several years.

The captain and his assistant were appointed by a state council of office-holders (*caboseros*). Nothing is known about the criteria that qualified an individual to serve as a captain or a lieutenant. Whether the state council represented a single polity (e.g., Asen) or a federation of small polities ("Acanij") is an unresolved issue. The captaincies functioned as places for wholesale and retail business, warehousing sites, sources of credit, and a regulating agency with rules and legal prohibitions. The captains and the other merchant-brokers had a favorable reputation as moneylenders. European factors borrowed gold from captains and their assistants just as readily as local military and political elites.

Many European trading stations included on their payroll resident captains of the Akani merchant-broker community as well as the captains' assistants or deputies. An account from 1670 describes the relationship between Akani captains and the trading stations.

> In the land of Fetu [i.e., Afutu or Efutu] the *Battafuen* [modern, *batafo*, long-distance, wholesale traders], or merchants, from the Kingdom of Accania [i.e., Asen], buy most of the merchandise from the trading Christians. Thus, each nation which trades with the Blacks intentionally strives to have at hand an eminent Accanisten (who is renowned and esteemed in Accania). Such an Accanist [Akani] lives therefore in the town nearest the Christians and receives from the latter not only a fixed monthly allowance but also such goods as says,

> iron bars, copper, tin, etc., and he is also given cheaper wares. He is called a captain, an honorable title among the Accani traders. So when merchants come [to the coast] from Accania in order trade with the Whites they report to this captain with a request: as they are obliged to lay out a certain sum of gold for merchandise, he should go in their place since he can strike a good bargain and gain the best price. (Müller quoted in Kea 1982, chapter 7)

Given the intense competition among the companies, no effort or expense was spared by the chief factors or commandants to retain (or obtain) the loyalty of a captain, who if offered more substantial payments (e.g., a monthly allowance, commissions, various gifts and fees, etc.) than a rival company's agents, might move his entire captaincy to another port.

The trading stations and local port authorities were expected to provide a secure trading environment for the captaincies. Both recognized the captaincy as a corporate entity with legal, social, and economic rights and privileges. Although merchant-brokers were commonly the biggest at the ports where they maintained captaincies, they did not enjoy monopoly rights over the trade of the ports. Rulers of coastal polities exempted captaincies from taxation (customs, tolls, war tax, etc.) although the captaincies were expected to make periodic "donations" to the rulers. However, Akani caravan-merchants were subject to various levies. The sources do not say whether the captains had to pay taxes to their political superiors in "Acanij"/Asen. Presumably, they did.

An interesting and perhaps atypical case is that of a well-known and particularly wealthy Akani captain named Jan Clasen Cutterique of Cape Coast. In his day he was one of the biggest and most influential merchants on the entire Gold Coast. He was one of the signatories of the commercial treaty concluded between the Afutu Kingdom and the English East Indies Company in January 1660. There, he was designated "Captain of the Accanies." Some idea of Cutterique's status can be gleaned from fact that he maintained a large and well-furnished house in Cape Coast. Another indicator of his wealth was his payment of a fine of nearly 1,000 ounces of gold to Aduaffo, the ruler of Afutu, in 1667 after he had killed a man in a duel. In the 1660s and 1670s, Cutterique received monthly allowances and other payments—collectively a form of rent—from both the English factors of Cape Coast and the Danish factors of the nearby port of Amanfro. He served two different chartered companies at the same time. His position was certainly unique, for there is no evidence that any other captain was ever employed by more than one trading company at a time. In addition, he traded with the Dutch at Elmina and aboard the interloper ships that anchored in the Cape Coast Road. For Cutterique to freely trade with the Dutch at Elmina and with interloper ships while receiving "rent" from two chartered companies was also highly unusual, even for someone of his status.

The merchant-brokers conducted their trade aboard ships and at the forts, castles, and lodges. The quantities and kinds of merchandise they purchased were largely determined by commercial and political condition in the Gold Coast interior and the security of the trade routes. A wide range of goods were bought with gold: textiles of different kinds, iron and lead bars, brass- and copperware, tobacco pipes, pottery, firearms, gunpowder, spirits, tallow, a wide variety of beads, knives, pewter ware, and much more. When there were military conflicts or political disputes, the captains suspended all trade until peace and order were restored. At other times, a captaincy's purchases were restricted to a limited range of goods because of the nature of inland market demands or because of slow sales at inland markets. Thus, in November 1645, the Elmina captaincy was interested only in iron bars, neptunes (i.e., large brass basins) and two kinds of cloth. On certain occasions, merchant-brokers would be interested in only one commodity, e.g., gunpowder, sheets, or neptunes. More frequently, merchant-brokers would buy an entire ship's cargo: lead bars, iron bars, carbines, a great range of cloths (Guinea brawls, says, paper brawls, sheets, coarse and fine sletias, perpetuanas, tapseal, narrow nicanees, etc.), rum, and pewterware of all sorts. The captaincies also conducted a big trade in salt and smoked fish.

The Elmina captaincy was one of the most important on the coast and is well documented. A few examples will provide an idea of the kind of information that can be found in the Dutch Company's daybooks. In October 1645 a new captain was appointed to head the captaincy at Elmina, the biggest town on the Gold Coast (resident population, ten to fifteen thousand) and the Dutch Company's chief commercial base in West Africa. A daybook register from the St. George Castle describes the arrival of the captain.

> A servant of the king of Fetuij [Afutu] arrived saying that the expected Accanist [Akani], known to us as Speck and to the Blacks as Quauw [Kwawu], will be here tomorrow or the day after with many Accanists from Futuij and a great number from Mouree. He is coming here to be captain over the Accanists ... (Kea 1982, chapter 7, p. 266)

The next day Kwawu arrived with one hundred of his own servants and one hundred Akani merchant- brokers who resided in the sub-coastal town of Afutu and the port of Moure. On the morning of November 2nd the new captain met with Dutch officials in the Castle.

> This morning, after the gate was raised, appeared the newly arrived captain, Quau, together ... the captain of the Accanists at Moure, besides other merchants. Quau informed us that he had been appointed by the *caboseros* [principal men] of Accanij. Whereupon we replied that neither side should suffer any problems but each should do its duty and that we shall treat him like all the former captains were treated. (Kea 1982, chapter 7, p. 266)

Kwawu assumed authority over a captaincy that had more than thirty senior, junior, and apprentice merchant-brokers—perhaps as many as fifty. His monthly allowance from the Dutch Company was one *benda*, or two ounces of gold. The allowance was customarily paid in gold and merchandise and occasionally in livestock (mainly cattle). His assistant received a monthly allowance of one-ounce gold in addition to "customary presentations." In addition, Kwawu received customs duties on each Dutch ship that traded at Elmina, apparently at the rate of two ounces gold per ship. He regularly received gifts of different kinds, usually luxury items (including cloths, beads, and weapons) and various other forms of remuneration included trade goods, gold, and livestock (cattle, sheep, and goats). The captain and individual merchant-brokers received fixed commissions on all commercial transactions. The Elmina captaincy, which had its own quarter ("Abcou"), received regular gifts from the Dutch factors as a corporate body—that is to say, the gifts were not intended for individual merchant-brokers but for the captaincy itself. The Akani-Dutch relationship was, in fact, reciprocal. On a regular basis, the captain presented Dutch factors with gifts of agricultural produce, livestock, and gold ornaments and jewelry.

In June 1645 a Dutch report from Elmina Castle noted that the general practice of Akani merchant-brokers was to buy a great quantity of imported merchandise at low prices and to sell them for gold at very high prices. One of Kwawu's very important duties was to come to a mutual agreement with the Dutch factors on the prices of the trade goods. It was a practice of the factors to draw up at regular intervals a *marckt-brief* or *prijscourant*, or a price list of all the goods to be sold at the Dutch Company's establishments. The goods included not only merchandise brought from Europe but also commodities purchased from the coasting trade. After the *marckt-brief* was made up, it was presented to the captain and the senior merchant-brokers. Discussions concerning the price list could last for several days and sometimes for weeks. Failure to agree on price adjustments could provoke the captain to suspend all commercial transactions at the Dutch castle and possibly all other Dutch trading stations and to direct the trade to the stations of other European companies.

Elmina was not Kwawu's first appointment as captain. His earlier captaincy or captaincies are not known, but it is likely that in the 1630s he resided in one of the sub-coastal towns. He served as the Elmina captain until 1652 at which time he was appointed by the Akani state council to head the Cape Coast captaincy. He held this post for three years at which time his superiors abruptly removed him from office. The documents do not explain why he was replaced. It is worth noting that Cape Coast, like Elmina, was a major West African port. A 1663 Guinea Company report described it as the "head factory" and residence of the company's chief agent for the whole of Africa. The Cape Coast captaincy was understandably a prestigious one, and as its captain, Kwawu enjoyed much influence among all of the coastal Akani captaincies. After 1655, there are no further references to him in the companies' records. It is likely he was appointed to an inland captaincy and never again served on the coast.

As captain, Kwawu's training and skills had to be considerable for his duties were manifold. He had to know Portuguese Creole, the commercial lingua franca of seventeenth century western Africa, as well as local coastal languages (e.g., Fante, Guan, and possibly Gã). He had to have knowledge of gold weights and measures, both European and local. The local gold weights were based on the Islamic gold and silver weight standards of Timbuktu and Jenne and some of these weights derived from weights used in the ancient Roman Empire (Garrard 1980). He had to know what goods were available at the trading stations and at what prices, when ships and inland caravans would arrive. He also had to know what goods were in demand in the inland markets and at what prices, and he had to know about the military and political situation in the interior of the region since the security of the caravans depended on a peaceful and stable environment. Kwawu would have "hosted" all Akani caravans arriving in Elmina. He adjudicated all disputes that affected his captaincy, especially in cases concerning credit and debt. He ensured that individual members of the captaincy did not deviate from the group norms established to promote their collective interests, for example, by trading gold below a fixed value. He served as a mediator in disputes between different captaincies, between European trading stations—the Dutch and English, for example—and between European trading stations and local rulers. At times, he settled disputes and conflicts between one coastal town and another or between a sub-coastal town and its dependent ports. He concluded commercial agreements with local rulers and the European factors, thereby ensuring rights and privileges for himself and his captaincy. These agreements covered a range of subjects, such as tolls, custom duties, commissions, preferential access to local markets and trading stations, security of merchant-brokers' property, liabilities, and so on. The captain could forbid members of his captaincy from trading with a European fort or factory and he could prohibit Akani caravans from traveling to a particular port or a sub-coastal political capital to trade. He was responsible for ware-housing goods purchased from ships and the port's trading establishment and organizing the caravans that transported the goods from the port to towns and markets in the interior.

One captain who enjoyed a long and distinguished career on the coast was a man named Korankyi. In the 1630s and 1640s, he was captain of the Akani merchant-brokers at Mankessim, a large sub-coastal political capital, and at the same time, he headed the captaincy at the port of Kormantse. In 1655, he was appointed to the captaincy of Cape Coast, succeeding Kwawu. He remained in charge of this captaincy until late 1658 or early 1659, at which time he became the captain of the merchant-brokers at Elmina. His successor at Cape Coast was the wealthy Jan Clasen Cutterique who remained captain there until 1696. For the period between 1632 and 1704, the trading company records refer to more than twenty captains, deputy captains, and more than fifty senior and junior merchant-brokers. These persons represent only a small percentage of the Akani merchant-brokers who resided in the ports and sub-coastal towns in the seventeenth century. Nonetheless, they offer some idea of the organizational scale of Akani trading operations during the period under review.

The International Gold Bullion Trade

From a global perspective, the 1629 Dutch map of the "regions of the Gold Coast" may be said to have constituted a spatial foundation for the Akani commercial formation. In 1679, a Dutch source reported that Akani merchants controlled all of the trade of the greater Gold Coast region. The commercial geography that defined the operations of the Akani captaincies corresponds to what geohistorian Fernand Braudel calls "economic life proper." He defines it as the realm of a market economy, town markets, provincial production surpluses, regional merchants, currencies, and prices. Akani commercial geography would seem to correspond to another level of economic activity, what Braudel designates the domain of merchant capitalism, the sphere of historical grandeur, grand profits, the international world of long-distance trade, and the site where kingdoms and fortunes are made and unmade. The Akani commercial formation was tied historically to transcontinental exchange networks that stretched eastwards towards the Nile Valley and northwards towards the Mediterranean seaboard and from the late fifteenth century onwards towards the Atlantic. To understand early modern merchant capitalism, Fernand Braudel comments, one needs to establish the topography of commodity exchange. Capitalist growth would not have been possible without the "liberating" action of the world market. Capital accumulation could only take place in early modern Europe only because of the high profits of long-distance trade. Merchant capitalism consists of the "places" where capital could be invested. Gold Coast ports were "places" where Akani trading capital, as well as European trading capital, was invested.

A late-seventeenth-century French source estimated that total gold exports from the Gold Coast amounted to 10,000 to 12,000 marks (80,000-96,000 ounces) annually. The Dutch company exported 5,000 marks (40,000 ounces), the English company, 3,000 (24,000 ounces), the interlopers or private traders, three-fourths of whom were Dutch, 1,500 marks (12,000 ounces), and the Danish, Portuguese, Brandenburgers, and French exported altogether 700 to 800 marks (5,600-6,400 ounces). Earlier in the century, the same report notes, yearly gold purchases totaled 14,000 to 15,000 marks (112,000-120,000 ounces). Throughout most of the century, the Akani captaincies were the principal exporters of gold. (For other exports [ivory, dyewood, gum, pepper, lime juice, hides, wax, civet, etc.] see Justesen 2005, vol.1; Law 2001; DeCorse 2001a; Chouin 1998. Akani captaincies did not as a rule sell captives to Europeans. For imports see den Heijer 2003a; den Heijer 2003b)

What happened to the gold supplied by Akani captaincies? Thomas Crisp, a founder and factor of at least two short-lived English companies and the Guinea Company, claimed to have exported half a million pounds sterling from the Gold Coast between 1636 and 1644, or between three and four tons of gold. Most of this gold would have been brought to the coast by Akani caravans. Presumably, Crisp sold some of his gold to the English East India Company. From the 1640s to the 1660s the company's commercial strategy was to acquire "rich Guinea gold" and ivory at the Gold Coast and to sell both in India. Its court of minutes contains numerous references to the Gold Coast–India trade. First enunciated in the late 1649s, the strategy was to join the trade of Guinea, that is, the Gold Coast, to the trade in India because gold was "so much in demand in the East." Another report relates, "it is agreed that the trade of Guinea for gold and teeth [ivory] shall be united with the East India trade in one body and regulation by the authority of the state." The East India Company had to contend with the rival Guinea Company, but in 1657, the East India Company took over the Guinea Company's Gold Coast trade. In 1660, Officers of the East India Company sent a petition to the Duke of York with the following declaration:

> The trade they enjoy on the Gold Coast serves their East India trade by supplying it with gold, which is carried thence direct to India.... As the Gold Coast trade cannot be made advantageous without the East India trade and the latter needs the supply of gold, it would be of service to all concerned if the two trades were united.

In 1669, the East India Company signed a warrant "to permit Edward Blackwell to export £40,000 to £50,000 of Guinea gold, custom free, to improve the trade in the East Indies." Between 1658 and 1663 seventeen East India ships transported a total of 43,736 ounces gold from the Gold Coast to India, or between one quarter and one half a ton. Yearly exports amounted to an average of 7,289 ounces. Once again, most of this gold would have passed through Akani captaincies. Between 1600 and 1700, 811 ships sailed from England to Asia and exports of silver and gold amounted to 1,300 tons. Akani captaincies would have been responsible for a substantial quantity of this gold.

According to one of its officials, the Dutch West Indies Company purchased at its Gold Coast trading stations 40,400 marks gold (323,200 ounces) between 1623 and 1636, and, according to another report, between 1635 and 1674 the company bought a total of 57,532 marks gold (460,256 ounces). In 1661 it exported somewhat more than 1,758 marks gold (14,064 ounces), in 1662, slightly more than 2,039 marks (16,012 ounces), and in 1673, a little over 902 marks (7,206 ounces). From 1668 to 1676 the Dutch Company exported a total of 3,125 marks (or 25,000 ounces), that is, 125 ounces a year (Anonymous 1652-74). From 1674 to 1696, the new West Indies Company exported an annual average of 1,700 marks of gold (13,600 ounces). An unspecified portion of Gold Coast gold was sold to the Dutch East Indies Company, which shipped it to Asia. Between 1600 and 1700, 1,770 ships sailed from The Netherlands to Asia and many of these ships would have carried West African gold. Of all the Dutch West Indies Company's exports from Africa, gold accounted for approximately eighty percent of the total value.

The Danish companies exported much less gold than the Dutch and English companies did but their records also provide interesting details about the gold trade. In January 1674, an inventory was taken of the gold in stock in the African Company's main trading station, Fort Fredricksberg. The inventory listed the following items: ten sacks of gold dust, each with 20 marks of gold; gold dust in miscellaneous bags; debased gold in miscellaneous bags; three gold neck rings; gold wire; gold amulets and debased gold; gold artifacts (hatbands, buttons, knobs, amulets, etc., whose total value was 237 marks 5 ounces and 13 angles [1,896 ounces]). The sacks of gold dust would have been sold by the merchant-brokers of the Amanfro captaincy. The debased gold and gold objects would have come from residents in the coastal and sub-coastal towns, such as traders, brokers, interpreters, boatmen, militia officers, and political officials. Danish gold exports were consumed in Denmark, although some gold was probably shipped to the East Indies.

In his detailed description of the African gold bullion cycle between 1300 and 1800 Ian Blanchard contends that during the years 1670-1760 West African gold producers played a significant role on international specie markets, following a period when this role was marginal due to the dominant position of American production on world gold markets. He connects the African cycles to "the rhythm of a series of environmental-economic cycles" and identifies its role in the world-economy.

> During these years from 1660-1710 exports of mercury to markets other than those supplying the Spanish American silver mines continued at a slightly higher level of about 1,500 quintals a year. Of this about half was dispatched to [West]

African producers, working beyond the Niger Bend where output of gold increased from about 1.5 tons a year in c. 1660 to 4.875 tons on average in 1690-1710. By far the largest part of this output (3.245 tons) passed to Europe by way of the trans-Saharan routes, controlled from Morocco, the terminal points of these routes—Tangier and Ceuta—attracting the covetous attention of the European nations. Only a diminutive flow passed to the West African coast. Here the trade grew from about 1.3 tons a year in c. 1660 to 1.628 tons in 1690-1710, attracting a host of Dutch, English, Brandenburg, Danish, Portuguese, and French traders to pick up the crumbs from the Moroccan Emperor's table. (Blanchard n.d.)

Blanchard probably underestimates gold exports from Gold Coast ports, for he does not seem to have included the Dutch and English trading companies' transport of "rich Guinea gold" to India and the East Indies. Still, his wider argument implies that West African and Saharan exchange systems were more significant for the Akani commercial system than exchanges at European trading stations along the coast. In the seventeenth century the export of gold from Gold Coast ports was never a substitute for the dense and long-established transcontinental trade.

Cultural and Symbolic Economies

What was the relation between the spatial and temporal functionality of the captaincy organization and the merchant-brokers' worldview and their conduct of life? Were the captaincies sites of enunciation, ethics and codes of conduct, reflexivity, and subject formation? What can be called the abstract dimension of the dominant, indeed hegemonic, Akani commercial system in the seventeenth century? What, in other words, can be said about the social imaginaries and mythopoesis of Akani captaincies? How did the gold trade affect the life of Akani merchant-brokers at the level of culture and ideology? What was the imaginative dimension of Akani socio-political and commercial life? What, in other words, were the theoretical components of the gold trade? What social imaginary did this trade generate and did the captaincy organization en-capsulate a dialectic interaction between the praxis of commerce and the texts and practices of culture? By social imaginary, I mean that which enables the practices of a society, the way one feels about societal institutions and relationships, or, in short, the way imagination figures into the construction of social institutions, representations, and prac-tices. Did the Akani captaincy organization contain and control the truth of the reality of a specific Akan or trans-Akan history? Was it a central formation in the history of the Akan world's origin? The above ques-tions bring to mind cultural and symbolic economies of the Akani com-mercial world (for relevant discussions see Konadu 2010; Wilks 2004). The questions cannot be answered with any degree of satisfaction until more evidence is generated.

Karl Marx stated, "the dialectical theory of truth and reality is insep-arable from a given society's actual conduct of life." The actual conduct of captaincy life would seem to entail the creation of cultural meanings, modes of classification, processes of valorization and de-valorization, and, perhaps, other worldly social visions. These would represent con-stituted and conceptual elements of truth and reality. In seventeenth cen-tury coastal and sub-coastal towns the politics and social imaginary of trade were lived, spoken, and visually expressed. How was this real-ized? The towns were places where the public display of material wealth by elites occurred several times a week. The ceremony of display was one of the socio-institutional contexts in which property relations ex-isted. In the towns the symbolism and symbolic order of gold organized dominant discourses about social statuses and human worth and in this sense the distribution of gold defined a cultural geography. The material and cognitive aspects of gold had a powerful presence among Akani merchant-brokers. The cultural arc that established the centrality of gold in quotidian life was realized in an annual ceremonial event. On this occasion, Akani captains and other senior merchant-brokers publicly exhibited their gold and other possessions in the most ostentatious man-ner possible. A case in point is the celebration of wealth possession in the capital of the coastal Afutu (Fetu) Kingdom. On the weeklong Ak-wasi festival which was held once a year, the senior merchant-brokers of the three Akani captaincies in Afutu publicly displayed their "splendor and magnificence" before thousands of people gathered in the state capital, according to an account dating from the 1660s. Thursday was the merchant-brokers' particular day of display. This ostentatious ceremonialism was an event of cultural and social placement and a personal identity marker. At the same time it transformed the public square into a "heterotopic" or sanctified space. It reflected the elevated position of gold in the social imaginary of those whose gold and property holdings were significant. It was indicative of gold and its representational claims on space, history, and social being. To Akani merchant-brokers, gold was a commodity to be exchanged but it was also a symbolic figuration with a cultural and ontological logic in its own right. The range of cultural, ideological, and symbolic trajectories associated with gold underpinned economic and social relations. The captaincies' public ceremonialism was a function of its role in Akani social relations of property.

Conclusion

Many years ago, Marshal Hodgson related in his discussion about the emergence of modernity in Europe. He places this phenomenon in relation to what he calls the "Oikoumenic Configuration."

> It was also necessary that there exist large areas of relatively dense, urban-dominated populations, tied together in a great interregional commercial network, to form the world market which had gradually come into being in the eastern hemisphere, and in which European fortunes could be made, and European imaginations exercised. (Hodgson 1993, pp. 47, 292)

The Akani captaincy organization and the wider Akani commercial formation may be said to have been embedded "relatively dense, urban-dominated populations" engaged in local and long-distance trading networks. The Akani captaincies provide a vivid example of the scale of commercial activity at seventeenth century Gold Coast ports and,

historically speaking, the captaincy organization and its interacting networks created the possibility and the actuality of a growing chartered
companies' trade in seventeenth century Atlantic Africa. There are implications here for understanding early modern (medieval) global flows
of gold, on the one hand, and the formulation of Trouillot's "North Atlantic universals," on the other. In other words, Akani captaincies cannot
be neglected in the formulation of theoretical perspectives on the formation of the early modern world and West Africa's place in world history historiography.

A Precolonial Political History of the Sefwi Wiawso *Oman*

STEFANO BONI

Stefano Boni teaches social and political anthropology at the University of Modena and Reggio Emilia, Italy. He has written extensively on the history of Sefwi and on anthropology.

Introduction

Very little has been written concerning the precolonial history of Sefwi. Holtsbaum, a colonial administrator, produced a first, brief attempt to reconstruct some aspects of Sefwi history in the 1920s. More recently, Quarcoo and Sieber wrote a short paper dealing with the Sefwi past. The important, pioneering works of Daaku in the late 1960s were centered on the collection of oral traditions. Published in the early 1970s, they have not been followed by further in-depth publications. Roberts' studies in the precolonial history of Sefwi remain unpublished, as is more recent research by Sefwi schoolteachers. The lack of documentation for the Sefwi area is due, at least in part, to the scarcity of archival evidence for Sefwi in comparison to regions closer to the coast which were in constant contact with the Europeans and to neighboring states that were more important politically and militarily. Sefwi lies in what is today the northern tip of the Western Region of Ghana, about 200 km from the coast; it covers an area of 2,695 square miles and is crossed by the Tano and Bia rivers. Sefwi currently comprises three Traditional Areas: Bekwai, Anhwiaso and Wiawso. Wiawso, the largest of the three, is the focus of this paper. With the sole exception of gold extraction, up to the late nineteenth century Sefwi was only marginally involved in productions aimed at transcontinental trade. The area was scarcely populated up to the first half of the twentieth century. Politically Sefwi exercised a very limited autonomy as it was under Asante control during most of the eighteenth and nineteenth century. It is no surprise that little attention has been devoted to the historical study of the region.

The precolonial history of Sefwi, and in particular that of the kingdom (*oman*, pl. *aman*) of Wiawso, however, deserves attention for several reasons. First, Sefwi history is fascinating in itself: it is important both for the Sefwi themselves and for academics to reconstruct the deeds of the earlier inhabitants of the region, to propose a plausible chronology of the reigns of the various kings and to revise the dating of some crucial events. Second, Sefwi history may be taken as an example of trends common across the Akan area. For example, the dynamics that led to the formation of the Wiawso *oman* may be profitably compared to the creation of centralized political units elsewhere in the Akan area. Third, Sefwi history may also prove helpful to historians of neighboring areas. The Sefwi Wiawso *oman* was part of wider dynamics (war, migrations, alliances) that linked it with other Akan states in a inter-regional framework.

The works of Daaku, based primarily on the collection of oral traditions, were pioneering in many respects but left out a great deal of archival evidence. Moreover, the narratives used by Daaku were limited to fewer than twenty stools and touched only on certain aspects of Sefwi precolonial history. In what follows, I draw extensively from the oral traditions gathered from 1993 to 2000 and from archival material. The national archives at Accra as well as the regional ones of Kumasi and Sekondi offer precious insights into the precolonial Sefwi past that complements the documents of the Sefwi Wiawso State/Traditional Council. Other evidence used are narratives from neighboring Akan states and nineteenth century accounts by Europeans traveling inland. Precolonial Sefwi historiography would certainly benefit from the systematic scrutiny of European records produced on the coast, here examined only superficially, as these may well throw more light on events discussed tentatively in the present paper.

Archives contain twentieth-century narratives concerning the precolonial past. These traditions are to be handled with care as narratives have a legal and political dimension: oral traditions are continuously altered and adapted to meet the requirements of current political struggles. Even though narratives are continually transformed by cumulative manipulations, oral traditions seldom lose completely the connection to the past that generated them. What follows is an exercise in historical reconstruction in which various sources are compared to deduce a likely past. While we can be reasonably confident of the occurrence of certain events, because we have several sources (perhaps from different areas and periods) that are in accord, the interpretation of other events, as we shall see, is more problematic.

Origins: From Afum Kroko to Amekye

Little is known of the seventeenth-century political dynamics of what is now considered the Sefwi area. Bosman offers little insights on areas and populations far from the coast; he uses the names "Encasse" and "Juffer" to describe the territories on the east of the Comoé River under Denkyira control. A similar indeterminacy on the identification of groups is found in eighteenth-century cartography. Daaku identifies "Great Inkassa" as the current Sefwi area. Meyerowitz speculates that Inkassa derives from the Guan suffix "nka" joined to "Saye" meaning "Sehwi." The identification of Sefwi with Bosman's "Encasse" seems however supported by little solid documentary evidence. While the identification of past ethnic or geographical labels with current groups and places is problematic, we have more reliable information on the economic and political transformations that occurred in the latter part of the seventeenth century in the southwestern Akan world. Wilks' argument on the formation of the central Akan states helps us to understand what might have happened west of Asante. Wilks sees the emergence of centralized political units in the course of the fifteenth and sixteenth century as an abrupt historical break "triggered off ... by Akan entrepreneurs who for the first time used gold to obtain labour." The accumulation of slave labour combined with the spread of agriculture and long-distance trade produced a revolution that gave rise to "big men" and later to village chiefs who were eventually absorbed into centralized political units. According to this model, the extraction of gold and its commercialization stimulated the emergence of centralized political units in the Akan world. There is evidence that similar dynamics took place in the forested areas that would later become known as Sefwi, albeit with a delay of a couple of centuries in comparison to Wilks' model. Kea holds that in the course of the seventeenth century large quantities of gold were extracted from the upper Tano and Bia basins, where Sefwi lies. The area was crossed by important trading routes linking the coast with Bighu, a large commercial centre inland. According to Kea, the trade between the Tano basin and the coast expanded consistently in the period between 1640 and 1700 and political centers were formed in the present-day Sefwi area. Around 1680 the region witnessed the expansion of the Aowin state and of Denkyira in the last decade of the century. Terray dates the establishment of forest states in the area to approximately the same period; he believes that the formation of centralized political units was generated by the increased trading with the coast and by the Mande expansion in the North.

The upper Tano basin was probably sparsely inhabited during the seventeenth century. Boinzan, Benchema and Tanoso are locally known as the oldest settlements and it is likely that these villages existed in the mid-seventeenth century. It is also probable that around 1680 Aowin control extended to the area and that Boinzan was under Aowin influence. It is likely that the peoples of this area, at this stage, did not perceive themselves as part of a distinct centralized state, an *oman*. Communities within the area paid allegiance to the more powerful neighboring states. The "ethnic" identity of the settlements, if any such identity existed, was transformed by the change of overlord.

The migration of the Asankera into the area and the consequent, gradual establishment of a centralized political unity can be tentatively dated at the early seventeenth century. The Asankera today present themselves as members of a matrilineage but their common matrilineal origin is dubious. Different Asankera branches claim different clanic affiliation (Bretuo and Oyoko) and several branches are said to have been incorporated through patrilateral links, oath swearing or through the assimilation of slaves. The Asankera may be more realistically seen as a shifting alliance between groups cemented by a matrilineal idiom. The term Asankera has more to do with issues of political identity and status than traceable matrilineal descent. Asankera groups are present in various parts of the south-western Akan world. In Sefwi, the Asankera are represented by a group of matrilineages holding several stools, amongst them the paramount stool of Wiawso.

Asankera oral traditions trace their origins to Takyiman. It is said that Kwakye Dapaa led them to Wassa Efiena and Bremang before their last northwards migration into present-day Sefwi that was then under Aowin influence. The Sefwi Asankera are still in contact with the Asankera family in Wassa. The movement of the Asankera along the Tano valley may have been produced by a period of great political and military turmoil in the southwestern Akan world. The migration towards little inhabited portions to the west of the Akan world continued in subsequent decades. The Asankera were followed by numerous groups that settled further west.

The Asankera group settled in the Tano valley. Its first settlements are known as Ahenkrom, Essamain, and Enwomaso. The man who led the Asankera into the area that would become known as Sefwi is remembered as Afum Kroko (also known as Kuroko, Kooko, and Koko-roko). The list of his successors is somewhat speculative. Some names are however recurrent as early ancestors of the Sefwi *amanhene*: Kwame Esomowe (also spelled Asomori); Ekyia (perhaps also known as Akyei Basani) who is known to have been destooled; Ohu Aben (also spelled Ehusaben); and Amekye. Very little is known about them and the order of their succession varies in different lists. Early twentieth century oral traditions and secondary sources state that these Asankera rulers were under Denkyira rule in the late seventeenth century. Very likely, these early leaders had a limited authority on both population and land. The Asankera had not yet moved to their present capital, Wiawso and at this stage controlled a very limited area and few villages.

Asante Conquest: Ebiri Moro and Bumankama

More information is available on Amekye's successor Kwasi Bumankama (also known as Oburum Ankama, Oburumankoma Fiakye,
Boomuncumma or Burum Kama). He is known to have transferred the
group's residence a few miles westwards, from Essamain to the present
capital, Wiawso. Moreover, Bumankama expanded the Asankera domains: he is remembered as a warrior king who established the
Asankera's domains as an emerging political entity in the southwestern
Akan world by fighting adjacent Aowin settlements. Bumankama's
reign can confidently be dated to the late seventeenth and early eighteenth century.

In this period, the Asankera became involved in larger scale politics:
Bumankama was, at first, under Boa Amponsem of Denkyira, but his
rule possibly lasted up to the time of the first Asante campaigns in the
area. An Asante source recalls a raid of Boa Amponsem (with the assistance of Osei Tutu) against Bumankama. In 1701 Denkyira was defeated by Asante. The forested areas of the upper Tano river basin were
probably shortly without an overlord but Asante gradually took over
Denkyira's domains including the present-day Sefwi area. To date the
beginning of Asante control over this region is important because it may
prove helpful to throw light onto another controversial event which occurred in those years: the raid of Ebiri Moro on the Asante capital Kumasi.

According to Fynn, in the early eighteenth century the Asante invaded the present-day Sefwi area, termed by the author "Great Inkassa
and Inkassa Igyima." Asante, however, did not keep control over the
area for long as the Aowin won it back and controlled it up to the
Aowin-Asante war of 1715. Terray dates the Asante invasion of Sefwi
in the same year. Daaku believes that Asante controlled Sefwi before
1715 and that the Sefwi fought alongside the Asante in the Aowin war.
C.-H. Perrot dates the beginning of Asante control over Sefwi between
1701 and 1710, following Daaku's work.

Even though there may well have been some Asante campaigns that
concerned the use of the Tano basin in the first two decades of the eighteenth century, I believe there is sufficient evidence to suggest that the

future of the region was shaped by a major Asante expedition some years later, around 1720, when the Asante moved their army westwards in their pursuit of Ebiri Moro. Dutch sources suggest that the period between 1715 and 1720 was one of great turbulence, as the Asante had not yet established a firm rule to its south-west: Wassa, Aowin and Asante were in a state of quasi-perennial reciprocal conflict. Within this framework, in 1718 the Dutch sources give evidence of an expedition of eight thousands "Ouwiens" to Asante, which would become known as the Ebiri Moro raid on Kumasi. The sources provide the following description of the campaign:

> It is reported about the Ouwiens that they have returned from Assiantyn with a considerable booty, including 20,000 women and children, that they found no resistance, and that they have exhumed the dead Assiantyns.

In the source, there is no reference to Ebiri Moro nor to Sefwi. Two years later there is evidence of an Asante expedition sent to find and punish the Aowin. Daaku and Perrot use the Dutch source reported above and Sefwi oral traditions to reconstruct the episode. Daaku, Perrot and Wilks are convinced that the Sefwi were not involved in the episode, as they are not mentioned in the source. Sefwi, according to this reconstruction, was already under Asante control and fought alongside their overlords against the Aowin. Below I compare sources to explore the use of ethnic labels with reference to what is now known as the Sefwi area and to date the establishment of Asante rule in the area.

Oral traditions of the nineteenth and early twentieth century give a different account of the Ebiri Moro expedition. The ethnic label "Sefwi" is used and associated with the raid, even though there is no agreement on the degree of the involvement of the population termed "Sefwi." Sources have been by Perrot who quotes Reindorf, Fuller, Rattray, Delafosse and Cheruy. I therefore limit myself to add a few other quotations on the episode from secondary sources and some archival evidence of the early twentieth century to suggest an involvement in the episode of chiefs who, at the time, resided in the present-day Sefwi area, raise a series of issues that are not easily solved. The cause of Ebiri Moro's

rampage is unstated. Opoku Ware and the Bantamahene are alternatively indicated as the leaders of the expedition against Ebiri Moro. The
identity and destiny of the women of the Asantehene's lineage captured
in the course of the raid is uncertain. The comparison of narratives on
other points, however, seems more relevant for the reconstruction of
Sefwi history and namely where did Ebiri Moro seek refuge after the
expedition on Kumasi and what was the ethnic membership attributed
to him by the sources. I will weigh the evidence in regards to these issues to suggest a possible involvement of the population of the area that
is currently identified as Sefwi in the expedition and an Asante campaign to the area, or to a neighboring one, around 1720.

Several sources hold that Ebiri Moro passed through Sefwi in the attempt to escape from the Asante army. The confrontation between the
group led by Ebiri Moro and the Asante is remembered as having occurred close or in the present day Sefwi area. Fuller states that the struggle took place close to the Tano river; Reindorf holds that the Asante
overran Ebiri Moro at Korowadaso and went on to destroy the capital
of the kingdom of "Safwi and Wasa." An oral source mentioned by Perrot holds that Ebiri Moro was caught close to the Sobore River, a few
miles from Wiawso. Sefwi oral sources mention Karnayerebo, a village
not far from Sefwi Awaso as the location of the confrontation. An en-
quiry held in 1922 aimed at establishing the land rights over the eastern
part of Sefwi and involving Sefwi, Asante and Ahafo chiefs dealt extensively with Ebiri Moro's raid and with the Asante pursuit of the fugitive. All chiefs agreed that the Asante expedition was crucial in
establishing land rights over the area. While chiefs declared that the
Sefwi Wiawso stool was not directly involved, they gave contradicting
information on the destination of Ebiri Moro's journey: Ahafo, Gyaman,
the Nkoranza forest (north of Sefwi), and Wassa (south of Sefwi) were
mentioned.

Wiawso *amanhene* at least from the 1920s onwards deny that Ebiri
Moro was a Sefwi *omanhene* and that were involved in the raid against
Kumasi. The Sefwi rather state that they were involved alongside the
Asante in the pursuit of Ebiri Moro and that is how they acquired a pres-
tigious position in the Asante empire. Sefwi narratives stress their faith-
fulness as allies of the Asante but it may very well be that even though

Ebiri Moro was not directly connected to the Wiawso stool, he and his supporters hailed from an area that was later identified as Sefwi. Sources based on narratives collected in the nineteenth and early nineteenth century in a variety of Akan states suggest some sort of identification between Ebiri Moro and Sefwi. Rattray, an Asante source reported by Wilks, and an Asante praise poem identify Ebiri Moro as a Sefwi. More often, however his ethnic identity is problematic, and often different labels are overlapped. Reindorf states that Ebiri Moro was the king of Sefwi and Wassa but he seems to put more emphasis on Sefwi. Fuller holds that he was a Sefwi king and the Sefwi are described as "a powerful tribe adjoining the Denkeras, and therefore in dispute with the Ashantis," he also believes that at the time Wassa paid tribute to Sefwi. Delafosse describes Ebiri Moro as "chef zema du Sahué." Ahafo narratives identify Ebiri Moro as coming from the Sefwi area or an adjacent one. Some Sefwi oral traditions recognize Ebiri Moro as a Sefwi *omanhene*, others as a chief connected to the *omanhene*, still others refer to him as an Aowin. Ndenye oral traditions recorded by C.-H. Perrot does not mention Sefwi as the ethnic group of Ebiri Moro. Fynn holds that at the time of the Asante expedition, the Sefwi were under the Aowin and that both collaborated in the raid against Kumasi and were victims of the Asante reprisal.

Sources are not in accord in many respects but seem to indicate that Ebiri Moro hailed from a region in or around present-day Sefwi and this was his destination on his way back from Kumasi. However, perhaps what is most interesting is that some sources suggest that territorial boundaries and political and ethnic membership were fluid: the groups west of Asante were connected by political links different from those of the twentieth century and ethnic belonging was not always easily distinguishable. The Asankera group had recently migrated from the Wassa area and it seems most likely that it maintained some ties with the former neighbors. This may offer an alternative explanation to that suggested by Daaku and Perrot for the omission of "Sefwi" in the Dutch source concerning the raid on Kumasi. Sefwi not mentioned simply because Wiawso and other emerging political entities at the time the source was written did not have name for themselves.

The ethnic identity of what is currently termed the Sefwi area was, in the early eighteenth century, not conceptualized and described with ethnic labels that are in use today. Along the Gold Coast-Ivory Coast boundary, the demarcation of clearly defined ethnic groups and boundaries was an arbitrary colonial operation of fixation and codification carried out in the course of the late nineteenth and early twentieth century. This unprecedented necessity to clarify and stabilize groups' identity and territorial possession was due at least in part, to the choice of an 'ethnic' criterion in the demarcation of the colonial frontier. Several of the works quoted above were based on narratives collected purposely to establish an ethnic history of the region which was then used by the two colonial powers to negotiate the establishment of the Gold Coast-Ivory Coast boundary. The colonial sources reported above show the difficulty of fitting informants' narratives concerning eighteenth century identities a European conceptual framework structured on well-defined and fixed ethnic groups and territories. Several British and French administrators came to term with the problem of giving an ethnic membership to Ebiri Moro by overlapping different ethnic names.

At the time of Ebiri Moro's raid on Kumasi the ethnic labels used to describe the present-day Sefwi area and its political heads were others (Aowin, Wassa, Denkyira, possibly Encasse) as a distinct Sefwi identity had not yet emerged. The rise of Asante produced the final demise of Denkyira and Aowin, the overlords that had controlled, in the course of the seventeenth century, the villages which would later come under Asankera rule. The fall of kingdoms that had been dominant in the south-western part of the Akan region opened new opportunities for political entities which had enjoyed limited autonomy and power. Chiefs who had been under Denkyira and Aowin authority gained more room for regional maneuver when they came under direct Asante control. The Asankera chief of Wiawso was one amongst other political heads (Boinzan, Anhwiaso and later Bekwai) who was able to expand control over clusters of villages in the course of the eighteenth century. Even though the prerogatives of the emerging political heads and the extent of their domains were often variable and unclear, they were able to gain recognition as heads of autonomous political units, of *aman*. These were legitimized ideologically and organized politically as units, albeit under ultimate Asante control.

Going back to Wilks's hypothesis concerning the emergence of centralized political units, the area discussed in this differs from several other Akan regions as the accumulation of labour and power did not occur in a political vacuum but in a period in which neighboring areas were already organized in structured, centralized units that imposed subordination on emerging political heads of the Sefwi area. An *oman* therefore emerged only when the political power balance in the western Akan world was transformed by Asante rule and allowed for the strengthening of local chiefs; this was much later in comparison to other Akan states. While the commercialization of gold and the accumulation of labour may have been crucial for the rise of political heads, these had to wait for a revolution in the regional political context to be able to form states.

The emerging *aman* shared cultural similarities produced by a peculiar process of acculturation in which the influence of their previous overlords and Asante overlapped. The Wiawso *oman* was therefore seen as sharing, besides geographical proximity, linguistic, political, ritual and religious traits with neighboring *aman* to an extent that merited an independent ethnic label "Sawee." The ethnic label was also used to distinguish an area comprising kingdoms strictly connected to the Asante empire from regions and groups settled or chased further west on which Asante influence was weaker and less structured. It may well be possible that "Sawee" derived from a name referring to a location or group that existed in the early eighteenth or seventeenth century but what seems crucial is that the ethnic label gained a fame and a currency only in the late eighteenth or early nineteenth century as a result of a new political framework established in the western Akan world.

The hypothesis of the emergence of both centralized political units and a new ethnic identity after and as a consequence of Asante rule must be tested with a more systematic scrutiny of the European manuscripts produced on the coast but, to my knowledge, the first known appearance of Sefwi as an ethnic name dates back to Bowdich, as "Sauee" or "Sawee," almost hundred years after Ebiri Moro's raid. The name will be transformed in the course of time into the present-day "Sehwi," "Sahue" or "Sefwi." From Bowdich's mission onwards, most studies restated the name as "Sawee," "Shouy," "Safwi," offered new particulars or simply reproduced his account. Maps of the Gold Coast and of Guinea began to include the name because of the information provided by Bowdich.

In view of the above, the argument excluding the participation to the Ebiri Moro raid of chiefs and groups whose descendants are currently part of the Sefwi political structure simply because an ethnic name identifiable as "Sefwi" is not mentioned in eighteenth century sources must be reconsidered. Oral traditions of the nineteenth and twentieth century, narrated at a time when Sefwi was an established ethnic unit, often describe the participation to the raid by linking the ethnic name 'Sefwi' to a group of people who were not termed Sefwi at the time of the events narrated. These narratives suggest that some relation existed between the participants to or supporters of the Ebiri Moro expedition and those who will later be termed "Sefwi."

While conclusive evidence of the participation of chiefs of the present-day Sefwi area the Ebiri Moro raid is problematic, the sources support more decisively the hypothesis that the Asante expedition against Ebiri Moro, occurred at the beginning of Opoku Ware's reign and interested what will become known as Sefwi. The military campaign of 1720 was however probably just one of several expeditions aimed at establishing firm Asante rule in the area. Wilks suggests that several "campaigns" against "Aowin, Wassa and Twifo" were needed up to the 1780s to affirm Asante authority in the area. Bowdich provides us with a key passage but of difficult interpretation: "Sai Cudjo defeating the Warsaws and Assins more decisively than his predecessors, first compelled them to acknowledge their fealty to Ashantee. He also subjected Aquamboe, and Aquapim, quelled several revolts of other countries, and was esteemed a great captain. The grandfather of Amanquatea Atooa, conquered Sawee, killing the king Boomuncumma; and Bakke, soon afterwards, subjugated Moinsea."

The identity of the "the grandfather of Amanquatea Atooa" and of "Bakke" is uncertain. It is also unclear if the occupation of Sefwi and the killing of Bumankama is to be dated, according to Bowdich, at the time of "the grandfather of Amanquatea Atooa" and of "Bakke" possibly in the first two decades of the eighteenth century or during the reign of Asantehene Osei Kwadwo (1764-1777). The later date would be in-

consistent with a considerable body of documentary evidence that suggest that Bumankama ruled in the late seventeenth and early eighteenth
century and that Okodom was the Asankera ruler at the time of Osei
Kwadwo. Dupuis is equally ambiguous on the establishment of Asante
control on the Sefwi area: "He [Osei Tutu, reigned 1701-1717] subdued,
besides Dinkira and Tofal, a great extent of country beyond the Tando
river"; however it was Opoku Ware (1720-1750) who increased the influence "upon the confines of Wossa" and it was during the reign of
Osei Kwadwo (1764-1777) that "The subjugation of Gaman ... laid the
Sarem country prostate at the feet of the conqueror, who penetrated
Shouy [most likely Sefwi], Ghombati, and Ponin." Reindorf and Claridge seem to combine various campaigns: Reindorf states that "King
Oburum Ankama and Abirimoro were taken prisoners and beheaded"
by Opoku Ware; Claridge holds that during the reign of "Osai Kujo,"
"Sefwi was also subjugated at about this time and its King, Burum
Kama (or Abirimoro), killed."

The sources are inconsistent in many respects, perhaps because they
feel the need to reduce the subjugation of Sefwi to a single invasion instead of viewing it as a slow process. Evidence seems to suggest that
the establishment Asante rule over the area was gradual: it possibly
began under Amankwatia Panin, before the expedition against Ebiri
Moro, and campaigns continued over several decades. These operations
shaped the history of the area over the following century as Asante established a firm grip on Sefwi; reorganized the balance of power in the
area; strengthened the position of the Asankera, with the nomination of
a new and more faithful ruler. These important transformations, in turn,
produced the demise of previous ethnic labels and the diffusion of a single name for the area: Sefwi.

Political and Territorial Expansion:
Okodom and Aduhene

Wiawso military defeat and the insertion in the Asante domains paradoxically marked the strengthening of its territorial expansion and political activism. Asankera narratives present Bumankama's successor,

Kwadwo Nkuah (also as Nkuah Paain and more often as Okumdom or Nkowa Okodom, destroyer of battalions), as the one who contributed most decisively to the expansion of the Wiawso stool. Okodom succeeded to Bumankama, perhaps after a political vacuum of some years after the immolation of the latter by the Asante. Numerous sources suggest that he ruled in the mid-eighteenth century. According to Sefwi narratives, Okodom ruled at the time of Asantehene Opoku Ware (c. 1720-1750) and Kusi Obodum (c. 1750-1764) and was the son of Asantehene Osei Tutu who visited Sefwi when Asante was still under Denkyira rule, probably in the late seventeenth century. Sefwi inclusion in the Asante domains is therefore coupled with the nomination of a son of the Asantehene to the stool of Sefwi Wiawso.

Sefwi became an active part of the Asante for over one and a half centuries. In the nineteenth century, Sefwi provided men to the Asante army. Wiawso, in exchange, received political legitimation and support for its territorial expansion. Asante moreover protected Sefwi when attacked. Wiawso was also given the authority to act as a political and administrative agent of the Asantehene for areas to the south-west of the Asante Empire. The Wiawsohene was asked to represent the Asantehene in relations with chiefs of the southwestern Akan world such as Ndenye and Sanwi. Wiawso was in charge of collecting tributes, supervising the political situation and stood for the Asantehene in the settlement of disputes.

The increased prestige of the Wiawsohene in Akan politics was matched by a rapid territorial expansion. The Asantehene probably directed the Wiawsohene towards areas occupied by the Anyi-Aowin to the north and west of Wiawso as the areas to the south and east were already under Asante control. The present geographical configuration of the Sefwi Wiawso *oman*, with Wiawso situated in the south-eastern extremity of its domains, is the result of this expansion. During the late eighteenth and nineteenth century numerous groups, mostly coming from east and south, migrated into Sefwi and asked to serve the Wiawsohene. The immigrants were asked to settle in the neighborhoods of Wiawso in an initial period and were later sent to fight and expand the territorial domains of the Wiawsohene. The expansionist drive initiated by Bumankama continued under Okodom. Numerous *ahenemma*, sons of the Wiawsohene, were sent with their groups to fight the Aowin-Anyi: the villages of Bodi, Amoyaw, Sui, and Akwantombra were all established during Okodom's reign and are a lasting testimony of Wiawso's expansion. The expulsion of the group that will form the *oman* of Sefwi Bekwai is dated by Sefwi narratives to the latter part of the first half of the eighteenth century.

One of the consequences of Wiawso's enlargement is the westwards migration of the Abrade. According to oral sources recorded by Perrot the Abrade resided not far from the Asankera at Asomukrom, near what is now the Sefwi village of Denkyemoase. Abrade and Asankera came into contact during Bumankama's reign but lived peacefully up to Okodom's time. The latter started a long-term confrontation against Ebembonnu, the Abrade chief. The conflict eventually resulted in the expulsion of the Abrade around the middle of the eighteenth century. According to Cheruy and Perrot, a peace settlement between Okodom and the Abrade was mediated by Boafo Nda, the chief of the Alangwa. Sefwi narratives identify the Aowin as the defeated party and Kwesi Prempren of Mmoronu and Bimpong (or Berempn, Bempong, Birmpong) as their leaders. Abrade and Sefwi narratives display some similarities as well as differences: Asomukrom is recalled as the battleground in both instances and there are some intriguing coincidences. Sefwi narratives also recall conflicts with the Wassa, to the south, during Okodom's reign.

The extent of Okodom's reign is not clear, nor is it clear if there were some Wiawsohene who were destooled before the next recognized Wiawsohene, Aduhene I (also known as Eduhin and often associated with the title *Okogyeabuor*, he who repels and collects bullets). We know that Okodom was enstooled while still very young and that his rule was very long but if Okodom's reign began at Bumankama's death possibly in the course of the 1720s or 1730s, it certainly ended within the eighteenth century. We have two sources that confirm that Aduhene was the Wiawsohene at the beginning of the nineteenth century but of course he might well have been enstooled decades before that. The first source is an Ndenye narrative that dates Aduhene's rule back to around 1810; the second is a Sefwi oral tradition that recalls Aduhene's participation alongside the Asante in the expedition to Fante of 1807. Numerous sources confirm that his rule lasted up to the middle of the nineteenth century.

The military activity and the territorial enlargement of the Wiawso *oman* continued under Aduhene. The northward expansion of Wiawso was temporarily halted by the confrontation with Boinzan. There is evidence that suggests that Boinzan was a separate political unit up to the early nineteenth century. Boinzan's incorporation in the *oman* of Wiawso was a slow process that coupled diplomacy with violent confrontation. At first Okodom married a woman from the royal family of Boinzan, the son of the couple Kwao Asiedu was nominated Boinzanhene. Conflict ensued when Wiawso tried to sanction Boinzan's subordination by demanding a tribute. The feud lasted several decades and was only settled with the intervention of the Asantehene. Boinzan finally accepted incorporation in the Wiawso *oman* around 1840 but only after being offered the prestigious title of Kontihene. After the incorporation of Boinzan, the area beyond the river Bia, scarcely inhabited up to then, was settled by Sefwi and the village of Debiso established.

Overall Sefwi expansion came to a standstill around the middle of the nineteenth century. Aduhene is said to have sanctioned a peace with the Aowin. The numerous groups that arrived into Sefwi in the late nineteenth century were no longer asked to participate in military struggles but were rather sent to occupy uninhabited portions of the *oman*. There is evidence of occasional struggles with the Aowin, some of which were still in progress when British rule was established, and of new settlements (such as Behiramwere and Ahebenso) on the western frontier but these were founded alongside existing villages and did not expand Sefwi territorial domains significantly.

During Aduhene's reign, Wiawso participated actively in Asante politics. Bowdich states that Sefwi could provide four thousand men for the Asante army besides having to pay a tribute of 450 oz of gold (Boinzan paid a separate tribute of 100 oz). Sefwi took part in wars alongside Asante: oral narratives suggest that Aduhene took part in an expedition to Akyem known as the "Brahyia" war and to a campaign in Fante. Sefwi oral traditions recall that, after the Akyem campaign, Aduhene was held in Kumasi because he proved valorous and the Asantehene refused to let him return to Sefwi unless he was replaced by a member of the royal family. The two successive Wiawsohene (Kwaku Kye and Kwaku Nkuah Kaa) are said to have resided at the Asantehene's palace in Kumasi and to have been called from there to succeed to the Wiawso stool. Asante control was obviously tightening on Sefwi.

During most of the eighteenth and nineteenth century, not only was Sefwi part of Asante imperial domains with regards to politics, rituals and judicial administration, it became part of a system of communication and trade centered on Kumasi. Sefwi was inserted, albeit with a marginal role, in a system of trade routes that linked it to Kumasi. Sefwi was explicitly asked to protect and favor Asante traders passing through the area. The lack of documentation concerning trade in the eighteenth century in the national, regional and local archives prevents any definite conclusion on the characteristics of Sefwi trade in that century. It is unclear if Sefwi traders commercialized their products directly with the coast or if they had to pass through Kumasi. Sefwi certainly exported some quantity of gold, as the area is rich in ore from its numerous mining areas. More reliable information is available on the late nineteenth century. Both contemporary sources and narratives suggest that gold was the principal export towards the costal centers while imports were mostly guns, gunpowder, cloths, salt, and tobacco from the coast and slaves, shea butter and cloths from the North.

The role played by Sefwi in the Atlantic slave trade is uncertain in many respects but sources suggest that it was a marginal one. Sefwi, as most other southern Akan states, did not pay a tribute in slaves to Asante and a narrative suggests that the Asante did not take Sefwi as slaves. It is also unlikely that the local expansion of Sefwi resulted in consistent slave raiding because, as we have seen, military operations were probably of limited scale and the defeated parties either migrated or were incorporated in the Wiawso *oman*. Oral narratives, referring probably to the nineteenth century, recall that slaves were mostly bought by Sefwi rather than sold. This evidence, together with the low population density, seems to indicate that in Sefwi slaves were mostly bought to be incorporated into families as dependants. In the nineteenth century, the gradual demise of the Atlantic slave trade and the military operations of Samori Touré probably favored the purchase of slaves by Sefwi "big men" and chiefs. There is evidence of a consistent number of Akan slaves being sold in Sefwi by the Asante in the latter part of the nineteenth century even though the principal purchasing centre was Bonduku. In the early twentieth century, the king of Wiawso and the chiefly establishment more generally strongly opposed the liberation of slaves as they argued that the population of the *oman* was to a large extent composed of slaves and their descendants. A return home of slave families would seriously diminish the local population.

Towards Colonial Rule: From Kwaku Kye to Ata Kwasi

Aduhene died the middle of the nineteenth century was succeeded by Kwaku Kye who had the nickname of "killer" (*Sampene diamo*) and ruled up to the mid-1880s. With Kwaku Kye, Wiawso further intensified its participation in Akan politics on behalf of the Asantehene. Around 1850, Kwaku Kye judged an Ndenye political dispute on behalf of the Asante. Under his reign, a Sefwi chief participated in with Adu Bofo. In the 1870s Sefwi took part in the Asante campaign to the coast. Six hundred Sefwi were involved in an unfortunate expedition to Fante in 1871. The chief of Boinzan "Ohourou Quami" or "Ahuru Kwame" is mentioned as having participated in the expedition both by Bonnat and by the oral tradition recorded in Boinzan. In 1872 over one thousand Sefwi figure amongst the army of Adu Bofo participating in the Asante occupation of the coast they were sent to Appolonia in Nzema. This was the last war of the Sefwi Wiawso *oman* alongside the Asante.

   With the British invasion of Asante in 1874, Kwaku Kye sensed that the power balance in the Akan area was tilting towards the British. Wiawso began to contemplate the possibility of severing its relationship with the demanding overlord it had served for over a century. Kwaku Kye established ties with the British and withdrew allegiance to Kumasi. In 1879 made his intention to be autonomous from Asante known to a British envoy. From then onwards Wiawso sought formal British protection. In 1881 Sefwi challenged Asante supremacy over trade by blocking the road from Kumasi to Assin. In the same year, Kwaku Kye sent a message to the British stating, "the King of Ashanti had troubled Safi enough and put a heavy fine on him"; he offered collaboration in the fight against Asante. Sefwi actually participated on the British side in subsequent struggles between the two and was later compensated by the colonial administration.

While waiting for the British to make a decision over the extension of the British Protectorate to the *oman* of Wiawso, Sefwi authorities used their unprecedented independence to control trade routes passing from Gyaman, through Sefwi, to the coast and impose themselves as middlemen in the trade. Costal traders complained that this had a negative impact on the price of goods. The colonial government became increasingly worried and decided to extend its rule over Sefwi. Kwaku Kye, however, did not live to see the treaty sanctioned it was Kwaku Nkuah Kaa (reigned c.1885-1892) who, on 18 February 1887, obtained British Protection for Sefwi. Kwasi Ata Gyebi (c. 1892-1900) was the first Wiawsohene to come under direct British rule: a District Commissioner was stationed in Sefwi in 1896. The foreign presence made itself immediately felt on Sefwi internal politics. In 1900 some Sefwi chiefs were prepared to side with the Asante against the British in the Yaa Asantewa war and were prevented from doing so from Ata Kwasi. When Ata Kwasi died in the midst of the rebellion, Hobart, the Acting District Commissioner, sensed danger. He decided, with the British administration's tacit approval, to intervene in the Wiawso stool succession and imposed the candidate he thought was most in line with colonial interests, Kwame Tano (ruled 1900-1932). Sefwi political autonomy had lasted just over two decades and the Wiawso *oman* found itself again subservient to a powerful, and perhaps even more intrusive, overlord.

Reflections

I arrived in Sefwi Wiawso for the first time in 1993 as a BA student in anthropology. My research focused on the spatial dislocation of kin groups in settlements within the Sefwi Wiawso kingdom, *oman*, and in houses within villages. The research showed that, at both levels, kingdom and villages, the occupation of the territory was organized on the combination of groups identified as matrilineal relatives of chiefs, *adehyee*, and sons of chiefs, *ahenemma*. To map genealogical ties in history, I began to record the oral traditions of villages that had little prestige and of the most relevant stools in the kingdom. By car or on foot, I reached remote settlements, presented myself at the palace and asked to hear the stool's history. With few exceptions, chief or elders offered detailed reconstructions. I was welcomed with courtesy by the elderly *omanhene* Aduhene II, eager, as most Sefwi stool-holders, to present his view of history. The information of the narratives was used to compare different perspectives on historical events, to draw the sequence of chiefs who occupied the various stool, to date events. As I proceeded in the project, striking incongruities between the various versions emerged, as well as substantial discordances between the oral traditions and the few written sources on precolonial Sefwi history. At times, even during recordings, elders would discuss passionately, disagreeing on the memory of events or on what was the appropriate version to be narrated to a young, and unknown, foreign researcher.

Over the years, I recorded 33 stool narratives; gathered archival material in Accra, Kumasi, Sekondi and London and ordered secondary sources on Sefwi history. By April 1997, I had become a familiar figure in Wiawso and was granted permission to view the minutes of the Traditional Council. In May 2000, the newly elected *omanhene,* Nkoa Okodom II, allowed me access to what remained of the palace archives. When I entered in the room with Francis Mensah, the richest body of evidence on colonial and postcolonial Sefwi history was deteriorating for lack of care: I worked patiently to classify files, made photocopies of what seemed most relevant for my research and locked up the originals in a library. Keys were handed over to the *omanhene* and a linguist but, to my knowledge, no researcher was allowed in the room since my last visit to the archives in 2003, because of the prolonged deposition case, still pending, on the Sefwi Wiawso stool.

I worked on this growing, albeit chaotic, set of information in two combined directions. On the one hand, building on previous historiography, I tried to elaborate a reconstruction of which we can be reasonably confident. The paper contained in this reader addresses the precolonial political history, others were focused on transportation; strength and style of political institutions; gender and inequality; relations of dependence (slavery, pawning, marriage); the social and political topography of Wiawso; the *momome* ritual. In all these papers, I compare available evidence from the precolonial period with ethnographic data from the late twentieth century, trying to outline persistence and changes in cultural praxis. Anthropology proved a valuable companion to historical analysis. The issue of Ebiri Moro's identity, discussed in the paper below, benefitted from a key debate in anthropology on the fragility, dynamism and political use of ethnic labels. The anthropological attention paid to local conceptualizations and symbolic framing of ties, promoted innovative understandings of dependence and inequality.

The second use of the historical evidence, common in the anthropological tradition, was aimed at examining how reference to the past was used to justify and legitimize power relations in the present. In this regard, the shifting interpretations of the genealogical composition of the Asankera, the group presented as the matrilineage within which successors to the Sefwi Wiawso stool must be selected, as well as swinging representations of the relation between the stools of Wiawso and Boinzan, a prominent settlement, now within the Wiawso *oman* with the position of Krontihene but with a long history of conflict with the capital, proved fascinating. The contents and style of what were presented as unalterable oral traditions, varied considerably according to the speaker and the state of the power balance between groups: narratives were rapidly altered and manipulated in depth to adapt to shifts in national politics. Similarly, the classification of who was to be classified as a "stranger," a non-Sefwi, proved to be dictated by changes in taxation policies on cocoa farming: since agricultural land began to be scarce, around the middle of the twentieth century, the genealogical background of residents, even of those who had long been considered Sefwi, has been scrutinized closely in search of "impure" ethnic ancestors, in order to include farmers in the list of "strangers" who are asked to pay tribute to Sefwi chiefs.

In Ghana, historical narratives are often the principal evidence on which land and political rights are legally evaluated, historical memory is thus continuously manipulated in order to advance claims in the present. Social existences leave traces that will be interpreted in the future. In trying to make sense of the past one can both privilege the, always problematic attempt to describe meticulously historical events, or privilege current readings of the past, focusing on the always shifting interpretations of what has happened.

State Formation and Intercommunal Alliances on the Gold Coast (17th to 18th Centuries)

PIERLUIGI VALSECCHI

Pierluigi Valsecchi is Professor of the History of Africa in the Faculty of Political Sciences, University of Pavia. He is the author of Power and State Formation in West Africa: Appolonia from the Sixteenth to the Eighteenth Century *(2011). The following essay was translated from the French original.*

A Preliminary Consideration

The connection that exists between the category "Akan," the Akan region, the Akan "worlds," and the geographic frame of reference of our study, southern Ghana, poses problems, which are not solely those of name designation. Southern Ghana coincides with a large portion of the Gold Coast (or Côte d'Or)—a name which formerly, before the Gold Coast was placed under British authority, included also the farthest zones of the southwest of Ivory Coast.

Undeniably, the Gold Coast includes a fundamental portion of that which can be defined as "Akan"; one can even say that it constitutes the historical cradle and the human and cultural heart of the Akan world. But it covers also the human and historical realities which are not Akan, or are only partially so. These are, for example, the groups of the central language Gã-Adangme and Guan, the Akuapem, the Winneba and the

Ewutu. However, one also considers the linguistic and cultural heritage which are specifically "Pre-Akan" of the Shama, Ahanta, Nzema, Sanwi, Aowin, Ndenye, Sehwi, and on the whole the forests and the lagoons of the West. Nevertheless, beyond their degree of "Akanness"—more or less pronounced—and beyond the entire other possible alchemy of identity, all these elements are closely linked, melted into the history and the culture of the region. As Metternich said on the subject of Italy in the first half of the nineteenth century, the pre-colonial Gold Coast is a "geographical expression" in the sense of it being an entity deprived of political unity and a "national dimension," yet the name nevertheless provides a unity and fundamentally logical integration of the communities of which it is composed. This integration stems from a common space of territorial, productive, commercial, political, cultural, religious, and linguistic connections, etc. But the degrees of mixing and of fusion vary noticeably in the different portions of this space. Even though the category "Akan" is neither essential nor exclusive in our discourse, it is objectively poignant in its diverse aspects. In particular, it allows us to define a prevailing element to which we refer explicitly in this paper.

A Historiography Dominated by Asante

Even outside of the milieu of professional Africanists, one hears often that in the second half of the twentieth century, the Akan region was one of the privileged objects on which the newly emerged historiography concerning pre-colonial sub-Saharan Africa trained and formed itself. That historiography dealt primarily with political history, but especially since the eighties the progressive openness of the themes and a sensibility of the "new history" has produced fruitful results in such disciplines as anthropology and history. A space was also made for questions of social history, history of ideas, of beliefs, of culture, etc.

Among the initiated, everyone knows how this observation is justified, but we also know that Akan is too often considered synonymous with Asante. Research activity is concentrated with unequaled intensity on the great system of power which established itself around the Asante capital, Kumase, starting at the end of the seventeenth century and which in the course of the two centuries following it, provided space for one of the most complex political formations of West Africa, until the European conquest. This apparent "nation," insofar as its tangible entirety of power, institutions, ideology, and culture are comprehensible, thus lends itself to being the defining and identifying structure of the pre-colonial epoch.

It is the presence and heritage of that "nation" which explains to a large degree the attraction which Asante history exerts on modern historiography of Africa, in context with decolonization and independence. To know that "some very great thing" had its seat in Kumase well before the arrival of the Europeans provides an easy foundation for historical representation, and can be promoted as specifically African-autochthonous as opposed to that which is perceived as imposed by European colonialism. This is a process that, according to some, could be the origin of a series of over-interpretations and weaknesses of "nationalist" historiography.

A clear-cut disequilibrium in favor of the Asante is altogether the "original sin" of these studies, but it is also their "blessed fault," since the result of such work is evident in the high level of production at which historiography has to inevitably confront the Akan "worlds," and more generally the studies of the nations and societies of West Africa. It suffices here to recall such works as *Asante in the Nineteenth Century* by Wilks (1975), *State and Society in Pre-Colonial Asante* by McCaskie (1995) and also *Asante and the Dutch* by Yarak (1900). In 2002, the establishment of a chair of Asante history at the Center of West African studies in Birmingham, the first of its kind, allowed McCaskie to represent his devotion to an imposing research activity, developed during several decades.

Numerous other components of the region's history in the seventeenth and eighteenth centuries—on the coast as well as in the interior—without a doubt received very sporadic attention, devoid of the systemic character that characterizes the past forty years' historical studies concerning the Asante. An exemption was made, however, for certain sections of the heterogeneous society of the Gold Coast (in the ancient sense of the term), notably the centers on the coast exposed to Atlantic trafficking, which were the scene of a European presence which emerged at least at the end of the fifteenth century. Concerning this, we refer particularly to the Fante and Gã zone, placed in the center of a rich historiographical tradition.

The "Beginnings": From Wilks to Klein

Once the distinctions are established, and boundaries are appropriately drawn, it is necessary to emphasize a fundamental element: the very strong homogeneity of the entire region, not only the Gold Coast, but the entire Akan world, which constitutes a basic historical process. Yet all the studies concerning the Akan world are characterized by being in their numerous aspects "ethnic," in that attention is concentrated on the region's particular characteristics. Obviously, it is practically impossible to separate the history of one of those regions from the specific common components of the Akan ambience: the environment (the forest), the trade between the coast and the interior, the presence, ambitions, and competition of the Europeans, the required presence of traders and marabouts, the great political adventures in the forest region, the migrations, and the continued interactions between different groups involved in the logistics of the network, which open up a macro-regional scale. Such a fact is obvious, but its positive reception by historiographers has not yet been realized. The historiography is often, on the contrary, characterized by "insularity," the origin of which is linked to the tradition of anthropological studies.

Nevertheless, such a regional homogeneity is underscored by a narrow fabric of connections between the different histories. It emerges with particular force in studies that aim to formulate reliable interpretive models concerning the "origins" of the societies in question and to clarify more precisely the crucial phase that preceded the arrival of the Portuguese at the coast (in the second half of the fifteenth century) and which corresponds to the start of the period which one is able to document, thanks to European sources. Casting a glance at these studies, one may be tempted to summarize the terms of the theoretical debate as intense, even if it limits itself to a precise number of participants. It unfolded especially during the 1970s and 1980s. In addition, when glancing through it, we may be inclined to use such expressions like "mode of production," which may appear obsolete to the ears of experts. But one cannot forget that it is precisely in this framework of the debate where the studies have achieved results that are particularly important and fruitful for the historical research and a better knowledge of the Akan society.

One should emphasize the lasting impact of the brilliant interpretive construction of Ivor Wilks, who worked out a fascinating argument for the way in which the Akan world of the fifteenth and sixteenth centuries underwent the transformation from an economy of the forest based entirely on hunting and gathering—thus a low population density—to a system based on agricultural production. The forms of the previous social organization (bands or groups) were replaced by institutions better adapted to the new productive context, and which required absorption into the social indigenous body an enormous demographic surplus, able to supply the large work force necessary to expand the arable land for agricultural produce, at the expense of the forest. These institutions are the matrilineage (*abusua*, pl. *mmusua*) and especially the great exogamic matriclan (*abusua kese*, pl. *mmusua kese*).

This process of transformation, and the revolutionary demographic explosion that came with it, was made possible and fueled by, according to I. Wilks, the conjunction between the increasing demand of gold on the world market and the local demand for labor. The area of the forest is this particular phase imported slaves of different origins. A portion of them was obtained through payment in locally mined gold. Those who controlled the production of gold, the *abirempon* (singular *birempon*) or big men, soon became the biggest importers of forced labor, which they reused in the expansion of mining and agricultural activities, namely for their own source of wealth and power. The territorial and demographic organization of the system of the enterprise, or the *birempon*, that which Wilks defines as *birempon-dom*, became a nation, and some of these domains were the immediate origin of the political units of the Gold Coast forest region. Among these entrepreneurial figures one finds, according to Wilks, the founders of the Akan region's political and historical entities.

This interpretive framework has become a widely accepted historiographic paradigm, even if Wilks's proposed chronology for the development of the forest population is put into doubt by archeological research, performed especially in the milieu of the eighties, which emphasized the presence of stable systems of great dimensions (of the order of thousands of inhabitants) going back at least to the tenth century CE, and found evidence of ironwork and probably agriculture.

One of the most convincing critics of Wilks's thesis is A. N. Klein, who maintains that the process of intense forest colonization by the ancestors of today's Akan groups can be documented at the early stages of our era. Apart from archeological data, Klein bases his assertion on a biomedical simulation, namely on the history of development of resistance to malaria, found among those groups which were exposed to pathogenic agents in the forest such as malaria. The Akan had practically lived in the forest for millennia prior to the epoch in which Wilks places the definite establishment of this type of society. Certainly the sixteenth and seventeenth centuries are, according to Klein, marked by a radical transformation, but in a sense contrary to that of Wilks's hypothesis. The data at hand demonstrate indeed that there was a process of population concentration, out of necessity to ensure its defense and survival, which from a demographic view was severely troubled by new pathogens derived from contact with Europeans, but also by the devastating conflicts unleashed by the development of the Atlantic trading. As Klein himself admits, the conclusive elements and the generally available data are still too scant to permit a detailed reconstruction. To achieve it, archeology, most likely, is invoked to play a role of primary importance.

The Transformations in the Seventeenth Century: The Proposals of Kea and van Dantzig

In the obscurity that surrounds the persistent question of "origins," there is only one fixed point in the current understanding of the history of the Gold Coast and the entire Akan region, both in the representation we have locally and that of academic historiography. That point is the shared awareness of the revolutionary impact of the great socio-political and economic transformation in the region during the second half of the seventeenth century. One deals here with a series of developments that transformed the entire political, human, demographic, social, and economic framework, emanating from the forest region of the interior and spreading to the entire region. A new social-economic order emerged from it, along with new political entities much larger and better organized than those preceding them, extending to the realization of a territorial, demographic, and economic expansion: the veritable "imperial projects." The most important are, according to their chronological order and their formation, Akwamu, Denkyira, and Asante.

This historic phase is the object of intense research in the framework of a more general interest: the question of "nation" and the socio-economic forms in West Africa. This research is based, especially in theoretical terms, on an analysis of the "mode of production." On this subject, the important work published in 1982 by Kea, *Settlements, Trade and Politics in the Seventeenth-Century Gold Coast*, describes in an incisive manner a series of structural changes, a consequence of which between the sixteenth and the seventeenth century were new political, economic and military figures that arose or gained strength. The author examines the relationship between the formation of the society's class structure, the system of production, and the presence of commercial interests of foreign origin. According to Kea, whose analyses I will cite, are largely indebted to the studies of Wilks. The process appears as a transition between two dominant forms of social production: a commercial-agrarian type (the leading groups are constructed in the oligarchic-commercial network) and an imperial agrarian type (whose leading groups are based on the concentration of military power).

These changes in the productive and commercial logistics were provoked and conditioned by the radical transformation of the region's geopolitical, military, and social framework. It itself was an effect of the development of the Atlantic economy, which replaced the old system of Mediterranean connections. The African market system changed profoundly. These new phenomena included the introduction of American money into the European market, the development of the plantation agriculture, which necessitated an intensive usage of labor and led to an exponential increase in the demand for slaves. In the Akan region, during the second half of the seventeenth century, slaves had become an export more in demand than gold. These changes coincided with the realization of the great process of socio-economic transformation, and the creation of the system of forest agriculture; the Akan societies therefore adapted rapidly and integrated themselves successfully into the new system of the Atlantic economy.

The political-mercantile power structure of the seventeenth century embodied by the famous political commercial system of the Akan did not resist the changes. While the demand for slaves surpassed that for gold, certain privileged interlocutors of the Europeans became political, militarily organized agents. They gained strength in the interior at the expense of the Akan network (which they had become part of), and which they caused progressively to dissolve. But the decline of the "mercantile" system is equally perceived in the intensification of social contrasts between the urban ruling groups and the rural society for whom the control of the agricultural surplus was an issue. In the framework of this crisis the relationship between town and country transformed itself to the advantage of the latter.

Kea emphasizes that the previous equilibrium collapsed as consequence of the new imperial formations and their newly emerging merchant groups. The old Akan network was replaced by great commercial intermediaries living in coastal towns, especially in the Fante region, each being at the head of a system of contacts placed in different centers of the interior. The reinforcement of the new network went hand-in-hand with the Fante political-military expansion. However, more generally, the dynamics of the military conquest on a huge scale, put into place by the "imperial" agents of the interior, determined a proportional increase in the number of prisoners of war, who, as van Dantzig asserts, were immediately employed to satisfy the increasingly strong demand for slaves by the Europeans of the coast. In this framework, a series of national formations arose and affirmed themselves, such as Akwamu and Denkyira, but the foremost was Asante. According to Kea, these were the prototypes of the new pattern of imperial-agrarian formations of the region.

From a socio-political point of view, such a dynamic marks the connection of two different forms of corporate organizations of the ruling groups. The previous form of social organizations that united the ruling classes concerning political "economic" subjects consisted of horizontal regroupings, established according to the order, which Kea defines as that of brotherhoods of nobles. Those united the socially important individuals, the *abirempon*, and therewith the different political entities and linguistic and cultural affiliations of the Gold Coast of the seventeenth and eighteenth centuries. Kea bases his own reconstruction on sources that describe the procedures of recognition of social ascension— "the Ennoblement"—through integration into institutionalized groupings.

In addition to the "brotherhoods," there existed other forms of corporative organizations in higher classes linked to commercial activity, as for example the organizations of the Akan merchants (*Akanist*). They reunited the merchants and the intermediaries organized into domestic "captaincies." Van Dantzig sees in these networks, but also in other similar organizations of the Akan world, systems of corporate connections between certain commercial operators on the level of the entire region, and forms the hypothesis of their crucial role in the origins of Denkyira in the second half of the seventeenth century. Kea maintains that as a consequence of the great political and economic changes of this same time period, the old forms of social hegemony rapidly lost importance, while the great exogamic matriclan, the *abusua kese*, established itself as the principal form of coordination among the ruling classes on the regional level, and consequently, as the structure which, better than the others, regulated the connections of the dominant elements and the elements dominated.

In the beginning, the *abusua kese*—according to Wilks's theory adopted by Kea—is linked to the control and the management of the land, namely production. It is a corporation of *abirempon* families, including their dependents, those of non-free status, and families combined between them. As noted previously, these groups were involved in commercial activities. However, according to Kea, they reproduced themselves socially, not like a class of merchants and intermediaries, but like landowners and authorities within the new political formations. Effectively, the *abirempon* adapted to the new context. They changed their proper means of subsistence and invested the revenues of commerce into land properties and forced labor:

> The *mmusua-kese* may be said to have emerged as a result of changing patterns in the ownership of the means of production.... Not only were they corporate organizations that assimilated persons of servile status; they were also class organizations that represented the new political identities and roles of particular *obirempon* families. (Kea 1982, p. 92)

This became the triumph of the matriclan as a universal form of structuring social hierarchy at the exclusion of nearly every other type of re-grouping, the end result of a process that had begun, according to Wilks, during the fifteenth and sixteenth centuries.

But concerning this point, the reading of Kea appears neither founded nor convincing. It bases itself on a thesis that rests on the essential difference between the preceding associative forms of the ruling groups, forms founded on class and social rank, the merchant "brotherhoods," and the subsequent forms that refer to family relationships. Nevertheless, Kea has not provided the likely elements to support his thesis and to document the presumable process of passage from one form of organization to the other. It does not suffice for this purpose that he denotes which procedures of admission to the "brotherhoods," described by European sources of the seventeenth century as the ceremonies of "ennoblement," were discontinued in the first part of the eighteenth century.

Logistical "Network"

An obvious fact for anyone who has contact with historiographic materials of the Akan region is the existence of a macro-regional scale of interactions between the ruling groups, through the associations and the networks which define the borders of different political entities, designating a "particular geography." That said, it is necessary to state that the research related to this type of connection rarely advances beyond the confines of a limited historical-political entity or "ethnicity." The bonds of "kinship" between the ruling groups have been researched in important studies concerning the formation and populating of the political Akan entities of the west in the seventeenth and nineteenth centuries, as for instance, those of Terray concerning the Gyaman, of Perrot concerning the Ndényé, of Diabate concerning the Sanwi, or of Viti concerning the Baule.

This attention to the macro-regional perspective, presented in the analyses of the "origins" of the political formations in the late seventeenth and early eighteenth centuries, was shifted nearly exclusively to the structuring of the new nation's political, social, and economic seats, and to a history of their relations with the exterior, which is conceived as a classic system of "international relations" between politically homogenous units. This characteristic appears in the historiography of the Asante, which is dominated, if this is comprehensible, by the intense attention given to the dynamics of this complex national and imperial organization. However, many of the crucial elements that emerge from analyses of the eighteenth- and nineteenth-century histories manifest themselves like a fundamental constant, although with an unequal intensity and importance according to the particular historical context.

The observable situation of the Western Akan region during the eighteenth century is particularly emblematic. One sees clearly in this case how, from a long-term perspective, the dynamics of different local ruling groups are difficult to isolate from the larger and more general circuits, perhaps only as the outcome, spatially and chronologically, of contingent and very specific analyses. Indeed, historiographic materials (written sources and oral traditions), tend to focus on contexts that decisively transcend the logistics of the territorial, political, or ethnic aggregation on the local scale. This suggests or blatantly affirms the existence and the operational characteristics of branched networks, to the point of making their disentanglement and decoding very difficult. The impact of that fundamental data may seriously limit the value of a localized study or even of "ethnic histories." The particularity of this situation, which concerns a vast array of political entities including the current Ahanta, Nzema, Egila (Edwira), Pepeesa, Wassa, Aowin, Sanwi, and Bassam, as well as the Ewuture (Mekyibo) and Abure (of Bonoua) areas, is reconstructed with relevance by J. P. T. Huydecoper, Dutch commandant of Fort Saint Anthony at Axim. In 1762, he rendered an account (translated by Furley) of the short-term character of the conflicts between the political entities and additional united groups, furthermore closely related and interconnected:

> Between them (the aborigines) they are all divided into dif-
> ferent Stammen (tribes) of which neither they nor us know
> the origin ... but which have a very strong influence on the
> life of the community.... Some of the tribes are closely linked
> to others, some of them are strongly opposed to one another.
> The consequence of this is that when ... something big which
> can cause disagreements between them, they have the custom
> to help one another against a third party. Their love for their
> homeland is alone strong enough to break this bond and in
> the defense of which no attention is paid to associations
> (based on common origin, concerning a tribe).

Primarily, the countries were political-territorial units, which were more
or less direct successors of the "traditional nations" present in the region. These units constitute a constant reference in the political dynamics of the region throughout three centuries. Secondly, in the position
of setbacks and constant potentiality of conflict among them, but with
equally fundamental implications related to the dynamics of social-po-
litical and fundamental order, there stands the entity that Huydecoper
defines as *stam* (tribe).

   The identification of *stam* with the matriclan (*abusua kese* in Asante,
and *abusua eku* in Nzema) is obvious. However, this identification is
not exhaustive. Diverse local and European sources allow us to reconstruct by inference some of the connections that are encapsulated by
Huydecoper in the expression *stam*; and we will see how those include
a very large framework of relations, complex, colorful, and not re-
ducible to a unilinear scheme of kinship. One can indeed speak of relations through belonging to the same *abusua* or *abusua kese*, but also
very often determined by the degree of patri-lateral kinship. The affinity,
which arises from a common affiliation with the maternal lineage, the
matriclan, or the paternal lineage, can be consolidated by sworn pacts
of alliance, usually sanctioned by matrimonial exchanges. Esawa constitutes here a significant example. Here we deal with a great group of
the *mmusua* present in a very large portion of the Western Akan world.
Esawa is represented by its members as if it were a grouping of matriclans: Aduana in Sehwi and Aowin, Asona or Bretuo in Ahanta,

Ndweafo in Egila, Axim and in the Nzema zones in the west of Ankobra, where they are closely related to the local matriclan Azanwule, especially in the Western Nzema. At the end of the nineteenth century, the
Esawa d'Egila consisted of a grouping in the region, which occupied,
to cite only the most important ones, the seats of Bamianko, Banso, To-
mento, and Essuawa, but also Salman, Kekame and Anwea in Eastern
Nzema. The Esawa of Bamianko were closely related with the exchange
of successors to the seat of Akatakyi, in Ahanta, and also at that of
Kwawu, in Aowin. The succession, in every seat, was potentially guar-
anteed by several *mmusua*, thanks to those who formed the network.

But this is not all: Certain seats could obtain the successors of the
abusua, who did not define themselves as being Esawa and who recognized the kinship bonds with one or several components of the Esawa
group. Very often, the particular bonds were formulated in lineages
united by a sworn pact. The character of the network, or, better, of the
hierarchy (but not necessarily fixed) in the alliance of different groups,
which resulted from precise historical contingencies, is present in an
emphatic way in the narratives relating to the origins of the Esawa
d'Egila. These narratives cover in detail the terms of pronouncements
of the pacts between the groups concerned, and the matrimonial inter-
changes that they enforced.

We are facing a galaxy composed of many solar systems supplied by
planets and satellites of which some participate simultaneously in several orbits of different matriclans. To say it differently, the language of
kinship translates in the obvious way in the case of the Esawa, a stratification of connections of a different nature: primarily the historical
context of the formulation of the bonds of alliance, equal or unequal,
between the groups, emphasized by precise matrimonial strategies. The
logistics that derive from these agreements of associations were sum-
marized in 1920 by an old *ohene* (king) of Bansu (Egila):

> The families become one, when the member of one family
> sits on the stool of the other and vice versa ... have made one,
> they don't separate. There are families of one blood, and fam-
> ilies of the same name but not of the same blood. In several
> cases, the groups, which were mentioned, act like a large en-

semble, according to a certain coherence and, in particular, according to the institutionalized forms, which serve the mediation of internal conflicts. They have recourse to the same *ntam*, that is to say to the same form of oath.

Dependence, Integration, and Language of Kinship: Yarak, McCaskie, Terray

However, studies of greater depth in this domain are not easy. On one hand, previous studies are not very numerous and the material and methodological points of reference are rare. On the other hand, the available sources are often too general or too indirect to solidify the dynamics they suggest. Lastly, the access to this domain of analysis presupposes that one pays great attention to a discourse that is complex and often elusive: that of kinship. The local sources present the history of bonds between the groups through the language of kinship: The different groups are being associated based on matrilinear (matrilineage and matriclan) and patrilinear relations, or because of alliances based on matrimonial exchanges. These categories are generally accepted by historians as reflecting the actual data of the local society, but are rarely (and only recently) removed from a timeless, "structural" anthropological treatment and analyzed in their historical dimension. An exact, groundbreaking inquiry in this sense is that of I. Wilks on the subject of the origin of the matriclan. The institution is enigmatic, and in Asante and other Akan regions it continued to play a crucial role in the great exogamic unity (but not, however, in Nzema, Ahanta, Aowin, Anyi, Baule and generally in the West). In Wilks's analysis, the matriclan presents itself as a system of alliance, more than one of descent. According to McCaskie, this fundamental characteristic of the history of Asante matrilinearity, matrilineage included, had critical implications on local perceptions of the hierarchy of relationships among individuals and member groups.

The classic anthropological interpretation of matrilineage within a broader matriclan as "a constituent equally derived from the principle of descent," McCaskie, based on the "theory of alliance," objects:

> The perception of the Asante *abusua* is in terms of alliance
> rather than that of descent... In the Asante political thought
> these 'lineages' [are interpreted] in terms of assumptions of
> inequality: in the lineage a distinction is made between the
> 'true' descendants and the assimilated and often non-free.

The implications of this reading concerning the historical plane are visible in certain interesting reflections of L. Yarak, which helped to con-
textualize the connection between alliance/kinship and nation. Yarak
analyzes the connection between dominant and dependent members in
the *abusua* as also being a system of mediation for access to the soil,
imagining it in terms of the connections between landowners and tenants
and relations between "free" members of matrilineage and those who
were "acquired." (Yarak defines them as "adopted": they are the
gyasefo, "the people of the hearth" of non-free or foreign ancestry.) The
gyaase (hearth), which include all the persons of non-free condition assimilated into the *abusua*, act like a group placed into direct service to
the chief of the family. It consists of his domestic helpers, servants, and
defenders, but also of his most intimate advisers (and influencers).
These are the sons of chiefs of the family, which rules the *gyaase*, be it
those that act as the sons of free mothers, related thus through maternal
lineages different from those of the chief of the family, or be it those
that act as sons of non-free women and thus are directly assimilated into
the proper maternal lineage of his. The member of the *gyaase* takes on
the responsibilities at the place of his lord: there he cultivates the soil
as local farmer, searches for gold on his behalf, enters trade and combat
for him, serves him, and after the lord dies, is made heir of his property.
   Yarak elaborates on his characterization of the connection between
the "free" lineages and the subjugated lineages in the context of important, theoretically useful findings with regard to the Asante of the seventeenth and nineteenth centuries. He leaves the Weberian category of
patrimonialism. Once again, great differences in matters of dimension
and the development of the political institutions, which distinguish the
Asante from all the other political formations of the region, are established. Several of his considerations can nevertheless be applied to a
general analysis of the Akan nation. More precisely, Yarak rereads in a

critical manner the interpretation of the Asante imperial administration system, which Wilks considered as a system of bureaucracy formalized in Weberian terms. On his part, he sees an Asante "patrimonialism" closer to an oriental variant ("sultanism"), than to an occidental variant, the expression of which is the feudal nation. Furthermore, he contests the interpretation of a "mode of production of slaves," specific to certain great Akan nations, such as Asante and Gyaman, which was proposed by E. Terray. In his critique, he notes the adequacy and efficiency of mechanisms that permitted rapid integration of slaves into the social body.

Yarak emphasizes forcefully the fundamental role played by the *gyaase*. To explain the connection between power, the system of slavery, and society, he uses the categories of the "mode of feudal production" (or coercive rent-taking) and the "mode of tributary production" (or tax-raising). This is revisited by C. Wickham based on a materialistic approach applied to the historical situations of Europe and Asia during the high Middle Ages. In the first case (feudalism), the landowner did not only receive from his farmer a rent payment in money or services, but he was able to exert over him a control in non-economic ways, either formal (e.g., the administration of justice) or informal. In the second case ("tributary"), the surplus of the products is extracted through a tax demanded by a "class of the state," founded on a public institution, which possesses the political right to exploit a sector of society, which it does not directly control through administration of the land. In practice the connection of chief/*gyaase* is a variant of the "mode of feudal production" placed into a very broad connection between the chief and society of the "tributary" type. Nevertheless, this intervention produces a subordinate position, given that the members of the *gyaase* have not only specific obligations but are, in spite of it all, subjected to taxes like the other subjects.

The institution of the *gyaase* had the permanent function to rebalance the societal constituency, subjected to continued absorption of a great number of individuals and groups, those of non-free origin, slaves, prisoners, strangers, refugees, relatives, dependents, etc. By associating closely, thanks to forms affected by kinship, lords and subjects, masters and slaves, rulers and subordinated allies, the *gyaase* were able to act—

in a most efficient manner—as a sort of filter of mediation and as a flotation tank between entreaties of their relatives and those of the social class. If one wants to fully understand this logistic, one cannot avoid paying attention to the *gyaase*, a fundamental social institution in the Akan society (at least during the sixteenth and twentieth centuries). I. Wilks stresses the crucial importance of the study of its members, the *gyaasefo*, from a historiographic point of view. Thus, he defines them as "this peculiarly servile, yet peculiarly powerful status."

By Way of Conclusion: Histories of the Gyaasefo

The observation, even if superficial, of the individual histories of numerous members of the *gyaase* is indeed full of interesting surprises. One of the most well-known is that of Amankwatia Panin, the first Bantamahene who possessed the Asante military power. He was an individual of non-free status, a servant (*akoa*) member of the *gyaase* of Osei Tutu, the first *Asantehene*. However, the history of Amankwatia Panin is linked to that of the beginnings of the great national and imperial Asante system and can be very well be read as a classic case of individual social promotion, within a framework of power centralization that occurred through the augmentation of servants who depended directly on the sovereign. It deals with a process firmly attested to in the case of the Asante. But other cases are documented in the regions of the Gold Coast where central institutions of the same power did not exist and where one did not assist in a comparable process of national growth. They also are more indicators of a situation in which the status of strong personal dependence is not considered incompatible with the possibility to ascend to the positions which assure the control of important political, military, and economic power, including the highest office, that of the king.

Aniaba, the famous hostage, who the Esuma of Assinie left as collateral in France in 1687, was baptized and raised in Paris like the godson of Louis XIV and "heir to the throne" of Assinie; he was at the same time a member of the royal matrilineage of the Ewuture [Eotilé] and member of the *gyaase* of the chief Esuma (to whom he was probably given as collateral at an early age). Esuma and Ewuture are two groups that live on the shores and islands of the Aby lagoon. At his return to Assinie in 1701, Aniaba found himself in situation which is difficult to define, because he was able to effectively advance his ambitions for the royal seat of the Esuma, as "son" of the king, and, at the same time, he was the candidate for the Ewuture royal seat which remained empty because of his relatedness to the royal matrilineage. His aspirations were crushed, however, in the complicated and conflicting political circumstances of the installation of the French in Assinie (1700-1702). In the conflict with the commander Damon, he lost the support of the French, and it cost him not only the prospect of occupying a very elevated function of power among the Esuma (even if this was not the royal position), but also access to the seat of the Ewuture for which he had been the most qualified candidate. The royal family and the chiefs of the Ewuture chose Coucocrou, "the favorite slave" of the preceding sovereign, an individual powerful and ingenious, who like the chief of the *gyaase* had taken control of the estate of the departed.

Histories of this type are not isolated exceptional cases, but they occur frequently in the society of the Gold Coast in the seventeenth and eighteenth centuries. As representing an institution which occupies a central position in the system of power of the region, the *gyaase* contributed to maintaining the system to be the same as the original condition of the *abusua*, namely those which one could be defined as *adehyee* (singular *odehyee*), the innocent ones (those born free). By default, among the *adehyee*, the acceptable candidates in the care of the chief of the matrilineage (*abusua panin*) were the "sons" of the *abusua* and in particular the *gyaasefo* who were supposed to provide the successor. An example of these logistics is given by Yarak, who tells about the particularly interesting case of Tannie Boreo, an acquired slave who competed for the succession of the head of an Elmina *abusua* in 1830. After the death of the master, in the absence of a male heir, the office of the *abusua panin* was occupied by a slave, according to the custom, but that one died very soon, opening the path to Tannie Boreo, who had already inherited one of the wives of his predecessors and had assumed the functions and privileges of this position like a presumptive heir. However, the members of the family did not agree with his name: one part of them did not want anything to do with him and questioned his capability for the position of *abusua panin* because he was too young and had no experience. Tannie Boreo found himself then in a difficult situation and tried to get out of it by demanding from his masters money and a woman to marry, and in case of refusal to be sold to the new landowners. He threatened to otherwise cause damage to the family by bringing them into debt and creating judicial problems.

It is a common characteristic of the persons mentioned. It seems to me as being fundamental: from the point of view of their position in the kinship system founded on matrilineage, one can consider all like the *gyaasefo* as "people of the hearth," "sons," or as assimilated. Their personal status is doubtful enough, if one considers them from the point of view of the category *odehyee* (Anaiba is an exception), but it essentially did not prevent one from legitimately aspiring and ascending to prestigious positions. It can be concluded from their history—whether in the case of Aniaba or Tannie Boreo—that the factors of dependency permitted one to occupy a position he aspired to, in the absence of an eligible heir in the noble branch of the *abusua* of the acquisition.

One detailed observation of the historical framework of the seventeenth and eighteenth centuries seems to contradict an image of the Akan society that was widespread in the twentieth century and to which colonial anthropology has contributed considerably: That image suggested that the scale of personal status and the scale of political and economic power tended to coincide. The observed situations show, on the contrary, how a condition of personal dependency and the eventual, high-level control of political, military, and economic power were not contradictory. It is difficult enough to identify (in the pre-colonial epoch) the existence of a condition of individual freedom. In an abstract manner, one can identify a concept of individual liberty in the Akan category, which is the basis for the condition of the *odehyee*. But in actuality to be born free results in an extremely precarious position: The individual very easily at a certain moment of his existence loses the condition of freedom, be it by force or his own will, and he enters into a category of strong dependency (as when taken as pawn, hostage, or prisoner, or as a voluntary guest or vassal of someone powerful). In addition, the condition of the *odehyee*, even if it is not lost, does not assure the continued enjoyment of guarantees and privileges. To say it in another way, it is effective in certain conditions shared by a portion of extreme minority of the social group: The citizen in the full enjoyment of his rights, the "free one" by definition, is the *abusua panin*, the chief of the lineage (man or woman), the one who in the language of the drums is defined as "the one who cannot be put up for sale," at least not until a superior power—as in the case of the Asante nation—decides differently.

However, even in this case, to detect and define such a condition in the concretely observed historical situations is another thing. The entire assertion of autonomy by connection to the strong powers is difficult to separate from the affirmation of a capacity of financial autonomy: he is free who is able to make guarantees for his subjects and himself in the ever-present eventuality of debt, demands, or ransom (in case of capture). Thus, very often, the *akoa* is able to preserve for himself spaces of autonomy, of "liberty" spaces very great and effective that the *odehyee* cannot, mainly because he is not rich.

The Expansion of the Fante
and the Emergence of Asante
in the Eighteenth Century

JAMES SANDERS

James Sanders completed his doctorate in the Department of History at Northwestern University. Some time thereafter, he joined the U.S. Department of Defense, from which he eventually retired. The following essay, drawn from Sanders's doctoral research, attempts to assess the importance of Asante influence in the consolidation of the Fante in the eighteenth century.

Two general themes form the background for the present study: external trade and state formation. A major historical question concerns the connections between the two: how far was maritime trade crucial to state formation in West Africa? In the case of the Gold Coast, one recent study has emphasized the formative influence of maritime trade. Another has investigated the effects of trade goods, such as firearms, on the process of state formation. Kea's study of seventeenth-century Akwamu shows how firearms contributed to forms of social differentiation associated with state building. Others still have examined the effects of the trade in slaves on the emergence of states. Fage, for example, argues that the slave trade facilitated the development of "unitary, territorial political authority" in eighteenth-century West Africa. Finally, a very recent study, taking a more detailed focus, explores the origins of a particular coastal polity. Henige's research suggests that the Komenda paramountcy developed from the commercial activities of the "merchant prince" John Kabes.

What follows below is a case study of the Fante, who, during the course of the eighteenth century, had begun to change from a disparate and loosely organized society to one in which political units were crystallizing and which recognized common economic interests. In the eighteenth century, the Fante, participants in the Atlantic trade from at least the early seventeenth century, served as middlemen through whom Europeans obtained slaves from Asante and beyond. The object of this paper is to look at the consolidation of the Fante in the eighteenth century and to assess the influence on that consolidation of two external factors: European maritime trade and the emergence of Asante.

Historians have stressed the relationship between the development of Fante in the early eighteenth century and the emergence of the Asante state in the area of Kwabre and Kaase. "The main factor that made the Fante hasten to unite," writes one, "was the political change that was brought about by the Asante intrusion into the politics of the southern states." Prior to this period, he argues, the Fante were a disunited people whose power had "atrophied" and who were further weakened by their form of government in which the "Braffo" could not exercise power over the other chiefs of the country. In this condition the Fante stood in danger of invasion by neighboring states. The rise of the Fante, he concludes, was a result of the threat of "imminent Asante encroachment."

Without attempting to deny that the emergence of Asante had an important effect on coastal politics, these arguments may be modified in several ways in the light of new research. First, the source upon which the description of Fante before 1700 is based is the very inaccurate 1705 English translation of Willem Bosnian's *Nauwkeurige Beschriving van de Guinese Gout- Tand- en Slaven Kust*. The English edition contains the following passage: "If the Fante were not in perpetual civil divisions, the circumjacent countries would soon find their power by the irruptions into their territories." This crucial sentence has been incorrectly translated. As Albert van Dantzig has made clear, this passage should read: "for this reason and because the *Fantyneans* are not divided among themselves, the circumjacent Countries think twice before they abuse them [the Fante], because they would have a sour time of it." It is a mistake, then, to argue that the power of the Fante had decreased. On the contrary, they were recognized by Bosman as one of the strongest peoples on the coast.

A second misconception lies in the argument that attributes "disunity in the Fante state" to the debilitating tendency whereby "a chief sometimes would scarce own the Braffo for his superior." Fante in the seventeenth century was not a monarchy, as some of its neighbors appear to have been. It was not a kingdom in decline. Instead, the Fante were undergoing a constructive process of political evolution during this period. The dispersion of groups of Fante from Mankessim and the formation by them of distinct political units each headed by a king-like figure is not to be construed as a mark of debility. The powers of these persons over their followers exceeded that of those authorities resident at Mankessim and Abora referred to in European sources as "Braffoes"—a term literally meaning "executioner" but used by the Fante to denote those functionaries wielding secular authority, apparently based upon religious sanctions. The dispersion of the Fante succeeded, it appears, mainly for two reasons. First, their great numbers helped them to overpower other groups; second, they were substantially aided with firearms by the English. The group divisions *(abron,* or wards) which had existed among the Fante at Mankessim (and according to tradition even earlier), thus acquired an expanded territorial basis, an individual political status and a permanent identity.

Finally, the relationship between the emergence of Asante in the area around present-day Kwabre and Kaase at the turn of the seventeenth century and the Fante wars with neighboring kingdoms fought between 1700 and 1724 is not one of direct causality. Boahen has argued that after the conquest of Denkyera the Fante were threatened with "defeat and absorption" and their middleman role between inland and European traders was placed in jeopardy. In response to the "dramatic emergence" of Asante, as well as to guard against Akwamu and Akyem, the Fante expanded in the period 1700-1724.

To what extent was Asante a threat to the coast during the period when the Fante fought against Asebu, Fetu, Cabesterra and Agona? In the aftermath of the defeat of Denkyera, disturbances broke out among those states that had formerly been loyal to Asante. Twifo, Akani (Asen), Wasa and Aowin did not immediately recognize the overlordship of Asante, but rather found themselves able to pursue their individual interests with impunity and began to block paths leading to the coast and to rob traders. During the early eighteenth century Asante became involved in campaigns against some of these states as a means of establishing its dominion over them. In 1712 it fought Twifo with the help of a number of coastal kingdoms, including the Fante. Thereafter a campaign was commenced against Aowin to the northwest; it was under way by 1715. While Asante was occupied with Aowin, the Dutch reported, "the entire lower coast at the east of Elmina was being threatened by the Akims." As Boahen points out, the response of the Fante to the Akyem threat was to make a defensive alliance with Agona, Acron, Akwamu and Akani. When Akyem, presumably those represented by the later Abuakwa, attacked in 1716 the alliance succeeded in defending the member kingdoms. Between 1716 and 1724 neither Asante nor Akyem was engaged in wars threatening the Fante directly or indirectly. It was perhaps this interlude from the designs of larger powers that allowed smaller ones to act in furtherance of their own ambitions. Agona thus attacked Acron in 1716. The attacks, which apparently occurred over a number of years, eventually included the Fante, who overran Agona in 1724 and gained control of that area of the coast.

Asante did not, then, directly threaten the Fante coast between 1700 and 1724. Nor do Asante activities seem to have been especially dramatic. After defeating Denkyera, Asante faced the difficult task of establishing its control over the territories it had come to dominate. The allegiance of states which had previously been loyal to Denkyera had to be secured. The disruption that had occurred on the coast after the defeat of Denkyera clearly touched the Fante, but they reacted to potential threats by making alliances, not conquests.

The wars of conquest are rather to be viewed against the background first, of commercial rivalry among states on the littoral that competed with each other in bringing down trade from northern regions, and second, of competition among the Europeans who wanted to see the trade coming down through districts where their forts were located. The English were keenly interested in Fante expansion, because most of their forts were situated in Fante domains.

The defeat of Asebu around 1708 by Fante forces can be considered the first important war of Fante expansion. Skirmishes between the two kingdoms had been occurring at least since 1653, one of which cost the

English their lodge at "Enchiang" (possibly Anashan). By the first decade of the eighteenth century, the attacks were still being made. In October 1706, the Dutch Factor at Moree noted, "the Fantes have attacked all the surrounding Asebu villages and set fire to them and have plundered everything that came in their way.... About two years later the Fante attacked again, beheaded the king, and killed most of the important chiefs. From this assault, the kingdom never recovered." In 1717, a Dutch report stated that, "We have nevertheless little advantage to expect from Asebu—a poor and little residue of people, of whom nearly nothing remains but the simple name of Asebu, and who above all are vassals of Fante."

After the defeat of Asebu the Fante mounted an offensive against Fetu and Cabesterra. "[S]purred on by gifts & presents from Sir Dalby," noted the Dutch, the Fante defeated Fetu and took its king prisoner. With Fetu defeated, they observed, "the Fante now becoming puffed up & rapacious for booty, further incited by the Knight [i.e. Sir Dalby Thomas] have marched inland to defeat the Cabes Terras & having done that, [intend] to ruin Akim country.... " By 1710 the Fante had come to dominate much of the Gold Coast. With a note of apparent regret the Director-General at Elmina reported that "there is hardly any state here which is not allied to the Fantynse; they would rather have both our Companies as their enemies than Fantyn alone."

A decade earlier Fanteland had consisted of four coastal towns and an inland district whose dimensions were only vaguely defined by the kingdoms surrounding it. By 1710, it had increased both in size and in influence. The campaign against Asebu divested that state of much of its territory, which the Fante through the course of the century gradually repopulated. Whether the war against Fetu also resulted in territorial gain is difficult to determine, but it is clear that after the war the Fante attempted to exercise political influence over the kingdom. They were in a good position to do so because they had captured Ahen Pompa, the Fetu king. However, because of the important position occupied by Fetu in the commercial geography of the coast, the acephalous kingdom became the object of intervention by the Europeans. The English Governor at Cape Coast, Sir Dalby Thomas, who sought to direct traders passing through Fetu exclusively to English factories, now saw his opportunity.

In 1708 he hoped to "settle Aquebah Braffo to be Queen of Fetue"; and in 1709 he aroused the anger of the Fante by threatening unilaterally to install a new king in the district, one who would favor the English. For some time after the initial conquest, Fetu was unsettled. In February 1717 the English reported that a new "Dey" (apparently next in authority to the Fetuhen) named "Sumapong" had been installed who "has been in Holland and liv'd at Elmina." By fall 1718, it was reported that a new king had been chosen on "Recommendation of the Dutch." In response to these developments the Fante began "prepareing to invade Fetue & restore the old Officers with fire & Sword. A second invasion thus became necessary to preserve the effects of the first. This invasion may have been that which occurred in October 1720 when James Phipps, the English merchant, reported from Cape Coast that the "Fanteens [are] in arms against the Fetues &c So [we] hope the officers in the Fante Country will soon be Established again for the advantage of the Company."

Expansion of the Fante in the east, in the same period, is more difficult to elucidate. According to traditional sources the Fante gained control over the kingdom of Gomoa (i.e. "Acron") early in the eighteenth century when they were called to assist the king of Gomoa, Kwaw Ehura Aku, in a war against Agona. Fante forces led by Kusiedu (i.e. "Kusa Adu"), succeeded in defeating the Agona king Nyako Ako and thereafter Kusiedu—a Fante man previously resident in the Abora village of Besabew—was made king of Gomoa. However, the correlation between these traditions and the documentary evidence is not especially strong. In December 1720 Willem Butler, the Director-General at Elmina, reported that the Fante had attacked Agona and driven its forces to the fort at Senya Beraku.

In 1724 Director-General Pieter Valcknier reported that the Fante had taken up arms against Agona. Perhaps several campaigns over a period of years were needed to subdue Agona. In any case, there is little evidence in these sources concerning Fante relations with Gomoa. A single reference in 1720 to a payment having been made to "Ashadoe, King of Accroa" tempts one to identify him with Kusiedu of the traditional accounts, but without more evidence, it cannot be certain that they were the same person. Therefore, it is difficult to know exactly when the

Gomoa region came under Fante influence. All that can be said with confidence now is that by 1720 Fante initiatives in the area were under way.

Fante expansion inland is even more difficult to reconstruct than in areas east of Cape Coast and Anomabo. While coastal conquests are to some extent documented, similar data are sparse for the more northerly areas. With the exception of Cabesterra, lying to the northwest, the kingdoms against which the Fante fought in the early eighteenth century lay on the immediate coast. It appears from the accounts of early visitors to the coast that in the north the main district lying between Fante and the area from which the Akani gold traders came was "Atti." "Atti," or better, Etsi, refers to a people who antedate the Fante in the coastal region. Fante traditions say that these people were encountered at various places throughout the coastal region when the Fante came into the area. Battles were fought against the Etsi from the very start of Fante expansion in the region. Apparently, the first encounters occurred as the founders of the present-day Egyas and Anomabo expanded along the coast. Later, as the Etsi were forced out of the littoral area, they became an obstacle for the Aboras, who moved to the northwest when they departed from Mankessim. Unable to defend themselves against the more numerous Fante, the Etsi were either absorbed by them or compelled to move out of their way. In 1629, it appears that the only main body of Etsi was that to the north of Fante territory, as depicted in the map of that date. This corresponds with traditional evidence in which descendants of the Etsi explain that as a result of conflict with the Fante, "our people dispersed, and in small groups settled at different places, such as Endo village in what subsequently became known as Assin Apimanim State, where the Chief controls more land than even the Omanhene himself; Busumadzi village in Assin Attandaso Division; Abaka village in the Ekumfi State; etc."

Dating what might be called the dislodgment of the Etsi from the area into which the Fante were moving is difficult, but it appears that by the end of the seventeenth century the process was in its final stages. Battles, however, were still being fought; for example, there was one in February 1692, which gave the Dutch Chief Factor Johann Staphorst reason to expect a considerable supply of slaves.

However, these were not, judging from the evidence, frequent and the territorial sphere of the Etsi in relation to kingdoms directly on the coast seems to have been roughly the area where the author of the 1629 map placed them. The evidence does not indicate whether in the period around 1629 the Etsi constituted a compact centralized state or were dispersed in small areas throughout the coastal region. Nor is there any data to confirm D'Anville's view that the Etsi were "subject to Akanni." On the contrary, at that time the Etsi inhabitants of what is now the Ayan area of Fante constituted the largest group of what remained of the original Etsi inhabitants of the coastal region. Although they did not become politically incorporated into any of the Ayan Fante paramountcies, the former Etsi Oman of Sunkwa ["Sonquaij" on the 1629 map] had become so weakened that it was a negligible political entity.

After the campaigns against the Etsi had been completed, the northerly movement of the Aboras and Ayans did not proceed by conquest. The area to the north was less densely populated than that in the south, and the Fante did not encounter opposition from strong kingdoms as they did on the coast. According to Romer, the Danish merchant resident at Fort Christiansborg, the area north of Fante in the early eighteenth century was a frontier. He wrote:

> Above Fante is Accron, which is probably inhabited some 20 miles from the seashore, or rather, there are Negro towns here and there; the remaining 30 miles are deserted. From this point, to the northeast, I believe, there must be a large stretch of high hills, which are impassible. From the foregoing I have arrived at the following conclusion: The Assiantes formerly had to go through the deserted country behind Fante and Accron when they wanted to travel to Elmina and other western forts in order to trade. It was on these roads or in this deserted country that the Fantees captured a great number of Assiantes and sold them on the coast. From 1745, the Fantees simply denied the Assiantes the right to use this road. The Akenistes [i.e. Asen] have lived in this country since 1744.

In 1817 when Thomas Bowdich travelled through Fante to Kumase the northern regions of Fante and beyond were heavily forested and sparse in settlement. After arriving at Abora Dunkwa, Bowdich noted that

> We remained there [Abora Dunkwa] the next day, to allow
> our people to procure four days subsistence, as they would
> not be able to meet with provision on the path during that pe-
> riod.

In the early nineteenth century, when Bowdich made his journey to Ku-mase, the Fante were establishing towns in the area. An observer ex-plained that

> they [the Fante] are striving eagerly and gradually to get mar-
> ket towns established at distances 20, 40, and 60 miles inland
> where the interior traders may bring their gold and Ivory and
> where they will meet them with Merchandize from the Coast
> as it was during the slave trade.

About twenty years later, in 1841, T. B. Freeman, the Wesleyan mis-sionary, noted that from Asen Manso northwards lay "the more thinly populated and less cultivated parts of Fante." Evidence, then, from a later period is consistent with Romer's view that the area above Fante was a frontier; one nineteenth-century visitor to the coast used exactly this term to describe it.

In conclusion, the territorial expansion of the Fante that occurred be-tween 1707-12 and 1716-24 is not to be explained by reference to the conquests of Asante. The Fante themselves considered the English to have been a more important influence for they "furnished Arms Am-munition & money not only to take possession of the lands now inhab-ited by us, but likewise to conquer all those little states around us at present Subject to our Dominion."

Although the assistance given the Fante in their wars of conquest by the English was of great importance, neither this aid nor European in-terest in slaves available on the coast fully explains why the Fante were interested in conquering their neighbors. The conflicts of the Fante with surrounding kingdoms had in some cases been taking place throughout nearly the whole of the seventeenth century, long before the English surpassed the Dutch as the primary European nation trading on the coast. These conflicts continued in the eighteenth century. The increased competition for trade among European nations on the coast and their involvement with coastal kingdoms provide insights into the economic interests of the Fante.

The Dutch and the English reacted with interest to the emergence of Asante. In 1699 the English dispatched presents to the kingdom, and after the victory of Asante over Denkyera in 1701 the Dutch sent David van Neyendaal to the Asantehene with gifts as well as a message stating that they hoped to be able to enjoy good trade relations with his country. In addition, Sir Dalby Thomas attempted to convince some of the smaller kingdoms near the English forts to allow Asante traders an un-inhibited passage to the coast. Thomas recognized how important the Asante trade would be to the Company and eagerly sought to secure it. It appears as if one of the routes taken by Asante traders to the coast passed through the Fetu kingdom and that this was one of the reasons why the English believed that "If Ffetue was subjected & a fort built there you would carry the whole trade of the upland Country." The same consideration probably motivated Thomas's scheme for "setting up a ffactory in the Braffo of ffanteens cheif town about 25 miles from hence and in the cheif town of Quomino Coffee in the Capasteras country about 30 miles from this place up the country" to "secure your trade at a distance." It is certain in any case that Thomas bought large numbers of slaves directly from Asante traders and that this angered the Fante. Thus from the viewpoint of the Fante the conquest of Fetu was war-ranted to secure the Asante trade which they apparently did not yet fully enjoy during the governorship of Thomas. By 1724 the Fante, through their conquest of Fetu and other kingdoms, had put themselves in a po-sition to control the inland trade in an area which stretched as far west as Elmina, Eguafo, and Abrem, and as far east as Akwamu. To become exclusive intermediaries who brought down the Asante trade, and to maintain this position, was surely one of the main objectives of the Fante during the remainder of the eighteenth century.

In the same period, Asante sought to consolidate its influence over the coast. From 1724 to 1806, the political condition of the coast continued to be unsettled as Asante attempted to establish its dominance over those kingdoms formerly subject to Denkyera. These campaigns were of concern to the Fante, who did not want to risk an invasion that would have given Asante access to the coast. Consequently, the Fante joined alliances with other kingdoms to protect themselves. At the same time, however, they demonstrated an interest in arranging regular relations with Asante in order to enjoy the profits of the trade coming down from that country.

The alternation of these two objectives in Fante relations with Asante is discernible in various events throughout the century. In 1726, when Asante attacked Wasa, the Wasa king, Ntsiful, fled to the coast with a large number of his countrymen to seek protection. The Fante initially gave him refuge and as a result were invaded by an Asante army which penetrated as far as Asebu. Instead of surrendering Ntsiful the Fante waited until the Asante army had withdrawn, then waged two attacks on Elmina in retribution for aid that the Elminas had given Asante. Ntsiful himself remained in Fante until about 1729. Before he departed, however, the Fante had begun to arrange peace with Asante. Instead of maintaining their support for Ntsiful and the Wasas the Fante ultimately made peace with Asante. It may have been that the Fante decided to dissociate themselves from Wasa to avoid another invasion. But if that had been their motive they could immediately have surrendered Ntsiful either to Asante or to the Dutch. Although Wasa would later be included in alliances against Asante, at this time it appears that the Fante believed peace with Asante was more valuable than retaining Wasa as a defensive ally.

After 1726, and throughout the 1730s, Asante did not threaten the coast. This period of peace however ended in 1742 when Asante defeated Akyem. Following their victory over Akyem the Asante army began to spread out along the coast. The Dutch merchants Verschueren and Raams reported to Elmina from Accra in late May 1742, about two months after the defeat of Akyem, "We expect a bloody war between the 'Assiantynen' and the 'Fantynen,' because it is said that 'Pockoe' [i.e. Opoku Ware] has drawn all his forces together and that he is advancing on Agonna." The crystallization of another alliance among

Fante, Abrem, Fetu, Akani and Eguafo occurred in the same year. By the end of the decade, though, the alliance had widened to include Wasa, Denkyera, Akyem and Twifo whose addition made possible the total exclusion of Asante traders from the coast. Boahen argues that in the years between 1742 and 1750 the Fante had been able to constitute these other states in their defensive system, and that the "Grand Alliance" which had emerged by 1750 was the result of Fante diplomacy.

Developments in Asante may have been just as important to the formation of this alliance. In 1746, according to Fynn, disputes had begun which were of sufficient severity to lead the Danes to expect civil war in that country. The reforms proposed by Opoku Ware to enable the Asante government to administer a state which now exercised control over many diverse peoples, met with resistance in Kumase. Jan van Voort, the Dutch Director-General, reported from Elmina in 1748 that "the king of Asante is embroiled too much with the great men of his land to be able to take to the sword." Opposition to Opoku Ware's reforms continued to 1750, the year he died. In that year another conflict surfaced. Dako, whom Opoku Ware selected as his successor, fought against Kusi Obodom for the office of Asantehene. This struggle, as Wilks notes, "probably reflected a deeper conflict between those who favored the administrative reforms proposed but abandoned by Opoku Ware, and those who resisted radical changes in the political establishment." Ultimately, Kusi Obodom defeated Dako and became Asantehene. His success temporarily removed the threat of an Asante invasion of the coast. Opoku Ware, whose expansionist policies are well known, had planned such an invasion, but Kusi Obodom, of whom Arhin notes that he was "not a fighter," did not act on Opoku Ware's designs.

In contrast to Boahen, Fynn argues that the impetus for the "Grand Alliance" came not from the Fante but from states recently conquered by Asante which saw an opportunity to revolt when disruption in the centre of Asante occurred, and that they allied to augment the injurious effects of these civil disruptions by impeding Asante trade to the coast.

The coincidence in a period of about five years of a defensive alliance among the Fante and states immediately surrounding them, and the defection of Denkyera, Twifo, Akyem and Wasa from Asante overlordship, facilitated the formation of a broad alliance. This alliance had important effects on coastal commerce. The Wasas blocked the passage of Asante traders because they feared that if allowed through to European ports the Asante traders would acquire arms to be used against them. In 1751 Governor Melvil reported that "the Ashantees who are the great traders on this coast, have not been at the waterside these 7 years [i.e. since 1744], upon account of a quarrel with Intuffer King of Warsaw." Seven years later in 1758 the Governor at Cape Coast, Nassau Senior, still could lament that "the Warsaws will not allow the traders to come to the water-side but insist upon acting as brokers between them and the forts."

The supply of slaves available on the coast was not severely affected by the exclusion of Asante traders from coastal trading ports by Wasa and its allies. Asante was not the only source of slaves sold on the Gold Coast. In a letter to the Royal African Committee Governor Melvil wrote that

> There are great expectations of the Ashantees coming down this year a little time will determine how they are founded if they do come... the success of the Ashantees will alter everything here and destroy the trade for many years to come, if not for ever for what will remain after the consumption of 250,000 men, women, and children is taken away a little gold, a few teeth, and some duncoe slaves we may get, but after Fantee is extermined, we must expect few or no more Gold Coast slaves.

Second, in 1754 Melvil reported an "Inundation of Duncoes" [i.e. *nnonkofo,* or slaves of northern origin]; and he also observed that the paths through Akyem were open. Third, a report from Anomabo, the most important port on the Fante coast, for the same period (about 1754), mentions a "vastly great" trade. There is no evidence of consistent shortages of slaves, the main object of trade, on the coast. However, those forts to the west of Cape Coast, on the "Windward" coast, were adversely affected by the actions of Wasa. "For these ten years bygone," wrote Governor Melvil, "the windward forts have been very little worth to the Nation, but when the Warsaws go home, and the Ashantees come down, they will perhaps become your most valuable possessions.... " Although the "Grand Alliance" did not in any sense constrict trade on the coast, it did at times interfere with trade to the disadvantage of the Fante. "Slaves are very scarce," noted Governor Nassau Senior, "on account of the palaver between the Fantees and Warsaws still subsisting." Because of this stoppage, the Fante talked of "driving the Warsaws to their own country."

By the end of the 1750s, the Fante were altering their position toward the alliance that kept Asante traders away from the coast. Their dissatisfaction manifested itself in threats to attack Wasa and in a boycott; they attempted to impose on firearms going to that country. The reason for this change does not seem to be that the Fante were suffering from a decrease in trade. Although the total volume of trade had declined, this decline was not significant enough to be an explanation for the change in Fante relations with Wasa. The evidence reviewed above shows that trade was still flowing. It appears instead that the Fante intended to attack Wasa because Wasa had pre-empted the role of the Fante as middlemen in the Asante trade. From Elmina, J. P. T. Huyde-cooper, the Dutch Governor, reported that

> it is not the Wassas alone who live in disharmony with the Asantes because they are allied with the Dinkeras, Akyems, and Jufferoes; and these four people together possess part of the country that stretches from the height of Axim to Accra, so that they are lying between the Asantes and the beach, and are able to keep all roads closed for the first. This is in their advantage because they do all trade first hand, while the Asantes are forced to yield their slaves to them so they may sell them, and this is now a big advantage for these united peoples and this is undeniable.

Although trade on the coast had not been severely affected by this situation, as long as it continued the Fante made smaller profits from the Asante trade than they would have otherwise. This is the most plausible reason why the Fante began to turn toward Asante as an ally against Wasa in 1760. "The mighty Fante country," Huydecooper reported in

February of that year, "has entered into an agreement with the Asante king, also, Wasa, who alone has stopped the roads and trade, seems to be near destruction."

In 1765, Asante marched toward Akyem. The threat to a member of the alliance might have been partly a result of the Asante desire to end the blockage of its traders. In addition, however, the Asante government wished to enforce the allegiance of Wasa, Denkyera, Akyem and Twifo. A year earlier it had made military plans to achieve this goal. The willingness of the Denkyerahene, Owusu Bore, to remain loyal to Asante appears to have provided the impetus for the war against Akyem. According to Fynn, Owusu Bore had tried to convince the allies to negotiate their differences with Asante. Having done this, he was suspected of collaborating with the Asante government. An attempt on his life was planned, but Owusu Bore crushed his malefactors before they could act. Governor Mutter then reported that Owusu Bore and "his people immediately sett out & have fixed their camp about half way between Warsaw & Ashantee," and that "The Ashantees now give out that they will join the Dinkirahs and then attack the Warsaws Akims & Tufferoes, in which case they will in all probability become their Masters & consequently force a trade to the Waterside."

Early in 1765, Asante did attack Akyem and by May were rumored to be behind the Fante town of Abora. This invasion of the coast broke up what was left of the alliance among Akyem, Twifo, Wasa and Fante. It also seems to have strained the agreement between Asante and Fante to the breaking point.

In the aftermath of the war with Akyem the Fante captured over one thousand Asante soldiers, and sold them on the coast as slaves. The Asante army was unable to retaliate immediately and remained until October in its base in Denkyera. Instead of taking steps to repair the damage done to Asante, the Fante began to organize yet another defensive alliance with Twifo and Wasa to protect themselves against the possibility of an Asante invasion.

For some years afterward the kidnapping of the thousand Asantes remained an issue of dispute between the two. Although the Asante army had left the coast, a second invasion seemed a real possibility, but the Asante Council itself was divided on the matter. Governor Hippisley reported from Cape Coast in March 1766 that "The Ashantee King ... meditates an invasion upon the Sea Coast. The oldest Councellors endeavour to divert him from his design, but the Young men are all for it.... " By April of the same year, Hippisley could report that another invasion was not likely. He wrote:

> There is indeed a great probability of the Shantees being induced to put up with the losses and affronts they have received from the Fantees. They cannot see with Tranquillity all access to the Waterside cutt off, and no way left to open it but War. The principal Councellors are firmly of Opinion that they should not attempt a second invasion on Fantee; and have (at least so the King of Akanny has sent me word) prevailed upon their Sovereign to think no more of it.

The Fante however remained apprehensive. "The principal Caboceers all along the Coast," Governor Hippisley noted in July 1766, "are much alarmed." By September, it was learned that Asante had recalled its traders from "the two market places where they meet and vend their Slaves to the Fantees & an Allarm to the Fantees was the natural consequence." No hostilities developed and trade eventually resumed though the Fante had begun to restrict the sale of firearms. "Parties of Armed Men," reported Gilbert Petrie, the Governor at Cape Coast, have been sent "into the different Trading Paths to enforce it [i.e. the prohibition of arms sales] by seizing the Goods and Persons of every Trader who should be found attempting to carry up any of the contraband Articles." It was, in fact, this practice the English feared would provoke another crisis, for in the autumn of 1767 an Asante trader, caught dealing in arms, was killed by the Fante. Governor Petrie subsequently observed that the affront to the Asante king may result in "the greatest Revolution ever known on the Gold Coast. Either the King of Ashantee will become sole and absolute Master of the Coast and extirpate the Fantees, or be overcome by them, & driven back to his own Country." Again, however, nothing happened. Instead, by the early 1770s relations between the two countries had acquired a degree of regularity. Trade, for example, was flowing again as Asante traders came down directly to Elmina and regularly visited the markets on the northern borders of Fante country. Richard Brew, a local slave dealer, observed that "except at the time of the Ashantyn warr in the year 1765 I never knew slaves so plenty in my life." However, Asante still had not secured the coveted through passage to the ports of Elmina and Cape Coast. In December 1775 David Mill, the Governor at Cape Coast, reported that "A Month ago the King of Ashantee sent down Messengers here to acquaint me that he wanted to open a Market nearer the Waterside than before." Throughout the remainder of the century, Asante exerted pressure on the Fante, ostensibly to achieve this goal. While the wholesale kidnapping of Asantes by the Fante did not prompt an invasion of the coast after 1765, evidence exists to indicate that Asante retaliated by providing Asen with troops to avenge its own disputes with the Fante. Governor Mill reported in June 1772 that the Asens "in whose Country the Markets are held have plundered the Fantee Traders of a great deal of goods, and it is thought by the most intelligent Blacks that they have committed those hostilities by order of the Ashantee King." A Dutch report from the same month is more specific, stating that two Asen "caboceers" had been given Asante troops by the Asantehene to avenge a dispute that the Fante had provoked with Asen twenty years earlier.

In the same period Asante attempted to obtain a free passage to the coast by peaceful means. Asante envoys made an effort to involve the English in their aim, apparently hoping that through them the Fante could be persuaded to let their merchants use the paths to the coast. Having been approached by them, the English ordered presents for the Asantehene and the Anomabohen and decided to send messengers back to Asante. They, as well as the presents, were detained because the Governor was reluctant to dispatch them until he could be assured of their safe passage. Ultimately, Amonu Kuma, Omanhen of Anomabo, was entrusted by the Council of Merchants at Cape Coast with the task of arranging for the passage of the messengers and presents to Asante and the resolution of differences with Asante. If Asante had originally hoped to acquire leverage on the Fante by appealing to the English their hopes were frustrated by October 1780. Amonu Kuma did not make any special effort to settle the dispute and arrange an unhindered passage, for by the end of 1780 the English reported that the Fante still blocked the paths. Although in 1775, the English believed that the Fante would permit Asante access to coastal ports, by the end of the 1780s Asante traders still could only come down as far as the Fante market towns in the northern part of Fante territory. This restriction was a continuing source of irritation, for in 1789 the Dutch noted that Asante and Fante traders had had a dispute at one of the northern market towns that was so severe that the town itself was burned to the ground. Unable to get direct access to the coast through Fante territory, thrusts were made in other directions, notably in the west where in May 1780 Asante was reported to have "opened a path to that place [i.e. Cape Appolonia] where trade is brisker than here [i.e. Cape Coast]."

In the last quarter of the century, up until 1806 when Asante invaded the coast, relations between Asante and the Fante were not especially good despite the fact that Asante did not launch another invasion of the coast. The evidence indicates that the conflict between the two continued even while their commercial relations were maintained. The level at which the struggle was waged may have been determined by events in Asante. Reports of civil disruptions reached the coast throughout the final quarter of the eighteenth century. The accession of Osei Kwame to the Golden Stool marked the beginning of a virulent conflict in Kumase between him and the Asantehemaa Kwaadu Yaadom. Not until Osei Tutu Kwame became Asantehene in 1804 did the unrest diminish. The correlation between these struggles and a long period during which the coast was not threatened by an invasion suggests that the Asante government was unable to execute an invasion at that time.

By the end of the eighteenth century, coastal politics had emerged into a form it would hold through most of the next century. In the period from 1700 to around 1726, the Fante fought wars with its immediate neighbors. In the course of the remainder of the century, these rivalries were submerged to the overriding necessity of bringing down the Asante trade. Neither this, however, nor the earlier wars of Fante expansion resulted in the evolution of a political community among the various Fante groups. Ward writes that

In Bosman's day, about the year 1700, the Fante country was remarkable for its disunity: 'every part of Fantyn hath also its particular Chief, who will sometimes scarce own himself subject to the Braffo, who hath the ineffectual name only of Supreme Power.' A century later these tiny Fante states had come together into a federation, under the nominal presidency of the chief of Abora....

But Henry Meredith, an early nineteenth-century observer, might agree. In his 1812 account of the coast he wrote that

In the Fantee country they very often change their forms of government on certain occasions, and unite, for their general safety, under particular persons to whom implicit obedience must be paid. When the cause of this union is annulled, they recede into their accustomed form of government.

It was to this characteristic that Meredith attributed the 1806 defeat of the Fante by Asante:

The late visit from the King of Ashantee has proved to them the weakness of their Government and disconnected most of its leading paths - Such Imbecility has been observed in the Policy of the Fantees, that it may be said without hesitation, that those who live under absolute Powers, are more happy than those poor deluded Men who consider themselves a free people.

There is little evidence in Fanteland of a connection between wars of conquest and political development, least of all of the kind discernible in Asante history. Growth in central administrative offices attendant upon the acquisition of new territories does not appear to be a feature of the Fante case. Although the development of a community of economic interest that achieved its definition through the pressures exerted by Asante in its effort to acquire a direct route to the coastal trading ports may be discerned, a different focus is needed to elucidate what was happening among the Fante politically at the time.

Lacking a tradition of centralized political community, the Fante settled areas left vacant by wars against hostile neighbors in their new environment along the coast. The formation of independent paramountcies by groups of Fante was influenced but not determined by Asante. External influences are important in studying the history of the Fante in that the economy was based largely upon the import of slaves from Asante and its hinterland, and their re-export via European traders to the Americas. The Fante region cannot therefore be taken as an isolated one. But while investigation of the significance of external factors is a necessary condition of an understanding of Fante history in the eighteenth century, it is not a sufficient one. Careful attention must also be paid to internal factors, but these are beyond the scope of the present paper.

Asante at the End of the Nineteenth Century: Setting the Record Straight

IVOR WILKS

Ivor Wilks is Professor Emeritus of History at Northwestern University and a specialist on the history of Asante and of Islam in northern Ghana.

Introduction

Osafroadu Amankwatia, who died in 1975, practiced law in Kumase from 1956 to 1972 before becoming legal adviser to the Northern Ghana House of Chiefs. He possessed a keen sense of history, and in early 1940 had contributed several articles to *The Ashanti Pioneer* under the title, "Ashanti Conquered—in what war?" His theme was straightforward. There was no Anglo-Asante war in 1896. Asante was brought into the British Empire by political intrigue rather than military conquest. There was, however, a war in 1900, but it was not an Anglo-Asante one. Yaa Asantewaa of Edweso declared her opposition to the British presence in Asante, leaders from the Kumase district took up arms, but the other Asante divisions remained for the most part uninvolved. It was an Anglo-Kumase war. How then, asked Amankwatia, could the defeat of Yaa Asantewaa have provided the British with "sufficient ground for a claim to the whole of Ashanti?" He resorted to proverbial discourse. "If you want to be a happy liver let the past be the past," he wrote; "but when statements are made, which do not seem to be very right the past must be recalled for the understanding of all who are interested." Half a century and more after he made this plea, numerous references to the

"Anglo-Asante war of 1896" that was not a war, and to the "Anglo-Asante war of 1900" that was not Anglo-Asante, continue to appear.

I shall review these matters here. I make much use of British Colonial Office records that have long been available, and extensively used by scholars. Not a few of these documents are of Asante provenance, such as the considerable number of letters originating from the Asantehene, and the correspondence of the Asante Embassy in London in 1895 (to the office files of which the Colonial Office seems to have gained clandestine access). An excellent full-length study of the events immediately preceding the promulgation of the "Ashanti Order in Council, 1901" has been made by Robert E. Hamilton. It is impossible to do justice in one brief paper to the extraordinarily rich and complex data, but I shall suggest, following Osafroadu Amankwatia, that received versions of Asante's passage from independent nation to colonial dependency are in need of very significant revision.

At the end of 1895, Asante remained an independent kingdom. It was ruled by a king, Kwaku Dua III (now better remembered as Agyeman Prempeh I), whose powers were checked if not quite balanced by two councils. The members of the one, the Assembly of the Asante Nation (Asantemanhyiamu), were drawn from all the regions (or divisions) that constituted the nation, and of the other, the Council of Kumase, from functionaries in and around the capital who carried out the day-to-day business of government. For several years one major issue had dominated the political agenda, specifically, should Asante become a British Protectorate? There was no single Asante view about this. A reading of the sources suggests that, in the decade of reconstruction following the end of the civil war in 1888, most mainstream Kumase politicians came to realize that it was inevitable that Asante would become part of Britain's empire, and that the principal issue was to secure acceptable terms. There were, however, also conservatives who opposed any sort of erosion of Asante sovereignty and, in contrast, radicals who advocated closer association with the British as a way of achieving the liberalization of the traditional political system and "privatization" of trade and production. Of the two wings, the radicals were the more vociferous, for they had access to the press in the Gold Coast Colony. Thus a writer in the *Gold Coast Times* in 1883 could comment, doubtless with considerable exaggeration, that,

Public opinion in Ashantee has taken a new departure. The
people say that it would be almost impossible for them to tol-
erate a monarchy without the co-existence of a British consul
in Coomassie, as they perceive that the presence of such an
individual would be the only sure means of keeping the kings
in order....

If Asante politicians were divided on the matter of a British connection, so too were British ones on that of an Asante one. There was virtually universal agreement in London that the French had to be
prevented from entering into a treaty of protection with Asante. The
threat acquired a new urgency when G. E. Ferguson's report of mid-
1892 from the Asante northern hinterlands was received. "I understand,"
Ferguson wrote with reference to the Asantehene,

that he derived his munitions of war—snider arms and car-
tridges—from the French at Assinie. I have conversed with
some Koranza messengers, and they inform me that France
is aiding Ashanti. Should this be so, I cannot but reflect that
the French are making a cats-paw of Ashanti, and after
Ashanti has conquered our rear, France would set a protectorate over that country and its dependencies, and so place
the Colony of the Gold Coast in a similar plight to that of
Sierra Leone.

Opinion ranged from those who thought it in Britain's interests to support a strong and independent Asante in the rear of the Gold Coast
Colony, to those who urged the invasion and conquest of Asante and its
annexation to that Colony. Policy differences between Colonial Office
and Political Service were covered up, but did not entirely escape the
attention of the small but active pro-Asante lobby in the House of Commons (with which the great Irish patriot Michael Davitt was associated).

Griffith's Unsuccessful Coup of 1881

On 8 March 1889, Lord Knutsford, Secretary of State for the Colonies, wrote to the Governor of the Gold Coast Colony, Sir W. B. Griffith. He outlined Colonial Office policy towards Asante. The wellbeing of the Colony, he claimed, depended on maintaining good relations with Asante, and its king, Kwaku Dua III, should therefore be "supported and upheld in organising and maintaining peace and order in the country." The British Government, Knutsford stressed, had "no desire or intention of annexing Ashanti, or even of placing it under British protection," though a Resident might be appointed to live in Kumase to facilitate friendly relations. Ignoring Knutsford's ruling, in March 1891 Griffith sent Acting Travelling Commissioner H. M. Hull to Kumase to offer British protection to Kwaku Dua III, and to distribute £400 in bribes to ensure a positive response.

The offer of protection is the subject of an excellent paper by Tordoff, and the terms of the proposed treaty have been conveniently reprinted by Metcalfe. Griffith's proposal was to station a Commissioner in Kumase, who would be responsible to the Governor of the Gold Coast Colony. This Commissioner would "advise" the Asantehene on matters to do with facilitating the penetration of Asante by British capital, or in the wording of Article 5, of "such trade or manufacture as may be approved by the Governor of the Gold Coast, or by any officer appointed for the purpose by Her Majesty's Government." Although the terms of the treaty appeared unlikely to win enthusiastic support in the Asante councils, it was in fact debated at great length. Hull presented the offer of protection to the Council of Kumase on 5 April, and noted that thereafter its members met almost daily. Griffith was so confident that the mission would succeed that he turned his attention to that abiding concern of colonial administrators: latrines. Griffith wrote to Hull in Kumase, instructing him to ensure that the Asantehene "should enforce sanitary improvements in his town for the sake of all concerned," and to advise him "as to the steps he should take for the erection of latrines and their compulsory use."

Hull thought that members of the Council of Kumase were wary about relinquishing sovereignty. "The 'young men,'" he wrote, referring

to the populist leaders, "wish for the treaty; many of them told my carriers as much, but the Chiefs for the most part do not, fearing they will
be deprived of their power and privileges." The Council of Kumase
lacked the powers to decide such important constitutional matter, and
the protracted process of convening the Asantemanhyiamu was begun.
Once assembled, it too met daily. Hull addressed the members on 28
April, and his remarks were, to say the least, highly imprudent. On 4
May, he learned from Bekwaehene, who had himself argued strongly
for acceptance of protectorate status, that rejection of the proposed treat
was likely. Despite the Asantehene's assurances that a decision would
be made on 9 May at the latest, Hull nevertheless announced that he
was returning to the Gold Coast on the 7th. Although the Council therefore made a special effort to conclude its deliberations on that very day,
the Travelling Commissioner had departed a few hours earlier. The Asante answer had therefore to be put together in a courteous and well-
constructed letter to Griffith. It referred to the "very serious
consideration" that had been given to the proposed treaty, and reported
the conclusion of the debates, that is, that the Asante kingdom "must
remain independent as of old, at the same time to be friendly with all
white men." The reply also laid out what must have been majority opinion to do with the economic dependence of Asante on the Colony and
the Colony on Asante:

> Ashanti is an independent kingdom and is always friendly
> with the white men; for the sake of trade, we are to bind to
> each other, so it is our Ashanti proverb, that what the old men
> eat and left, it is what the children enjoyed.

It was not until 3 June 1891 that Griffith finally informed Knutsford
that he had made an offer of protection to Asante, and that it had been
rejected. The final paragraph of his long letter tells it all. "I do not lose
sight for a moment," he wrote,

> of the grave responsibility I have assumed with regard to my
> action in sending a mission to Ashanti for the purpose indi-
> cated without having previously submitted by proposal for

your Lordship's consideration, but I venture to hope that in all of the circumstances leading up to my course of action I shall not incur your Lordship's severe displeasure for having taken advantage of the favorable opportunity which presented itself for benefiting that country and once more endeavouring to control the unceasing internecine dissensions which have so long distracted Ashanti.

It took a month for the letter to reach the Colonial Office, and an immediate reply was dispatched by the Permanent Under-Secretary, R. H. Meade. "Lord Knutsford," he wrote,

> desires me to state that, whilst he is fully aware that you were actuated in the course you adopted by a sincere desire for the welfare and advantage of the Gold Coast Colony, and although he appreciates the force of many of the reasons which have assigned for it, he regrets that he is unable to approve of the action which you took in the matter.

Clearly Griffith had attempted to carry out a coup. He sought to extend his authority as Governor of the Gold Coast Colony over Asante, thereby presenting London with a *fait accompli*. The Secretary of State had no illusions about this, and was much angered by what he saw as the usurpation of powers that belonged to the Colonial Office by a high-ranking member of the Political Service. Meade made the point precisely:

> Looking to what has passed with respect to Ashanti, his Lordship cannot consider that you were justified in proposing to the King of Ashanti without previous authority a treaty which, if it had been accepted, Her Majesty's Government could hardly have declined to approve.

Asante as a British Imperial Matter

W. B. Griffith remained Governor of the Gold Coast Colony until early 1895, but F. M. Hodgson increasingly assumed the burden of administration. Although Hodgson's reputation was later to be sullied by his mishandling of Kumase affairs in 1900, he was in fact a man whose knowledge of local affairs was considerable. He had been Colonial Secretary of the Gold Coast Colony since 1888, and had served as Acting Governor for considerable spells of time. Much to the point, he was acutely sensitive to the matter of relations between Governor in Accra and Secretary of State in London, for he had been party to Griffith's *folie de grandeur* in 1891.

In mid-September 1893, rumors were reaching the Colonial Secretariat in Accra that Asante forces were poised to occupy Atebubu, a northern dependency of Kumase that had come to be regarded as under British protection by virtue of a shabby treaty that had been "signed" on 25 November 1890. On 28 September 1893 Acting Governor Hodgson, with the backing of his Executive Council, created the Atebubu Expeditionary Force, and placed it under the command of Colonel F. C. Scott of the Gold Coast Constabulary (who had fought in Asante as a major in the Black Watch in 1874). On 8 November Scott, whose force was no further inland than the Kwawu town of Abetifi, wrote to Hodgson. The ambitious colonel recommended that an ultimatum should be sent to the Asantehene ("the King of Kumasi"), to the effect that Kumasi must become a protectorate of the Gold Coast Colony. "I feel sure from all I hear," he informed Hodgson, "that the time has now arrived, if the British Government is so minded, to take the whole of Ashanti into the Protectorate, and I firmly believe it can be done without bloodshed." Hodgson, who undoubtedly already coveted the governorship he was ultimately to obtain in 1898, saw the danger signal.

Hodgson forwarded Scott's letter to the Secretary of State, now the Marquess of Ripon, on 18 November 1893, and in a covering note expressed disagreement with the colonel's view that Asante could be brought into a Protectorate without war. In this the Acting Governor had the advantage of the reports of the network of spies that he had authorized G. E. Ferguson to set up, in order to collect information on the

Asante army. In his response to Scott, Hodgson pointed out that in London "what is known as the Ashanti question is regarded as an Imperial question, and that this Government [of the Gold Coast Colony] has no power to deal with it." It was, he stressed, for London to decide on what form a settlement with Asante should take, and until that was decided, "no countries of the Ashanti confederation, such as Mampon, Juabin, Nsuta, and so forth, can be taken into protectorate...." Hodgson wanted this principle thoroughly understood not only by Scott, but by all those who, on Gold Coast Government business of one sort or another, roamed the northern hinterlands of Asante. G. E. Ferguson, currently engaged in trying to persuade the Nkoransahene to accept British protection, was one such. He was made to understand, Hodgson wrote,

> that the Ashanti question is an Imperial question and cannot be dealt with by this [Gold Coast] Government; and that under the circumstances it is not in my power to take any step such as that of extending protection to Nkoranza which might, and probably would, have the effect of forcing the hand of the Imperial Government.

Britain as an Asante Imperial Matter

On 9 October 1893, Acting Governor Hodgson met with Yaw Nkroma, who had been sent to Accra by Kwaku Dua III with assurances that no Asante attack on Atebubu was projected. The Asantehene, said the envoy, wished to have good relations with the Queen and the English Government, for "he is the grandson of Agyiman, and he only likes peace and trade." Kwaku Dua III thus linked himself with Fredua Agyeman who, as Kwaku Dua I, had reigned from 1834 to 1867. It was a period when "the peace party" was dominant in the councils, and was looked upon as the historical golden age of Anglo-Asante relations. Kwaku Dua III returned to the theme ten days later, when Hodgson's envoy, Travelling Commissioner H. Vroom, was in Kumase. "I wish," he said,

to remain always on good terms with the Governor as my
grand uncle Adjuman did with Governor Maclean [1830-43].
I want to encourage trade as Adjuman my grand uncle did in
the time of Governor Maclean.... Adjuman is my grand uncle,
I wish for peace and quietness as Adjuman did in the time of
Maclean. I desire to cultivate and maintain the good will of
my good friend [Hodgson] and the Great Queen.

Kwaku Dua III and his advisers were well aware that a distinction
had to be made between the Government of the Gold Coast and the
British Government. Asante enjoyed, so they firmly believed, friendly
relations with the latter, but they were disconcerted by the capricious
swings in policy of the former. In no sphere was this more evident than
that of territorial jurisdiction. In 1891 Governor Griffith had informed
the Asantehene that "the British Protectorate is very extensive, and Her
Majesty's Government does not desire to add largely to the enormous
responsibilities it already has on the Gold Coast...." Yet in the late 1880s
and early 1890s, the Government of the Gold Coast in fact extended its
protectorate over peoples who were undoubtedly subjects of the Golden
Stool. "May I ask," Kwaku Dua III wrote in a letter to Griffith, "is it
fair for Her Majesty's Government to deal so with me. I, whom you call
as a friend, is it fair to take all my subjects from me.... I wanted my
Juabin people, Adansi people, Quahoo, and Attabubu may be returned
to me as my subjects before." He was later to reprove Colonel Scott for
the disruption of trade resulting from the forays of his Atebubu Expeditionary Force. Knowing that Scott was a Gold Coast Government ap-
pointee, the Asantehene wrote, "I am sorry I have reported the matter
officially to his Excellency the Governor, for I am a peaceful king with
Her Majesty the Queen of England."
    In late 1893, Hodgson offered Ripon some observations about current
Asante politics. This was about a month after Kwaku Dua III had explained that he considered the good relations enjoyed by his forebear,
Kwaku Dua I, and Governor Maclean, to be exemplary. The point of
the comparison appears to have escaped both Griffith and Hodgson, either through their ignorance of, or willful disregard for, history. Hodgson informed Ripon that Kwaku Dua III—or Prempeh, as he now begins

to refer to him—lacked any following in much of Asante. "Although," he wrote,

> the principal Kings of the Ashanti Confederacy desire peace by incorporation with the Protectorate I am decidedly of opinion that King Prempeh and his party, which consists of the Kumasis, Adjisus, Ofinsus, the remnant of the Mampons under their new King, and a few others, wish to keep Ashanti entirely independent of this [the Gold Coast Colony] Government.

Hodgson added that, in the event of an invasion of Asante, he did not anticipate that much resistance would be encountered. "It might prove," he wrote, "that British troops would not be wanted but such a contingency has to be provided for, and I am not prepared to advocate the despatch of a further ultimatum to Kumasi unless it is."

Ripon agreed totally with Hodgson's assessment. Ruling out military action, he turned to that other instrument of British policy, bribery. Hodgson was instructed to offer generous "stipends" to the Asantehene, Asantehemaa and various divisional heads and other high functionaries. Reciprocally, the Asante Government would agree that an agent (with a strong "Hausa guard") should be stationed in Kumase to represent British interests there in ways to be fully worked out. Vroom presented the new proposals to the Asantehene and Council of Kumase on 19 March 1894. He explained them again nine days later, when *akyeame* from Mampon, Bekwae and Nsuta were present. It was only at a later meeting on 7 April that, reluctantly, he addressed the question of stipends. Following Hodgson's instructions, he announced that if the proposals were accepted, the Asantehene would receive £600 a year, the Asantehemaa £80, and "the other Kings," specified as Mamponhene, Kokofuhene, Bekwaehene and Dwabenhene, £200 each. It was not the Asante way of doing things, as Vroom well knew. The acquisition of money was a virtue, but this was tantamount to being put on the Governor's payroll.

It was time for the Asantemanhyiamu to review the whole matter of Anglo-Asante relations. "I beg to state," Kwaku Dua wrote to Hodgson, "that my District Kings, Chiefs, and principal men, will be here about the middle of this month for some of our very important business, when the subject of the British Government, which is not a small case, will be discussed...." The "important business" that took precedence over British affairs was the completion of the funeral customs for Kwaku Dua II (who had died of smallpox in 1884), so permitting Kwaku Dua III's own installation on the Golden Stool fully to be completed. This ended on 11 June, after which the Council turned to the British proposals. On 28 June, two messengers were dispatched to Governor Griffith, carrying a letter that gave some account of the proceedings. The decisions were those of the Asantemanhyiamu, the sentiments those of the Asantehene, and the rather impressive prose style that of John Owusu Ansah, his personal secretary and adviser. "I pray and beseech my elders," Kwaku Dua III affirmed,

> as well as my gods, and the spirits of my ancestors, to assist me, to give me true wisdom and love, to rule and govern my nation, and I beseech you, my good friend, to pray and ask blessings from your God to give me long life and prosperous and peaceful reign, and that my friendship with Her Majesty's Government may be more firm and more closer than hitherto had been done, that bye-gones will be bye-gones, that Ashanti nation will awake herself as out of sleep, that the hostilities will go away from her, that the evils which the constant wars has brought upon her, like destroying our jewels, may die everlastingly from her, and that I shall endeavour to promote peace and tranquillity and good order in my Kingdom, and to restore its trade, and the happiness and safety of my people generally, by making it to the advantage of the refugees to return, inhabit, and cultivate their respective countries, and thus raise my Kingdom of Ashanti to a prosperous, substantial, and steady position as a great farming and trading community such as it has never occupied hitherto, and that the trade between your Protectorate and my Kingdom of Ashanti may increase daily to the benefit of all interested in it.

It will be remarked that this impressive document envisages Asante and the Gold Coast Colony as trading partners, but does not address the issue of Asante's future political status.

When Vroom was in Kumase only a few weeks earlier he had obtained leaked information from the Council of Kumase to the effect that opinion regarding British protection was split three ways. There were, he wrote,

> (a.) Parties who oppose the establishment of British agency in Kumasi.
> (b.) Parties who favor British agency in Kumasi.
> (c.) Parties who advocate the extension of British protection to Ashanti provided the Government recognizes the suzerainty of the King of Ashanti over the countries already under our protection; provided certain Kings and Chiefs are not compelled personally to attend British Courts on the seacoast; provided also that the Government does not interfere with domestic slavery in Ashanti.

Whatever the strength of the first of these "parties" in the Council of Kumase, the final deliberations of the Asantemanhyiamu seem not to have favored so unyielding a stance. The issue was not one of patriotism but of political realism. Many realized that the nation was far from recovered from the ravages of the civil wars of 1884 to 1888; that Asante military technology had fallen far behind that of western European powers; that the modernization of manufacture and mining, and infrastructure, required inputs of European capital and skills; and that elements in the population had become radicalized to the extent of seeing the traditional monarchical state as a barrier to progress. In April 1894, John Owusu Ansah had written personally to Governor Griffith explaining that he wished to see matters between the British Government and Asante "arranged." "I shall," he added, "be proud to live to see, and for the future welfare of my people, that Ashanti Kingdom is one of Her Majesty the great Queen of England and Empress of India's territories."

In mid-1894, the Asantemanhyiamu saw the main political agenda as one of damage limitation, that is, of procuring the most advantageous terms from any Treaty of Protection with the British Government. John Owusu Ansah's younger brother, Albert, was perhaps not so optimistic as he might have seemed when, in a letter to Griffith, he remarked that it was time for the British Government "to formally acknowledge Ashanti as an independent native empire." Displaying a useful knowledge of world affairs he suggested that a model to be followed might be "the understanding now existing between Her Majesty's Government and the Ameer of Afghanistan by which annexation by any Power is rendered impossible."

The Council of Kumase seems to have discussed for the first time, on 5 April 1894, a plan to send a high-powered embassy to the Governor of the Gold Coast, authorized to negotiate all current misunderstandings. By the time of the meeting of the Asantemanhyiamu in June, the idea had been upgraded: the embassy would be accredited to the Queen and not the Governor, and would proceed to London. The names of the eight members of the embassy were announced, and authority given for a special tax to be levied to defray their costs. John Owusu Ansah was designated Ambassador Extraordinary and Minister Plenipotentiary (to follow the English text of his commission), and Albert Owusu Ansah his deputy. The Kumase Kyidomhene, Kwame Boaten, headed the embassy, with Kwaku Fokuo (of the Boakye Yam Panin group) serving as *okyeame*. Four other functionaries of the Asanthene's administration made up the complement. We have the Asantehene's own testimony that they were not to divulge the details of their mission to the Gold Coast Government: "These 8 persons were ordered to inform the Governor before taking ship to go to England that they are sent by the King and chiefs to discuss certain matters in England such as the nature of the facts they were not order to disclose the Governor."

The logic of the Asante decision was impeccable. Since the Colonial Office insisted that Asante affairs were Imperial ones, then the embassy had necessarily to deal with the Court of St. James. The Council of Kumase dealt with the day-to-day business of government, and when occasion arose, it was appropriate enough that communications should be maintained with the Government of the Gold Coast Colony. The Asantemanhyiamu, however, determined (Asante) Imperial policy, including matters of war and peace, and in such matters there had to be direct contact with the British Government.

No Grandeur for Griffith?

In 1891, Governor Griffith had reacted viscerally to the reprimand by the Secretary of State for the Colonies. He saw the Asantehene, because of the rejection of the offer of protection, as the author of his fall from grace in London. He orchestrated a virtual campaign to discredit the Asantehene and his advisers, and bombarded the Colonial Office with dispatches and enclosures containing defamatory statements—especially ones about "human sacrifice"—intended to force the Secretary of State to authorize military intervention in Asante. He became obsessed, in communications with Kumase, with matters of rank. On 5 February 1894 two messengers from the Asantehene, carrying a letter having to do with Atebubu affairs, had arrived in Accra to meet with the Governor. Hodgson was in fact administering the Government at the time, but felt obliged to express, on behalf of Griffith, displeasure at the lowly rank of the two. They should, he said, "tell King Prempeh that the embassy was not such a one as should have been sent to the representative of the great Queen of England, that I had some hesitation in receiving it, and that in future he must pay more respect to the Governor of the Gold Coast if he wanted his letters to receive attention."

By the second half of 1894, it is doubtful whether Griffith was any longer capable of effectively carrying out his duties as Governor. We have noted above that he was the recipient of a letter of 28 June 1894, in which the Asantehene had stressed his desire for peace and trade with Britain. Kofi Bua of the *afenasoafo* and Ofori of the *nseniefo* carried the letter, and on 9 July arrived at Praso, on the Gold Coast border, where they were detained for no more sinister a reason than that Griffith was arriving there on tour the next week. On arrival, Griffith refused to see them, informing Ripon that "their rank was not such as to make them worthy of having an interview with me," and suggesting that "underlying the circumstances of such men being sent is the intention of the senders to be disrespectful to the Government." Griffith did, however, accept the letter, and brought it to the attention of his Executive Council in Accra and of Ripon in London. It would be charitable to think that Griffith had subsequently decided that the letter was a forgery by John Owusu Ansah, and discounted it. There is, however, no evidence for this. He appears simply to have suppressed all memory of the document. Thus, on 31 October 1894, Griffith is to be found writing to Ripon as if he was still awaiting a reply from the Asantehene. "I think your Lordship," he commented,

> may rest assured that the declaration from Ashanti, in reply to the message sent, will be that the proposals of the Government made to them in March last by Mr. Vroom are declined, and that Ashanti elects to remain as she is. Should this be so, it will only be a waste of time to parley with Ansah or his principals. Therefore it seems to me that strong measures should be enforced without undue delay to compel the obedience of Ashanti to Imperial control.

A few cases must suffice to illustrate Griffith's attempts to have the Colonial Office agree to a military takeover of Asante. He duly forwarded to Ripon, for example, an extract from the *Gold Coast Methodist Times* for 31 August 1894, drawing attention, *inter alia*, to the following item:

> *A dreadful slaughter of human victims.*—It being customary with the new King of Ashanti, on his enthronement, to observe a general funeral custom for royal relatives deceased, Prempeh also, being now installed, kept the hereditary custom by slaying some 400 human beings in cold blood.

As Prince [*Ohenenana*] of Asante, Albert Owusu Ansah wrote to a Colony newspaper on 29 September 1894, "I cannot allow such a fabrication, since that there's not a particle of truth in it, to pass un-contradicted. I consider it a pure bogus trumped-up business to get Christian world against our nationality...." When the *Gold Coast People* also repeated the story on 24 September, Ansah complained directly to the Governor. "I am confident," he wrote, "that your Excellency, from your great knowledge of Gold Coast affairs, will not be misled by reports such as these to take any hasty course of action." The note of sarcasm could scarcely have escaped Griffith, who must have been virtually apoplectic at the threat that followed. "I must mention that I am for-warding a copy of this to my agents in London," wrote Ansah, "to have same published in Mr. Labouchere's paper the 'Truth,' and also a copy each to such of my correspondents in England as I may consider advis-able." Griffith sent a copy of this letter, along with that to the *Gold Coast Methodist Times*, to Ripon, and added a short resumé of Ansah's career, particularly stressing his "insolence, irregularities, and disobe-dience of orders" when he had worked as a telegraph clerk in the Colony in 1884.

On 25 January 1895, Griffith summed up his view of the Asante for the benefit of Ripon. "As the Ethiopian cannot change his skin," he wrote, "so also the Ashanti cannot change the natural bent of his mind in the directions of deceit, hypocrisy, mendacity, treachery, and unreli-ableness." An indiscreet personal letter, written by someone on Grif-fith's staff, survives from this period. "The Ashantee palaver," it reports,

is now in the following state—the Govr. is holding Council Meetings almost daily and sending cablegrams to the S[ec-retary] of S[tate] to try and bluff him into sending an expe-dition to hoist the flag at Kumassi consisting of Hausas and bluejackets but the S[ecretary] of S[tate] won't take it on or hasn't at present.

The Colonial Office must have been well aware of Griffith's progressive derangement, but was under pressure from many other quarters to change policy. The appalling F. Ramseyer of the Basel Mission, who had been a rather well-treated prisoner of Asantehene Kofi Kakari from 1869 to 1873, pursued, through the Colonial Secretariat in Accra, Field-Marshall Viscount Wolseley in hospital in Kilmainham, Dublin, and the Colonial Office in London, a campaign of his own to have Asante brought under British rule. "If things are remaining as they are," he told Wolseley, this means *constant quarrels and troubles in the interior*; it means *the continuation of human sacrifices,* which have never ceased; and it means *the country shut up for commercial purposes* and *educa-tional* work." And to the Colonial Office, Ramseyer made a quite unre-strained plea:

For God's sake, *for humanity's sake, for* THE PRESTIGE the English Government has still on the Gold Coast sake, may the Government act *at once* before it is too late, and bring peace in the whole Ashantee country and open it for the work of civilisation, for the work God has laid in their land, and for which it has been so much blessed. And these hundreds and thousands of poor innocent people who have been sacrificed in the street of Coomassee, are their voices not loud enough?

There were doubtless many mandarins in the Colonial Office who welcomed the idea of opening up Asante to the Christian god, but a more pressing lobby was that of businessmen. In early 1894 Chambers of Commerce, in London, Liverpool, Glasgow and no doubt elsewhere, began to urge that Asante be taken under protection in order to facilitate "the large development of trade," as the Secretary of the London Chamber put it. They wielded formidable power, and held a trump card: the knowledge that the Gold Coast Colony had an excess of revenue over expenditure, and could therefore finance at least limited military operations. The Asante that they wanted was one annexed to the Colony, and made safe for British and other companies to exploit its gold, and to develop an infrastructure of railways and roads. Later in the year, the Cape Coast Chamber of Commerce entered the fray. On 4 December 1894, Governor Griffith received a petition signed by nineteen businessmen, African and European. A document laid out a program of action with respect to Asante that was realistic enough to be negotiable. "Your petitioners pray," they wrote,

> that, in reference to the kingdom of Ashantee, it may be definitely brought within the sphere of British influence.
>
> That your Excellency may deem it advisable to place its administration upon a footing that should embrace some form of permanent Residency, under an experienced officer of a diplomatic and military training.
>
> That the King of Ashantee be allowed to reserve all the rights and powers which he now exercises over his people.

> That the Resident shall act as an adviser and chancellor to the King, and at the same time put down and do away with all barbarous practices and customs.

Griffith heard the petition, said that he knew little about the current intentions of the Asante Government, and asked that the document should not be circulated in England for the present. He then simply filed it, obviously regarding it as much too favorable towards the Asante. Griffith's successor, rummaging through the files, found the petition six months later, and decided that should be sent to Ripon. It is salutary to compare the measured tones of the businessmen in the Gold Coast Colony with the tirades of those mandarins in the Colonial Office who had apparently been affected by Griffith's unremitting harangues. Tordoff draws attention to a memorandum of February 1895, drawn up for the Cabinet by A. W. L. Hemming. "The continued existence," Hemming commented, "of a savage and barbarous power like Ashanti is a constant menace to the safety of the Gold Coast Colony, is a formidable hindrance to its development and the advent of civilisation, is an obstacle to trade, and is, moreover, a disgrace to humanity."

Ripon remained unprepared to advocate military intervention in Asante, but was aware of the political embarrassment that the arrival of the Embassy in London might cause him. On 30 November, he telegraphed Griffith:

> Inform King of Ashanti that Special Embassy will not be received here. Her Majesty the Queen can only communicate with him through Governor of Gold Coast, who is Queen's representative, to whom he should at once reply to message sent to him; in no case would she receive mission from a ruler who is accused, on apparently good grounds, of allowing human sacrifice.

When news of the arrival of the ambassadors at Cape Coast reached Ripon, he confirmed by telegraph that Griffith should "forbid them going on to England." Then, perhaps remembering certain basic principles of English law, sent off a second telegram to him the same day:

"You will, of course, while forbidding the Ashanti messengers to come to England, not make use of force to prevent them from doing so."

The Asante ambassadors arrived at Cape Coast on 10 December 1894, and met with Griffith on the 12th, 13th and 15th. Spokesman Kwaku Fokuo made the official Asante position quite clear:

> The King is very anxious that perpetual peace be effected in Ashanti. His Majesty thinks that if he keeps writing to your Excellency that will not settle matters for good. Therefore he has deputed them to Her Majesty the Queen, so that every matter may be entirely settled. Mere letters will not settle matters, so His Majesty has sent them [the ambassadors] to go and see the Queen so that peace may be perpetually effected in Ashanti.

At the meetings, Griffith publicly cast doubt on the integrity of John and Albert Owusu Ansah, reiterating that he did not recognize Agyeman Prempeh as Asantehene but only as "King of Kumase." He announced that London had already notified him that "in no case would her Majesty receive a mission from a ruler who is accused on apparently good grounds of allowing human sacrifices"; and—as if unsure that his position was clear—added that in the sight of "Her Majesty the great Queen of England and Empress of India.... you and your King are as nothing." No member of Britain's Political Service should have reacted as Griffith did. It seems likely that his mind was seriously unhinged. In the depths of the Colonial Office one high official, E. Wingfield, minuted, "The Governor's tongue wagged a little too much I think." The ambassadors protested with that combination of courtesy, logic, and firmness that seems so greatly to have infuriated Griffith. "We do not know," they said,

> whether Her Majesty's Government has ever exercised the right of forbidding visitors from any part of the world into their country, or whether the Government has acquired any special rights of this nature over the Kingdom of His Majesty our King; but, as an Embassy, we believe your Excellency

will see with us that we have no alternative but to obey the commands of our King.

They further clarified their position in a letter to Hodgson of 3 January 1895, "that considering the unfriendly attitude already assumed by Her Majesty's Government on the coast to the kingdom of His Majesty (and His Majesty deeply regrets this should be the case), it is impossible that mutual sympathy and understanding could be looked for, or arrived at in this Colony, to prevent war and bloodshed."

John Brew ("Brew of Dunquah, Prince-Chief of Abakrampan and Dunquah, Gold Coast"), who had agreed to act as the embassy's solicitor in London, wrote to the Colonial Office five weeks later, asking whether the Gold Coast Government would use force if necessary to prevent the Asantes from leaving for London. In a highly charged paragraph, Brew skillfully raised a new issue. "I have addressed your Lordship," he wrote, "as being the direct head of Her Majesty's Colonial Department, although it may have a more correct course to have addressed the Foreign Office on the subject." It may have been this communication that led Ripon's Under Secretary to read a statement in the House of Commons on 14 February, to the effect that "the King of Kumasi is not a Chief or ruler of sufficient importance to be allowed to send ambassadors to the Queen." In any case, he continued, "Her Majesty could not receive a mission from a ruler who, there is good reason to believe, allows and countenances the practice of human sacrifices."

Prelude to a War That Wasn't

In late 1894, Ripon had initiated a search for a new Governor. Hodgson, a strong candidate, was rejected, in part at least because he was seen as being too closely associated with Griffith. The choice fell upon William Edward Maxwell. He was then Acting Governor of the Straits Settlements, and Hamilton has usefully described his career of thirty years with the Political Service in Malaya (where his father had also worked from 1856 to 1871). Maxwell was deeply interested in development, which meant in effect the promotion of European enterprise in mining and rubber. There were two corollaries to this. First, Maxwell thought that the power of the British Residents should be increased, and that of the Sultans whom they advised, decreased. Second, he believed that a land policy must be evolved such as to afford legal protection to European concessionaires. It requires little imagination to see why Secretary of State Ripon, facing the growing demand for the establishment of a Residency in Kumase, and unable to ignore commercial pressures to open up Asante to trade and industry, saw in Maxwell the right man for Accra.

On 15 March 1895 Ripon briefed Maxwell. Griffith's advocacy of an immediate invasion of Asante had, he wrote, been rejected: "Her Majesty's Government would desire to avoid the necessity of warlike operations if possible, and you should therefore direct your first attention to the possibility of bringing about a peaceful settlement." A new diplomatic initiative should be developed, and a military solution considered only in the event of its failure, Ripon ordered, but the expenses of an expeditionary force would fall upon the Gold Coast Colony.

Maxwell took over the governorship on 7 April 1895. A month later Brew informed the Colonial Office of the arrival in London "of the Embassy dispatched by His Majesty Kwaku Dua III., King of Ashanti, to treat with the Government of Her Britannic Majesty on matters affecting the relations between the Empire of the Queen and his kingdom." The situation seemed auspicious. Both British and Asante governments professed a desire for peace and commercial intercourse. Ripon, however, had left himself little room for maneuver, and was unable radically to change policy by affording the embassy recognition. Meanwhile, in the Gold Coast Colony, Maxwell had been carefully assessing the situation, and his report was received by Ripon on 8 July 1895. It was, the new Governor wrote, very difficult to obtain intelligence about affairs in Asante as political activity was at low ebb pending the return of the embassy from London. He did not think that there was any great opposition to the presence of a British Resident in Kumase, though any attempt to change the status of servile groups ("the manumission of slaves") would be strongly resisted. Maxwell thought that the ambassadors might return home via Paris and Berlin, to explore the terms on which France or Germany might afford some form of protectorate status. Both powers would, he was sure, acknowledge that Asante was in the British sphere of influence. Maxwell was unsure whether the embassy would meet with him upon its return, or proceed directly to Kumase. Either way, he thought that "the proper place for the discussion of the future of Ashanti is Kumasi itself," and he expressed readiness to go there (with "a sufficient guard of Hausa Constabulary.") Only in the event of these talks breaking down would an invasion of Asante be launched. Any such military operation should be planned for the dry season of 1895-96.

On 25 June 1895, Joseph Chamberlain became Secretary of State for the Colonies in Salisbury's new cabinet. Since the Colonial Office had refused to recognize the embassy, little pertinent information was on file. He procured the services of a Member of Parliament, H. C. Richards. John Owusu Ansah's understanding of the situation was that, Richards,

> acting as intermediary, was deputed by Mr. Chamberlain, the Secretary of State for the Colonies, to see us. Mr. Richards wrote that, 'if the mission will put into writing their answers to the Queen's message, their reply to our demand for a Resident, and their pledge for a discontinuance of all human sacrifice, he will receive such communication through me, and return to them, through me, the answer of the Government.'

Richards, and a Mr. Bigham, Q.C., subsequently invited the ambassadors to the House of Commons. Claiming, falsely, that Chamberlain had not sent them, they obtained copies of the embassy's credentials and of various other documents. These they immediately dispatched to the Colonial Office, whereupon Chamberlain, of course, reasserted his refusal to recognize the ambassadors.

It is difficult to determine precisely when the Secretary of State, presumably in consultation with Maxwell, decided to invade Asante. As early as 5 September 1895 John Owusu Ansah informed the Colonial Office that news had reached him, from a reliable source, that the Governor of the Gold Coast was preparing an expedition against Kumase, "warlike or otherwise, we know not." The Colonial Office neither confirmed nor denied the report. The efficiency of Asante intelligence, however, should not be underestimated, and it is not at all unlikely that Maxwell was already making the first preparations to put the Colony's Constabulary on a war footing. On the very next day, 6 September, Chamberlain telegraphed Maxwell, instructing him to send an ultimatum requiring the Asantehene to accept a British Resident. The Governor was also asked to inform the Colonial Office of the number of troops required should Asante be invaded and occupied. Maxwell chose Captain Donald Stewart and Vroom to carry out this mission. They were well received in Kumase, and delivered the ultimatum on 10 October. Not surprisingly, the Asantehene refused to take any action until his ambassadors returned from London. It was about this time that Maxwell, acting on orders from Chamberlain, moved a strong detachment of the Hausa Constabulary to Praso, on the border of the Colony and Asante. This would not have escaped the attention of the Asante, but they could not have known that Scott—formerly of the Atebubu Expeditionary Force and now to have command of an Ashanti Expeditionary Force— had been summoned to London for discussions at the War Office.

It was the likelihood of war that led the ambassadors to push forward their business schedule. There were other than political matters on the agenda. They had assembled a team of associates that included the solicitor Jonathan E. Harris, the barrister Thomas Sutherst, and two public relations men, Arthur B. Chamberlain and Kendall Robinson. Questions of development were given priority. In 1892 the Asantehene had approved a concession negotiated by Dr. J. W. Herivel, setting up the Ashanti and Prah Mining and Trading Company. Governor Griffith regarded it as a French bid for influence in the Colony's hinterland, and used the Gold Coast Customs Department to make its operations impossible. On 20 September 1895 the ambassadors entered into an arrangement with a concessionaire, George Reckless, to establish a British Company for the development of Asante. It was, in many respects, a more ambitious version of the Herivel Concession. Jonathan Harris wrote to the *Times* to inform its readers that the Asante king "is prepared to open his country to British skill, and does not seek to hamper trade." Then, on 21 October, in the presence of solicitors, the ambassadors issued a document defining the scope of the Company's activities. The charter, so it read, would be, for the purposes of giving mining and other rights to the said Company, for the purposes also of railway construction and other public works, to employ skilled and other labour, to build manufactories, lay out townships, construct water-works, and waterways, to appoint and maintain a resident agent or agents; to organise a constabulary, to erect a mint and issue coinage, establish factories for trading and other purposes, to establish banks, to grant licenses for trading, mining, and other purposes, to impose such duties as may be deemed expedient on goods imported into the country, to lay out and cultivate plantations for all kinds of vegetable and other products, to establish schools for elementary, technical, and scientific education, to publish newspapers, to aid in the organisation of the military forces of the Kingdom, to assist the King in his government, including the administration of justice and the codification of laws, the King to undertake to protect life and property and the rights and privileges ac-corded to the Chartered Company as herein-before men-tioned, the King to receive an annual grant from the Company of one-fourth of the nett profits.

Harris, on behalf of the Embassy, wrote to the Earl of Selborne, Under Secretary at the Colonial Office, to draw his attention to the fact that the situation,

is in a sense altered, for your Lordship by now has been ac-quainted with the fact that the King, by his representatives here, has agreed to grant to a British company a charter for the opening up of Ashantee to British enterprise and skills, and in fact, the company will inherit even greater control over the country than the Government asks for.

Four days later Messrs Grundy, Kershaw, Saxon, and Samson, repre-senting Reckless, sent a copy of the document to the Colonial Office at its request. Maintaining an unbending stance, on 11 November the Colonial Office informed the solicitors for both the Embassy and Reckless that the "alleged concession" would not be recognized by the British Government. This was, to say the least, disingenuous.

In 1890 three Fante concessionaires had launched the Ashanti Exploration Company, leasing 100 square miles of land around Obuase. Edwin A. Cade of Smith and Cade, London, bought them out in mid-1895, and incorporated the concession into his Côte d'Or Mining Company. He claimed that both Bekwaehene and Adansehene had agreed upon the arrangement. The Asante ambassadors in London learned something of Cade's proceedings from "friends who are our informants." On 27 September, they sent off a memorandum to the "Kings and Chiefs of Ashanti," including Mamponhene and Bantamahene, recommending that Cade's mining operations should be suspended pending the return home of the Embassy. Whether Cade knew of this action or not, he certainly took the precaution of writing to Selborne at the Colonial Office. "In the event of a purchase not being at present possible," he suggested, "the position may still be a desirable one in the event of annexation taking place." This was on 22 October 1895, when Cade must have known the ongoing talks between the ambassadors and Reckless. Whatever the case, some sort of deal was made with Cade. Only a few weeks after Maxwell seized power in Asante, Chamberlain was to inform the Directors of the Côte d'Or Mining Company that its concessions in Asante would be recognized as valid. The Company was liquidated on 3 June 1896, and reborn as the Ashanti Goldfields Corporation.

Governor of the Gold Coast Maxwell Seizes Power

On 16 November 1895, Sutherst wrote to the Colonial Office, giving brief but tellingly constructed profiles of the leading members of the Asante Embassy, and enclosing a document it had issued that day. "Acting on behalf of Kwaku Dua III, King of Ashantee," it began,

> and as his envoys with full powers contained in the documents of which you have seen a copy, we have the honour to acknowledge the receipt of the Queen's ultimatum to our King, and we now, on his behalf and on behalf of the Chiefs

and people of Ashanti, tender submission thereto. We agree to accept a British Resident at Kumasi, and to conform to all the terms of the Queen's ultimatum, believing that all the promises made on behalf of the Queen, by Her representatives, will be faithfully carried out. The King and Chiefs desire the alliance and friendship of the Queen, and they desire, through the British Governor, to open up their territory to trade and commerce.

The Colonial Office replied on 18 November that the ambassadors should telegraph a message to the Gold Coast, to be forwarded to Kumase, that they had accepted the British ultimatum, and that they would proceed home. Maxwell, they understood, would then arrange to meet with the Asantehene "to receive his final submission and to enter into a formal agreement as to the conditions on which the affairs of his country will thereafter be conducted." Sutherst replied the next day, reporting that the ambassadors accepted the suggested program. They do, however, he wrote,

> desire me to protest against the preparations and lavish expenditure which is being incurred by the British Government, for no other purpose, as they allege, than a demonstration of strength, which is quite unnecessary, seeing that the King, Chiefs, and people have already accepted to the fullest extent the demands of the British Government.

Sutherst endorsed the protest. To make the Asante pay for the cost of the expedition appears to them, he wrote, "like firing on a flag of truce." The reply was immediate. Chamberlain did not trust the Asante, thought that they were procrastinating until the arrival of the rains, and was "of the opinion that the Resident to be appointed at Kumasi must now be installed by a sufficient force to secure his safety, and to convince the King of the futility of resistance." In fact, Chamberlain's "a sufficient force" was a euphemism for no less than a full-scale Expeditionary Force. On 21 November, Chamberlain telegraphed Maxwell: "It has been decided that expedition must go to Kumasi at all events. Do not relax preparation."

On 12 December 1895, Chamberlain made several suggestions to Maxwell. One was that Scott should seize the Golden Stool, "as the possession of this Stool will strengthen the [Gold Coast Colony] Government in the eyes of the natives...." A second was that the Asantehemaa Yaa Kyaa, mother of Asantehene Agyeman Prempeh, "a noted intriguer and a power in Ashanti," should be brought down to the Colony. And a third was that Agyeman Prempeh might be replaced as Asantehene ("King of Kumasi") by Yaw Twereboanna, "who is likely to be pliable in the hands of a strong Resident," but only on condition that he revealed the location of Asantehene Kofi Kakari's treasury that had supposedly been buried since 1874. It is unlikely that Chamberlain had any idea of the can of worms he was opening at this point, for Yaw Twereboanna had been a strong contender for the Golden Stool during the civil wars of 1884-88. Be this as it may, Chamberlain made it quite clear that these were actions "which it might be advisable to take in the event of hostilities with the Ashantis actually taking place," in which case "the future conditions of the Kingdom of Kumasi would be dictated by Her Majesty's Government."

In the event no hostilities occurred. The Embassy returned to Kumase and, in Agyeman Prempeh's own words, had "announced that a reply has been given to the Governor of the Gold Coast that the English flag has now been accepted...." It seems to have been understood that the Agyeman Prempeh had next—and again in his own words—"to send the prime minister to go and sign the treaty of accepting the British flag in Ashanti." The "prime minister" must here refer to Asafo Boakye, one of the most experienced of the functionaries of Kumase. Accompanied by Kwaku Fokuo, member of the Embassy, a meeting was held with Stewart at Odaso, only 7 miles south of the capital. Asante would, they said, pay the indemnities and "come under the white men's government." Stewart replied that the Expeditionary Force nonetheless intended to enter Kumase, but that the Asantehene would not be deposed if he complied with British demands. Agyeman Prempeh's own recollections of the event were similar. After the envoys had returned to Kumase, he wrote, Stewart heard that rumors were circulating that the British intended to destool the Asantehene. Stewart dispatched a messenger to Kumase to say that this was "a very false complaint." There is no doubt that Agyeman Prempeh and his councilors believed that the troops would enter Kumase, a "palaver" would be held, a new agreement formally signed, and that a Resident and a small guard would be left in the capital after Scott's forces had withdrawn to the Colony.

The Expeditionary Force entered Kumase on 17 January 1896, and was afforded a state reception by the Asantehene. Governor Maxwell arrived the next day, and announced that a public "palaver" would be held on the 20th, at which the Asantehene and Asantehemaa would be required publicly to kneel before him as an act of submission, to agree to pay the whole balance of the war indemnities incurred since 1874, to identify with notices the location of all stool treasuries, and to supply Scott's troops with 1,000 buckets of fresh water daily. What happened was quite different. At the "palaver," Maxwell took the submissions, and then demanded *instant* payment of the indemnities. When this proved impossible, as he knew full well that it would, he ordered the arrest—following a list that had obviously been prepared in advance- of the Asantehene, Asantehemaa, Mamponhene, and many of the leading Kumase councilors and two of its sub-chiefs, Edwesohene and Offinsohene. Colonial Secretary Hodgson graphically described the situation. "It was with dismay," he wrote,

> that the Kumassis and the Kings of those of the federated tribes who supported Prempeh, found that they had entirely miscalculated events, and that the British Government not only intended to remain, but made demands which were unexpected and which, without previous preparation, they could not comply with. Opposition was rendered impossible, because the whole system of native administration was paralyzed by the removal as political prisoners of Prempeh and the principal members of his Court, as well as the Kings who were his chief and open supporters. The young men, doubtless eager enough to fight for their king, were thus reduced to impotence. They were without leaders.

Agyeman Prempeh wrote that, "as soon as the King and others were made prisoner, orders were given to the soldiers to plunder and they plundered everywhere where tickets were placed and plundered all the properties in the King's palace and in the houses of the chiefs." A fever seemed to grip the new rulers of Asante, and the relentless quest for "treasure" continued long after the Expeditionary Force had withdrawn to the Coast. As news of this reached the Gold Coast Colony, it incurred widespread outrage. The Editor of the *Gold Coast Chronicle* was far from a lone voice when he wrote:

> The rumoured goings on of Government officials at Kumasi are most disquieting. Their arbitrary measures, especially their disturbing the graves of Kings, chiefs and others in insatiate search for gold … are reported to be indulged in by men boasting of the civilization of the nineteenth century and of the nationality of the most enlightened country in the world, representing Christian England, and probably professing the Christian Religion—these are certainly not calculated to give the Ashantees a very exalted opinion of England as a power, a Nation, and a Religious centre, nor promote the pacification of Ashantee.

The "prisoners," as the British referred to the Asantehene and those others they had forcibly abducted, were escorted from Kumase on 22 January 1896, and taken to Elmina on the Gold Coast (and subsequently, of course, to Sierra Leone and the Seychelles). The Governor of the Gold Coast Colony had carried out a veritable *coup d'état* in Asante. He had taken into his own hands, without a mandate from his superiors, the political authority of the Asantehene and his councils. Chamberlain was stunned when Maxwell explained his action by cablegrams of 19 and 20 January. A minute by Chamberlain dated 21 January reads,

> Remind Maxwell of the statements made here on behalf of Govt. to the effect that if Prempeh agreed to ultimatum and paid indemnity no further steps would be taken against him.... Mr. Maxwell must give us much better reasons than any adduced at present.

The Secretary of State's reply was dispatched the next day. "Deportation or detention as political prisoners not contemplated by ultimatum, or Sutherst correspondence," he wrote; "having regard to submission by the King, what grounds are there for insisting on a British Protectorate, with all its legal consequences rather than the establishment of British protection to the extent defined by the ultimatum?"

In the negotiations that were to follow, Maxwell had an advantage, for Chamberlain could scarcely disown the Governor's actions by ordering a return of the prisoners to Kumase. Maxwell, however, needed rapidly to consolidate his position by setting up some system of government for the occupied territory. He announced quite openly that his aim was "the destruction of the central power of Kumase," and appointed Donald Stewart as Resident. He decided to set up a "Native Committee of Administration," and various notables ("the chief men remaining in Kumasi") were consulted about its membership. On traditional constitutional grounds, they recommended the senior divisional rulers, Mamponhene and Kokofuhene. This, so we shall see, was not in accordance with Maxwell's grand strategy. His three appointees were all from the Kumase division. Opoku Mensa, Kumase Gyaasewahene since 1884, was the senior member; Kwaku Nantwi Kaakyera, Akankade *okyeame* since about 1877 the second; and Atwemahene Antwi Agyei the third, whose death late in 1896 led to his replacement by Toasehene Kwame Afrifa.

Maxwell decided to use the instrument of the Treaty of Friendship and Protection to extend his authority over the various outlying divisions, or *aman*, of the Asanteman. On behalf of the Queen, he, as Governor of the Gold Coast Colony, would take each under the protection of Great Britain. A treaty that had been signed on 18 October 1895 with the Adanse (though in fact with only a rump of the state) was taken as a model. On 26 January 1896, he requested permission from the Colonial Office to negotiate treaties with Mampon and Nsuta, the only two divisions mentioned. The mandarins were somewhat mystified, but concluded that, "as we have had to send an expedition to Kumassi we are under no obligation from extending protection to any of the tribes formerly belonging to Ashanti...." In point of fact Maxwell had already seized the initiative, for treaties had already been made, before permission was received, with Bekwae and Abodom (11 January 1896); Nsuta (18 January); and Nkoransa (30 January). The second wave of what I shall call, for convenience, the "Maxwell Treaties" soon followed: Dwaben, Kokofu, Mampon, Agona, Offinso, Edweso, and Kumawu, all on 10 February. The rulers of the *aman* who affixed their marks to these documents did not see themselves as casting off allegiance to the Golden Stool, but as acting in conformity with Asantehene Agyeman Prempeh's decision to accept British protection. In British law, however, the validity of the Maxwell Treaties was doubtful. Anglo-Asante relations rested upon a series of treaties with various Asantehenes, Osei Tutu Kwame in 1817, Osei Yaw in 1831, and Kofi Kakari in 1874. Any new treaty, specifically, one of protection, should have been signed by Kwaku Dua III (Agyeman Prempeh), for his *de facto* abduction could not nullify his *de jure* sovereignty.

It is unclear precisely how Maxwell conceived the links between the Native Committee of Administration and the powerful rulers of *aman*. Hodgson, Colonial Secretary at the time, later observed that

> the arrangement appears to have been considered suitable, to deal with the outlying tribal districts by means of a Committee of Native Chiefs, who were to confer with, and work under the orders of, the Resident, and to keep him advised of all matters affecting the welfare of the country, or acts likely to disturb the peace. Administration by means of a Native Committee was doubtless considered to be the most likely means of inducing the Ashantis generally to fall in with the altered state of things, but otherwise the arrangement had nothing to commend itself, and there was no guarantee that the members of the Native Committee, who by their position and residence in Kumassi were often able to ascertain the movements of the Government, would on their part act loyally and with a strict regard to British interests.

Whatever the intention, the Native Committee of Administration certainly dealt with matters that were Asante rather than purely Kumase ones. Vroom was in the capital once again in May 1897, and reported that Opoku Mensa brought forward an agenda for the consideration of the Governor that included the return of the Asantehene from exile, the restoration of certain towns and villages to Kumase that had changed hands during the civil wars, the distribution of Great Oath fees, and so forth.

One other matter required immediate attention, that of the relationship of Asante to the Gold Coast Colony. Many Chambers of Commerce had been pressing for the annexation of the former by the latter, and the extension of the jurisdiction of the Supreme Court of the Colony to embrace both. In a despatch to Chamberlain of 28 January 1896, Maxwell argued that it would be unfair to require Asante traders to travel to the Gold Coast continually, in order to attend summonses from the Supreme Court. The jurisdiction of the Supreme Court should not extend north of the Pra, and the Resident in Kumase should be trusted to administer justice "on ordinary principles of equity and common sense."

Maxwell had, in fact, succeeded in creating what began to look remarkably like a personal fiefdom in Asante. He had installed a Resident who, with his Native Committee of Administration, exercised the functions of an Asantehene, but was responsible solely to him, Maxwell, rather than under the jurisdiction of the Supreme Court of the Colony. Moreover, Maxwell had conferred on the Resident powers that were illegal, being grounded in neither an Ordinance of the Gold Coast Colony nor an Order in Council in London. It was all very irregular. Chamberlain could not dismiss or even transfer Maxwell without stirring up a hornet's nest in Parliament, where the occupation of Asante had not been universally acclaimed. The Colonial Office took a time-honored way out of the dilemma. Resident Stewart was given home leave from March to October 1896, and Major C. B. Piggott of the 21st. Hussars acted in his place. Governor Maxwell was likewise given home leave, from April to October 1896, and Hodgson once again took over as Acting Governor. I have, unfortunately, been unable to find any record of what transpired between Maxwell and Chamberlain, but it is clear that Hodgson was instructed to maintain a low profile in Asante, relying on the (Acting) Resident and the Native Committee of Administration for the exercise of civil government. Asante was, as it were, put on hold—or left to the attention of the concessionaires. The main thrust of British policy was directed, first, to preventing the Muslim reformer, Almami Samori, from establishing himself in the old savannah provinces of As-ante, and second, of turning them instead into the Protectorate of the Northern Territories of the Gold Coast. The legal experts in the Colonial Office had, however, continued to puzzle over the status of Asante. Fi-nally, in December 1896, Assistant Under-Secretary of State J. Bram-ston produced a succinct but authoritative answer. "We do not hold Ashanti," he wrote, "either by conquest or cession—both terms imply annexation and we are there only in exercise of H.M.'s jurisdiction in a foreign country."

The Gold Coast Governor and the Kumase Resident returned from leave in October, and at the end of that month Chamberlain instructed Maxwell to send a small force to counteract a possible French thrust through Wagadugu to Gambaga. Stewart was appointed its head, and occupied Gambaga—over 300 miles from Kumase—on 24 December 1896. Maxwell was apparently required to intervene in Asante affairs as little as possible. He turned his attention to the development of the gold mining industry in—supposedly at least—the Colony. On appoint-ment as Governor he had, on 28 March 1895, written a memorandum, "Coolie Immigration. Gold Coast," and raised the matter with Cham-berlain again in March 1896, *after* the coup. In January 1897 he sought permission to bring in Chinese miners from Malaya, not as labourers, but as investors. W.H. Mercer, Assistant Private Secretary at the Colo-nial Office, evaluated the proposal. It was, he thought, carefully worked out, "and Sir W. Maxwell from his Eastern experience is the right man to carry it out." He did not recommend, however, that Chamberlain should approve the scheme. "The Chinamen," he wrote, "who would be brought to the Colony at the cost of colonial funds would not be or-dinary labourers but capitalists or the representatives of capitalists, and they would report their opinions to their employers and not to the Colo-nial Government. This is not what is wanted." Nevertheless, Maxwell was allowed to draw £1000 from the Colony's treasury to finance a pilot scheme in the Colony. Shortly after his son, George Maxwell, arrived in the Gold Coast with 16 Chinese miners in tow. Their venture in Akyem Abuakwa was not successful, and all left the Gold Coast to-wards the end of the year. Maxwell, however, was not present to witness the failure. He had left Accra on a journey to what had become known as "the Hinterland" on 26 July 1897. He was in Bonduku in September when, very seriously ill with malaria, he applied for leave of absence. He arrived in Accra in early November 1897, and was, according to Hodgson "shattered in health, and totally unfitted to write a report." He sailed for Liverpool on 3 December, and died at sea, off Grand Canary, on 14 December.

In London, the Assistant Under-Secretaries became busy. Was Hodgson the man for the job? "Sir W. Maxwell," wrote Antrobus,

> recognized Mr. Hodgson's capability but he suspected him (I think unfairly) of disloyalty to the Governor. It is notorious that they didn't get on well together; but Sir W. Maxwell was not an easy man to get on with, and Mr. Hodgson was apt to put forward his own views more persistently than he was justified in doing. The tone of some of his minutes during Sir W. Maxwell's absence was certainly open to objection.

Nevertheless, Hodgson had already administered the government of the Colony for over two years, and he was duly appointed Governor in April 1898.

Hodgson made it clear that he would not necessarily follow Maxwell's initiatives. The matter of the Supreme Court was of special concern. "Now that capitalists are turning their attention to the gold reefs in Ashanti," he wrote, "and many Europeans are likely to be employed in connection with the gold mines, it is, I venture to suggest, more than ever desirable that the Supreme Court should exercise jurisdiction over Ashanti...." This was a total reversal of Maxwell's policy, and Hodgson explained how he had come to change his mind. He was on leave during the first half of 1898. "I returned to the Colony in July, 1899," he noted,

> having during my leave done all I could by personal interviews to ascertain what capitalists and merchants intended to do with regard to the development of Ashanti. I was more impressed than ever with the necessity, in the interests of

trade and mining capitalists, apart altogether from political considerations, of formulating a more complete system of government.

Chamberlain none the less rejected Hodgson's recommendation. It would be preferable, the Secretary of State replied, "that the Resident should be entrusted with judicial as well as executive functions." Realistically, he observed that the Resident would inevitably be largely concerned "with questions connected with the development of the gold-mining industry." Chamberlain entered two caveats; first, that the Governor of the Gold Coast should have power to legislate for Asante by proclamation, and second, that the authority of the Concessions Court of the Colony should extend there.

Hodgson also made it clear that he considered the Maxwell Treaties of early 1896 to have been questionable policy. "It is necessary," he wrote,

> to maintain the position as it stands at present, namely that this Government has taken the place of the Native paramount authority, that the Resident as representing the Government stands in the place of that authority, and that—Agreements notwithstanding—the Tribal Kings and Chiefs are under the same obligations of service to the Government as they were to the King paramount before the change took place.

Yaa Asantewaa Saa: Kumase's Attempted Countercoup

Robert Hamilton has explored at length the roots of the widespread dislike of the regime of Resident and Native Committee of Administration between 1896 and 1900, particularly with respect to the use of conscripted labour. Any such account has largely to be built on the later testimony of Governor Hodgson, who saw in the Resident system many of the causes of his own misfortunes. "The West African native," wrote Hodgson, holds very tenaciously to ancient customs, and the inability of the Ashantis to obtain slaves seriously interfered with their means of livelihood. They found themselves unable to obtain a sufficient number of labourers to work in the native gold pits and to carry on their farming operations, and further they were, at the same time, called upon by their chiefs, under application from the British Resident, to supply labourers for public purposes, as far example the construction of roads, and the conveyance of Government stores....

The responsibility of fining rests entirely with the Resident, who has not been required to report to the Governor this exercise of power on his part. I became aware that there was discontent arising from this cause when, on my way to Kumassi, the King of Adansi having made it a matter of complaint when I met him at Kwisa. It was also mentioned to me by Opoku Mensa, the senior member of the Kumassi Native Committee.

In fact the Resident in Kumase had assumed (like the Asantehenes he had replaced) powers of life and death, and had used his Constabulary as a firing squad to execute those condemned to death. Attorney General Geary of the Gold Coast Colony learned of this, and was shocked. Maxwell had acted, as we have seen, quite illegally, having no authority to confer such powers on the Resident (who, thus, according to Geary, might be charged under British law with homicide, manslaughter, or false imprisonment).

In early February 1899, reports were reaching the Resident in Kumase that a rising was being planned by no other than the members of the Native Committee. The Resident did not wish to be an alarmist but pointed out that, with most of its soldiers and armament deployed in the interior, the garrison was reduced to a single officer and 189 men. This, he thought, was "encouraging any malcontents to try a rising," but added, "nearly the whole of Ashanti would be against the Kumasis if they were ever foolish enough to do so." Stewart probably felt confident in this judgment since his informants were Dwabenhene Yaw Sapon, Bekwaehene Yaw Boakye, and Mamponhene Kwasi Sekyere.

In the event, he soon decided to discount the reports, especially when reinforcements of 100 men arrived from the Gold Coast, to be joined by another 100 from the north. Governor Hodgson was on leave at the time, but on his return to Accra in July 1899 found no cause for alarm. He was radically to revise this opinion with the outbreak of hostilities the following March:

> The whole course of the outbreak has, I think, made it abundantly clear that the malcontent Ashantis … had for some time been secretly preparing for revolt. The collection of the enormous quantities of warlike stores, which the siege of Kumassi, and the determined opposition to the gallant force under Colonel Sir James Willcocks, showed them to be possessed of, must have been spread over a long period. It is in itself evidence of a pre-determined outbreak.

There is no doubt that, whatever the situation earlier, a resort to arms became inevitable after Hodgson made a public statement of policy in Kumase on 28 March 1900. The major issues he raised were as follows. First, he announced the abolition of the Asante monarchy. Neither Agyeman Prempeh nor Yaw Twereboanna—nor, by implication, any other royal of the Golden Stool—would ever rule Asante. "When the Government assumed the control of this great country of Ashanti," he explained,

> it took over also the powers which were previously possessed by King Prempeh. The paramount authority of Ashanti is now the great Queen of England, whose representative I am at this moment. In order that the powers of the King paramount may be exercised properly, inasmuch as the seat of the Government is far away at the Coast, it is necessary to place here a white officer, who bears the title of "Resident." Under the Governor the Resident at Kumassi exercises the powers of King paramount.

Second, Hodgson announced the introduction of a new tax of 2,000 peredwans (or £16,000) annually, which he described as *interest* on the sums spent by the British and Gold Coast Governments on the expeditions of 1873-74 and 1895-96. Third, he demanded surrender of the Golden Stool. "Why am I not sitting on the Golden Stool at this moment?" he asked. "I am the representative of the paramount power...." Hodgson ended his address famously: "Kings and Chiefs ... I want you all, as I have told you just now, to look on me as your friend as well as your Governor."

Hodgson's first and third announcements both had to do with one constitutional issue, that of paramountcy—or sovereignty. There was, of course, a hidden agenda, to which the Governor alluded in a letter to Chamberlain of 7 April 1900. He referred to his announcement that the Queen was now the paramount power in Asante, and wrote,

> Although I felt sure that this announcement would not be a palatable one to many, it appeared to me to be necessary to make it, having regard to the large number of gold mining concessions which are being obtained and also worked in Ashanti, and so that there might be no misapprehension in the minds of the Kings and Chiefs as to the position which the Government holds towards them.

Four days later, on 11 April, Hodgson again wrote to Chamberlain, explaining that he intended to stay in Asante until affairs there were completely settled. It is, he wrote, "essential in the interests of trade and of the gold mining concessions that what has to be done here should be of a permanent and lasting character." By that time a small force under Capt. C. H. Armitage, searching for the Golden Stool, had already been attacked, on 2 April, near Bare. It is beyond the scope of this paper to describe the escalation of this "collision of forces" into a major military confrontation, but Claridge's account remains remarkably informative.

Titular command of the Asante army belonged, traditionally, to Mamponhene. The Kumase war leaders therefore insisted that Mamponhene "must come and be their head." He, however, was already actively working, with Dwabenhene, Kumawuhene, Nsutahene and others, to persuade the Kumase people and their supporters to "stop their foolishness or evil doing." In this they were unsuccessful. Two members of the Committee of Administration openly joined the insurgents, but the British prevented Opoku Mensa from doing so by detaining him in Kumase Fort. In a post-war inquiry that had to do with the punishment of the defeated leaders, the three were described as the "principal instigators" of the war. Yaa Asantewaa, however, was said to have been "elected to command Ashanti forces," and Kofi Kofia—a chief of no great importance except because of his military capacity—to have taken a "very active part in direction of military operations."

Yaa Asantewaa, Edwesohemaa, or "Queenmother" of Edweso, was by no means unknown to the British Administration in Asante. She and her grandson, Edwesohene Kwasi Afrane Kumaa, had granted a concession over "Obbuassi Mines" to G. A. Robertson, the Winneba chief, and Amma Sika. Her grandson, however, was among those seized and exiled by Maxwell at the beginning of the year. It was, accordingly, Yaa Asantewaa who, by one of the Maxwell Treaties of 10 February 1896, committed Edweso to Britain's Friendship and Protection (though it seems unlikely that she conceived these terms in anything like the way Maxwell did). On 19 November 1896, the Kumase Resident questioned her about the concession. The indomitable old lady said first, that she knew nothing about the concession, second, that if she had been party to it she would have asked for more money, and third, that the land in question had been given to Edweso by Agyeman Prempeh as a reward for its support in the civil wars. Strangely enough, Stewart seemed unaware of Cade's negotiations for the Obuase lands, and appears to have thought that Kokofu (rather than Bekwae or Adanse) was the proprietor. When exactly Yaa Asantewaa decided actively to take to arms is uncertain. Willcocks referred to her as "one of the most capable of Ashanti rulers with a reputation for commanding in the Field." She was, he added, "one of our bitterest foes, and it was tolerably certain that she meant to have one fight with our troops."

Kofi Kofia, who was singled out with reference to his military prowess, is better remembered as Kofi Fofie Kaserepa. He was Kumase Nkonsonhene. There was, however, a more powerful figure behind him. Kofi Kofia is described as "the lieutenant of Kobina Cherri," that is, Kwabena Kyere. In the mid-18th century Awua, a son of Bantamahene

Apraku Panin and himself later to become Bantamahene, settled a part of his family at Odumase some 75 miles from Kumase on the Bonduku road. Their descendants retained the right to advance their candidacy for the Bantama Stool, the occupant of which served as commander-in-chief of the Kumase army. Kwabena Kyere belonged to this group. As "2nd Odumassi" he was one of those who attested to the Treaty of Trade and Friendship—another of "Maxwell's Treaties"—made with the "King of the Country of Borumfo" (that is, of the Bron people) on 4 March 1896.

In 1900 it was noted that Kwabena Kyere "had been lately anointed King of Bantama." Fuller referred to him as "the chief-designate of Bantama," using this description perhaps because Bantamahene Amankwatia Kwame was still alive although in exile. The election of a new Bantamahene in such circumstances was, we might be sure, intended to supply the Kumase forces with a "traditional" commander when Mamponhene had refused to assume "traditional" command of the forces of the whole Asanteman. Thereupon the war of 1900 became an Anglo-Kumase and not an Anglo-Asante one. This crucial distinction escaped Armitage and Montanaro, who referred to Kwabena Kyere as having been "elected Commander-in-Chief of the Ashantis." It also escaped Compton who was, however, well aware of Kwabena Kyere's status. "... Kobina Cherri was a militant fetish man, and the actual and able Commander-in-chief of the Ashanti army;" he wrote; again, "most important potentate of all—Kobina Cherri, now known to have been the chief pillar of the insurrection;" and again, "Kobina Cherri, the rebel generalissimo, commander-in-chief and Confederate King."

In the second half of August, the Kumase divisional forces, augmented by some troops from Kotoku and Adanse, maintained their offensive. It was not until 1 September 1900, after severe fighting, that Colonel James Willcocks finally succeeded in concentrating his Field Force around Kumase. He then immediately struck in a northwestern direction, through Atwema where the main Kumase strength lay. Odumase was reached. Its chief, according to Compton, "was awed by the great and crafty Kobina Cherri, the Czar of the Confederation, now hiding in these parts whose whisper still was almost as good as any other chief's will, and whose frown had not yet lost its fierceness or foreboding." As it turned out, acting on information, Major J. G. Browne surrounded Sunyani on 13 November, and captured Kwabena Kyere. He was brought into Kumase on 23 November, tried by Military Commission for having countenanced the massacre of some 80 rubber traders, and was hanged on the 25th. The Resident, Stewart, uneasy about the wisdom of executing prisoners of war, wrote, "no chiefs actually murdered any one with their own hands, but orders were given by the Heads of the rising and promulgated amongst the other chiefs.... There was near universal admiration for the courage with which Kwabena Kyere met his death, which, Compton wrote, "knocked the last nail into the coffin of rebellion."

In the House of Commons on 18 March 1901, Chamberlain made a perspicacious comment on the hostilities of 1900. The Asante, he argued,

> are ready to accept defeat, but they are not ready to accept the consequences of defeat without actual conflict. If you want to get to the bottom of the recent disturbances, you will find it in the fact that these people were called upon to suffer the consequences of defeat without having been defeated.

What has become known as the Yaa Asantewaa War was an unsuccessful countercoup much inspired by Edwesohemaa Yaa Asantewaa, and led by Bantamahene Kwabena Kyere, intended to achieve a return to something like the pre-1896 situation. We may assume that none of its leaders believed that the British suppression of the rising would be construed as a *conquest* of the whole Asanteman. But Compton made an almost eerily prescient comment on the death of Kwabena Kyere:

> With a fine, lion-like dignity that lifted him above the vulgar noose, died King Kobina Cherri, and with him the ambition that would have revived a Pagan Empire in Western Africa to slash the opening pages of the twentieth century with its satire on civilisation.

The opening pages of the 20th century were in fact to be "slashed" by the "Ashanti Order in Council" given at the Court of St. James's on 26 September 1901, which begins:

> The territories in West Africa situate within the limits of this Order, heretofore known as Ashanti, have been *conquered* by His Majesty's forces, and it has seemed expedient to His Majesty that the said territories should be annexed and should henceforth be part of His Majesty's dominions....

It had been, as Lawyer Osafroadu Amankwatia saw in 1940, all something of a fraud.

Slavery and Abolition in the Gold Coast: Colonial Modes of Emancipation and African Initiatives

KWABENA OPARE AKURANG-PARRY

Kwabena Opare Akurang-Parry is Professor of African and World History in the Department of History and Philosophy, Shippensburg University. He specializes in comparative slavery and abolition, colonial rule and African responses, and the social and economic history of Ghana.

The British abolished servile institutions in the Gold Coast after the nominal conquest of Asante in 1874. The formulation of the British policy of abolition for the Gold Coast is well known: Raymond Dumelt's study is the most exhaustive to date. However, historians of the Gold Coast have portrayed the official British-Indian mode of emancipation as the only one that manifested and the various analyses that inform it remain exiguous. Gerald McSheffrey indicates that slave desertions undermined the effectiveness of the British-Indian model. Dumett and Marion Johnson, whose conclusions suggest that the British-Indian model was successful because the majority of former slaves chose to stay with their holders, have disputed his view. More recently, Akosua Perbi has affirmed the conclusions of Dumett and Johnson.

Thus, compensation, self-redemption, and emancipation by degrees, all proposed by the Colonial Office, and kin redemption, an African initiative are missing from the literature. This study reevaluates the British-Indian model, investigates the other modes of emancipation, and discuses how some of them became vehicles of freedom and why others paled into insignificance. It offers a more detailed analysis of slave and pawn desertions and the alteration in the British-Indian model. It delineates that this mode of emancipation operated only in the vicinities of coastal forts and castles and the Christian missionary enclaves in the interior. In addition, it reveals that self-redemption, based on land tenurial arrangement, and kin-redemption also occurred. These affected post-proclamation relations of production and land tenure. Further, this study expatiates on African responses and initiatives in the emancipatory process. Lastly, it shows that the failure to compensate holders led to various forms of protest politics, while emancipation by degrees faded into obscurity.

The discussion of modes emancipation between the Colonial Office—derived from parliamentary debates—and the colonial government had two major interrelated objectives. One was to prevent a cataclysmic response to abolition, and consequently a crisis in the social structure and alterations in the political economy, while the other objective was to prevent any economic cost to Britain. In the end, the Colonial Office chose the British-Indian model, but authorized that compensation, emancipation by degrees, and self-purchase should be studied as alternatives. However, the ending of "slave dealing by importation" and the freeing of "all children born at the end of this year [1874]" were to take immediate effect. The terms of reference from the Earl of Carnarvon to Governor Strahan were as follows:

> [Bear in mind that the question at issue is not whether the legal status of slavery shall or shall not cease, nor indeed whether emancipation shall be deferred to some indefinite and distant date ... but by what modes of proceeding the many difficulties in the way may be surmounted without sacrifice to those objects which are essential to public order and the peace of society on the Gold Coast.

In addition, the colonial government was instructed to pay particular attention to "the views and sentiments of the chiefs" in "giving beneficial effect to the changes" the government intended to introduce.

The British-Indian Model

The British-Indian model had been utilized to abolish slavery in India more than thirty years earlier. The British-Indian model forbade slave dealing and provided that courts "should not take cognizance of any right over the liberty or person of a servant. Thus, it sought to abolish slavery without disrupting the existing forms of servile labor. In theory, it included the abolition of pawnship, but in practice this institution was marginalized. The Colonial Office posited that the application of the British-Indian model would benefit emancipation in the Gold Coast. It declared that this mode of emancipation would forestall disruptions in the social structure and allow contented slaves to remain with their holders. The Colonial Office averred that the British-Indian model would allow old and infirm slaves to stay with their holders. Further, it would accommodate conjugal and parental relationships built on slavery and pawnship, therefore sustain continuities in the social structure. Additionally, it would not disrupt labor, nor foment agitation for compensation. It was calculated that the British-Indian model had succeeded in India, which had a larger population; therefore, it would succeed in the Gold Coast, where the population was smaller. Lastly, the Colonial Office concluded that abolition in the Gold Coast would he uneventful because the servile institutions were benign and assimilationist.

Governor Strahan was enthusiastic about the British-Indian model. Presenting an overview of it to the Colonial Office, he opined that there "[were] many favorable conditions," though he acknowledged that "due precaution against risks" had to be taken. However, he revised the "due precaution" with a differing rationalization that "emancipation may be speedily or almost at once obtained." Proclaiming that slave-dealing would not pose a problem to the British-Indian model, he explained that

> The sale of domestic slaves within the Protectorate has not at any time, as I am informed, been a matter of common practice: on the contrary, it is against the hest standard of native feeling and is discountenanced by their laws, unless under exceptional circumstances in which it is permitted.

In addition, he contended that the importation of slaves into the Colony "for the purpose of being sold did not "take place to any very great extent." He noted that those persons who were brought into the Colony as slaves were "generally the captives of wars or periodical raids amongst interior tribes." Comparing slave-dealing with slave-holding, he delineated that problems were more likely to arise with the latter than the former. He explained that the prohibition of slave-dealing would end wars that had generated captives for sale and concluded that

> the changes in the condition and mutual relation of the population will be much less rapid and sudden in fact than in theory might be supposed. Nothing can be more complete than the change which is contemplated, but its actual operation will, in all probability, be gradual.

Accordingly, slave desertions would be sporadic and the penurious state of the servile population, coupled with their "established associations" with their holders, "would combine to prevent any general or wide spread [sic] exodus." In addition, local conditions, including long distances that set communities apart, would prevent desertions. He averred that holders would acquiesce to abolition because the coastal states were accustomed to incipient British rule. In addition, the British defeat of Asante, their foe, would strongly influence that decision. Lastly, he asserted that the colonial government would meet any resistance "with the judicious exercise of the force," and that there would be no "difficulty in repressing and promptly punishing lawless acts of whatever nature."

Governor Strahan, however, pointed out some problems that were likely to arise. He elucidated that the British-Indian model might prevent holders from supporting old and infirm slaves. In addition, holders might use punitive measures to restrain slaves from seeking their freedom. He declared that the "idlest and disorderly class" of slaves would readily desert, and, having no means to maintain themselves, they would form "marauding parties to commit robberies on the roads, and in other ways prey upon the more industrious of the population." He concluded if all or some of these problems manifested, an arrested development and disruption in social relations of labor could occur. Having weighed the benefits and costs, Governor Strahan endorsed the British-Indian model.

McSheffrey has argued that the gradualist approach of the British-Indian model failed because slaves took advantage of the abolition and deserted. In contrast, Dumett and Johnson have pointed to the success of the British-Indian model because slave chose to stay with their holders. However, their conclusions are only true for the colony, especially the Cape Coast-Accra administrative area, and the interior regions, such as Akyem Abuakwa, where the Christian missionaries operated. The region between the coastal enclaves and Asante was nominally affected by the implementation of the British-Indian model. But for the anti-slavery enthusiasm of the Basel Mission in the Eastern Province, slave-dealing there would have continued on a larger scale. By the mid-1880s, the implementation of the British-Indian model in the Colony had become ad hoc and erratic. The problem of slavery in the Protectorate was seriously addressed from 1889-90, when Firminger and the Aborigines Protection Society (APS) criticized the laxity in the administration of the abolition ordinance there. This spurt in policy critique had to await a more serious implementation from the late 1920s, when the anti-slavery societies and the League of Nations put additional pressures on the colonial government.

Not all the envisaged advantages of the British-Indian model manifested; several problems beset its implementation. During the early months of the abolition, some of its principles were abridged. Slaves and pawns who did not prove cruelty from their holders were freed by colonial officials. In addition, the anti-slavery fervor of the Basel Mission encouraged slaves and pawns to desert in large numbers to the mission quarters or suktattrz as converts or refugees. As well, slaves, independently and encouraged by their kin, took matters into their own hands and deserted. Labor disruptions which were evident in the early years of the abolition, continued through to at least the cod of the last decade of the nineteenth century. In carefully nuanced statements, the colonial government minimized the extent of the disruption in labor, but there are strong indications in such reports that bore ample testimony to the fact that serious disruptions had indeed occurred. Examples of such formidable indicators were "a series of [slave] migrations ... ['exodus'] going on to and from different parts of the country." Also, families took advantage of the abolition to free their relatives, and "cases of this nature constitute at least nine-tenths of all that have occurred in connection with the emancipation scheme ..." In addition, a significant number of slaves sought freedom through the colonial courts before the First World War. From the equivocal standpoint of the colonial reports, the massive slave desertions led to an orderly process of change. However, a close reading indicates a devastating alteration in the social structure and social relations of production. As a policy, the British-Indian model disregarded pawnship, hence its expansion in the post-proclamation colonial economy.

Self-Redemption

The Colonial Office contemplated self-redemption, but in the end it was abandoned. Consequently, it was not officially implemented but was seized upon by holders and slaves in their post-proclamation arrangements. The Colonial Office had recommended it as a mode of emancipation because the Basel Mission in the Eastern Province had set a precedent during the pre-abolition period. In his instructions to the colonial government Carnarvon clarified:

> It appears from the evidence taken before the Committee of the House of Commons in 1865, that the German Missionaries in the eastern Districts of the Protectorate have been enabled to effect the liberation of a considerable number of slaves amongst their Christian converts, by inducing Christian masters to agree to the gradual self-redemption of the slaves.

The Colonial Office justified that since slaves could possess property, they should be made to purchase their own freedom:

> [T]he right of a slave to hold property does not appear to be questioned.... Every slave who ha[s] the means should be in-

vested with the right of purchasing his own freedom and that
of his wife and children.

It also pointed out that in order for it to be effective, the self-redemption
scheme should be uniform:

[S]ome scale of evaluation should be devised founded in the
case of self-purchase as well as in that of compensated manumission upon present values.

Further, the Colonial Office explained that holders might resent "valuable slaves" buying their freedom, and as a result might not support
"burdensome" or infirm slaves who could not do likewise. Consequently, it was "necessary to secure some provision for those of the old
and infirm" who could not depend on their holders to support them. To
solve this problem, the Colonial Office suggested that "valuable" slaves
should make an annual contribution "by which [they] should be indemnified for the subsistence of others [the infirm slaves]."

Having considered the Colonial Office's views, Governor Strahan
argued against self-redemption. He surmised that problems would arise
if payment extended for long periods. In addition, he stressed that in
"the absence of education accounts would be impossible, and innumer-
able disputes would arise as to whether the amounts fixed as the price
of redemption had been paid or not, which it would be impossible-to
solve." Lastly, he averred that

[I]t is not to be expected that the slaves in any large numbers
would avail themselves of opportunities of self-redemption
and only very slowly would this method operate (if ever it
sufficed) to wipe out the reproach of slavery in the Protectorate.

Thus, self-redemption would prolong the period of the emancipation.

The discussion of self-redemption remains a gap in the extant literature. Once it was rejected as a mode of emancipation, colonial officials
relegated it to an abysmal background. Consequently, there is a dearth

of information about it in the official records. Durrett and Johnson claim that most slaves settled in comfortably with their former holders, and more recently. Perbi, with a more detailed analysis, has reached a similar conclusion. However, these conclusions are not informed by an analysis of the actual post-proclamation arrangements that arose between former slaves and former holders. Thus the implications of this immense economic change for the social structure and land tenure are barely explored.

Oral history and Basel Mission records show that in the post-proclamation period some former slaves who stayed with their holders worked out schemes that were closely linked with land tenure to redeem themselves, and to ease the transition from bondage to freedom. Both sources pinpoint that the type of post-proclamation arrangement described by Dumett and Johnson, and recently Perbi, was not based on the usufruct use of land. Rather, it was a lopsided arrangement that allowed former holders to expropriate the labor of former slaves. Some former slaves rented land from their former holders, while others engaged in sharecropping. Such post-proclamation arrangements entailed export commodity production, including kola, oil-palm products, and cocoa. In addition, former slaves produced local staple food, such as cassava, yam, plantain, pepper and cocoyam and so on, for subsistence, for both themselves and their former holders, as well for the local, markets. In addition, arrangements included exploitation of head porterage services that supported the transportation and marketing of local food staples and export commodities. In some cases, former slaves and their families worked for their former holders, during the weeding, planting, harvesting, and marketing—transportation—seasons.

These post-proclamation arrangements were established especially in the burgeoning export commodity and staple crops producing areas of the Birim-Densu-Pra basin of the Eastern Province. The evidence emphasizes agricultural activities as the medium of self-redemption. But paucity of data makes it difficult to determine the duration of self-redemption. It is likely that the duration was based on the peculiar circumstances of former slaves and the particular choices of their former holders. What is certain is that in most cases, such arrangements broke down, leading to new forms of dependency.

Historiographically, self-redemption is significant for several reasons. It strongly indicates that forms of labor that emerged as a response to the emancipation were equally demanding and exploitative. This disputes Durrett and Johnson's position that capitalist demand for the production of export commodities resulted in the growth of a prosperous, independent peasantry. Rather, it escalated and did not change the matrix of power and exploitation in the social relations of production. Indeed, Robertson and more recently, Crier and Austin, have variously affirmed a post-proclamation expansion in female slavery and pawnship. Some former slaves became smallholders producing for the local and external markets. This was predominant in the burgeoning agricultural economy of the Pra-Birim-Densu basin. The production of staple foods for the local markets, facilitated by the availability or land and cheap labor, but excluding huge capital, credit facilities, and duties, aided accumulation by former slaves engaged in self-redemption. In some cases, this led to a crisis of adaptation. In the comparative literature, analyses of the crisis of adaptation paradigms have tended to rely on overseas export and long-distance trade without it taking cognizance of the implications of the local and inter-community trade and exchange. In sum, former slaves utilized the resources—land, agricultural activities, trade, and mining ventures—of their holders as a means of individual accumulation.

As noted, the self-redemption process described above, which occurred in the backwaters of the burgeoning agricultural regions, may have escaped the attention of colonial officials. As a result, it was hardly mentioned in the official records. Self-redemption tended to perpetuate the dependency of former slaves on former holders. In fact, while more research is warranted, the exaction of such dependency was not substantially different from the pre-abolition conditions of involuntary servitude.

Kin-Based Redemption

It is worth pointing out that the primary data on kin-based redemption is scarce; however, the few available ones are authoritative. They include court cases and special colonial reports furnished to the Colonial Office. Kin-based redemption entailed kin-groups and individuals who capitalized on the abolition ordinance to free their relatives in bondage. This took several forms, including outright redemption that excluded payment for the price of the relative held in bondage, court cases, and the ritual normalization of preexisting servile-based marriages. The difference between kin-based redemption and self-redemption is that the former tended to lead to the total liberation of persons in servility, while the latter perpetuated their servility in other forms.

Kin-based redemption, entailing the use of the courts, and excluding monetary exchange for those being, redeemed, began soon after the inception of abolition. For example, in a report to the Colonial Office, Governor Strahan wrote:

> Very numerous instances have occurred, and are still occurring, of persons seeking the intervention of the Courts to aid them in removing their relations from distant parts of the country.... Cases of this nature constituted at least nine-tenths of all that have occurred in connection with the emancipation scheme, and deserve a word or two special remark, throwing, as they do, a curious light on the internal history of the Gold Coast.

Apart from the illustrative figure of nine-tenths, Governor Strahan also described it as "a series of migrations ... going on to and from different parts of the country." The kin-based intervention was built on the strong winds of change launched by the abolition. Governor Strahan noted that it would "come to a natural termination in the course of no [sic] very long time," but did not indicate exactly when. McSheffrey has observed that it "continued unabated." But it is more likely that the current of such kin-based emancipation was ephemeral. First, the evidence suggests that initial forays by kin-groups to redeem their family members in servitude were successful within a short time frame, at most by 1878. Second, was drowned by the colonial government's preoccupation with popular anti-colonial resistance and the Asante question from the mid-1880s. Lastly, and most plausibly, the inept implementation of the abolition laws curtailed the popular impulse to use the courts as a vehicle of freedom. With the realization that the colonial administration was not wholly supportive of the abolition laws, the enthusiasm for kin-based emancipation waned. There is a reasonable presumption to suggest that by the mid-1880s, such kin-based interventions, driven by the force of colonial policy, had become a thing of the past.

Historiographically, the kin-based redemption mode is illuminating. First, McSheffrey has emphasized the importance of the figure of nine-tenths as indicative of the widespread desertion of slaves. In addition, those emancipated by their kin were likely enslaved in the locality; in other words they were not people from the north—the so-called *donkos*. This suggests that a large number of such slaves were autochthonous war captives from the Colony and the Protectorate. This may partly explain the ability of kin-groups to trace and liberate their family members in bondage.

Second, this mode calls for a reassessment of the interrelated, well-known paradigmatic, yet polemical issues of slavery, kinship, and outsider status. If as the evidence dictates, slaves lived in relatively close proximity to their kin, then theoretically they were outsiders only to their holders' kinship groups, as in reality they maintained kinship ties with their families. In fact, as Governor Strahan clarified the matter, the slaves

> and their descendants would continue in all time coming to be looked upon as slaves of the captor or purchaser. But the families to which these prisoners belonged have never ceased, though generations may have passed, to have their eyes upon the members whom the force of circumstances had separated from them; and now when emancipation has given the opportunity, it is the aim everywhere of the heads of families to collect within the circle of their own authority every person connected with their family by ties of blood.

What is worth emphasizing is that a similar situation is described in the Basal Mission sources. For example, the Basel missionaries wrote, "People are also coming from Akim villages to fetch home their ex-slave relatives." Indeed, it is likely, as the evidence indicates, that kin-groups could not redeem their slave relatives prior to the abolition because, as the vanquished in the "petty wars," captivity of their kin was one way they could maintain peace with the victor. Again, the fact that such captive-slaves were sometimes sold by the victors complicated the issue of redemption in the pre-abolition period.

Third, it suggests that such slaves could have originally been pawns who had not been redeemed, and hence had fallen into perpetual bondage. This may also help explain why their kin were able to trace and liberate them. Toyin Falola and Paul Lovejoy's theoretical considerations support this: pawns removed from the "immediate vicinity of the debtor" and when "sufficient time [had] passed without prospect for the payment of the debt," could traverse into slavery. Thus, it may be presumed that the nine-tenths of the emancipated servile population redeemed by their kin included a large number of pawns. Though warranting further research, this line of reasoning suggests that the pawn population was larger than previously thought. Hence, it queries the view that pawnship only expanded in the post-proclamation period to replace slavery.

Fourth, in their introduction to the studies on the demise of slavery in Africa, Richard Roberts and Miers, suggest, based on "new research," that those who left their holders were not wholly welcomed by their kin. This study offers a variation of that conclusion, but delineates that in this instance, slaves were encouraged and assisted by their kin-groups. What needs to be assessed is the degree of reintegration of such redeemed slaves into their kin-groups. Though warranting further research, it was likely conditioned by their status in the social structure prior to being enslaved.

Lastly, Robertson, in her study of post-proclamation slavery in Accra notes that the courts were instrumental in the freedom attained by slaves during the early years of abolition. In fact, the court cases continued throughout the period of abolition to about the end of the First World War. What needs to be emphasized is that the courts failed to mount comprehensive programs to help freed slaves make the adjustment from bondage to freedom. Also, during the initial phase of the abolition, most of the court cases took place in the major axis of colonial administration along the coast. Even those cases that occurred in the interior were tried in either Accra or Cape Coast. This is not to ignore the fact that some traveling commissioners adjudicated some of such cases during their tours of duty. Thus, the servile institutions continued to thrive more in the interior, until total administrative control was affected over there in the early twentieth century.

Another facet of kin-based redemption was the complete ritualization and reenactment of pre-abolition servile-based "marriages." Pertaining to mainly females, it was rooted in the social structure and served as a vindication of the stigma of servile status. Immediately following the inception of the abolition, kin-groups in their quest to legitimize the marriages of their slave/pawn-relations, were able to induce former holders married to such slaves/pawns to perform the full marriage rites. In a report that detailed the effects of the abolition, Sir David Chalmers, the brain behind the abolition ordinances, observed:

> I have even known instances, and I believe there has [sic] been many of them, in which the sentiment attaching to free marriage was so much appreciated that persons who had been married as slaves previous to the promulgation of the Emancipation Laws have subsequently gone through the ceremonies of native marriage a second time as free persons.

Apart from the issues of emancipation and legitimization of marriages, this new arrangement sought to reinforce the pivotal role of kin-groups in such marriages:

> In marriage it is a discernible feature that it is now more frequently than formerly contracted through the interposition of the blood relations of the woman given in marriage, and there are proportionately fewer instances of its contraction through the master or mistress [holder] of a household.

While such ritualization of marriages may have conferred a sense of autonomy and the removal of the stigma of slavery, it did not better the lot of such women, as male/husband exploitation of female/wife remained an ingrained aspect of the social structure.

Thus, the colonial administration was aware of the actions of kin-groups in emancipating their members in bondage, and which challenged the aims of the British-Indian model. Primarily, these kin-based interventions were a part of the African initiatives in the emancipatory process.

Compensation

The extant literature shows that holders agitated for compensation, but does not reveal that their agitation was long-lasting, continuing well into the 1890s. Compensation was a focal point in the discussion of the abolition in the British parliament, and central to the debates was the amount to be paid to holders and the cost to Britain. For example, J. Lowther, the Under-Secretary of State for Colonies, suggested during a parliamentary session that

> If the Government were totally and unconditionally to abolish domestic slavery upon the Coast, then they ... must ask for something like £1,000,000 for compensation to the owners of slaves, or they must spend a similar sum in keeping a body of troops from the coast.

Lowther's assessment was revised by E. Ashley, who argued:

> If the question should turn out to be one of money, the whole population of the Protectorate not being more than 250,000, and the average price of the best slave, the Houssas [Hausa] being only £5, it was by no means a question of paying £1.000,000 ... but paying £100,000 would be quite sufficient for the purpose.

Also, in a speech to the British parliament, Carnarvon cautioned that unless the British government was prepared to pay about £1,000,000 compensation, the abolition should be gradual. Furthermore, an allusion was made to compensation in the British West Indies, but it was dismissed. Commenting on this issue, the influential *African Times* explained:

> For there is no ... analogy whatever between the slavery destroyed, with compensation, in the West Indies and that existing on the Gold Coast; not only because of the absence of creative supervision and protection in the latter case, but because, also, there are no such industrial results derived from the Gold Coast slavery as were derived from that of the West Indies.

Eventually, the issue of compensation paled into insignificance. The arguments adduced against it included the benignity of the servile institutions, the financial cost to Britain, and the undefined nature of the British territoriality in the Gold Coast.

In spite of the weight of parliamentary debates and public opinion against compensation, the Colonial Office recommended that the colonial government reassess its merits. Thus, on August 21, 1874, Carnarvon proposed for consideration "the payment of small compensation in money" to holders after seeking the "willing cooperation of chiefs and large slave-owners." The Colonial Office further proposed a computation for the compensation scheme, based on the price of the slave at the time of purchase—else it "would become more costly in proportion as the country became more prosperous." Further, it noted that the price of an able-bodied adult male ranged between £8 and £9, for example, therefore the computation had to be streamlined by a framework that would consider sex, age and health, as price determinants for compensation.

Carnarvon stipulated that compensation would lead to the "extinction of legal slavery at the end of a short term of years." To reach this goal, the indigenous rulers and holders were to be warned that whether they compromised or not the servile institutions would be abolished. Therefore, the holders would have to accept the colonial government's compensation scheme, or else gain nothing in the end. Compensation was not only assessed as a scheme to abolish slavery, but pawnship as well.

Carnarvon advised:

> For the purposes of such an arrangement it would he proba-
> bly equitable that pawns should be taken to be the slaves of
> their present possessors, unless the indebted owner is able to
> pay his debt, including the arrears of interest, in which case
> the compensation should he payable to him, and the right to
> the services of the pawn should revert to him for the ap-
> pointed term.

Having considered the compensation proposal, Governor Strahan rejected it on the following grounds. First, he magisterially explained that
the British defeat of Asante during the Anglo-Asante war 1873/74 was
a form of compensation. He surmised:

> Her Majesty in the sacrifices she has made in rescuing the
> owners of slaves—with the rest of the inhabitants of the Pro-
> tectorate—from defeat and disaster, and from slavery under
> a savage and blood-thirsty monarch which was impending
> over all of them, has already done far more than made com-
> pensation for all the interests in their slaves these owners
> could possibly claim.

Second, using the labor of slaves as his unit of analysis, he proclaimed
that the servile classes by their labor had paid for the "amount of a redemption many times over, especially in the case of pawns." Thus, there
was no need for the colonial government to pay compensation to the
holders.

The refusal of the colonial government to compensate holders led to
opposition and protest politics that took three forms: collective action,
local press protests, and individual action. All three forms of opposition
highlighted the fact that the emancipation had led to the loss of slaves
and pawns, who were property and a source of wealth. Emphasis was
also placed on the fact that slaves/pawns who did not show cause for
cruelty had been freed by colonial officials, contrary to what Governor
Strahan had told the indigenous rulers. As a result, holders declared ve-

hemently that the government had to compensate those whose slaves/pawns had been manumitted. The case of compensation to holders in the British West Indies was cited to support their demand:

> Slavery was introduced on this Coast by and for the gain of the West India planters—they were compensated for their property; there were no fixed bayonets on them.

Apart from these general reasons espoused in the collective quest for compensation, the individual protest by Robert Hansen of Accra, affords a unique case study. Hansen addressed a petition for compensation directly to the Secretary of State for Colonies. He believed that he would not obtain a fair treatment in the hands of the colonial administration. This suggests that either there was a popular distrust of the colonial government, or the latter had already refused compensation to others in Hansen's situation. The second explanation seems more plausible: the colonial administration had rejected compensation, a focal point in the holders' anti-abolition petitions of 1875.

Hansen's submission for compensation highlighted his family's military roles and material contributions toward the British administration, beginning with the Anglo-Asante war of 1824 and ending with his own participation in the Anglo-Asante war of 1873-1874. In addition, he pointed out that his family had been instrumental in preserving the stability of the Gã states during the pre-colonial period. For example, when Captain Maclean arrived in 1831, his father "helped [Captain Maclean] with 50 men [probably including slaves] to garrison the forts effectively." Pointing out that his father and some of his siblings lost their lives in the service of the British Empire, he stressed that when his father died, Captain Maclean deprived them of their wealth by "selling off houses, land, plates, furniture, herds of cattle ... even attempted to sell the slaves." He advanced stronger reasons for compensation based on the emancipation of his slaves. First, he noted that chieftaincy in the Gold Coast was not absolutist: therefore, Governor Strahan erred by seeking only the consent of the chiefs to abolish slavery. Second, he opined that he "never bought or sold a slave in [his] life"; rather, he had acquired them "by inheritance and [they were] lawful property." Third, he held that compensation would "enable [him] ... hire labour" to use on his land and repair his house which had been destroyed by the earth-quake of 1862.

In a letter calling Governor Stanford Freeling's attention to Hansen's petition Carnarvon, though critical of Hansen's disparaging comments against Governor Strahan, instructed:

> I should also wish you to consider whether under the peculiar circumstances of the case, some pension of very small amount or a gratuity in recognition of the past services of his family and himself might not he granted to him.

In a reply, Governor Freeling, acknowledged the import of Hansen's petition, as well as the adverse impact of abolition on the Hansens' wealth. However, he explained that the Hansens had "since made no effort as others have done to maintain their positions by trading in other pursuits." He advised against any form of compensation to Hansen, stat-ing that the colonial government would he "inundated with claims of every description many of which it might be difficult to refuse when a precedent had once been established."

It should be emphasized that the popular call for compensation con-tinued throughout the post-abolition period, despite the unequivocal po-sition of the colonial government. Thirty years into the abolition, in the midst of a labor crisis, the local press, patronized by the African intel-ligentsia, remained relentless in its crusade for compensation.

Emancipation by Degrees

Yet another mode of emancipation proposed by the Colonial Office was emancipation by degrees, based on gender, "classes," and age. Unlike other modes that were left to the colonial government to determine their suitability, the Colonial Office took the initiative to abandon it. Eman-cipation by degree was in fact first considered in 1833, when various schemes were examined as vehicles of emancipation in the sugar colonies of the Caribbean. From the standpoint of the Colonial Office, its objective in the Gold Coast would be to provide slaves with "a small portion of immediate freedom, the power of reaching total and ultimate emancipation through the exercise of industry." Its underlying working principle would be that

> upon each class and sex, a price per head should be fixed by law, arbitrarily, but founded as closely as was possible upon the average market price borne during the last ten years by slaves of the like age and sex.

Such prices per head would be divided into six equal parts, with each of the six parts representing a slave's labor for a working day. The colonial government would purchase from holders one of such working days for each slave between the ages of six and seventy years. Thus, the government would pay one-sixth of a stipulated price for a slave, and then

> the slave should be left, by his own exertions in this one free, to gain the means of purchasing for himself a second free day; by his own exertions in the two free days to effect the purchase of the third: and so on till he should have accomplished the purchase of the remaining working days of the week, when he will be altogether free.

However, some allowance was made for those under six and those over 70 years of age. The government would purchase the sixth day for child slaves "as soon as they should reach [the] age [of six]." Those above 70 years old were to have the "option of gratuitous freedom or retaining their claims of support by their owner and continuing under the obligations of slavery." For children born to slave mothers the proposal outlined that the "progeny thenceforth horn of slave mothers were to inherit the sixth day, which should have been purchased for herself previously to the period of the birth."

Such emancipation by degrees was abandoned by the Colonial Office because of several factors. First, it was posited that the predial slavery in the West Indies, on which the emancipation by degrees was based on, was different from slavery on the Gold Coast. The second factor was that slave labor in the Gold Coast procured "small money value," suggesting that slaves would not be able to work to pay off the remaining five-sixths of the prices at which they were bought. Lastly, it was estimated that slaves and their holders would "maintain existing relations," thereby rendering the government's payment of the stipulated one-sixth of their price ineffectual. Thus, emancipation by degrees, as spelt out by the Colonial Office, was abandoned.

Conclusion

The colonial administration in the Gold Coast was instrumental in the decision to utilize the British-Indian model. During the initial phase of abolition, it became effective in the Colony, where the colonial administration was more forceful, but not in the relatively isolated Protectorate states. The British-Indian model created problems, as the servile-holding class and the servile population adjusted to abolition. Alterations in social structure and political economy occurred despite the pre-abolition postulations and calculations of benign response. African initiatives manifested in the other modes of emancipation and in the post-proclamation arrangements between former slaves and former holders in areas of land tenure. Considering the Gold Coast as whole, African initiatives in the abolition of servile institutions eclipsed those of the colonial administration, especially in the Protectorate states.

"My Arse for Okou":
A Wartime Ritual of Women on the Nineteenth-Century Gold Coast

ADAM JONES

*Adam Jones is Professor of History and Culture in Africa,
University of Leipzig, Germany. He has published extensively
on West African history before 1900, including a number of
richly annotated European source materials.*

Mmàrimâ nni hô à, mmàbasiâ yi wônho kyèré
("When men are not present, women expose themselves")

If women are mentioned at all in studies of precolonial African warfare, it is usually with reference to nineteenth-century Dahomey, where several thousand female soldiers fought in many military campaigns. Elsewhere there are a few recorded instances of women taking part in battles, for example among the Mbundu in the seventeenth century, among the Igbo in the eighteenth century and in nineteenth-century Ethiopia. In much of Africa, however, war formed part of the "exosphere" from which women were automatically excluded. Yet even if the waging of war is more often than not a man's affair, its impact is usually felt by society as a whole. It seems to me that those who have written about the history of African women have frequently neglected the ways in which their peacetime and wartime roles might differ. Most of the classic ethnographic descriptions we have of social organization in Africa were written during peacetime and these take this situation more or less for granted. However, historical records suggest that peace was the exception rather than the norm in the nineteenth century and probably before. As Dozon has argued, war represented not so much a breakdown of the precolonial sociopolitical system, but rather a "regulatory practice tied to the movement of social production": moreover, it was through war that the "differential relation" between men and women was most clearly demonstrated, since it provided a clear-cut means of regulating among men the control of women. As in other parts of the world, war played a crucial role in "drawing the lines" between male and female.

In this paper I propose to discuss how warfare affected relations between men and women on the Gold Coast (the southern part of modern Ghana west of the Volta and a small adjacent area of Cote d'Ivoire). I shall he concerned with several ethnic groups, each with its own forms of kinship and political organization, notably with Akan-speakers (Fante, Asante, etc.) and with the Get who live further east. As far as the topic of this paper is concerned, however, ethnic differences do not seem to be of crucial importance.

Women and Warfare

Although the history of the Gold Coast offers nothing comparable to the Amazons of Dahomey, women were certainly sometimes involved in military affairs. The best documented example is that of the small Fante polities, whose military organization (*asafo*) was divided into a number of "companies"; membership was inherited patrilineally, so that the companies formed a structural contrast to the matrilineally organized descent group, *abusua*. Women, like men, belonged to their father's company, and the strength" of the women in a company was something to boast about, if only because it implied that the men were even stronger.

Several Fante communities also had a separate women's contingent, *adzewa*, whose main task was to dance and sing on certain occasions, including some funerals, and to keep up the men's morale in wartime. The head of the *adzewa*, known as the *adzewafuhene*, must have been of some sociopolitical importance: Dutch documents mention presents given in the late eighteenth and early nineteenth centuries to the "women of the quarters" or the "Great Quarterwomen," terms which apparently referred to the *adzewafuhene*. Presumably the "queen" (*mannye*) of a Gã town played a similar role, together with her female officers: according to a nineteenth-century source, she had to "lead the women in any public business or in war."

Rivalry between the different "quarters" of a town often led do demonstrations of collective female militancy. In 1764 fighting broke out in Moure because of the aspersions cast by women of one quarter on those of another. Nearly a century later, after a quarrel between the people of English Accra and Dutch Accra had been settled, the women of the two places kept hostility alive by exchanging insults; and in the twentieth century riots between Fante *asafo* companies have originated in a similar manner. Such outbreaks, although triggered off by particular events, could only have occurred against a background of well organized solidarity.

It is unlikely, however, that Gold Coast women took an active part in any fighting outside their own villages. Quite apart from anything else, male fears of contact with menstruation would probably have made it difficult for young women to go to war. Oral traditions in the Akan-speaking interior of the Gold Coast celebrate several queen mothers who participated in wars fought between 1820 and 1900; all were old women, presumably beyond menopause. One contemporary account of the "Asante War" in the early 1820s states that the Queen of Akyem was "in the hottest part of the action," and there are a few references to women of high status accompanying Asante armies. Otherwise nothing suggests that women saw active service in this region. Those who went to the front at all did so not as soldiers or in order to make it hard for the men to retreat (as in Ethiopia), but as a sort of commissariat, carrying food for their husbands or male kin.

Should the war result in victory, women generally took part in the celebrations. In the seventeenth century women as well as men on the central Gold Coast trod on the skulls of enemy warriors that were brought back, and on the anniversary of a victory the successful general and his wives might stage a mock battle in celebration.

Mmobomme

From what has been described so far, it might seem that the wartime role of women was limited mainly to that of supplying and congratulating their menfolk. On an ideological level, however, their position vis-a-vis men changed significantly. This change was expressed through a ceremony (or set of rituals) known in Twi as *mmobomme* or *mmomo(m)me,* aspects of which are mentioned in at least twenty sources written by European observers between 1784 and 1903, covering the whole region between the lower Bandama River (in what is now Cote d'Ivoire) and the Volta. Although many of the details varied over time and space, certain frequently recurrent features can be picked out. These include "dance," praise and execration, "prayer," symbolism, "obscene" behaviour (including nakedness), and inversion of gender roles, including the abuse of male "cowards." I shall deal with these in turn, although they were closely linked.

Dance

After the men's departure, women painted their skin white with kaolin powder and (according to some sources) put on white clothes—white being, among many other things, the colour of victory and of liminality. In doing so they were no doubt consciously marking a contrast to other occasions, notably funerals, at which women daubed themselves with red earth. Dressed in this manner, women would parade through their village or town at least once a day, shouting, gesticulating, beating drums (a musical instrument normally reserved for men) or brass pans and performing dances reserved for such occasions, similar to the men's war-dances: "They walk in a circle, singing and keeping time, moving their bodies in a peculiar manner and from time to time acting as if they intended to attack the nearby enemy." For European observers such behaviour must have been confusing and somewhat alarming, and their reports do not often give a clear picture of what happened or what the purpose was. Most observers were struck by the amount of noise; this, they wrote (probably correctly), was intended to "frighten hostile spirits" or "influence the fetish."

Praise and Execration

In its narrowest sense the word *mmobomme* refers to the songs sung on such occasions. Some of these were exhortations addressed to the soldiers, such as the song reported to have been sung by Gã women in 1826:

> "Sons of heroes, get hold of your guns!
> The King's white men say, When you get to fight, you will fight!
> (When the war breaks out, you will be able to fight!)
> Sons of heroes, get hold of your guns!"

Other songs extolled the leading men of the village and poured scorn on the enemy in a manner reminiscent of European soldiers' songs such as "Colonel Bogey." A few "samples" extracted from songs of this second type were recorded in the Baule country by Maurice Delafosse, probably in 1894 or 1895. Unfortunately they have survived only in the form of an expurgated French translation:

> Okou est un ennemi, qu'on lui coupe la tête.
> Okou est Pexcrement de mon derrière.
> Okou se fait aimer charnellement par les chiens.
> Okou est complètement impuissant.
> Les femmes d'Okou ne veulent pas se laisser approcher par lui.
> Les parties génitales d'Okou sont pourries et ont l'odeur des excréments.
> Quant à Kouadio, il est un homme. Toutes les femmes d'Okou partagent la couche de Kouadio.
> Kouadio peut renouveler dix fois de suite ses exploits amoureux sans être fatigué.
> Aoussou aussi est un homme. Kouadio et Aoussou sont forts et leurs homes sont forts.
> lls couperont la tete et les parties génitales d'Okou.

According to Delafosse, the women concluded the ceremony by making violent thrusts of the buttocks in the direction of the enemy country, singing: "My arse *(mon derriere)* for Okou" (or whomever the enemy happened to be). Although this gesture is not mentioned explicitly in other sources, it seems legitimate to regard it as embodying the key significance of *mmobomme*: women made use of their bodies—the one thing over which they had unlimited control—to demonstrate their power as women, in this case by "defecating" upon the enemy.

Prayer

Prayer, according to many sources, was another essential element: in their songs and speech women invoked the protection of (or sought to propitiate) "the gods," "the God of War" or "the fetish." In Akropong prayers were addressed to the spirit dwelling in the large tree *(Ficus voge-liana)* in front of the king's court, known as Mpeni, whose shade was symbolically associated with peace and "coolness":

"You are our father Kofe! You are great! You are the Old One! You sent our men to war; bring them back. We fall down before you and place the matter in your hands; you are our hope."

Symbolism

The symbolic significance of this ritual is alluded to in many accounts, each very different from the others. When the men of Accra went to war against the Anlo Ewe in 1784, "[their women] sat down in the canoes which lay upon the beach and acted as if they were paddling them, throwing some [i.e. other women] into the sea; they also took bricklayers' trowels and laid bricks. All of this was allegorical: the paddling on the sand meant that our men [i.e. those of Accra] were to cross the River Volta, engage the Augnaer [= Anlo] in combat and drown them. The bricklaying, on the other hand, signified the building of Fort Konigstein [at Ada, near the mouth of the Volta]" (Isert 1788: 227).

In 1838 a French visitor to Elmina wrote: "Imagine hundreds of bacchantes, each holding the end of a string 3 ells long, both ends of which are knotted, and along which there are at intervals some grains of gold or pieces of glass, like the chaplets of pilgrims or Calabrian bandits. They pretend to exert all their energy to break the string, calling out:

'My husband / my brother / my cousin / my beloved is still alive'"
(Douchez 1839: 97-98).

Other authors, referring mainly to the Akwapim region (further east),
describe different forms of symbolism. Women might spend the day
pouring water on the ground, with the aim of thereby quenching the
enemy's fire in battle or (put in more philosophical terms) in order to
"cool the matter." They might place pots of water in the streets of the
village, to ensure (by analogy) that their own men would not suffer thirst
during the campaign. A creeper tied firmly around a bundle of grass
from top to bottom served as a representation of the fate that awaited
the enemy. Women carried *fufu* pestles to the crossroads outside the
town, in order to remove misfortune. They might also stage a mock battle: in 1784, for instance, the women of Accra fought one another with
wooden sabers while their men were at war; in Akropong a century later
the women, having tied cords and other objects around their feet, fought
one another with whips shaped like guns. In some villages women
painted large fruits black and threw them, as if to hit the enemy with
cannon balls; they might also stab pawpaws (representing the heads of
the enemy) with knives.

Obscene Behaviour

Several sources indicate the importance in *mmobomme* ritual of gestures
that would normally have been considered disgusting; and three authors
(all referring to Cape Coast or Elmina) state that women went naked,
at least at the time when a battle was anticipated. When asked by European men why they had done this, women at Cape Coast replied: "What
does it matter? We were all women at Cape Coast. The men have gone
to war." (It was somewhat naive to expect that women would—or
could—deconstruct" their own symbolism for the benefit of curious
outsiders.) Interestingly, according to Ellis, on such occasions some of
the leading women might wear two hens' eggs fastened above the pu-
denda.

Inversion of Gender Roles

As this last detail might suggest, war made it possible (or necessary?) to invert or reverse some of the etiquette which normally governed gender roles. This was the one occasion on which a woman might be seen wearing men's clothing or carrying an implement associated with men, although to do so was not essential. In some cases they carried knives, old flint-locks, imitation weapons carved out of wood, or simply long sticks, which in this setting were regarded as guns. Other implements used included paddles, fly-switches, machetes and (in the case of non-Christian wives of Christians) books.

Gender inversion among the Baule and their Anyi neighbors was even more explicit. Women adopted the name of their husband or of a male relative and addressed one another with salutations normally reserved for men. Seated on the ground, they would tell tales of their alleged exploits in battle, each one giving lewd details of the (masculine) pleasure she would have in sleeping with the women she had captured. In addition, led by the chief's senior wife, the women poured libations of water, drank water in the way men would drink palm wine or spirits, and then thanked the chiefs wife with the words "Father X, thank you."

Elsewhere women temporarily filled the political offices occupied in peacetime by their husbands, unless the latter were among the very old men who had remained at home. Similarly, as missionaries noticed to their surprise, even a few "heathen" wives of Christians attended church in their husbands' stead as long as the war lasted.

Furthermore, a woman could act more aggressively than was usually considered proper (i.e. without danger of being regarded as an *obaa banyin,* or "female man"). The objects of attack were not only the enemy but also any man fit to bear arms who had remained at home, including sometimes Christian catechists and even white men. During their dancing the women would encircle such a man, shower him with ridicule and abuse, and then perhaps beat him with sticks, stones, whisks cut from palm fronds or whips made of cotton threads. Women in Asante sang special songs (called *kosa-ankomee,* "coward") which could drive war-shirkers to suicide. Alternatively, according to two sources (both referring to the central Gold Coast in the early nineteenth century), they might castrate him.

Thus a large number of different elements are mentioned in connection with *mmobomme* ritual. It would probably be wrong, however, to assume that all of these constituted an essential part. Some are mentioned in only two or three sources. In my opinion their absence in other accounts is significant, and they may therefore be considered "optional" according to the situation. These include the use of noise to "frighten the hostile spirits," the praising of one's own side and cursing of the enemy, the use of "disgusting" gestures and nakedness, and the adoption of male roles in public life. However, other elements feature in the majority of sources: the importance of the colour white, the performance of a dance or parade, the role of prayer, the need for symbolic actions (albeit of widely differing kinds), the use of male clothing or implements, and the adoption of aggressive behaviour towards those men not actively engaged in warfare. These we are probably justified to consider "core" elements of *mmobomme* ritual.

The earliest reference I have discovered to such ritual dates from the seventeenth century. A German surgeon who lived at Fort Nassau (Mouri) on the central Gold Coast from 1617 to 1620 wrote:

"While the men are at war, their wives at home make green wreaths, dance with them and call on their god Fytysi [i.e. 'fetish'] for help, until they see a sign one way or the other, such as heads which one of the men of high rank may send home to delight the women" (Brun 1624: 83-84).

Here we already have three elements mentioned in nineteenth-century accounts of *mmobomme*—dancing, prayer (for protection or victory) and symbolism (in this case "green wreaths").

Problems of Interpretation

To offer an interpretation of the complex symbolism embodied in such behaviour lies beyond the scope of this paper. One difficulty is that the function and outward form of *mmobomme* have changed considerably. Since 1900 no wars have been fought in this region, and inevitably this has transformed the meaning of rituals such as *mmobomme*.

Nowadays a community occasionally feels itself threatened in its very existence, and then it is the responsibility of women to ward off the danger by means of *mmobomme*. If, for example, two villages are engaged in litigation, if an epidemic breaks out, if a bad omen for the village as a whole is seen or if the rains are unusually heavy, women in rural areas may perform *mmobomme* songs and dances, marching from one end of the village to another in ways similar to those described in nineteenth-century accounts. The best documented case is that of the Anyi. When a woman dies in childbirth, it is believed that all other pregnant women are in danger. They therefore gather at one end of the village, wearing only a loincloth and holding branches of the ginger lily (*Costus afer*). Other women join them, wearing male clothes and making threatening gestures with objects belonging to their husbands or with large pieces of wood. The women set out to "wage war" against the power which has caused a pregnant woman's death, shouting imprecations and begging the tutelary deities to protect them. They insult the men of the community, who are obliged to hide and whom they temporarily replace; for it is the "defection and impotence" of the men which have caused all the evils current at this time.

Mmobomme today has different meanings and purposes among different groups, in part perhaps a reflection of the divergent twentieth-century histories of these groups, but also no doubt a result of local differences that already existed. Perhaps the "half naked men and women" who demonstrated in Accra against the Ghanaian government's claim to have won the 1992 elections were drawing inspiration from *mmobomme*. In Aowin it can serve to demarcate more clearly the boundary between the village community ("cool," "white") and the bush ("hot," "red"). The rarely performed *aworabe* rite in Akwapim, in which "nude women pound the street with pestles at night" in order to keep away disease or bring rain seems to be in essence a variation upon the same theme. Among the Fante the word *mmobomme* refers only to mourning songs performed after the death of a chief. Elsewhere it can designate prayers which people (mainly women) may hold when a relative is taking an examination.

These modern examples indicate that today, as in the past, the rite draws upon "women's dangerous creative power" in various ways. Yet given the new meanings which *mmobomme* assumed during the colonial and postcolonial period, it would be futile to expect detailed information on its significance in precolonial times from oral tradition. It is possible that what happens today also occurred in the nineteenth century, or at least that the form of the ritual has remained constant while its function has changed; but we simply do not have enough evidence to demonstrate that this was the case. Of course it would be useful to know more about the significance attached to *mmobomme* today; but given that even those scholars who have lived in the region for many years have not found out very much, I do not consider a fieldwork project focused upon this question a viable proposition. Nor have I been able to discover sources for the first half of the twentieth century that might indicate what sort of processes turned *mmobomme* into what it now is.

In order to understand what it meant in the nineteenth century, therefore, we are obliged to rely principally on the written sources cited above. Surprisingly, these have been largely neglected. Virtually the only scholar who has discussed *mmobomme* with reference to precolonial warfare is Arhin (1983: 96):

> It is unclear whether the dances and songs were expected to have magico-religious effects on the enemy. But they had the practical effect of shaming potential war dodgers.... The situation can be summarized by saying that the essential female military role was to give encouragement to the men.

This assessment may be challenged on three counts. Firstly, there can be no doubt that the dances and songs *were* thought to have "magico-religious effects." Were this not the case, it is hard to see why in Asante, at least, the women responsible for *mmobomme* were obliged to lead the same sort of ascetic life as the men in the war camp—eating no tomatoes, for instance, and bathing only in cold water. Furthermore, the old men who remained in the village insisted that the women perform *mmobomme,* urging them to redouble their efforts whenever gunshots were heard. If a battle was lost, this was attributed to the women's failure to act at the moment when it took place; hence the need to avoid lengthy intermissions if the war were being fought too far away for gunshots to be heard.

Arhin's comment also pays too little attention to the fact that the women themselves clearly cherished participation in *mmobomme*. As Delafosse remarked: "This custom constitutes simultaneously an amusement and a duty." The women, he observed, looked happy at the time and later recalled such occasions with pleasure. No doubt they would have enjoyed other kinds of charivari too, but this one had a special significance. In my view, the roots of this practice lay in the tension that existed, at least latently, between the sexes: *mmobomme* offered women—within a carefully delimited framework—an opportunity to "turn the tables." As one observer commented in 1839: "It is not surprising that the women are so exacting with regard to men [in wartime]; for they themselves are treated quite harshly, in circumstances where in our country they are coddled" (Douchez 1839: 22).

Above all, to refer to the women as if they were merely cheer-leaders, who gave the men "encouragement," fails to explain why—at least according to some report—they went naked. The extreme case was that of Baule women, who at such times of crisis performed a dance *(adjanu)* in which their body was covered in white cloth and only the genitalia were exposed—a reversal of the normal state of affairs, when such exposure was considered (by men) almost as dangerous as menstruation. Was this explicit emphasis on sexual symbolism merely a form of "encouragement", or did it not also serve as an ominous manifestation of female power?

The significance of this "psychological mobilization of the female population" becomes clearer if we compare it with forms of female militancy in other parts of West Africa. An obvious example is *anlu,* a "disciplinary technique" employed in the past by Kom women in the Cameroun Grassfields against men who had committed certain offences that were considered obscene. The women would appear "donned in vines, bits of men's clothing and with painted faces to carry out the full ritual. All wear and carry the garden-egg type of fruit which is supposed to cause 'drying up' in any person who is hit with it. The women pour into the compound of the offender singing and dancing.... Vulgar parts of the body are exhibited as the chant rises in weird depth ... "

Similarly in the famous Women's War of southeastern Nigeria in 1929 Igbo and Ibibio women "used their bodies to 'insult' men; and they adorned themselves in 'the wild,' thereby utilizing the armoury of

Nature to convey their belief in the life-giving powers of the land with which they associated their own powers of reproduction."

These parallels, which could be taken further, suggest that *mmobomme* was not altogether a unique institution. Certain elements—notably singing, dancing, symbols of masculine social roles, nakedness and/or sexual insult, and the use of greenery or fruits with specific connotations—appear to have been common to other forms of collective female activity at times of crisis.

It is possible to detect further parallels in African and European rituals of status reversal, where "groups or categories of persons who habitually occupy low status positions in the social structure are positively enjoined to exercise ritual authority over their superiors.... They are often accompanied by robust verbal and nonverbal behavior, in which inferiors revile and even physically maltreat superiors" (Turner 1969: 167, 185).

Human societies, Turner has argued, refer to two contrasting models of society—one as a structure of jural, political and economic positions, the other as a *communitas* of idiosyncratic individuals who are equal in term of shared humanity. Behavior in accordance with one model tends to drift away from behavior in terms of the other, for instance when those in authority misuse the incumbents of lower positions. Rituals of status reversal are designed to bring social structure and *communitas* back into harmony. This may be done at a fixed point in the calendar: some Zulu, for instance, used to have rites that ascribed a dominant role to women for a brief period when crops had begun to grow. Likewise in May (the month when women's desires were considered to be at their most immoderate), women in rural Franche-Comte "could take revenge on their husbands for beating them by ducking the men or making them ride an ass; women could dance, jump, and banquet freely without permission from their husbands; and women's courts issued mock decrees."

Alternatively, such rituals can be employed, for instance in southern and eastern Africa, to avert a natural calamity.

> Put briefly, structural superiors, through their dissensions over particularistic or segmental interests, have brought dis-

aster on the local community. It is for structural inferiors—
representing communitas—to set things right again. They do
this by symbolically usurping for a short while the weapons,
dress, accouterments, and behavioral style of structural superiors—i.e., men. But an old form now has a new content....
Structural form is divested of selfish attributes and purified
by association with the values of communitas. (ibid.: 184)

Although it is doubtful whether war was regarded as resulting from
a "social sin," *mmobomme* was evidently closer to this second kind of
inversion. The main difference is that the status reversal was not sym-
metrical: although *mmobomme* women might in some cases adopt
men's roles, there were no men to play the part of women. But among
the Bete, who live to the west of the Baule, the death of a woman in
childbirth is seen as a threat to the community as a whole and is therefore followed by a ritual ceremony in which "naked women drive men
out of the village and assume power for a few days, subjecting the men
to hunger and isolation." Here we can certainly speak of status reversal,
and it may be that the thinking behind *mmobomme* was somewhat similar.

In order to test this interpretation, it is worth examining whether Gold
Coast societies also recognized the notion of status reversal in the first
sense, i.e. in connection with the calendar. One indication that this was
the case has already been pointed out by Turner: at Axim in the late seventeenth century an eight-day festival was held annually, during which
people had "the freedom to sing all sorts of bad things about anyone,
no matter whom—be it to recall his frauds or knavery, or whatever
pleases them" (Bosman 1704: 148). Two centuries later, Rattray
(1923:153) witnessed something similar in northern Asante; its purpose,
he was told, was that: "Once a year ... every man and woman, free man
and slave, should have the freedom to speak out just what was in their
head.... When a man has spoken freely thus, he will feel his *sunsum*
['soul'] cool and quieted ... "

Neither author referred specifically to the structural relationship between men and women in this context, but there can be little doubt that
gender was one of the issues. In the coastal town of Elmina in the mid-

nineteenth century a "beating custom" took place annually on three con-secutive Tuesdays, giving women a brief outlet to express resentment at their position:

> The fair sex has the right on these days to give the men a good thrashing with lianes ... , unless one wishes to redeem oneself with a few bottles of rum.... However, in order to ren-der the gentlemen harmless, the women have a gentler or at least less painful custom: during the preceding week they [the men] are permitted to cool their anger by scolding the women to their heart's content.

Another account referred to the same practice in Elmina a generation earlier:

> The native believes in a false god *(afgod)* called Enzan, on whose account the women must be scolded by the men; and thereby, on account of the goddess Iadodo, the women have the right for a week after the opening of the river to beat the men who exercised this injunction upon them.

Moreover, at certain annual festivals the norms regulating female sexuality appear to have been temporarily relaxed, so that it was ac-ceptable for a woman to approach a male stranger at a dance and pro-pose sex to him openly. This was quite different from *mmobomme:* the rule in Asante, for instance, was that if a *mmobomme* woman committed adultery in wartime, she was to be immediately executed.

It would be wrong to explain the role of nineteenth-century *mmobomme* ritual in terms of a single "function." For one thing, we know so little about many vital aspects of it: were all women involved, for instance, or only a special group? In addition, was nakedness re-garded as a means of shaming men, or did it have some other signifi-cance? Indeed, ought we to speak here of nakedness ("a state of being undressed which causes shame, disrespect, and harmful results in one's social surroundings") or of nudity (a term referring to "liminal situations in which a person passes from one social status to another")?

Moreover, the little we do know about *mmobomme* indicates that its meaning was multi-faceted and highly complex. No doubt under certain circumstances *mmobomme,* like annual husband-beating, might serve to consolidate male dominance in "normal" social life by offering an outlet for the expression of resentment by women with regard to their culturally defined role. Although they were supposed to be a deliberate exception to the norm, they may have presented people during a period of social upheaval with an alternative way of viewing the structure of society and of the family.

Archival Fragments:
Ntamoba and the Political Economy
of Child-Rearing in Asante

JEAN ALLMAN

Jean Allman is Chair and J. H. Hexter Professor in the Humanities, Department of History, at Washington University in St. Louis. Allman has written extensively on matters of nation and national identity, gender and colonialism, and indigenous belief systems in Asante and elsewhere. The following essay, a revised version of an article published in the journal Africa, *explores through the problematic concept of* ntamoba *the changing dynamics of child-rearing in Asante. This essay seeks to historicize and explain the multiplicity of meanings and the eventual disappearance of* ntamoba *by examining the ways in which a father's rights of use over his children were transformed into rights of ownership.*

Introduction: The Case

In the early 1990s, as part of a broader study of gender and social change in colonial Asante, I found myself plowing through volumes of customary court cases at Manhyia Record Office—the archive attached to the Asantehene's (king's) palace in Kumasi. I was there more or less against the advice of several senior scholars who, at the time, warned me that there was really not much "on women" in the records. As I was soon to discover, however, nothing could have been further from the truth: Much of the material dated from the late 1920s through the early 1950s, but there were even four or five volumes that antedated the Native Juris- diction Ordinance of 1924—the British colonial statute, which sought to systematize and regulate so-called "native tribunals" as part of the implementation of "indirect rule." Together, the volumes opened up for me an extraordinary window into gender, generation and the political economy of family life in late nineteenth and early twentieth century Asante.

It was in one of those rare early volumes that I came across a case, Kojo Asamoah v. Kojo Kyere, which involved an extremely puzzling dispute between a matrilineal uncle, acting as head of family, and his niece's husband. It was heard before the Native Tribunal of Bompata, Ashanti Akyem, on 18 February 1921. The plaintiff, Asamoah, charged the defendant, Kyere, with having "falsely accused Plaintiff of depriving [him, the defendant, of] his two children." According to Asamoah, his niece, Abena Esien, was married to the defendant and had two children with him. One day the niece complained that the defendant was not treating the children properly. The next morning one of the children came with a message from the father that he was claiming *ntamoba* fee. The uncle replied that he was not claiming the children, and the husband swore that he was.

In his opening statement the husband, as defendant, testified that his wife had earlier complained that he was depriving her of the children and that he had replied, "They are my children, and the only work I am getting from them is my water for my bath." A few days later, according to Kyere, the uncle came to his house and asked if he were claiming *ntamoba*. The uncle agreed to "pay including any other expenses," if he were. Kyere decided to make a claim, but testified that he did not receive any compensation. According to his account, the plaintiff swore that he was "not claiming the children and I swore that he is claiming them." The Kyeres' son supported his father's testimony by stating that his uncle "claimed back the children and Abena Esien to his people and he is the head. Plaintiff afterwards swore that he is not claiming the children, and my father the Defendant swore that he is claiming them." Unfortunately, the court reporter did not record, as in many other cases in the volume, the tribunal's justifications for its finding. The case concludes abruptly with the tribunal having "entered judgment for Defendant with costs hereunder assessed for depriving Defendant of his children."

What struck me immediately about this rather strange case was the word "*ntamoba*," which was obviously central to the claims being put forth. It appears that, if the matrikin were claiming back their own, the father had the right to demand *ntamoba*, a sort of compensation for the loss of his children and their services. If such were the case, not only would *ntamoba* be central to the criss-crossing web of obligations, responsibilities and rights which bound a matrilineage (*abusua*) to the husbands/fathers of its members, but it would be singularly important in defining a father's responsibilities toward and rights in his children vis-a-vis the matrikin. There was, however, a hitch here, and it was a big one. At the time I found this case I had been working for nearly a year on the changing dynamics of mothering in colonial Asante and I had never once come across the term *ntamoba*. How could it have been so crucial in mediating these primary social relations and yet have left so few traces in the historical record? While it is difficult and often risky to construct an hypothesis, much less develop an historical argument, when the sources are so slim and further digging seems only to turn up confusing and contradictory testimony, sometimes archival fragments are all the historian has to work with. If *ntamoba* had been central to defining and mediating the economy of childrearing in precolonial Asante, it had, by all indications, disappeared in the course of the late nineteenth and early twentieth centuries, perhaps earlier. Its disappearance, I suspected, just might provide clues to the ways in which family economy in Asante was transformed over the past century.

Some Contradictory Pieces of the Puzzle

Since first discovering the Bompata case I have looked through a host of written sources, from mission and government reports to early twentieth-century ethnographic works, and I have incorporated questions about *ntamoba* in life histories collected in several Asante towns, including Kumasi, Tafo, Effiduasi, Asokore and Agogo. Most written sources, primary and secondary, including the works of R. S. Rattray, make no mention of the term. Of the one hundred or so Asantes I interviewed in the 1990s between the ages of 68 and 100+, a good many could provide no definition of *ntamoba* at all. Those who could offered many and contradictory meanings and only a handful of these seemed applicable to the original Bompata case. Fortunately, among the few written sources there is some consensus on meaning. The second edition of Christaller's *Dictionary of the Asante and Fante Language* defines *ntamoba* as "indemnification to parents for a child that refuses to stay with them and runs away to the relations, to be paid by the latter." This definition obviously works in the Bompata case, although the father was the only parent being "indemnified." J. B. Danquah provides a more elaborate but similar definition, which warrants fuller quotation:

> A father has right of use over his children, but the true ownership is vested in their maternal family. The tie between mother and child can scarcely be broken; but the relationship between father and child can be destroyed by a customary process. This is the process involved in "Tamboba." It not infrequently happens that a father has to part with his "right of use" over his children in favour of their maternal relations. This demand is generally made by the wife's family.... For the father to part with his life interest in the children our customary law provides that a sum of money fixed by law and called Tamboba should be paid to him in respect of each child so taken away by its maternal relations.

Danquah's explanation of *ntamoba*, though derived from his experience in the neighboring Akan state of Akyem Abuakwa, obviously resonates strongly with the details of the Bompata case in suggesting that a father's rights in his children could be terminated by the payment of compensation known as *ntamoba* by the maternal family. So far, so good. But what of the oral sources?

Here is where the difficulties begin. Of those older Asantes with whom I spoke, a majority did not recognize the term at all. Of those who recognized *ntamoba* and could define it with some confidence, most remembered it as a marriage payment of one sort or another. A few, like Grace Amfum of Tafo, remembered *ntamoba* as a payment by the husband-to-be to the future wife's matrilineal family. Others recalled a marriage payment either to the mother or to the father of the future wife. "The parents give birth to a child," explained Yaa Abrebrese, "and they raise the child up.... In the course of raising up the child, the child might urinate on them, do all sorts of terrible things. Therefore, to compensate for that, you give *ntamoba* to either of the parents to compensate them for the trouble they have taken in bringing the child up." That the father of the wife-to-be was the sole recipient of this payment is the more common response among those who recall *ntamoba* as a part of the rites of marrying. It is a response I found to be particularly common in Kumasi, especially around the *ahemfie* (palace) at Manhyia, where the reminiscences of many echo those of Akosua Mansah:

> If a man wants to marry a woman he goes to see the mother, and the mother says he should go and see the father. The father will ask that you pay the ntamoba.... It is the father who receives ntamoba. That is to let him know that he has a daughter who is married to someone.

The recollections of Nana Kyeame Owusu Banahene, one of the Asantehene's senior linguists, provide additional detail:

> The one who begets the woman is called banintan [father; parent]. Now this man, whether he begets a girl or a boy, will be nursing the baby while the woman is cooking. Some time, that child will be urinating on him. When the child grows up, and someone wants to marry her ... that pain that he endured ... means the man was really banintan paa [a good parent]. The money, you call boba. So when the man is now coming to take the daughter, he has to pay for the pain. That is called *ntamoba*. It is for the girl's father ... [and] if anything happens in the family, he [the father] will know that the man has really married his daughter.

Nana Baffuor Osei Akoto, another of the Asantehene's senior linguists and age 92 when I spoke with him, associated *ntamoba* with marriage and the payment of a fee by the husband-to-be to his future father-in-law. But other older Asantes, many of them outside of Kumasi proper, connected *ntamoba* not with rites of marriage but with rites of birth. Yaa Dufie of Effiduasi explained that "when you give birth to a child and you are going to name the child, the things that the father brings to the child after the naming are called *ntamoba*." Efua Tebiaa of Agogo provided a similar definition, along with some etymological detail. She suggested that the term comes from the phrase *tan a wo ba* (the father who has given birth to a child) and that, in order for a man to be recognized as *tan a wo ba*, he must meet certain financial obligations: "If the father gives birth to a child and he doesn't look after the child, and the child grows, and he wants to go for the child, he will be asked to pay all the expenses that the woman incurred in looking after the child."

While Efua Tebiaa's definition of *ntamoba* seems to bear some relation to the kind of exchange being acted out in the Bompata case, the two concepts are certainly not identical. One is related to the establishing of rights in a child and the other is related to the termination of those rights. In fact, I initially encountered only three oral accounts of *ntamoba* that parallel the meaning implicit in the Bompata case. In 1992 Ama Nyarko of Kumasi explained that if a man married a woman, had children with her, and did not take care of those children, the woman's family could remove the children from him. If the man then swore that the children should not attend his funeral, that is, that he was severing all connection with them, it was called *ntamoba*. Ama Nyarko did not link the term with any specific payment, just to the severing of a father's rights. Thomas E. Kyei, an Asante educator who worked with Meyer Fortes on the Ashanti Social Survey, remembers *ntamoba* in much the same way as Danquah reported it in 1928, as a sum "paid by the family to the father to signify that the father has been relieved of all the fatherhood responsibilities." Kyei recalled only one such case from his childhood in Agogo. "There have to be extraordinary circumstances," he explained, "for a father's rights in his children to be totally severed."

When I had nearly given up finding anyone who could help me make sense of the Bompata case, I stumbled upon a man whose definition of *ntamoba* not only paralleled the meaning implicit in that case, but derived from his own personal experience. Kwame Nkansah, a 90-year-old man living in Agogo, explained: "You have given birth to a son. You have raised him and then he says he will not serve you. Then you have to get *ntamoba*. You will get it from his family." He recalled being told as a child that *ntamoba* was demanded of his family. His grandmother had given birth to his mother and an uncle. Instead of serving their father, the two went to stay with their uncle in Akyem. "When they came back," he recalled, "the father said, no, he would not respond, and they asked why. He said now they know where they come from, and he will demand *ntamoba*. He demanded [from the family] £3 for each of them."

Aberration or Artifact:
Historicizing the Conflicting Fragments

So what is one to make of these conflicting and contradictory definitions—*ntamoba* as any number of marriage payments, *ntamoba* as a rite connected with birthing and naming, and *ntamoba* as marking the termination of a father's rights in his offspring? That the definition of *ntamoba* as a marriage payment to the wife's father was widespread in Kumasi, especially around the Asantehene's court, and that the definitions closest to the Bompata case seem to derive, like the Bompata material, either from Asante Akyem or from Akyem itself, may suggest that the inconsistencies here are simply geographical. This simple formulation, however, would not explain why many older, long-time inhabitants of Agogo (Asante Akyem) unequivocally define *ntamoba* as a marriage payment, or why the informants in M. J. Field's 1938 study in Akyem offered similar testimony. The problem may, indeed, be one not simply of location but of time and of social rank. What happens if, rather than dismissing the 1921 Bompata case as local aberration, we investigate it as archival fragment, as historical artifact?

First of all, we should recognize that the multiple definitions emerging in both oral and written sources are not entirely disconnected. They all seem to share an underlying concern for a husband/father's reciprocal obligations and rights vis-à-vis his wife's and/or his children's family, or *abusua*. All these definitions situate *ntamoba* as a mechanism through which an *abusua's* relationship with the husbands/fathers of its members is mediated. That the connections among definitions may be quite close—indeed, that they may begin to collapse one upon the other with closer inspection-is suggested by Akua Senti's remarks:

> You see, normally they do the [marriage] rites twice-once for the uncle and once for the father. In fact, the one for the father is called *ntamoba*. In the olden days, about a week after a child is born, a father will name the child. If a girl, he will give her a cloth to lie on. It is called *ntam*. So when it is time for the girl to get married, and the man is doing the rites, the man will pay back the father's *ntam*, that which the father paid when he was naming the child, his daughter.

For Senti, all of *ntamoba's* definitions seem to boil down to one transactive meaning. Indeed, it may be useful for the moment to take this sort of generic notion of *ntamoba* and situate it among the fragments of evidence we have regarding a father's rights in and obligations toward his children in the pre-colonial and early colonial periods. This process may provide at least some clues to the disappearance of *ntamoba* from the historical record. And what do we know of fathering in pre-colonial Asante? Our best sources on a father's rights remain the works of the anthropologist R. S. Rattray. Admittedly, Rattray paints a picture of the "Ashanti father" in a rather normative, unchanging world. However, his early twentieth-century informants do open an important window onto the last half of the nineteenth century. Much of Rattray's presentation on the "status and position of the Ashanti father," as he terms it, consists of quotes from "fathers and mothers and uncles themselves" and those individuals were drawing on experience from the last decades before colonial rule. From them we learn that, while it was expected that children, especially sons, would live with their father once they passed infancy, a father by no means owned his children. He could not pawn them, and they could be removed from his care by the uncle, should the father be "too poor to bring up the child properly." One informant reported, "A father has no real [legal?] power over his grown-up children. If they wish to go to their *abusua* [blood] he cannot prevent them." While a man passed on his *ntoro* (spirit) to his children, was responsible for naming them and, at the other end of the life cycle, his children were responsible for providing a coffin upon his death, obligations and rights over the intervening years were not rooted in notions of absolute ownership or final authority. In short, a father was expected to raise his children, to discipline them and to train them; in turn, he could expect to be served by them, but under no circumstances did he own them.

Ntamoba in its generic form makes complete sense in the late nineteenth/early twentieth-century framework sketched above, particularly if life cycles are drawn into the picture. It seems to articulate the kind of exchange in marriage and parenting whereby a husband/father and an *abusua* entered into an ongoing process of transacting responsibilities for rights of use. We can see, for example, that a father's right of access to his children was initiated with his completion of the rites of naming. As a result of naming his child, the father accepted the responsibility for training her/him. He now had certain legitimate duties toward and claims upon the child that the child's mother and her *abusua* were bound to recognize. If, after the child had reached an age when he/she should be serving the father and did not, the father could demand the return of *ntamoba* in compensation, because he had met his obligations, but was being denied his rights of use, either by the child's behavior or by a decision of the *abusua*. Paternal obligations and rights, therefore—the father's connection with his child's *abusua*—could be terminated by the father demanding and receiving *ntamoba* or by the mother's family offering and the father accepting *ntamoba* as indemnification. Finally, we can see *ntamoba* mediating the relationship between a father and the man his daughter intended to marry. This may be seen as the penultimate manifestation of *ntamoba* in the life cycle of a father/daughter relationship, the final one being the daughter's obligation to contribute to the cost of her father's coffin. In this context the father, as *banintan a wo ba*, as the one who parented this girl child, was compensated by the husband-to-be and, in turn, was now released from any obligation to his daughter. The primary reciprocal relationship (obligations in exchange for rights of use) involving the daughter would now be between her *abusua* and her new husband (who in some senses replaced the father). Of course, what is particularly interesting about this transaction is its gender specificity. There was nothing similar to mark a transformation in the father's responsibilities toward and rights of use in his grown son. Indeed, much of the evidence we have suggests that a father's reciprocal relationship with his son and his son's family was far more enduring than that with his daughter. A father, according to Rattray, was supposed to find a wife for his son and pay the "head-money" for him. "The father will give his son a *dampon* (sleeping room) ... and a *pato* ... in which the wife will cook. He will stay with his father until his father dies, and then may go to his own uncle." In other words, a father's active reciprocal relationship with his son/son's *abusua* was maintained throughout the father's lifetime. That with his daughter and her *abusua* virtually ended with the daughter's marriage, the only remaining service due being the daughter's obligation to help pay for her father's coffin.

The generic *ntamoba* that I have interpolated into Rattray's early twentieth-century evidence gives us some sense, normative though it may be, that ownership of children in Asante was supposed to rest firmly with their *abusua*. A father's rights in his children were supposed to be rights of use only, despite the fact that a child, particularly a male child, might spend his entire life in his father's house. That a father's rights of use were so defined is best evidenced by the fact that a father could not pawn his children, though he could receive them in pawn. That his rights, moreover, were temporally circumscribed is evidenced in the role of *ntamoba* in his daughter's marriage. Over the course of a life cycle, a father's rights of use in and his duties and obligations toward his children changed according to the children's age and gender. *Ntamoba*, we can hypothesize, may have been transacted in many forms, but its basic role as definer and mediator of paternal obligations and rights of use appears remarkably consistent, from naming to marrying. Indeed, these dynamic and complex processes of exchange seem much less confusing when one recalls the proverb *Gyadua si abontene ne hi wo fi*. We are reminded, quite simply, that in a normative world "the *gyadua* [tree] stands in the street, but its roots are in the house."

The Disappearance of *Ntamoba* and Transformations in the Family Economy of Child-Rearing

And so what happened? How and why did this notion of *ntamoba* disappear from the historical record? Unfortunately, Rattray provides us with few clues. Though he gives us a late nineteenth and early-twentieth century canvas from which to speculate, the picture he paints has no historical dimension and conveys little sense of place—social or geographical. It is worth noting briefly, moreover, that, of all the roles and relationships Rattray investigated during his time in Asante, fatherhood and fathering were among the most troublesome for him, and he ended up relying far more on direct testimony than on his own observations and analysis when he put together his chapter on "Father and Children" in *Ashanti Law and Constitution*. It is clear that Rattray had a very difficult time getting past his own notions of the "natural" father and the "natural" affinity between fathers and their children in this section of his work. For him, matrilineal affiliations were "man-made," while a father's role was original, essential. This is particularly evident in the last paragraphs of his discussion:

> *Patria potestas* in Ashanti dwindles to rather vague unsubstantial claims, based on the natural, no less than the supernatural, forces at work in his favour, but opposed by all the man-made customary laws of the tribe.... It would perhaps not be far from the mark to suggest that an Ashanti passes through two distinct periods in his life: childhood and youth, which are spent with the natural father, to whom he gives a natural obedience and affection; these are later to be weakened by the materialistic and kindred considerations which are to draw him ever farther from his natural parent and towards his uncle...

It is not implausible that Rattray may have missed the mark here. *Ntamoba*, already declining in social importance, may not have been visible to him or to his European contemporaries because their understanding of fatherhood was rooted so firmly in essentialized notions of natural rights and affinities, of natural ownership eroded by materialist matrikin. But if we can, for the moment, accept the basic premise that *ntamoba* existed at some time in some parts of Asante (but that European writers, for whatever reasons, could not always "see" it), then how may we begin to explain, historically, its disappearance from certain parts of the social fabric?

I would like to propose here a two-stage hypothesis that attempts to foreground time and social place/status as key variables in explaining the disappearance of *ntamoba*. The first stage is based on the postulation that *ntamoba* is of great antiquity, that as a mechanism for mediating the relationship between a man and his wife/children's *abusua* it may very well date back to the creation, in the fifteenth and sixteenth centuries, of the great Akan matriclans. Ivor Wilks has argued, quite convincingly, that we can associate the emergence of the *abusua-kese* (big lineage) with the clearing of the forest and the development of food crop cultivation. The matriclans, quite simply, served to "facilitate the assimilation of strangers and ... of the unfree labor being drawn into the forest country." Yet the labor necessary during peak periods in the cycle of cultivation (the felling of large trees or the clearing of land) required co-operation among several domestic groups. That co-operation, Wilks argues, was "the most common between groups linked by marriage: that is, that a man obtains the help of his wife's brother (and thereby often procures the services of his own grown son)." *Ntamoba*, I would suggest, makes complete sense in this framework as a way of mediating and articulating a father's access to the labor of his wife, his children and their *abusua*.

But does *ntamoba* continue to make sense, as we move from Asante's immediate protohistorical period (*firi tetemu*) to the historical? The answer is—for some, yes, but for others, no. The emergence of the Akan state (*oman*) coincided with the emergence of specific social groups or classes for whom *ntamoba* would have made little sense. Again, Wilks's work on Asante's early history provides some important clues. In "Founding the Political Kingdom," he argues for the critical role of entrepreneurs ("big men" or *aberempon*) in the founding of the early Akan state. "Those who controlled the production and sale of gold," he proposes, were those able to procure a supply of unfree labor. Those who procured unfree labor were those able to create arable land within the forest. Those who created the arable were those who founded the numerous Akan polities. We see, in other words, a class of Akan entrepreneurs emerging: a class of those able to use the strength of the world bullion market and the availability of labor locally (whether through Wangara or Portuguese suppliers) in such a way as to create the new agrarian system. The descendants of these early developers became the nobility, the *adehyee* of the state, and were distinguished from both free settlers (*amanmufo*) and from the unfree. Many from among this latter group, Wilks hypothesizes, were incorporated into Akan society as members of the *gyaasefo* ("the people of the hearth"), who were the servants of the nobility. Certainly, for the nobility and for the unfree, *ntamoba* could not mediate transactions surrounding marriage and child-rearing in the same way it did for free-born commoners. For example, the slave wives of an *oberempon* gave birth to children who were incorporated into their father's lineage, not into the lineage of their mother, who was considered kinless. While *ntamoba* as a marriage payment to the *oberempon* father may make sense here, little else does, for the father and his royal lineage quite clearly owned such children and had rights over them that a male commoner married to a female commoner simply did not. The meaning of patrilineality, in other words, had to become class/rank-specific. I would like to suggest, therefore, that the first stage in *ntamoba's* fracturing and eventual disappearance coincided with the emergence of the state in the Akan forest. While *ntamoba* could continue to articulate the ongoing exchange between a common man and the *abusua* of his free wives and children, it was obsolete in the realm of power, wealth and privilege in which both *aberempon* and *gyaasefo* operated.

Certainly *ntamoba* would not have been the only social transaction reconfigured or even undermined by the emergence of the Akan state. Adultery (*ayerefa*) may provide an interesting parallel. We know from our very earliest sources that, among commoners, when a man's wife had a sexual connection with another man, the husband was entitled to a small compensation (*ayefare*). The case was considered a domestic matter (*efiesem*). To have a connection with the wife of an officeholder, however, was a crime against the state (*oman akyiwadie*) and compensation was awarded based upon the rank of the man whose sexual rights in his wife had been violated. Compensation could range from a substantial quantity of gold to capital punishment for the offender, the wife and members of her family. Adultery compensation came to reflect and articulate power relations within the Asante state. *Ntamoba* may have been reconfigured in similar ways. For those with power, it seems to have become a simple marriage payment, but for commoners it probably continued as an important mechanism for transacting exchanges between a husband and his wife/children's *abusua* well into the nineteenth century. That the meaning of *ntamoba* may have been class/rank-specific for a very long time could very well explain why those so close to the Asante court today insisted on *ntamoba's* exclusive rendering as a marriage payment, while those further from the court, both in physical distance and in terms of social identity, were more likely to posit a range of definitions, including the one so central to the 1921 Bompata case.

But, that particular case notwithstanding, by the time we reach the restoration of the Asante Confederacy Council in 1935, if not decades before, *ntamoba* clearly exists only in a rare, vestigial form and primarily as a type of marriage payment. Even among commoners we have only scant evidence of its existence. Why? It is my speculation that *ntamoba* vanishes among commoners in the late nineteenth and early twentieth centuries for the same reason it was reconfigured among Asante's ruling classes hundreds of years before. To put it quite simply, *ntamoba* no longer made sense for anyone—rulers or ruled, noble or commoner. And it no longer made sense because a commoner father's rights in his children, like an *oberempon's* rights over his non-free children, had become inalienable. His role vis-à-vis his children had been transformed from one of rights of use bound to reciprocal obligations to one of outright ownership. His relationship to his offspring was no longer part of a complex process of exchange with their *abusua*. It stood alone as fact; it no longer worked as process. In this new configuration, how could a father be compensated for the loss of use rights in his children when those rights had been transformed into rights of ownership that were, at once, inalienable?

The forces behind this more recent transformation are undoubtedly many and multivalent and a full account would require a detailed social history of Asante's late nineteenth- and early-twentieth-century past. What we can do is identify areas worthy of investigation on the basis of existing evidence—evidence gathered primarily from customary court records, missionary and government documentation and personal narratives. These sources suggest that we should look closely at (1) the impact of cocoa and cash on Asante family economy, (2) the ideological influence of missions on Asante conceptions of marriage and family, and (3) the specific effects of schools and school fees on family economy. These areas of investigation are far from discrete; they overlap and are mutually constitutive. However, for the sake of clarity and organization in this brief discussion, it may be useful to treat them separately.

That cocoa and the broad-based exchange economy that followed in its wake upset the "old order of economic relations between wife and husband," as Katherine Abu has written, would be disputed by few. The relations of production in cocoa seemed to erode, though certainly not destroy, Asante notions of matrilineal inheritance and to lend primacy to economic relations among members of the conjugal family. As Gareth Austin and others have shown, the labor necessary for the initial expansion of cocoa into Asante came "very largely from established, non-capitalist sources," including "farmowners themselves, their families, their slaves and pawns, co-operative groups of neighbors and, in the case of chiefs, *corvée* labour provided by their subjects." After the abolition of slavery and of pawning in 1908, wives' and children's labor became increasingly important, particularly for the establishment of farms on the cocoa frontier. By the end of World War I there was little land available for cocoa cultivation around Kumasi or to its south and east, so the industry began to spread westward, and in these frontier areas, particularly when farmers had little access to cash, there was heavy reliance on the labor of wives and offspring. Quite early, therefore, the conjugal-centered nature of the labor process on the cocoa frontier pitted wives and children against their husband's/father's matrikin. The labor invested in husband/father's cocoa farm could yield no long-term security, since the husband owned the farm and product and fully controlled the proceeds, and members of his matrilineal family, by Asante customs of inheritance, were to succeed to the property.

Throughout the first decades of the twentieth century wives, children and, at times, even husbands challenged matrilineal inheritance on the grounds that wives' and children's labor investment in a cocoa farm contributed to the husband/father's wealth. Many argued for the right of wives and children to inherit at least a portion of the estate. At times, husbands willed cocoa farmers to their wives or children to prevent their matrikin from inheriting the property and in acknowledgement of the labor invested by their conjugal family. Many women and children were not so fortunate, however, and their experiences mirror those of Akua-Addae of Tafo, who, with their daughters, assisted her husband on his cocoa farm for many years. When he continually refused to give them even a portion of the farm, or to include such provision in his will, Akua divorced him. "I would not continue to marry him," she recalled. Personal reminiscences like these make it abundantly clear that cocoa and the exchange economy did not automatically lead to the destruction of matrilineal inheritance, and Christine Okali is certainly right to argue that much in "male-female interactions [is] still determined by matrilineal kinship ideology and practices." But surely something was fundamentally transformed within the conjugal family economy when joint labor produced a cash crop for sale and not food for consumption! A woman's labor (not to mention that of her children), as Roberts suggests, was now compensated "only in the continued obligation of her husband to provide part of her subsistence from his own earnings." The reproduction of the family was now based in production and exchange, and the husband/father became the central, mediating figure through whom the value of wives' and children's labor was realized.

Most European social scientists in the mid-twentieth century recognized that cocoa had done much to alter the family in Asante. Meyer Fortes, after completing work on the Ashanti Social Survey of 1945-46, argued that cocoa, among other things, fuelled the tendency "to leave property to children instead of nephews and nieces." But Fortes, like Danquah in discussions of Akyem Abuakwa, believed that ideological forces were at work as well, that missionary activity was as important a force for change in inheritance patterns as cash cropping. Although we are only beginning to understand the complex and conflicting ways in which missionary activity impacted on Asante life (and

Asantes, in turn, shaped mission efforts), few would deny that most missionaries came with clear ideas about the importance of the conjugal unit and of the centrality of the father to that unit. All mission groups active in Asante in the early twentieth century encouraged their members to marry under government ordinance, which limited a husband to one wife, made divorce much more difficult and entitled a wife to one-third of her husband's estate and children to one-third of their father's estate. (The matrikin were left with one-third.) The Wesleyan Methodist Mission Society, for example, one of the more active in the region, reported in 1931 that all its African ministers were married under the ordinance, as well as all its trained catechists and most of its teachers and circuit agents. Yet how to encourage ordinary members of the church to marry under the ordinance remained a difficult task, and much of the Methodist mission effort in the early 1930s seems to have been devoted to facilitating this process. C. Eddy, who taught at Wesley College in Kumasi, pleaded with mission headquarters in the late 1930s for permission to bring his wife and young twins to Kumasi. He argued that their presence would serve as an example "that we hope to set to our staff and students of Christian family life" and that it would provide a place where students from the neighboring girls' school (Mmofraturo) could receive training.

Eddy's remarks highlight the importance of education in the missionaries' ideological battle against Asante marriage. The success or not of that battle is very much an open question, although the evidence I have encountered suggests that missions were not particularly effective in their struggle against Asante customs of marriage. But what did reach from the mission school right into the web of crisscrossing obligations and rights within the family were school fees. Although a much more narrowly defined field of investigation than cocoa or missionary ideology, school fees, I would argue, cut right to the heart of daily negotiations over child-rearing. Indeed, nearly every older Asante with whom I spoke in the 1990s mentioned school fees—for boys and for girls—as a never-ending source of conflict between mothers and fathers. A focus on this new family expenditure, therefore, can lend important insight into transformations within family economy, particularly in the changing rights and obligations of fathers. Before the advent of mission schools in Asante, a father was responsible for the training of his children, particularly his sons. It is not surprising, therefore, that, when mission schools and fees entered the picture in the early twentieth century, most understood the fees to be the responsibility of the father. But a father's cash expenditure on education could not simply replace a father teaching a son, for example, to farm or to hunt. It brought with it an assumption of greater rights of use in, and perhaps even ownership of, children. In other words, cash investment in a child's education transformed a father's role within his conjugal family. We can catch glimpses of this process in a 1936 case heard before the Asantehene's Divisional Court B. Kwasi Quansah filed suit against R. A. Mensah for £100 damages. He claimed that his daughter, Mary Quansah, while engaged to another man, was impregnated by Mr Mensah, a teacher at his daughter's school in Kumasi. The future husband subsequently refused to marry Quansah's daughter. The £100, according to the plaintiff, represented the expenses he had incurred as a result of supporting his daughter through her pregnancy and after the birth. They also reflected the fact that the defendant had "spoiled my daughter's school time," thus adversely affecting her future economic well-being. In many ways the facts of this case are telling. Mr Quansah filed the suit alone; no representatives of Mary's matrikin were present. None, apparently, assisted her during her pregnancy. Moreover, unlike the daughter in Rattray's account, who was trained in her father's house, served him and then went off to marry, Quansah's daughter went to school. Quansah had invested heavily in her education and appeared to exercise full rights of ownership over her. As a result of the pregnancy, his cash investment in her future had been jeopardized, so he sought legal recourse.

Kwasi Quansah was certainly not alone. Colonial era documentation, from customary court records to district commissioner diaries, is replete with stories of individuals seeking recompense amidst the chaos and conflict generated by the factors highlighted here: by cocoa, mission ideology or the simple introduction of school fees. The testimony recorded in those cases provides invaluable insight into the ways in which broad social forces could play out in an individual's life. The judgments, moreover, allow us to look for trends, for changes in so-called "customary law" in colonial Asante. For our purposes here, they provide an important, though tentative, index of social change. For example, reviewing cases from the very earliest pre-1924 volumes through World War Two, we see a gradual trend in the kinds of judgments rendered in child custody/child support cases—a trend away from insisting on the reciprocity of a father's rights and a father's obligations to the recognition of paternal rights independent of the fulfillment of any obligations toward wife and/or children. The very earliest of these recorded cases (before 1910) were heard before colonial officials who seemed to be utterly confused. They understood that children "belonged to the mother's family," but were in complete disagreement among themselves over what that meant in terms of a father's rights. An incident in 1906-07 in which the Adansi *omanhene* claimed the child of a deceased Adansi woman on behalf of her family demonstrates the depths of misunderstanding and discord among British officials. The woman had been married to an Assin man, and the man refused to give up the child. The Adansihene demanded the child's return. For months colonial officials forwarded reports and traded minutes on Asante "customary law" regarding ownership of children. Virtually no one agreed with anyone else. Unfortunately the case disappears from the historical record before a judgment was rendered.

After 1924 and the implementation of the Native Jurisdiction Ordinance in Asante, colonial administrators empowered chiefs and their councilors to rule on "custom," so it is after 1924 with the establishment of native tribunals throughout the region that we encounter a wide range of customary court documentation that allows us to chart changes in so-called "customary law." Certainly, from the very beginning of this period, we see numerous cases in which native tribunals ruled on inheritance cases in favor, at least partially, of a wife's and/or children's claim on a husband's/father's estate. These cases reflect a growing social tendency to recognize an inalienable connection between fathers and children. In child custody/child maintenance cases, however, a noticeable change in judgments occurs more slowly and less dramatically. Many of the judgments from cases of the late 1920s and early 1930s seem to echo what we know of rights in and obligations toward children in the pre-colonial period. In these cases reciprocity was upheld. For example, in Kwadjo Safo v. Kwame Antwi, et. al., the plaintiff claimed

£100 in damages from his wife's family because, as he testified, "they had deprived me of my children." When subsequent testimony proved that the father had not supported his children over the years, the plaintiff was non-suited with costs "in that his action is inconsistent with Native Customary Law."

Other cases, particularly as we move toward the Second World War, were less likely to enforce reciprocity and therefore more likely to uphold paternal rights independent of paternal duties. Ama Manu v. Kwasi Buo is a case in point. Here Ama Manu claimed £8 5s 0d in maintenance and subsistence from her ex- husband. She testified that she had been married to the defendant's brother, but that the brother had gotten quite sick and was unable to support her and their children. She asked for a divorce, but his family asked her to wait. When her husband died, his brother agreed to take her as his wife. "Nine months passed," Ama testified, "and nobody subsisted me and so some man had sexual connection with me." Kwasi Buo then demanded that she name the offender, so he could collect an adultery payment. In his defense Kwasi Buo argued that he was "not liable to pay any subsistence or maintenance fee to her, especially as her husband was sick and she was misconducting herself with other men." The court ruled against the plaintiff, finding that her "behaviour toward her sick husband" meant she was "customarily not entitled to any subsistence by the defendant." The judgment in this case is particularly telling because the reciprocity in earlier cases is simply not enforced here or, from another perspective, is enforced but in one direction only. Ama's and her children's right to subsistence was made dependent upon Ama's fidelity. Paternal rights, however, stood alone. They did not rest on the ability or the willingness of either her first husband or his brother (second husband) to provide Ama and her children, with subsistence.

In cases like this, and countless others, *ntamoba* makes absolutely no sense, because paternal rights were, at once, severed from paternal duties and transformed from rights of use to inalienable rights of ownership. Indeed, a father's relation to his child and to his wife's and children's *abusua* resembled nothing less than the relations that prevailed in pre-colonial and early colonial times, when a father held his child as a pawn—a practice technically outlawed by the British in 1908. As Rattray wrote, a father could not pawn his child, but he could receive the child as a pawn from the child's *abusua*. When this occurred, a different set of rights and duties was conferred upon the father. He was now entitled to half of any profits made by the child and he had a "legal right [inalienable right?] to the child's services and ... might take him away without asking the permission of the *abusua*." In the case of a pawned daughter, the father's role in any marriage arrangements became paramount. He received the largest share of the *aseda* (thank-you offering) and retained "more control over the daughter than either the husband or the woman's *abusua*" after the marriage. A father also became responsible for half his child/pawn's debts. A father was not liable for the debts of his free child (*adehye wo*). These points are particularly important because we begin to see customary courts of the post-1924 period rendering judgments that uphold, in quite explicit ways, the sorts of rights and duties that were associated with fathers and pawn-children—but long after the abolition of pawnage, when all children, at least in the eyes of the law, were freeborn. For example, in the 1929 case between Akosua Adae and Kwaku Ahindwa, the plaintiff complained that her ex-husband was not paying the debts incurred by their children. The court ultimately ruled that Ahindwa could have no "right of commanding his children" until he paid half the debts incurred by his children. While the judgment in this case upheld some sort of reciprocity, it was the reciprocity of a father/pawn-child relationship, not that of a father and a freeborn child.

That pawnage, rather than being effectively abolished, became hidden within a changing family economy is certainly evident in the path-breaking works of Gareth Austin and Beverly Grier. Both scholars explore the ways in which pawnage became a means of mobilizing the labor of children and wives in the rapidly expanding cocoa economy of the early twentieth century. Indeed, Austin writes of the "feminisation" of pawning in Asante and Grier of a "coercive and exploitative precapitalist relationship ... [becoming] re-legitimized and harnessed to ... accumulation." Both, moreover, explore in some detail the payment of *tiri sika*—a marriage payment by which a husband loaned his wife's *abusua* a given sum of money. It was the payment of the *tiri sika* in the period before 1908 that rendered a freeborn wife essentially a pawn-wife. After 1908 the payment continued as one of a variety of marriage payments, but at least one missionary observer in the early 1930s reported that it was being increasingly emphasized in all marriage ceremonies as the "essential ceremony in a native marriage contract." Such an emphasis surely suggests that pawning and marrying were becoming overlapping systems of exchange, as were pawning and fathering. But what were the long-term implications of this overlap? What did it mean for fathers and mothers, husbands and wives, daughters and sons, that pawning was rearticulated in colonial family relationships? Because Austin and Grier trace pawnage as labor acquisition, they are not specifically concerned with the ways in which marriage and parenting, broadly speaking, were impacted. But the repercussions here, I would argue, were tremendous and enduring. As pawnage was collapsed into the categories of son, daughter and wife, rights, duties and obligations in Asante were broadly recast. The rights of the colonial father/husband became the rights of the nineteenth-century pawn-holder. And those rights, in turn, became increasingly detached from reciprocal obligations and duties. We need to connect the final disappearance of *ntamoba* in Asante, therefore, with the conflation of subordinant categories or, more specifically, with wife/pawn, daughter/pawn, son/pawn. That *ntamoba* survived in Asante only in a vestigial form, as a marriage payment from son-in-law to father-in-law, makes sense in this context. Only in this form did *ntamoba* not challenge or undercut the inalienable rights of ownership of the colonial Asante father. As a one-way marriage payment from son-in-law to father-in-law, it was given in recognition of all that the father had endured in raising the child and marked the moment wherein (certainly not the process whereby) the daughter/pawn became wife/pawn, as well.

Concluding Thoughts:
Matriliny, Patriliny, and What's Lost in Between

Some of the social processes described in this chapter have been treated elsewhere, largely by anthropologists, who have tended to frame the discussion in terms of an inevitable, ongoing battle between matrilineal and patrilineal tendencies in Asante society. Rattray ruminated on the *ntoro* (spirit) inherited from one's father v. the *mogya* (blood) one inherited from the mother. Fortes described a "submerged descent line" and cast the matri- v. patri-battle in terms of continued efforts to "adjust the jural and moral claims and bonds arising out of marriage and fatherhood to those imposed by matrilineal kinship." But, "left to itself," Field predicted for Akyem, matrilineality would "die a natural death." What these sorts of discussions have in common is a tendency to view domestic power as part of a zero-sum game, with patrilineal forces of the twentieth century inevitably prevailing over the matrilineal. In other words, if matrilineality and avuncular power eroded or diminished, then patrilineality and the power of the father must have increased by precisely the amount the other decreased. This equation does not get us very far and obscures much that is going on. The evidence we have surrounding the disappearance of *ntamoba* in fact suggests that a society like Asante can be tenaciously matrilineal and at the same time display an increasing degree of patriarchal power—and I use "patriarchal" here in its most literal sense as "rule by the father."

That matriliny could accommodate growing patriarchal power should come as no surprise. Anthropologists and historians alike have long understood the incredible flexibility of matrilineal organizations. Wilks, in particular, makes a convincing case for locating the very origins of matrilineality in an Akan agrarian revolution that required a flexible mechanism for mobilizing and incorporating vast numbers of unfree laborers into an expanding agricultural society. The subsequent emergence of the Akan state (*oman*) and increased social differentiation based on wealth and political power did not render matrilineal organization obsolete. Indeed, Douglas's 1969 conclusion that matriliny is not necessarily doomed by increasing wealth still seems to hold more than a quarter of a century later. "Matriliny would be capable of flourishing in market economies," Douglas wrote,

> whenever the demand for men is higher than the demand for things. Because of the scope it gives for personal unascribed achievement of leadership, matrilineal kinship could have advantages in an expanding market economy. In my view

the enemy of matriliny is not the cow as such, not wealth as such, not economic development as such, but economic restriction.

But the flexibility or adaptability highlighted by Douglas and others requires historicizing. We must not mistake the durability of matriliny in Asante for immutability. For example, when we try to make sense of *ntamoba* in the context of a domestic economy of child-rearing in colonial Asante, we see fundamental transformations occurring in the power of husbands/fathers vis- a-vis their wives/children. These transformations occurred without undermining the basic structures of matrilineal kinship. This was no zero-sum game.

As a father's rights grew increasingly inalienable in colonial Asante, they were detached from any reciprocal obligations to his children. A father owned his children whether he provided them with subsistence or not. This transformation occurred at a time when the economic cost of rearing children, particularly as a result of school fees, was rising dramatically. That cost would not be integrated into an ongoing system of exchange between a father and his children's mother and their *abusua*. A father would not be obliged to meet them in order to retain his rights of use in his children. Indeed, there were increasingly fewer ways to encourage/force/persuade a father to view those costs as his obligation, because none of his actions or inactions could threaten his ownership of the children. Fatherhood was now a position endowed with inalienable rights; it was not something you did, that you negotiated via extended processes of exchange involving rights and service.

The implications of these developments were obviously far-reaching and even a brief consideration would take me well beyond the bounds of this chapter. It is, however, important to note in concluding that much of the burden of these profound transformations in the domestic economy of child-rearing fell quite squarely on the shoulders of Asante mothers. While some women were fortunate in that the their children's father assumed responsibility for school fees, provided funds for clothing and feeding those children and cared for them in their absence, others were certainly not so lucky: the fathers of their children did not contribute to subsistence, much less to school fees, yet what recourse was there? What pressure could be brought to bear? The obligation to parent (*-tan*) and to sustain children was now primarily a woman's alone. Thus the final disappearance of *ntamoba*—even with the sketchy bits of evidence we have—tells us much about the ways mothering in colonial Asante was transformed alongside fatherhood. Though by appearances Asante mothers were doing much what they had done in the nineteenth century—feeding, bathing and clothing their children—they were doing it in a world in which there were far fewer safety nets for them or for their children. It was a world in which more was expected but less was obliged. As eighty-year old Efua Sewaa of Tafo remarked, "You begot the child. You delivered that child. It is the duty of the mother, whether she likes it or not, to look after the child. An uncle, or aunt, or father, or anyone else, they just look after a child when they feel like it." Trying to make sense of *ntamoba*, if it achieves nothing more, should at least make us stop and reflect on statements like these. Are they mere essentialist ponderings on the inevitable and eternal burdens of motherhood, or have they been historically constructed in ways we should try to untangle?

Connecting with the Past, Building the Future: African Americans and Chieftaincy in Southern Ghana

SUSAN BENSON

The late Susan Benson was a Fellow at New Hall (Murray Edwards College), Cambridge University. As an anthropologist and social scientist, her work focused on matters of race and gender, especially with regard to West Africa and the African diaspora. The following essay was part of a larger project, before her death in 2005, where she had planned to combine the history of transatlantic slaving with the memory, real and imagined, of Africans in the American diaspora.

Introduction

In January 2003, Accra played host to a major international conference exploring questions of chieftaincy and governance across the African continent. Later in the same year, in August, the Panafest Foundation, supported by Asantehene Otumfuo Osei Tutu II, hosted what was billed as the first Conference of African Traditional Leaders in Kumase, bringing together chiefs from Nigeria, Togo and South Africa, as well as from every part of Ghana. Over three days of speeches and deliberations, many claims were made for the enduring importance of chieftaincy institutions both in maintaining cultural traditions in the face of social dislocation and in facilitating local development. At the same time the Ghanaian press continued to debate the implications of the five million dollar World Bank grant negotiated by the Asantehene for traditional authority capacity-building in the Ashanti region. The place of tradition and the role of traditional rulers in development, it seems, is suddenly very much on the political agenda.

Now it is a commonplace of contemporary scholarship that "tradition" conceals considerable invention. In this paper, however, I am dealing not so much with invention as with the effects of a deliberate and explicit innovation in Ghanaian traditions of chieftaincy: the incorporation of non-Ghanaians, especially African Americans, into the chieftaincy institutions of the Akan areas of southern Ghana. Many such individuals have been enstooled as *nkosuohene*, "progress" or "development" chiefs, a title initiated in 1985 by Asantehene Opoku Ware I and adopted widely both within and outside Asante at different levels in the hierarchy of traditional office-bolding. Some hold other titles. Public opinion in Ghana is sharply divided on the usefulness and appropriateness of this involvement and this is one of the themes of this paper. But I also wish to address the question of what such chiefs, few of whom are resident in Ghana, intend when they enter into such binding commitments. What is at stake here, I argue, is not only the question of how best to mobilize resources for local community development, nor even the broader question of building effective collaborative relationships between Africans of the Diaspora and those in the continent, between "those who left" and "those who stayed behind," as various informants put it. What such innovations and the debates occasioned by them also reveal is the interplay between the creative possibilities of contemporary transnational connections and the ongoing importance of particular and quite distinct historical understandings and political interests. In this paper, I begin at a rural community; I then examine the history of this institution as it has developed since 1985 before considering the factors that structure the institution today.

"We came to bridge the gap": Nana Yaa Twumwaa in Assin Nsuta

It is noon on a cool August Saturday, 2001, and I, along with several hundred others, am sitting on the Durbar ground in Assin Nsuta, one of the chain of Assin villages strung out along the Cape Coast to Kumase Road. We are there to witness the enstoolment of the Reverend Dr. Barbara King, founder and leader of the Hillside Chapel and Truth Center of Atlanta Georgia, as Nkosuohene of the Benkum Division of Assin Apimamin, of Nsuta, a small community of some 5,000 people, is the center. Around me are some of the 72 African Americans who have made the journey from Atlanta with Dr. King; for them, this is the climax of a whirlwind tour of Ghana lastly scarily seven days. Facing us are the people of Nsuta, while to our left, making up the third side of the square, are seats for the chiefs and their elders, as well as representatives of local government. At the center sits Nana Kwame Nkyi XII, paramount chief of Assin Apimamin, and his entourage. It is thanks to his visit to Hillside Chapel earlier this year that Dr. King is being enstooled.

We have been waiting for some time. Many of the Americans, bussed in early this morning from Coconut Grove Beach Resort where they are spending a couple of nights, are getting hungry and thirsty, but no one around me wants to buy the hardboiled egg and bread or the water that is on sale. Their tour guides have warned them that village food will make them ill. Suddenly there is the sound of drumming: the new *nkosuohene*, wrapped in *kente* cloth, is carried in a palanquin into the ground. Around her, in a great enfolding surge of movement, are Nsuta people and those of her own people who have accompanied her into the *ahenfie*, the palace, for the sequestered part of the ritual. Nsuta women are wearing "white" cloth, as is appropriate for the occasion; and so too are Dr. King's people. Theirs is truly resplendent—yards of white brocade, elaborate head ties, heavily embroidered shirts, much obviously bought specially for the occasion, outnumber the white t-shirts and trousers. As Dr. King is carried round the ground, radiant with the force of the occasion, those who are sitting around me get to their feet and join in too. The noise is terrific, the dancing energized. Then, as Dr. King is ushered to her seat the speeches begin. Nana Kwame Nkyi, to whom Dr. King must now swear her loyalty, announces her new name: Nana Yaa Twumwaa I, the name of the founder of the village: "Your name is rooted in the history of Asante, of which you are justifiably proud." He acknowledges that enstooling an African American as

nkosuohene is a controversial matter—"Some people are not comfort-
able with this institution"—but for him, it is a positive thing: "it is only
the misfortune of the slave trade which divided us." This sense of the
corning together of those who share a common identity is a theme too
in Dr. King's speech. As she says, "we came to bridge the gap"; "we
came home"; "we are together." At her request, the Hillside Chapel people get to their feet and face the Nsuta people: hands raised in front of
them, they spun round in a complete circle and in, unison call out "Na-
maskar Assin Nsuta! I salute the God within you!" Dr. King continues,
"We came to tell you that we are not tourists, we are you and you are
us! As pledge of her intentions, she donates $3,000 (21 cedis at 2001
rates) to initiate work on a new agricultural secondary school; plants a
tree on the site; and then, at the end of a long day, returns with her party
to Elmina and the luxurious quiet of Coconut Grove, to Accra, and then
to America.

Nana Yaa Twumwaa is one of three Africans of the diaspora honored
with chiefships in the Assin Apinamin area. One, Nana Essie Boah I,
Mrs. Minion Phillips, had been enstooled earlier in 2001 as Gyaasehema
of Apimamin, in recognition of her role in organizing the return of the
remains of Sister Crystal, one of the two African slaves whose ceremonial reburial at Assin Manso formed a central element in Ghana's first
Emancipation Day commemoration in 1998. The other, Professor
Brown, Nana Kojo Amuah I, formerly a lecturer at Cape Coast University and now resident in the United States, had been honored by Nana
Kwame Nkyi for his work in supporting educational projects in the area,
an area in which he continues to offer substantial assistance. Each case
is different, drawing upon different kinds of transatlantic connection,
focusing different ideas of engagement and offering different kinds of
benefits to the communities and individual protagonists involved. As
the material presented above suggests, there are a number of complex
agendas in play here: agendas that draw upon ideas of identification
and difference, of beneficial reconnection and of common purpose and,
perhaps most importantly, upon the linking of such common purpose
to ideas of a shared historical identity. There are also again, as the account of Nana Twumwaa's enstoolment indicates, questions that immediately arise around any simple notion that, as far as rural Ghanaians

and African American visitors are concerned, "we are you and you are us." Before, however, considering these issues as they play out in the contemporary context I want to look a little more closely at the history of the *nkosuohene* concept and its changing place in late twentieth century Akan political thought and practice.

Nkosuo in Kumase: An Innovation in the Traditional Manner

In contemporary Ghanaian public discourse there is a powerful strand that casts chiefship as heritage, a traditional institution valuable as a repository of enduring cultural and political values and currently besieged by the "batterings of modernity." It is not surprising, then, to find that objections to non-Ghanaian *nkosuohene* are often framed in terms of an unwarranted break with sacred tradition. However, an informed reading of Akan history would suggest, rather differently, that innovation is very much a feature of Akan political culture: institutions of governance always in motion, dynamic rather than fixed, resilient in the face of new circumstances. As Ivor Wilks (1998) has argued, it is important, then, to see the ways in which innovation may draw upon understandings of the past, and how key political concepts may thereby be subtly transformed, As Wilks demonstrates, ideas of *nkosuo*, progress, or—in today's preferred formulation, "development"—have been central to Asante political culture over the past century: but what work do such ideas do now, in the context of contemporary Ghana?

Significantly, it was in the course of the 1985 Golden Jubilee celebrating the 50th anniversary of the restoration of the Asante Confederacy that the then Asantehene Otumfuo Opoku Ware II announced his intention of creating an *nkosuo* stool. Such "invention" of chiefly office was no late twentieth century innovation: indeed, as the late Nana Antwi Buasiako pointed out to me, it has been customary for all Asantehene to set their mark on their reign by creating a new *okyeame* stool, and it is always open to them to create others, as Nana Opoku Ware's predecessors had on occasion done: "Every Asantehene can create the stool he likes." In fact Nana Opoku Ware himself created two other significant stools that reflected the changing nature of the *Asanteman* (the Asante nation) in the late twentieth century: the Aboafo stool, conferred upon a leading member of the Asante community in New York, and the Dwadwafo stool, similarly conferred upon a loyal supporter of the Golden Stool.

However, in the creation of the *Nkosuo* stool, Nana Opoku Ware was focusing renewed attention, albeit in a very different political and economic climate, not only on the needs of the future but also on the enduring legacy of the Asante past: on the politically weighted ideas of unity and progress foregrounded by his predecessor Asantehene Otumfuo Prempeh II in the context of the restoration of the Asante Confederacy 50 years before. This moment too had been explicitly signaled by the creation of a stool, that of *Nkobom*, unity. I use the term "signaled" advisedly. As Nana Buasiako again put it: "Nana Prempeh made the stool [*Nkobom*] *to show that he has made unification possible*" [my emphasis]. The creation of this new stool was not, in short, merely a mechanism for honoring a particular individual (the first incumbent, Nana Akwasi Boakye, was an individual recognized to have offered outstanding service to the Golden Stool) but was an act intended to set its mark on the times. Similarly with the *Nkosuo* stool: the intention was to focus and frame the attention of the Asanteman: it spoke of direction. Indeed, Nana Opoku Ware intended others to follow where he led, and urged that his own paramount chiefs as well as chiefs outside Asante should appoint such chiefs.

What, precisely, was the original purpose of the *Nkosuo* title? The first incumbent, E. K. Osei, was a wealthy businessperson, "very active in the service of the Golden Stool," from a family connected to the Palace. His task was "not to sit down" but "to go around the Paramountcies and report back" on questions of economic progress. The *raison d'etre* of the stool, then, was Nana Opoku Ware's concern with the future prosperity of Asante, and how best this might be achieved. In Kumase, *Nkosuo* was established as a division within the Gyaase (Household). After E. K. Osei's death, his stool was "blackened" (i.e., consecrated) and he was succeeded by his son, the current Ghanaian High Commissioner in Britain, Mr. Isaac Osei. Like *Nkobom* this was, in other words, no "honorary" stool but a *mmamadwa*: in the gift of the Asantehene but in the usual course of things "for the family: whether son or sister's son."

Nkosuo since 1985

In Kumase the *Nkosuo* stool was thus incorporated into the structure of palace offices—an innovation, so to speak, in the traditional manner. Outside Kumase, the title has been used less restrictively to draw those not eligible for chiefly office into the public life of their towns and villages: to recognize contributions made and elicit future commitment to community well-being. In an increasingly dispersed and globalized Asante nation, the office has undoubtedly served to tap into the resources and energies of Ghanaians living away from their home communities, elsewhere in Ghana or abroad. In this broader sense, *Nkosuo* chiefships could be seen as a kind of solution to dilemmas faced by traditional office-holders and their communities in the late twentieth century: how to bridge the gap between rural needs and urban resources, between those eligible for chiefly office and those with management and development skills, between traditional resource bases and new forms of wealth and accumulation. Nana Arhin Brempong (2001) and others have written cogently about the challenges faced by chieftaincy in the twentieth century: the ongoing crisis in funding the public responsibilities of office, the increasing volatility of succession disputes, and the growing importance placed upon managerial capacity and educational skills as well as upon personal wealth in the selection of a chief. Attracting a wealthy and dynamic *nkosuohene* is an appealing prospect for a chief wishing to take his community forward; as it is for one beset by financial difficulties. However, if *nkosuo*, in its original conception and in its association with *nkobom*, unity, focused very strongly on the idea of mobilization, of coming together to progress, in many cases— especially in the case of non-resident African Americans—it has come to acquire a narrower focus. As one divisional chief succinctly put it to me in discussing the proliferation of *nkosuohene* in the paramountcy he serves: "they come to donate."

Nearly 20 years after Nana Opuku Ware's declaration, it is clear that the *nkosuohene* position has developed in ways unthought of by its originator. Even within the *Asanteman* there are significant numbers of what one could call do-it-yourself Nkosuohene: village chiefs or sometimes even village elders who have acted upon an expression of interest or taken the initiative and approached an individual on their own account, rather than going through their divisional or paramount chiefs or informing the appropriate *okyeame* in the palace. Some *nkosuohene* have been selected because of their long association with a particular place, or their involvement in educational or development projects there, as was Nana Amuah in Assin Apimamin; others, like the Rev. Dr. Barbara King, have been chosen more speculatively for their potential as donors and mobilizers. Some enstoolments reflect the seriousness with which some chiefs and their communities take the institution and involve vetting by the male and female elders of the community, *aseda* fees, seclusion and instruction. Others are performed hastily in the course brief visits of a few days. In some cases, the new chief has been expected to supply the necessary regalia and cloth for his or her enstoolment, an outlay of many hundreds of dollars; in others cloth, regalia, the stool itself are given by the community—which again involves considerable expense—or might be loaned for the occasion.

Not all non-Ghanaian *nkosuohene* are Africans from the Diaspora. There are also British VSO workers or Gap Year students who have been enstooled in the villages in which they have worked, as well as businesspersons who have been awarded such titles in recognition of the assistance they have offered to particular traditional authorities. In 2002, a retired US army career officer, a dentist, was enstooled thanks to links between his Catholic congregation in Long Island and Wadie Adwumakaase Kese in Offinso north of Kumase. However, it is Africans of the Diaspora who predominate in the Akan areas, and these are recruited a multiplicity of ways. Sometimes connections are made through quite formal linkages at paramountcy level between Ghana, traditional area organization in the USA and prominent African American individuals. 1999, for example, Mamponghene Nana Osei Bonsu II enstooled three African Americans; all were important figures in public administration the USA and had attended the 1999 African American Summit in Accra, but the particular links between them and Mampong were said to have been activated by members of the Mampong royal family and the Mampong community, including their Nkobomhene, resident in the USA. In other cases, church connections are important and Ghanaians attending particular congregations in the US have "led" parties from those congregations to their home town or village. Others emerge from workplace contacts or personal friendship networks. Yet others develop in the course of a visit to Ghana in a manner that can only be described as opportunistic, from a chance encounter, or when individuals interested in "making a contribution" have been led to a particular community by professionals involved in the tourism industry.

Consider, for example, the diversity of bridging connections involved in the recruitment of African Americans into chiefship positions in and around Elmina, in the Central Region. As the site of the earliest and one of the historically most significant European fortifications on the Gold Coast, Elmina, together with its neighbor Cape Coast, regularly attracts a large number of Diasporic visitors and is home to a small but politically active community of settlers. One of the earliest of these, Mr. Ben Robinson, was enstooled as Safohene Nana Okofo Iture Kwaku Ababio I in the small fishing village of Iture in 1989 in recognition of assistance rendered. Subsequently his daughter too was enstooled in another part of the Central Region. Other developments were set in train by the late Nana Kojo Eduakwa IV, Akwamuhene of Edina. Nana Eduakwa had nieces and nephews living in the USA and visited there several times in the 1980s. In 1987 he accompanied them to the Bosom Dzemawodzi in New York, established by Nana Yao Opare Dinizulu, whose quest for his African roots had led him in 1965 to the Akonedi Shrine in Larteh and who, after training at the shrine, had established a centre for the worship of Akan gods and the promotion of Akan culture in New York. Nana Eduakwa invited members of Nana Dinizulu's organization to Elmina and led them to one of the Tigare shrines in the town, where his sister was the officiating priestess. One—who through the good offices of the shrine took both Tigare and Mmoatia back with her to the USA—was later enstooled (in 1988) as Nkosuohene in Atonkwa, his village just outside Elmina. Another was enstooled in Ampenyi, Nana's father's village, a little way down the coast. In the 1990s Nana Eduakwa was also centrally involved in the development of the Elmina elements of the biennial cultural arts festival Panafest. It is perhaps unsurprising, then, that Amperiyi later secured a second African American as chief, a university administrator from Maryland introduced there by Kojo Yankah, the Chair of the Panafest Committee. Ampenyi's third African

American chief, a Chicago businessperson and academic enstooled in 2002, arrived by a different route, when his daughter, recently married to an Elmina man, asked a friend to find him land for hotel development on the beach. Meanwhile connections made through another prominent Elmina family with a member resident in the American north-west secured a development chief for Kwaprow, just over the border in Ogua traditional area.

What all this indicates is the increasingly salience in the last third of the twentieth century of a whole series of interlocking spaces of contact and association that span the Black Atlantic. African American engagements with Ghana and Ghanaian engagements with America are of course as old as Ghana itself, and some of the actors now holding traditional titles have connections with Ghana stretching back to the 1960s. However, the past twenty years have witnessed not only the growth of an increasingly diversified African American settler population in Ghana—business people and retirees as well as political activists and those seeking reconnection with the culture of the motherland—but also the arrival of a much large number of short-stay visitors. It is estimated that 60% of Ghana's burgeoning tourism industry, now the country's third biggest source of foreign exchange, comprises visitors from the Diaspora. This not only reflects the rise in the USA, of a black middle class with money to spend but also the re-situating of all things "African" within the practices and politics of African American identity, a process in which Ghana has come to play an especially important role: as the home of Pan-Africanism, as the site of powerful kingdoms and their rich material culture and—as for Nana Dinizulu—as a place to explore "African spirituality." At the same time, the last third of the twentieth century witnessed a massive Ghanaian exodus not only to Britain, Germany, the Netherlands and other European countries but also to Canada and the USA. Akan civil society institutions are no longer encapsulated by the borders of the Ghanaian state; and Akan chiefship institutions now incorporate the Akan populations of the New World.

The NDC government that ruled Ghana between 1992 and 2001 was not slow to see the political and economic potential of such transnational connections. The development of Panafest, arguably increasingly oriented towards the Diaspora and especially towards an American audience, Rawlings' adoption of the more somber Caribbean celebration of Emancipation Day in 1998 and his enthusiastic endorsement of African American involvement in Ghana in the African American Summit in 1999 all attest to a lively awareness of the benefits to be reaped. But here I am concerned not with connections cultivated at the level of the state or of big business but with those mediated by the idiom of chief-ship and the idea of personal connection with particular places. Such engagements certainly speak the language of development, progress and coming together to build a better future that is the currency of government-led transnational initiatives. But they also promise a re-newed—and publicly recognized—incorporation into a heritage of which, in Nana Kwame Nkyi's words, one might be "justifiably proud": a recuperation, for African Americans, of a lost past.

The context in which the concept of *nkosuohene* is being set to work is thus located at the point of intersection of two very different historical trajectories and on a terrain defined by a number of distinct if overlapping political and cultural agendas. On the one hand, there is the ongoing historical trajectory of Akan chiefship and its changing character in the context of the colonial and post-colonial state. Critical here is the increasingly problematic and fractured relationship between chief, community and viable resources; critical too are local ideas of what chiefs are, what they are meant to do, and the difficulties faced by chiefs in meeting these expectations and obligations. On the other hand there is the historical trajectory of the African populations of the New World— a history in which things African occupy a complex and shifting space, and in which the politics of race and the politics of culture have become closely intertwined.

Disparity and Connection

The advantages for local communities in acquiring a non-Ghanaian *nkosuohene* are obvious. The resources of individuals are modest in comparison to those of the international donor agencies; nor in totality do they begin to approach the level of economic support generated by remittances sent from abroad by Ghanaians themselves. A couple of thousand dollars would be a large individual donation. But they go directly to the community concerned. "They send to the village," as one chief put it, whereas Ghanaians living abroad generally "send to their families." And, in comparison to NGOs, there is no money lost to Nissan Pajeros, no computers for staff in Accra offices, no money set aside for seminars and workshops on implementation. Such modest sums will restock a clinic, help build a school, buy books for a library. African Americans have also acted as mobilizers, finding sponsors for needy children's school fees, paying teachers' salaries, raising money for school equipment or medical supplies and researching ways to initiate small-scale development projects. It is precisely the ongoing disparity and disjuncture between Ghana and America that is being put to productive use here, with *nkosuhene* acting as a bridge across which resources—material or otherwise—can flow.

Some Diasporic African chiefs spend a considerable part of their year in Ghana, or visit several times a year, some have acquired or are planning to build houses in or near the communities in which they are enstooled, but most I have knowledge of visit Ghana for relatively short periods of time annually or even biennially. Some come with large parties on carefully planned tours, of which an important element will he one or two days visit to the "adopted village" of the party leader an opportunity for celebration, for consultation, for donations, or for physical participation in community projects. Few stay there overnight. Indeed many local people took it for granted that African Americans, like European *aburoni*, were incapable of drinking local water or sleeping in local houses without getting a testimony to the enduring power of colonial hygiene discourses.

Absenteeism of this kind has been the basis of some objections to non-Ghanaian *nkosuohene*. As all Ghanaians know, residence is no guarantee of effective leadership and absence does not necessarily mean disengagement. As for "sons of the soil," if some who live elsewhere neglect their communities, many others fulfill their responsibilities energetically. It is, nevertheless obviously true that African American chiefs are, on the whole, less likely to have long-standing relations with the communities in which they are enstooled than *nkosuohene* chosen from amongst the local population—or even than development workers accorded such titles. The discourse of natural kinship—"we are you and you are us"—as well as the sense of spiritual reconnection experienced by some Diaspora chiefs on their enstoolment or even on their first visit to their adopted community elide the fact that strangers can know little about outstanding disputes and local reputations. It is one thing to "come here and romance the chiefs," as one tough-minded *nkosuohene* put it is another to engage in the hard work, of learning Fante or Twi, understanding local priorities and getting to grips with the robust and intricate *realpolitik* of Akan political institutions. Some *nkosuohene* do not even attempt to try, like the man enstooled in Akyem who vanished never to be seen again, or Gary Byrd, an important figure in Panafest 1992, enstooled in the Central Region but apparently entirely inactive. None of the prominent individuals enstooled in Mampong in 1999 had returned by 2003, nor showed any sign of serious engagement, and were publicly roundly condemned as "useless" by the Mamponghene who was inclined to take a cynical view of their motives. Then there are those content to rely upon the good (or bad) offices of mediators and to visit for a day once every year or two with money, second-hand clothes and a default-mode donation of school supplies. Others, however, are well aware that they have a lot to learn and are encouraged to do so. Critical in this respect are the personal qualities of the Nkosuohene and his chief, be that a humble *adikuro* or an important traditional ruler, and their capacity to collaborate effectively in the interests of the population they serve.

If "bridging the gap" was important in some cases, in others that gap was seen as offering strategic advantage. As one Nkosuohene who now spends a good deal of her time in Ghana described her early experience: "people in some ways want you to stay foreign if you don't know the language you don't know what's going on, you can be controlled." Others had withdrawn from situations where, it became absolutely clear, the resources they had brought for football clubs, school development projects or—in one case the celebration of Kwanzaa by the village's children—were being diverted into other pockets; in one particularly difficult situation, to fund the construction of a fine cement-block house for the *odikuro* (as of my last visit in the summer of 2003, I am glad to say, still "under construction"). The possibilities of productive partnership are there, then, but so too are the possibilities of misprision, of wasted efforts and downright exploitation.

Culture and Politics

The material exchanges in the *nkosuo* institution are undoubtedly important. However, there are other resources at stake here, particularly among those whose decision to involve themselves in chieftaincy is only part of a broader political project of reconnection with the motherland. Consider here the picture presented by a cluster of development chiefs enstooled in the 1990s in Asante, Akyem and Kwahu, a loosely knit network of friends and fellow Afrocentrist scholars, many of them holding university posts in the USA. These include individuals now in their sixties who grew up in Georgia, South Carolina, Alabama, or New Jersey—in an America untouched by civil rights activism and who played and continue to play a salient role in the Black cultural politics of the US. These include Molefi Asante, doyen of Afrocentrist studies, who runs the African-American Studies department at Temple, enstooled as Kyidomhene Nana Okru Asante Peasah at Tafo in Akyem Abuakwa in 1995; and—perhaps the most important of these figures in the Ghanaian political context—Leonard Jeffries, former Director and tenured professor in the Africana Studies program at City University New York. A founding director and current vice-president of ASCAC (Association for the Study of Classical Civilizations), Jeffries first visited Africa with the Crossroads program over 40 years ago. His close association with Ghana specifically dates back to 1982 when Nana Akuoko Sarpong, paramount chief of Agogo in Asante, visited New York on behalf of the late King of Asante, Otumfuo Opoku Ware II to enstool a member of the Asante expatriate community as chief. Interest generated by the visit of the king himself for the opening of the *Asante Kingdom of Gold* exhibition in 1984 reinforced this link. It is at this point that City—and Agogo—became focal points in an emergent field of transnational social relations which endures for much of the NDC period: individual Asantes traveled to City to teach courses on textiles or dance, while, led by Professor Jeffries and others, African Americans came to Ghana to learn about Africa. In 1995 and 1996 Professor and Mrs. Jeffries and six others of their network were enstooled in Agogo with a variety of titles: as divisional chiefs, as Nkosuohene, as Nkobomhene and as Dompiahene. The Jeffries too have titles in Elmina, Leonard Jeffries in one of the Asafo companies, while Rosalind was enstooled by the Edinahene as "Chief of Education and Progress" in 2001. There are also plans to enstool one of his nephews as Nkosuohene in Anomabo, a site, like Elmina, critically bound up with the history of the Atlantic slave trade and where Jeffries now plans to develop a cultural center dedicated to the memory of the pioneering African American scholar John Henrik Clarke.

Then there is a younger cohort, now in their forties and fifties, whose activism was shaped by the turbulent conditions and social transformations of the 1960s and 70s. These include a number of individuals—Asa Hilliard, Na'im Akbar and Wade Nobles—closely involved with Association of Black Psychologists and particularly interested in addressing the corrosive effects of racism and the history of enslavement on the black psyche. Hilliard, Akbar and Nobles, for example, founded the Enyimyam Program, now in its ninth year, with the explicit aim of encouraging a positive reconnection with Africa through an engagement with Ghana; they lead yearly study groups to Accra, Cape Coast and Elmina and Kumase. Nobles was enstooled in 1996 as Nkosuohene at Akwasibo, in Kwahu, where he has been involved in some interesting small-scale projects as well as offering support for education; Akbar was enstooled in 1995 at the resonant but conflicted site of Abonu on Lake Bosumtwe. Hilliard and his wife have been more recently enstooled as Nkosuohene at Mankranso, part of the Kumasi division within Asante, where they have ambitious plans for local development. Dr. Patricia Newton, another member of this network, and also active in bringing parties to Ghana, is enstooled as Dompiahene in Agogo, where she is regarded as their most active non-Ghanaian chief. For each of these a visit to their "adopted" communities is part of the tour agenda.

To dismiss these individuals, as some Ghanaian critics do, as "tour guides" only interested in making money ("it is a business for them") would be too seriously to misunderstand their motivation. Most, as I indicate above, take their position as chief very seriously. They also, however, have a broader agenda. These are advanced with cultivating, securing and transmitting a particular vision of the Africa past, and present. This vision is reflected in the care taken in the structure and organization of their tours; in the literature they donate to village libraries; and in their plans and dreams for further projects. If, in Wade Nobles's words, "Ghana requires African Americans," Africans in America also require Ghana: "We didn't sell or give away our birthright—continental Africans are holding in trust our spiritual heritage for us.... Engagement with Ghana is not merely, then, a matter of establishing a channel along which material resources and technological knowledge can flow, it is also about recuperating and protecting a shared heritage upon which [the] future of both Africans in Ghana and Africans in America will depend. "The circumstances of history have broken up the African family ... the question is how to re-knit the ruptured psyche of the African world."

In important respects this vision marks a significant departure from the ideals of the modernizing Pan-Africanism that informed the politics of the first generation of American settlers in Ghana, men like Padmore and Du Bois, or, still living in Accra, Robert Lee, who came, in his words, "to build Ghana and to build Africa." For many—though not, of course, all—of those intellectuals, artists and professionals who looked to Ghana in the decade around independence the concern was to build an African modernity—a process—that would inevitably entail sweeping away "reactionary" forces and abandoning "backward" practices. In that older political tradition, the focus was firmly on the future, and race consciousness was invoked as the basis upon which individuals might be mobilized to come together and build it. Thus for Robert Lee, looking back at the failure of that Pan-African vision, Africans' commitment to particular histories and particular traditions was no asset but a major obstacle to achieving that kind of collective consciousness: "They're not into the skin game, they are into the culture game."

Now that idea of a Pan-African future is undoubtedly still important—indeed it is a central trope in all the public speeches made by Ghanaian public figures and by African American activists in the course of Emancipation Day and Panafest celebrations every year. Equally important is the idea of an Africa valued precisely as a container of the past: for its traditions, its time-honored institutions, and its moral and religious values—valued, in short, as living heritage precisely for its difference from a "developed"—and deformed—America. The focus, in short, is not solely or necessarily upon Ghana and the possibilities of economic progress, but also upon Africa as a cultural resource for both for Africans in America and for Africans on the continent, a resource that must serve as the basis upon which black pride and self-respect—especially masculine self-respect—will be forged and which can heal the wounds of colonialism and imperialism on the one hand and enslavement and racism on the other.

It is in this light that we should understand Molefi Asante's commitment to building a $1 million "Pan African Cultural Center" in Tafo: plans include a theater, an art museum, a traditional medical center, rural broadcasting facilities, performance space and seminar rooms, as well as a children's library. Hence also the importance of those memorable village encounters, when, fleetingly but seductively, gaps are closed and "we" indeed "are you" (if not "you" [are] "us").

Now this vision of what Africa in general and Ghana in particular represents for Africans of the Diaspora is also deeply attractive to many Ghanaians too, particularly in a context in which the economic hardships and uncertainties of the last third of the twentieth century have undermined confidence in the projects of modernity that dominated the independence period. For Nana Kobena Nketsia V, for example, Omanhene of Essiado Traditional area, African Americans' commitment to a traditional Africa is an important counterweight to the "misdirected elite that has run away from Africa ... provoking the Africans to think about themselves—to move us into our Pan-African identity that will save us." It certainly appeals to a position commonly described in Ghana as "traditionalist": more pragmatically it also appeals to traditional rulers seeking to maintain and reinforce the importance of chieftaincy in changing times. In this sense both Africans of the Diaspora and the traditional authorities and cultural brokers with whom they engage are drawn into what Bayart, in his astute account of the long-run characteristics of African state structures calls "extroversion": the creative deployment of external resources in the legitimizing and maintaining of internal political agendas. For both traditionalism in Ghana and cultural nationalism in the USA, ideas about the authenticity, rootedness and spirituality of Akan traditions are resources that can be drawn into localized political and cultural projects on either side of the Atlantic. In a more direct sense these connections are in and of themselves a resource: something that can be mobilized to demonstrate political and cultural capacity, the capacity to draw the other—whether that be Africa in America or America in Africa—into the personal ambit of the individual concerned. Chiefs demonstrate to their communities their connection to "outside"; the stool names of Diasporic Nkosuohene appear on web sites along with their publications, their lecturing engagements, and their professional biographies.

Dissenting Voices: "The spiritual links are not there"

This is not, however, to say that such alliances, and the view of history and identity upon which they rest, are uncontested. In the United States context, there are many other strands of African American politics: not all African Americans identify with an Africa of Kings, Queenmothers and chiefs, nor are all Ghanaians traditionalists. Indeed, as one Ghanaian intellectual put it to me, the demand that Ghana remain different is "a source of worry" to many: "We are supposed to live traditionally ... they have created images of Africa and want to find them." There is considerable irritation around Diasporic accusations that "'you people'—and at this point it is always 'you people'—are straightening your hair, wearing western clothes, wanting a western lifestyle."

Such conversations point to the limits of those powerful metaphors of unity and shared identity that play a central role in public narratives of connection between Africa and its Diaspora. It is worth pausing for a moment here to consider in more detail just how these ideas are being modeled. For many African Americans, what underpins these exchanges is the idea of natural kinship, of shared corporeal substance. In Nana Yaa Twumwaa's words, "We are you and you are us": a single people divided by a painful history but united in essence, now coming "home." For African Americans of this persuasion, the debate about "foreign" chiefs is mis-framed: they are *not* foreign, while the idea of European development chiefs is a contradiction in terms: how can people who are not Africans become African chiefs? In parallel fashion, chiefs with Diasporic Nkosuohene often invoke both the idea of home-place and of common kinship: in the words of the Tafohene, "we don't recognize him (Molefi Asante) as a foreigner but as a brother who has got lost and come back."

Others have a very different view of what constitutes the bonds of kinship—and, more particularly, of the importance of descent in circumscribing the participation of non-royals in chiefship institutions. Some traditional rulers as a result choose to make a sharp distinction between "honorary" chiefship titles—here meaning positions such as of *nkosuohene*—and what one could call the "real thing": an entitlement that rests on community of substance with those who have "gone before." As one individual put it to me: "These are not blackened (consecrated) stools. And they do not see the blackened stools of my family. That would be unacceptable."

Others see the issue in harsher terms. Eguafohene Nana Kwamina Ansah IV, for example, has both publicly and privately expressed his strong opposition to the involvement of Diasporic Africans: "An expatriate is not of royal birth…. My ancestors got rid of local murderers by selling them into slavery." Thus if a descendent of one of these came back and was enstooled "it would cause an unholy spiritual link with my ancestors." Such a chief would be "a pervert in our tradition ... the spiritual links are not there."

Paradoxically both African American ideas of racial unity and these controversial views of non-negotiable difference draw upon similar ideas of perduring and essential identity. It is a sense of the unalterable essence of what is transmitted from the past that informs both Nana Kwamina Ansah's opposition to the conferring of chiefship titles on those outside the *Ahenfie*, and in a very different way, African American ideas of natural kinship. One, however, focuses upon the idea of shared racial essence, fusing together "those who left and those who stayed behind" while the other draws upon a more particularistic idea of kinship, transmitted through blood (*mogya*) and encoded in descent. Neither, however, leaves any room for the idea of connection as process, or for prospective rather than retrospective ideas of common identity.

Yet as I have tried to demonstrate above, the successes and failures of these new chiefship arrangements have much less to do with questions of natural connection (or otherwise) than with the capacities of individuals and the collaborative relationships they can build. In this respect perhaps it is useful to focus on a rather different aspect of Akan traditions of personhood: the idea that character (*suban*) can be cultivated as well as inherited from ancestors, whether noble or base. In this the conferring of names, as is customary in the enstoolment of a chief, plays a critical part. To confer a specific name may involve the detection of observable qualities that link the original possessor to the namesake, but it is also intended to conduce resemblance: the identity between name and person shapes the *suban* of the one who bears it. In this sense, one might see the enstoolment of Diasporic chiefs as a space for the recognition and cultivation of *suban*, *suban* manifested in conduct (in Fante, *edze*; in Asante Twi, *abrabo*), in which present actions and prospective connections speak louder than the past: in other words as recognition of a future, as well as a past, of which, in Nana Kwame Nkyi's words, people might be "justifiably proud."

Conclusions

In 2003, two years after Nana Twumwah planted that tree in Assin Nsuta, the site was overgrown. Concrete blocks, bought for the new school, had appeared, then vanished. Also vanished were any references to Assin Nsuta or visits to Ghana on the web site of the Hillside Chapel, though Dr. King still chooses to describe herself there as "a.k.a. Nana Ya (sic) Twumwaa I of "Ghana, West Africa." In Abira, by contrast, in the massively eroded and impoverished countryside to the east of Kumase, visitors can inspect the newly completed library built thanks to the efforts of the town's two Nkosuohene: the only one, the town's Krontihene tells me proudly, in Kwabre district. The town's Nkosuohene come every year, and stay in the town; the library is only one of the ways in which they have contributed. Other projects continue, some haltingly, some steadily. There is, in short, no single story that can be told about this relationship.

This notwithstanding, there are some general points which can be made. What I have been exploring are the tensions and creative possibilities that have developed around the transnational connections of the late twentieth century—a period that has witnessed the emergence of a multiplicity of contact spaces that span the Black Atlantic. I have argued that the development and expansion of the *nkosuohene* institution must be seen as the outcome of two distinct and intersecting trajectories: the changing role played by Africa in general and Ghana in particular in the African American imagination and the vicissitudes and challenges faced by Ghanaian traditional rulers and their communities in the harsh economic conditions of the late twentieth century. In this sense the proliferation of non-Ghanaian chiefs in the Akan areas of Ghana is only a part of a broader process of strategic deterritorialization, in which survival and prosperity critically depends upon the creation and sustaining of resource networks that link home-places to outside whether that be Accra, London, or New York. Paradoxically, I would argue that links with "outside"—in this case Ghana—may also be valued as a critical resource by African Americans engaged in projects of racial uplift and cultural pride in the USA. In this sense one can see these developments as a process of mutually beneficial extroversion. The construction of common ground—of a way, to go back to the original idea of *nkosuo* as imagined by Asantehene Otumfuo Opoku Ware, of going forward together—might, however, be more difficult to achieve. While the language of the networks that link the fields of the Ghanaian diaspora together is the language of particularity—family, home-place, region—in the case of Diasporic Nkosuohene a different language is being mobilized: that of racial solidarity and of reconnection with a ruptured past. How and if these languages of identity will mesh remains very much to be seen. Just how these particular transatlantic connections develop will, of course be for Ghanaians and African Americans to decide: but, to quote the proverb, this is a path that will only be made by walking it.

What's Tourism Got to Do With It? The Yaa Asantewa Legacy and Development in Asanteman

LYNDA R. DAY

Lynda R. Day is Associate Professor of African History and Chair of the Africana Studies Department at Brooklyn College-CUNY. She has written a book and several articles on women's political leadership in Sierra Leone. The essay below focuses on historical memory and the Yaa Asantewa Centenary in Asante.

Introduction

The year 2000 marked the centenary of the anti-colonial war led by Yaa Asantewa, the legendary female ruler of Edweso, a small town near the Asante capital of Kumase. An explosion of centenary events brought attention to her life and legacy, and took on the added dimension of boosting tourism and furthering development in the Ashanti region. In an economic climate where tourism is the third-largest foreign-exchange earner, both government officials and outside observers agree that packaging historical events and people for tourists has great potential as an income-generating activity. However, can a community create or re-create their heroic figure in a way that will attract people from all over the world? Can interest in the leader of a bygone political struggle really stimulate increased tourism? How should a historical legacy be promoted and sold? How much more so when the definition of this historical legacy is closely tied to the actions of one individual? What impact will increasing tourism have on the local communities? If hundreds of foreigners from the industrialized world travel to the Ashanti region and bring hard currency, how can that money best be used to promote sustainable development? This paper seeks to explore the challenges of linking the Yaa Asantewa legacy to the promotion of tourism and development in the Ashanti region.

Theoretical Background

A discussion of the impact of increased tourism in the Ashanti region intersects an ongoing debate about the benefits and negative consequences of global tourism. The World Tourism Organization, a United Nations agency, has defined tourism as: "the activities of persons travelling to and staying in places outside their usual environment for not more than one consecutive year for leisure, business and other purposes." Since the 1950s, the numbers of international tourists and their expenditures have grown from an estimated 25 million arrivals in 1950 to more than 500 million in the late 1990s. Victor T. C. Middleton, a British tourism theorist, projects that global tourism will grow 3 to 4 percent a year between 1995 and 2010. If one considers the amount of money spent in travel, lodging, food, and entertainment, then tourism is currently the world's largest industry. But the question arises: what will be the impact of increased economic activity of this type on the Ashanti region? Tourism, unlike more measurable commodities (i.e., minerals, cocoa, and coffee), provides services to visitors who travel to the source to consume them. What, in fact, will the guests be offered? What choices will tourism bring to the residents of the host region? Will it affect the local culture? If so, how? Will it lead to economic development?

Immediately after World War II, economic planners saw tourism as a beneficial, "smokeless" industry, a "passport to development—a clean, green industry with lots of jobs and no factories or fumes." One of the expected benefits of tourism was that it is renewable: "Unlike oil, tourism is sustainable." Furthermore, it was expected to lead to world peace and international understanding among diverse peoples. But since the 1970s, it has been clear that, particularly in developing countries, ecological and cultural damage can result from increased tourism. Indeed, many observers have pointed out that local people have not benefitted economically from increased tourist activity. More recently, rather than merely assuming that it will improve local economies, policymakers have begun to focus on ensuring that tourism projects are constructed in ways that in fact improve the lives of local people. The potential for both long term benefit and harm was so apparent that in 1999, tourism was an important component of the agenda of the United Nations Sustainable Development Commission and a global code of ethics for tourism was proposed by the World Tourism Organization.

Indeed, at another extreme, some theorists posit that tourism in developing countries amounts to another type of colonization, "the final stages of colonialism and empire" as people from the "developed" world travel to poorer regions to enjoy the remnants of indigenous cultures that have managed to resist the onslaught of globalization and modernization. From this perspective, tourism "exploits the ... [majority of the people], pollutes the environment, destroys the ecosystem, bastardises the culture, robs people of their traditional values and ways of life and subjugates women and children." In contrast, some observers assert that a tourist presence strengthens local traditions and reinforces local identities. They contend that because of the outside world's attention, and with local resources being marshaled to re-create and institutionalize historical events, artistic achievements, or personalities, that a "pride of place" emerges in the local population, leading to an enthusiastic and self-conscious retention of that culture. And then of course planners stress the potential practical benefits of providing jobs for people, markets for local industries, and tax revenues, and otherwise raising the standard of living for people in the tourist destination.

Much of the discussion addresses the issues of cultural change and cultural "authenticity." Questions arise as to whether the cultural heritage preserved by the local people represents a genuine cultural identity; whether the culture is being preserved artificially; or whether change is occurring because of outside pressure. Many authors have noted the irony that in some tourist destinations, indigenous people maintain ancient cultural practices primarily for the tourist market and not for any inherent role it plays in their lives. One example is the Kagga Kamma resort in South Africa's Western Cape, at which forty San people (the so-called Bushmen) spend their days working at a re-created Bushman village, where they practice their ancient crafts for the benefit of tourists—but away from work, they live in more contemporary structures and wear Western-style clothing, bought with the money they earn at the re-created tourist village. Bruner and Kirshenblatt-Gimblett's incisive deconstruction of Maasai "tribesmen" recreating their ancient lifestyles for tourists under the direction of a British ex-colonial family at their ranch in Kenya demonstrates the irony of tourist tableaux that valorize the colonial imagery of African primitivism and British civilization. Whose version of local history and culture is being presented? What is the value of a culture if it is being kept alive self-consciously for a profit and if it bears little relationship to real life? Where is the "authenticity" in this scenario?

In spite of the risk of distorting indigenous cultural expressions, the reality of a globalized economy seems to mean that local history or folk arts can only be maintained if they are marketed and generate an income. Indeed, "Tourism has been a driving force over the past fifteen years in taking cultural heritage into the economic mainstream," and the only remaining question is how that marketing will be done, because tourism "can be a boon for a country's heritage as long as the law of the market is applied in moderation." In the current climate, enhanced tourist revenues tend to flow out of African countries because multinational corporations usually own the hotels, airlines, and resorts that generate the most tourist money. Nevertheless, few doubt that tourism has real potential as the growth industry of the future. With a careful assessment of the needs of the people of each locale as well as good management on the part of government planners, it might be possible to maximize the positive effects of tourism and minimize or limit its negative effects.

In Ghana, government officials at the national and regional levels have determined that tourist development is an important goal for the country as a whole and the Ashanti region in particular. Given their commitment, it remains to devise and shape visionary policies regarding tourism. Middleton, the British tourism policy theorist, details a marketing plan that stresses a collaborative process involving public and private sectors to make sure that tourism is sustainable. Middleton posits that , it is only with the joint cooperation of all segments of the affected society that tourism can help the community and fulfill its potential for non-exploitative economic and social uses *Ecotourism,* the term now widely used to describe such sustainable tourist travel, implies that with broad and farsighted planning, international visitors will benefit the indigenous peoples and the environment. Applying the ecotourism model, travelers will help preserve the biodiversity and cultural authenticity that still exist outside the world's industrialized regions. At the same time, observers must consider that cultural authenticity is a contested and fluid construct. The culture that tourists come to see will likely reflect hybrid forms of identity that evolve from the global flow of ideas and values and their reflection in the local sphere. In the application of the same model in Ghana, the sustainability of cultural authenticity at tourist destinations will include public presentations of local history and culture that genuinely reflect the community's needs.

Historical Representation and Tourism

Widely ranging voices on the global impact of tourism make it clear that all over the world, and not only in the Ashanti region, cultural and historic re-creation is central to boosting tourism. Of course the focus on marketing history is not without precedent, since packaging and promoting historical figures and historic sites for tourists is a tried-and-true technique. For example, the town of Williamsburg in Virginia, the re-created home of some of America's founding fathers, has attracted millions of visitors since it opened more than thirty years ago. Every year, tourism offices in local towns and villages publish glossy printed brochures that include historic houses along with the golf courses and amusement parks. And the huge entertainment complex at Disney World in Orlando, Florida, includes a robotically animated re-creation of the U.S. presidents discussing the Constitution.

In spite of how commonly historic tourist attractions may be offered for public consumption, visitors are typically unaware of the compromises that have been made in preparing these historic sites. This discussion of the representation of public history in the Ashanti region is foregrounded by my experience as a curator for the museum services department of Nassau County, in Long Island, New York. The museum division, a government agency, was supposed to educate the public about history and the arts, generate income through the gift shop by increasing tourist traffic, and help get the incumbent politicians reelected. As the person responsible for mounting exhibits and writing visitors' guides, I was constantly aware of the balancing act that promoting these different goals entailed. In particular, was the problem of attracting visitors to learn about a history that included the unpalatable and embarrassing realities of the conquest of the Native Americans and the enslavement of people of African descent? One example of how the museum division handled the latter will illustrate the problem. For years, the professional staff had struggled with the issue of how to present slavery at the county's historic re-created farm village. The curators knew that there had been slaves of African descent in that farm village in the 1700s. But how could the staff re-create or dramatize this reality? For one thing, no one was sure if historical accuracy would dictate that the slaves are dressed in rags, or behave in a subservient manner, or speak some sort of "broken English" dialect. Would the poor living conditions of the slaves have to be shown? If they were, would that upset the tourists? Another problem was that none of the African-American employees of the museum system wanted to portray slaves. The solution: date the house to 1800, when the census was silent on the presence of slaves at the farm. The result: tourists come to the village and leave still blithely unaware that black people ever lived on farms on Long Island in the colonial period, or that there ever was slavery on Long Island. The unpalatable history was sanitized. The tourists were missing an important aspect of history, but the curatorial staff could breathe easier.

The foregoing example illustrates the point that public representations of history are subject to the political needs of the moment. Historical accuracy is typically sacrificed in the interest of promoting tourism, or for maintaining the prevailing political status quo. To re-create the Yaa Asantewa story, comparable historical compromises had to be made. Knotty issues had to be soft-pedaled or skirted around. For example, how would the districts and traditional leaders who did not join Yaa Asantewa's resistance movement be represented? How could one explain the traitors who told Yaa Asantewaa's secrets to the British? Are there both heroes and villains in this story? What about the claim that Yaa Asantewaa provided magic that caused the British guns to mis-fire? Should the tourists be told that? Or that she had slaves? Could any of the foregoing be explained in a guided tour? In a brochure? On an exhibit panel? In fact, would not the "real history" have to be tidied up, even sanitized to serve as an attraction to tourists?

The Yaa Asantewa Festival and Development

During the centenary year, government officials in the Ashanti region openly acknowledged that the Yaa Asantewa legacy was part of a long-range plan to boost local tourism and development. Mike Gizo, the Min-ister of Tourism that year, noted that 350,000 foreigners had visited the country in 1999 and generated $340 million for Ghana's economy. He projected that by 2010, Ghana would host approximately one million visitors generating an income of 1.5 billion *cedis.* The regional tourist boards were largely charged with implementing ambitious and thought-ful strategies for making sure that foreign visitors would generate local development. One key component in the strategy was to revive or even create festivals that would attract tourists and lead to sustainable local development.

The Director and Deputy Director of the Ashanti regional office of the Ghana Tourist Board, Jacob Oty-Awere and Ekoe Sampson, in in-terviews conducted at their offices, contended that festivals were critical to any plans to draw tourists to the region, but they stressed that as fes-tivals are designed and launched, they must contain measures to pro-mote sustainable development, and they stressed that any infrastructural development must be centered in the villages outside urban areas, so as to pump any increased revenue into the rural sectors of the economy.

Their hope was that new festivals would generate construction projects, as well as launch forums and colloquia on issues, which would raise the consciousness and awareness of local residents. Oty-Awere and Sampson stressed, with no attempt at humor, that festivals can no longer be merely opportunities to dress up and socialize, but should be the locus of change, material improvement, and cultural reclamation.

Two such festivals illustrate this effort. The biennial Pan African Historical Theater Festival (Panafest), launched in 1992, has been attracting thousands of tourists to Ghana over the years. The festival brings together artists, musicians and dramatists who open new productions at this time. The artists give classes and workshops on traditional Ghanaian arts and crafts, and the festival has helped support a permanent performing-arts village on the coast. Emancipation Day is another example of an annual celebration designed to attract visitors from the Americas. In 1998, it included a youth forum, an international conference, the reenactment of a slave procession to the Cape Coast dungeons, a wreathlaying, a concert, a memorial service, and a craft bazaar. The awareness of this celebration is growing in the African American community in the United States, and several groups in July and August of 2000 planned their travel dates to Ghana to coincide with the events scheduled for it. Both of these celebrations have demonstrated the potential for drawing international visitors to attend cultural events of this type.

Though Panafest has drawn many thousands of people to Cape Coast, these visitors have not necessarily traveled to Kumase, even though they have come all the way across the ocean to Ghana. Indeed, Panafest seems to have taken on the expectation of being a festival for Greater Accra and the Central Region. At the same meeting where the Minister of Tourism presented the statistics referencing the number of visitors to Ghana, the Deputy Central Regional Minister pointed out that 40 percent of the tourists who come to Ghana stay in the Central Region. Thus, the goal of sustaining a biennial Yaa Asantewa festival centered at Edweso in conjunction with a Kente festival centered at Bonwire is to boost tourism in the Ashanti region, just as Panafest and Emancipation Day do for Greater Accra and the Central Region.

In August of 2000, the Yaa Asantewa festival was launched with great fanfare in the region and in the country at large. Not only was 2000 the centenary of Yaa Asantewa's war of resistance, it was also an election year, and the ruling National Democratic Congress party needed to boost its popularity in the Ashanti region for any hope of returning Jerry Rawlings to the presidency. Official government sponsorship of the popular Asante heroine's commemoration was a way to generate good publicity for Rawlings. The week-long celebration included a wide range of components, some that were planned just for the launching, and some that were to be expanded in the future. The week's events included an international conference, a football match, the inauguration of a Yaa Asantewa museum, a mass gathering of women, a funeral and reinterment of Yaa Asantewa's remains, an interdenominational church service, a tour of the craft villages in the region, and a mock battle at the Army Museum fort in downtown Kumase. Two ambitious ventures, opening the museum and staging the mock battle at the fort, provide particular insight on the challenges involved in creating venues and opportunities for shaping the Yaa Asantewa legacy and linking it to tourist development. Both of these events involved a cooperative effort on the part of multiple segments of the community, and served a variety of goals through the avenue of historical re-creation.

Yaa Asantewa Museum

One of the most ambitious projects launched during the centenary celebration was the opening of the Yaa Asantewa Museum in Edweso. The construction of this museum was a unique endeavor, involving disparate elements of the regional community, including the traditional ruler of Edweso, the District Chief Executive, the Regional Minister's office, faculty members from Kwame Nkrumah University of Science and Technology, and a local architectural firm. The museum was projected to be the cornerstone of a tourist village, which, when complete, would contain accommodations for tourists, shops, restaurants, and a hotel. It was hoped that the tourist village would necessitate, and perhaps help pay for, infrastructural development, such as improved access roads, better lighting, expanded plumbing and toilet facilities, and improved signage. Similar improvements were projected to take place in

Bonwire, Edweso's sister town and the center of the Kente weaving tradition.

The opening day of the museum attracted a crowd of thousands, including numerous tourists and many dozens of dignitaries. At least two large groups of African Americans had traveled to Kumase from Accra as part of their Emancipation Day tour package. The special guest of honor was the first Lady of Ghana, Nana Konadu Rawlings, who had brought two of her daughters, including the one named Yaa Asantewa, to grace the occasion. A bust of Yaa Asantewa, especially commissioned to be erected in front of the structure, was unveiled on the day of the opening by the First Lady. Speeches were made by the Regional Minister, the District Chief Executive, the Offinsohene, the traditional ruler who is considered the patron of the town of Edweso, and the First Lady herself. Musicians and dancers performed for hours in front of an appreciative crowd.

Probably the most impressive part of the event was the museum itself. It occupied a handsome and visually striking building, which purported to re-create a typical Asante royal residence of the years around 1900, a residence in which Yaa Asantewa might have lived. From the sloping thatched roof, to the rich earth-colored finish, to the gleaming *adinkra* symbols boldly painted on the outer walls, to the delicate bas-reliefs decorating the lower portion of inner and outer walls, the building was a beautiful and graceful structure incorporating many features of Asante traditional architecture. Indeed, rare design elements such as the bas-relief carvings, no longer used on modern buildings in the Ashanti region, gave the structure historical significance. This demonstration of traditional architecture was expected to attract local school groups and current residents of the region, as well as international visitors. Thus, the building encapsulated and expressed Asante history and culture in a way that, while eliciting admiration from foreigners, was expected to elicit a self-reflexive pride in their heritage from the Asante people themselves.

The building's interior layout, with its central courtyard and rooms lined up one after the other in a rectangular shape around the courtyard, were supposed to depict the living space of an Asante female ruler. The arrangement of the living space and its assumptions about who lived where and how is more problematic. Though the details of furnishings might indeed have been historically accurate, the working concept seemed more to reflect modern sensibilities about how a single, financially secure older woman might have lived than the realities of Asanteman during the war years of the late nineteenth century. For example, the large windows would belie the need for defensive measures against arrow attacks. And the site plan made no provision for rooms, space, or accommodations for slaves, which wealthy royal families of this time were known to have had. With the museum building, a new tourist destination was created, one that was a construction of local history that would be attractive to visitors while reflecting the community's need to honor and celebrate its history. This public presentation both asserted its own history and reflected the best in universal values. In a global marketplace that upholds the values of female efficacy, power, and independence, Yaa Asantewa is in the forefront, exemplifying these values. Visitors to the site saw a re-creation of Asante architecture from the late nineteenth century that functioned as a shrine to an independent woman who defended her nation's honor while displaying universal values of self-sacrifice, loyalty to one's country, defense of one's home and family, as well as newly evolving values of female strength, autonomy, and economic self-sufficiency. Slavery, warfare, and summary executions, all part of nineteenth-century Asante life, are absent from this picture. These historical realities would be frightening to foreign guests and embarrassing to local hosts. In this presentation, their locality is global: they are not behind, nor do they have anything to be ashamed of. The newly constructed museum, like the newly constructed history, was attractive, and was expected to draw and satisfy the expected guests as well as the hosts.

The museum was thus an example of how cultural re-creation served the needs of the moment, and how such re-creations can form a bridge between the realities of the past and how our current values are refreshed, renewed, reinforced, or promoted. The beauty of the building, not to mention the strength and power captured by the bust of the queen, established, enhanced, and preserved the heroic image of the figure the community had determined to honor. The fact that, after the Centenary, the site quickly fell into decay and a few years later was burned to the

ground reflects on-going local political rivalries that the Centenary celebrations merely papered over, but did not resolve.

Mock Battle at the Fort

In many ways, the mock battle staged at the old British fort in downtown Kumase during the centenary week of the celebration encapsulated
the issues addressed at the outset of this paper. It serves as a nexus for
considering such events as cultural constructions, tourist attractions,
and the potential for promoting development goals. The many players
in this event—the army, the media, the Asante royal bureaucracy, national and regional government officials, and the students from the Yaa
Asantewa Girls' High School—were brought together ostensibly to develop a program of interest to tourists, but with tourist development as
the catalyst, the event seems to have been most notable for generating
new cultural and historical understandings, and perhaps for becoming
a vector of social change.

The mock battle attempted to re-create an assault made by Asante
warriors on the fort during a siege in the final Asante war against the
British. Triggered by the British governor's insistence that he be allowed to sit on the Golden Stool at a meeting of Asante chiefs in March
1900, the war was the nation's last armed resistance to colonial rule,
and cost the lives of thousands of Asante fighting men. After the meeting, the elderly queenmother of the town adjacent to Kumase, Edweso,
is reported to have exhorted the chiefs to resist this further humiliation
to Asante national pride. She was later appointed war commander (*os-
ahene*), and under her leadership, an alliance of many of the Asante
kings and their respective militias fought a seven-month war of resistance. The staged attack as it was presented at the commemoration was
a fascinating presentation of history as entertainment. The ominous and
insistent pounding of huge war drums quickened the pulse of thousands
of observers and heightened the anticipation of the battle to come. Each
observer could feel something of the fear and awe that thousands had
felt one hundred years before. The loud crackle and rattle of the muskets
and the deafening sound of the cannons alternately startled, frightened,

and amused the crowd. The sight of the "warriors" dressed in their war gowns with their faces painted, brandishing ancient but fierce-looking guns and charging the fort with no visible defense against the booming cannons being fired from within, elicited the crowd's admiration and sympathy. Furthermore, the re-creation informed the spectators, with no need for narration, why, at least on military grounds, a frontal assault on the fort could not have succeeded. The numerous "wounded" men being carried off the field of battle after every cannon blast dramatized the losses the Asante nation suffered for the dream of maintaining their independence. The emotion in the crowd was palpable. Bringing the historical event to life made the conflict of one hundred years before somehow fresh and immediate; it was clearly a successful effort. But at the same time, the re-creation reflected the ways in which the representation of the past is shaped and compromised for public consumption in the present.

As effective and riveting as it was, the drama of the attack was weakened by depicting only a handful of "enemy" personnel inside the fort. A good drama has to have villains, and the few white people (*aborofo*; sg. *obroni*) in green tee shirts moving around inside the fort provided no true representation of British imperial might. There was no clear picture of whom the Asante were fighting. In fact, they had fought not merely disembodied guns, but a multitude of real people, including Governor Hodgson of the Gold Coast and his wife, other British officers and missionaries, and their wives, as well as hundreds of Hausa troops, who had occupied the capital of the Asante kingdom. Having more people inside the fort, perhaps wearing vintage uniforms, would have heightened the tension and sense of conflict. We should have seen characters portraying British soldiers and their African allies from other regions of the Empire, soldiers who would be dressed quite differently from the Asante warriors outside the fort. The attack as staged portrayed no visible, certainly no powerful "enemy." However, the question arises, though such a dramatization would have enhanced the entertainment value of the mock battle and would have been more historically accurate: would it attract more tourists? The portrayal of British soldiers in uniform and white missionaries with their long bushy beards might bring home, more forcefully than anyone cares to remember, the brutal reality of colonial racism and its military and cultural domination.

In fact, cultural compromises have long since been made. The Asante are now Christian, and adopted the cultural trappings of modernity after the British conquest of 1900. White people are now welcome guests in Asanteman. Not only are the British no longer the enemy: they are principal trading partners with Ghana. A British firm owns nearly half of Ashanti Goldfields, the gold-mining concern that brings in the lion's share of the country's revenue. The negative impact of British colonization on Asante is far from the forefront of collective memory, and no one seems to be interested in dredging up that part of the past.

The depiction of the 60-year-old Queen Yaa Asantewaa, as played by a lithe 18-year-old student, further problematizes the question of cultural construction. Most accounts of the Yaa Asantewa War suggest that the queenmother played a symbolic role, planning strategies, organizing supplies, and rallying fighters with her rhetoric, magic, and personality. Some accounts say that all during the war, she never left Edweso until she was forced to flee to avoid arrest. But those who observed the spectacle that day at the fort might now say with confidence that she fought at the head of the troops in battle. The Yaa Asantewa at the fort was tall, strong, and dynamic, leading the charge in trousers and battle dress, carrying and shooting a musket. Is this the way tourists and the Ghanaian public want to see their heroine? Would a tiny, elderly woman, who took no active part in the fighting, fit the bill as the Asante war leader? The accuracy of historical re-creation was sacrificed to the needs of the public and the global marketplace to see a vigorous action-heroine.

Fostering women's empowerment, a corollary goal of festival organizers, was admirably enhanced by the brilliant exhibition by the Yaa Asantewa Girls' High School Drill team that afternoon. They demonstrated extraordinary discipline and skill with their crisp and complex moves, making it abundantly clear that young women have the talent to perform well in areas of endeavor stereotypically restricted to men. And of course the subtext—women's leadership in war, or at least of one woman war leader—was updated by the inclusion of the young women in modern military uniforms carrying automatic pistols. Having them as a "curtain raiser" to the mock battle led by Queen Yaa Asantewa, transformed the historical thematic subtext of a woman at war into a contemporary message of women's empowerment, thus promoting a current goal of social and political policy. In this way, the program became a vehicle for the construction of new cultural values while linking them to selected cultural threads from the past.

In spite of the event's effectiveness as spectacle, very few tourists attended. However, it may be more important that the event sustained the rapt attention of a few thousand Kumase residents for several hours. The visibility of the fort, an historic set piece that usually sits ignored in the heart of the city, seems to have been raised in the consciousness of the public. It thus had the effect of transmitting historical knowledge and awareness to Kumase's citizens. Furthermore, the mock battle provided good public relations for the army, which trained the volunteers and conducted the "battle," as well as for the Yaa Asantewaa Girls' High School, which not only fielded an excellent drill team, but also demonstrated courage "under fire," as the girls portrayed Asante warriors attacking the fort. Later in the program, prominently seated national and regional National Democratic Congress (NDC) government officials were introduced, and gave remarks from the stage. Thus, one way to consider the "mock battle," as it was configured, is that it functioned more as a vehicle for national integration, boosting the national leadership and building a consciousness of Ghanaian nationhood than as a mechanism for promoting tourism, and certainly more than as a mechanism for re-creating historical accuracy. Though some may have been afraid that an event highlighting Asante's history of resistance would stoke the embers of Asante regional and ethnic nationalism, the omnipresence of the regular Ghanaian army, led by a northern general, clearly made this a government event, a national event. The NDC goal of women's empowerment, as commonly articulated and embodied by Nana Konadu Rawlings, was central to the program. The public coverage of the afternoon's events, the many dignitaries up from Accra and other regions, and Ghana Television (GTV) video cameras guaranteeing a national television audience, lifted the Asante war against the British out of the realm of local legend and into the ranks of national myth. The staging of the mock battle ensured that a broad spectrum of Ghanaian society could be self-reflectively proud of its history.

Both the Yaa Asantewa museum in Edweso and the staged battle at the fort used historical and cultural re-creation to empower today's community. Both efforts took liberties with historical accuracy; but whether consciously or unconsciously, these interpretations advanced larger social goals. The goal of using the Asante cultural heritage as a mechanism through which to raise the consciousness of the public and build social cohesion and political integration was most successfully met. Both of the examples discussed in this paper are part of a process of reconfiguring identity through the integration of global and local cultural maps. The economic push for increased tourism was a catalyst for this process and a marked increase in tourist visitors may be the future outcome.

Conclusion

The Yaa Asantewa festival has great potential for bringing visitors and income into the Ashanti region. Reconfiguring a regional figure as a national heroine could boost domestic tourism, seen by many planners as a potent force in contemporary international trade. This image of Yaa Asantewa should be attractive to Ghanaians from other regions of the country, as well as to transnational Ghanaians and their children from other regions who now live in the United Kingdom or the United States but regularly visit "home."

A growing number of the visitors who now bring in the tourist revenue are African Americans and Afro-Caribbeans. For these people, the cultural identity constructed in the Asante region is critical to their interface with that society. Black people from the diaspora already travel to Ghana moved by a historical construction that identifies Africa in general and Ghana in particular as a "motherland," an ancestral home. Ghana becomes a palette on which to paint their missing memories of "home": for this group more than any other, visits to Ghana become a means to "stroll down memory lane" and "become immersed in the past and dream of it as the future." For diasporic blacks, the cultural destinations and events constructed by Ghanaians are critical to building new definitions of identity, and can lend themselves to new global linkages.

Today, most residents of the Asante region are not aware of a historic or cultural connection to Africans in the Americas. For them, African Americans are *obroni,* just like other Americans and all people of European heritage; however, black people from the United States or the Caribbean are motivated to visit for reasons different from those of Caucasians from Europe or America. Blacks from the diaspora are on a pilgrimage to their supposed ancestral homeland, and they visit Ghana almost exclusively as consumers of historical representation, culture, and heritage. Even if they buy souvenirs, the objects they buy are fraught with significant cultural meaning for them. One response to the Deputy Minister of Tourism, who called on local communities to raise their consciousness of the needs of a growing tourism industry, is to encourage a greater awareness of and appreciation for the historic and cultural connections of Asante people and Africans in the Americas. Yaa Asantewa, in her persona as an anti-colonial freedom fighter, a woman proudly upholding the traditions of her people in a fight to the death, is a marvelous symbol of shared struggle against political and cultural oppression. The positioning of Yaa Asantewa as an international heroine during the centenary year was part of a process of global integration tying the people of the African diaspora into the cultural heritage of the Asante region. By thus constructing alliances of cultural heritage and connection for both groups, African diasporic guests and their Asante hosts are poised to find each other in the "empty meeting grounds" of global culture.

Diaspora Discourses

KWASI KONADU

Kwasi Konadu is Professor of History at the City University of New York. The following essay is a revised excerpt from his The Akan Diaspora in the Americas *(2010), focusing on the uneven dialogue between diasporic Africans and Akan peoples in North America, and the claims which both make to culture and diaspora in the Akan homeland and abroad.*

> *Nnεmmaafoɔ se tete asoɔe yεnsoɔ hɔ bio.*
> *Na adεn nti na yεntu tete-muka mmiεnsa mu baako*
> *na ɔnka mmienu?*

> Children of today say we should not do things
> in the ways of our ancestors anymore.
> So why is it that they do not take out one of the three stones
> used to hold up the cooking pot and just leave two?
> —An Akan proverb

Born in 1930 in Augusta, Georgia, under the name Augustus or Gus Edwards, Nana Yao Opare Dinizulu entered a world marked by the Great Depression and the interim of two world wars. Proximate to the Georgia–South Carolina border, Augusta is divided by the Savannah River. Just as the Atlantic Ocean separates North America and Ghana, so the Savannah River could have divided Georgia and South Carolina—states, particularly the latter, that have had a historic Akan presence—for Nana Dinizulu would cross both ocean and river and become transformed. In so doing, Nana Dinizulu helped to change the landscape of Akan spirituality and culture as practiced in North America. The phenomenon of diasporic Africans' historic engagement with Akan culture and spirituality form the parameters of this essay, and herein I telescope this concern by focusing on the efforts of the late Nana Dinizulu of New York and raise two significant issues for the study of the African diaspora in the Americas. One issue is an imperative for internal dialogue on both sides of the Atlantic Ocean, since most opportunities for dialogue and the interrogation of diaspora are left to osmosis rather than seized by diasporic Africans and Akan migrants, who have now become part of an unfolding diaspora beyond the confines of Ghana. Unfortunately, even scholars (of Akan cultural origin) that attempt to examine the "new African diaspora" in North America fail to grasp the significance of the parallel practice of indigenous Akan culture and spirituality among fewer Akan persons and a growing number of diasporic Africans. These scholars are more concerned with the immigrant narratives of Africans who have made North America their new "homeland" and their often ill-informed perceptions of diasporic African realities. Another issue is that many diasporic Africans have traveled to and taken up residence in the Akan homeland since the early twentieth century, and they have recently problematized the "slave castles" of Ghana. These edifies have become contested sites of meeting and reinterpretation, a crossroads at which diasporic Africans are adopting Akan cultural institutions and spiritual practices, and Akan persons are seeking to depart from Ghana and those practices. The latter are also becoming increasingly steeped in Pentecostalism and a "prosperity gospel" that equips them, at least ideologically, in their outbound desires for North America and parts of Europe. As the Atlantic Ocean becomes a path frequently crossed and re-crossed by both groups, these phenomena associated with the Akan diaspora strongly suggest that the study of a composite African diaspora must be one of ongoing movements and transformations in specific and shared dialogue among Africa-based and African diasporic communities.

Comparative Histories and the Akan Lens

The Akan experience in the Americas and West Africa during the nineteenth and early twentieth centuries provides an important "diasporic" lens, for in comparative perspective, that experience linked North America and West Africa and revealed similar processes that were unfolding among African and African-descended communities. New York became a nexus for these experiences and the similar paths pursued by converging, Westernized, and elitist segments of both communities. In Manhattan, the significant number of businesses and churches owned by prosperous families of African descent created a contrast between the pomp and quasi-pageantry of those Westernized families and the poverty of the larger number of formerly enslaved persons, who worked as waiters, domestic workers, and dockworkers around the port districts in Manhattan. In North America the nineteenth century began with the gradual abolishment of the international enslavement enterprise, though domestic enslavement increased—New York abolished slavery in 1827. As "freed" Africans and their descendants shifted from chattel in the homes of former owners to wage laborers situated in cellars, and as competition for jobs and survival escalated in a period of heightened industrial transformation in New York City, violence and acute racism affected many lives. In fact, a decade after the Dutch attempted to restore the "slave trade" in the 1850s, many of the foregoing issues continued into the late nineteenth century. When the anti-draft riots of 1863 forced diasporic Africans from Manhattan to independent African-descended communities in Brooklyn, they came to neighborhoods like Weeksville and Carsville, which had been established around the 1830s in the vast, semi-rural region of Brooklyn's Ninth Ward.

These communities provided economic opportunity and charitable institutions, such as the African Union Society and its African School no. 2, which were established by and for diasporic Africans. Such institutions became a place of refuge for those who migrated to Brooklyn due the anti-draft riots of 1863, in which poor whites blamed the hated Civil War draft on diasporic Africans residing in Manhattan. Determined to defend their lives and homes against an attack during these violent protests, the diasporic Africans of Weeksville, for instance, took up arms and posted guards. The part of Manhattan that became known as Harlem, as well as sections of Brooklyn in its own right, became key cultural, political, and residential centers for African descendents from the U.S. South and the Caribbean in the late nineteenth and early twentieth centuries. With the "betrayal" of Reconstruction and Jim Crowism in the South, a nationalist spirit found expression in movements to establish all-African-descended towns and Oklahoma as an all-African-descended state. In 1879 Benjamin "Pap" Singleton's migration crusade from Tennessee toward the West mobilized as many diasporic Africans in North America as in the movement led by Marcus Garvey in the 1920s, if not more. Those efforts to find strategic alternatives to injustice, violence sanctioned by custom and the law, and the need to protect the interests of families and communities in Oklahoma and Tennessee would foreshadow the appeal of the so-called back-to-Africa movements envisioned by Alfred Charles Sam (also known as Chief Sam) of the Gold Coast and Marcus Garvey of Jamaica, two Akan-related persons whose movements were based, not by happenstance, in Harlem and Brooklyn.

Diasporic Africans entered the twentieth century poised for a new political, cultural, and institutional vision beyond personalities such as Booker T. Washington, who opposed "going back to Africa" but sponsored programs and opportunities for those who desired a return to the African continent. Yet, it was Booker T. Washington who inspired Marcus Garvey to come to North America and whom Garvey wanted to meet; however, Washington died before Garvey arrived. The Garvey movement, with its focus on unification and ridding the African continent of colonial rule, and the Communist-oriented African Blood Brotherhood (ABB) influenced the contours of a Harlem renaissance where culture and identity took center stage. This revitalization drew the likes of Langston Hughes, Countee Cullen, Alain Locke, W. E. B. Du Bois, Richard B. Moore, Arturo Schomburg of Puerto Rico, Hermina Dumont Huiswoud of Guyana, and Claude McCay of Jamaica. Cyril V. Briggs founded the ABB in 1919 because of a split from A. Philip Randolph's *Messenger* publication over definitions of "radicalism." Members of the ABB included notables such as Richard B. Moore and Hubert Harrison, who originated the Harlem street-corner orator tradition that Malcolm X later embraced, fashioned the slogan "Race First," and provided an important platform for Marcus Garvey when he arrived in Harlem. While Garvey represented the sentiments of pan-Africanism and a nationalism that advocated Africa as the true homeland of diasporic Africans, his movement was preceded and can be better understood by the movement that Alfred Charles Sam initiated. In fact, Chief Sam's movement also anticipated the wave of diasporic Africans who settled in Ghana during the 1960s and thereafter, and who were primarily from the Caribbean and North America.

Born to Nana (James) Kwakye Sam and Akosua Twumasiwaa Buaa in 1879 or 1880, Alfred Charles Sam departed from the path of a missionary worker envisioned by his father and became a trader who inherited the chieftaincy of Apasu a few years after his first trip to North America. In 1913 Alfred Charles Sam envisioned first commercial and then diasporic voyages to the Gold Coast through his Akim Trading Company Limited, which was incorporated in South Dakota. Alfred Sam served as its president after liquidating his interest in the previous Akim Trading Company, established in 1911 and chartered in New York. According to reports in the *New York Times*, Sam procured a vessel named the *Liberia* (formerly the *Curityba* and purchased for $100,000) with a capacity of five hundred passengers. Only those diasporic Africans who held membership in the 130 "clubs of negroes" across the country could buy shares, and two of these shares (at $25.00 each) provided free passage to the Gold Coast for a husband, wife, and children under sixteen. A non-shareholder, A. E. Smith, was "the only white man connected with the company," though he merely acted as its agent. All officers of the trading company were "Gold Coast inhabitants" of Akyem, including Chief Sam, who was born and reared in Akyem and later schooled by the Basel Evangelical Mission schools at Kyebi and Akuropon, capital of Akuapem.

The idea for the voyage originated from Sam's ownership of land endowed with gold, rubber, and mahogany resources, which he purchased from *omanhene* Kwame Dokyi of Akyem-Abuakwa, and his leased lands from local Akan leaders. Those lands would be offered or rented to diasporic African settlers for an unstated amount. On the vessel's return, it would carry African products (e.g., mahogany, cocoa beans, rubber, and coffee) for sale in the United States. Sam had enjoyed some success in commerce as a cocoa and rubber trader, and news of his aims, including the prospects of land, spread to the United States, particularly

Oklahoma. The success of Chief Sam's message and interactions with prosperous African-descended businessmen and farmers in Oklahoma and other parts of North America was, in part, facilitated by the message of Bishop Henry McNeil Turner, who visited West Africa and South Africa. Here, the commercialist interests of Chief Sam converged with the emigration-minded aspirations of diasporic Africans, and, to that effect, the Akim Trading Company Limited urged the emigration of the best farmers and technicians among diasporic Africans in North America to further the goal of greater autonomy for Gold Coast commercial interests vis-à-vis the British monopoly of Gold Coast imports and exports. Interestingly, as Chief Sam and sixty passengers departed on the *Liberia* for the Gold Coast via several U.S. states and Barbados, a group of nine African-descended men from Brooklyn—with no connection to Sam's project—formed the African Union Company to engage in business on the Gold Coast through a concession of land granted by "three of four native chiefs," as Sam had done in the effort to procure the same African products.

Chief Sam and those who came to the Gold Coast eventually settled at Saltpond, near Kormantin, prior to being seized by a British warship and held in Freetown, Sierra Leone, despite the most obvious fact that the *Liberia* flew the British flag as a registered British vessel. The group of diasporic Africans were well received and cared for by several indigenous community leaders and their people—some of whom actually gathered monetary donations for the settlers and their stay—but a number of the settlers fell ill to malaria after inspecting and even clearing some of the land Chief Sam had purchased. The next year, however, Sam Chief's plan began to unravel with official restrictions and legal proceedings, debt incurred by the *Liberia*, and British authorities at Cape Coast castle, who refused to provide Sam and his cohort with coal for the vessel. Because of the cumulative effect of these barriers, the *Liberia* was abandoned and sold to the Universal Transportation Company, whose ship, the *Zealandia*, towed the *Liberia* from Cape Coast to New York. Amid a wave of discontent due to limited resources and a multitude of other issues mounted by opposition forces, many of the emigrants, who were mainly prosperous male farmers and a few married couples, returned to the United States aboard the *Abosso* after ten or more months on the Gold Coast. Meanwhile, Sam became a cocoa buyer and abandoned the project because of acute duress and the associated legal, political, and diplomatic costs. Chief Sam and his second wife, a diasporic African from North America, produced a child named Kwakye Sam—no doubt named after Chief Sam's father, Kwakye Sam, in a manner wholly consistent with Akan naming patterns found in Ghana and the Americas. Some diasporic Africans of Sam's expedition stayed and settled in Winneba, Accra, and Cape Coast and developed tobacco and rubber plantations, manufactured local gin (Gã: *akpeteshie*) and gunpowder, and developed engine-driven boats that were used along the coast.

Many, however, were suspicious from the outset, and some, such as the British government and its Gold Coast colonial authorities, attempted to thwart Sam's efforts. In the United States, W. E. B. Du Bois warned readers of the *Crisis* about Sam and his "scheme" just as the local press on the Gold Coast did the same. The local press in West Africa, however, reconsidered when Sam modified his emigration plans to include sixty rather than five hundred would-be settlers. Sam's modification was in response to official British opposition—specifically, the British threatened to deny his vessel British registry. In an unprecedented act, the British enacted an ordinance on the Gold Coast in order to "regulate those not born in any part of West Africa" and, in doing so, compelled "each Afro-American immigrant to deposit five pounds as a security bond." Both the Gold Coast and the Sierra Leone press, including the nationalists who wrote for them, became fervent supporters of the "African movement" after Chief Sam modified his plans under British and Gold Coast colonial pressure. In spite of that pressure, Sam's African movement contributed to the development of pan-Africanism and nationalism in West Africa and the wider African world. It also anticipated Marcus Garvey's movement, though, as Sam and the movement's main intellectual proponent, Orishatuke Faduma, would admit, it was built upon earlier efforts of Daniel Coker, Elijah Johnson, and Paul Cuffee (whose father was Akan and who advocated emigration), as well as nineteenth-century nationalists Edward Wilmot Blyden and Bishop Henry McNeil Turner.

Despite its apparent failures in the eyes of some, Chief Sam's movement and those that came both before and after it provide important insights. First, Chief Sam's efforts and those of his supporters and allies demonstrate the ways in which European or white sentiments functioned as a catalyst in the birth or reemergence of nationalist aspirations and strategies. Second, Sam's efforts provided a sense of the great measures that international and domestic European forces and their colonial agents took to proscribe African and diasporic African engagements and relations, especially those that threatened the capitalist hegemony and the global order of things. Such measures included the British, North American, and Gold Coast campaigns as well as efforts by their ideological agents to discredit Sam's claim to land and chieftaincy, dissuade diasporic Africans from emigrating, compel Gold Coast shareholders in the *Liberia* to resign, and convince people that diasporic Africans would disrupt the so-called racial peace on the Gold Coast. Finally, diasporic Africans in North America provided the most powerful lens through which to apprehend the deep, almost irreconcilable contradictions in a country governed by whites who projected themselves as guardians of "civilization" and "freedom," though they engaged in and sanctioned racialized slavery and segregation, lynching, disenfranchisement, sharecropping or peonage, and an attendant psychological violence in print and visual media (e.g., caricatures and minstrels).

Faduma surmised that the African movement led by Chief Sam had precedent and that improvements in its administration—the establishment of provisions for the accommodation and welfare of the emigrants, as well as thorough organization and periodic fiscal accounting of the Akim Trading Company—would have been the key to its success. Nonetheless, a decade after Sam's project, forty-nine-year-old Nana Amoah III of Cape Coast came to the United States to study the "progress of the Negro race" and "the centres of Negro population," though, in actuality, he came as an entrepreneur seeking financial backing for cocoa shipping to enter the Gold Coast cocoa trade. Nonetheless, he started with Harlem, one of the early bases of Chief Sam and his ideological successor, Marcus Garvey. After arriving in Virginia and then traveling on to New York on the *Aquitania*, Nana Amoah was scheduled to "visit Chicago, Philadelphia, and Baltimore [and other parts of the United States] to see what men of his race have accomplished ... [and to help] bring about a closer understanding between the negroes of the two continents." Nana Amoah was enstooled among a Fante community in 1914 (though the actual enstoolment occurred in 1919) and probably knew of Chief Sam and his African movement, since Saltpond was within the Fante coastal territories and both men shared or at least supported pan-African ideals (Nana Amoah participated in the third and fourth Pan-African Congresses in 1923 and 1927).

Nana Amoah and Chief Sam established or were part of a line of trader-nationalists who sought both economic support from diasporic Africans in North America and their technical assistance to combat the British commercial monopoly on the Gold Coast. They also hoped to bolster the status and institutions of the Gold Coast's "educated native elites." The *New York Times* noted that "the educated natives," of whom Nana Amoah was one, "dominate the thought and action of their people" although their numbers were small relative to the larger population, even in the urbanized areas. At a lecture at the Episcopal City Mission Chapel of the Messiah in Harlem, Nana Amoah was joined by "Prince Kojo Tovaluo-Houenou of Dahomey [Bénin] ... and Dr. J. E. Kwegyir Aggrey" of Achimota College. That evening Nana Amoah not only urged his audience of diasporic Africans to "cultivate racial pride ... [as] African" but also referred to an 1897 treaty with the British that allowed land to be held in trust for diasporic Africans so that they could "claim land where their ancestors in Africa died intestate." Whether such a treaty, in scribal or oral form, was actually made is unclear, though it would hold implications for those diasporic Africans who have returned to Ghana and engaged government and local officials about the very issue of land and the right to return to Ghana as one of several possible homelands. Nonetheless, Nana Amoah's appeal to diasporic Africans to contribute their technical knowledge and skill toward the "development" of the Gold Coast, as well as his and Chief Sam's suggestion of available lands and a homeland free from racism, was part and parcel of what Nana Amoah represented on the Gold Coast via his Westernized identity and commercial aspirations.

Nana Amoah's identity is critical to our understanding of the purpose of his trips and the nature and intent of his orations to largely African-descended audiences while in New York. Nana Amoah, popularly known as Chief Amoah III but named Kwamina Faux Tandoh, ended his medical studies in Britain around 1900 to become an entrepreneur in timber and import-export commerce. He "helped negotiate the concession that produced the Ashanti Goldfields Corporation." The *New York Times* reported that Nana Amoah was a "member of the Church of England" and spoke English fluently, and that Gold Coast authorities, who refused to fund his efforts, distrusted him as a "colonial" African. In the end, Nana Amoah was unable to secure the financing he needed and was deported to the Gold Coast after collapsing from a brain disease in the winter of 1929, and being found on the New York streets by the police. Nana Amoah, like Chief Sam, sought to break away from British commercial hegemony but failed largely because he, as part of the early twentieth century Gold Coast intelligentsia, appealed to the very authorities that maintained foreign control. Steeped in the Christian and Western orthodoxy of the day, the Gold Coast intelligentsia saw its numbers and impact increase in the mid- to late nineteenth century and this turn of events convinced Amoah his fluency in the language, religion, dress, and mannerisms of the British would earn him the desired respect and resources from British officials and capitalists alike.

The likes of Chief Sam and Nana Amoah provide a significant backdrop for an Akan experience that is still unfolding, with more than ten thousand Akan persons in New York City and many diasporic Africans from North America and the Caribbean visiting, taking up residence, and forming relationships with the Akan homeland through New York airports and seaports. The Akan experience also reveals how the broader processes of Westernization, Christianization, and elitist formation among segments of both African and African diasporic communities in West Africa and North America, respectively, were on parallel trajectories during the nineteenth and early twentieth centuries. The quest for partnership with the established colonial order on the Gold Coast and in North America created factionalism among and within Gold Coast and diasporic African elites, and two divergent visions began to emerge on both sides of the Atlantic Ocean. In the Gold Coast and North America, nineteenth-century diasporic African converts split from the ordinary non-Christian folk along class lines, and developed an acute yet ambivalent distaste toward things "African" (e.g., African-based spiritualities, cultural practices at odds with Christianity, and African names). On the North American side of the equation, the foregoing process was evident by the first or second quarter of the nineteenth century, when "black elites" sought "admission into the club" (i.e., equal rights and full acceptance by whites), and while the majority of the African-based community saw racism and its insidiousness as deeply rooted in their fight for human and civil rights, the elites viewed slavery and discrimination as obstacles that prevented *their* progress and not necessarily collective advancement. The parallels for both groups, bridged by the Atlantic Ocean but bounded by shared concerns of a cultural and spiritual nature, were more than striking at the turn of the twentieth century.

Nana Dinizulu and the Reemergence of Akan Spiritual Praxis

At the dawn of the twentieth century, close to 90 percent of all diasporic Africans lived in the U.S. South. However, large migratory waves between 1910 and 1940 and again from 1940 to 1970 accounted for more than half of that once 90 percent residing in the northeastern region of North America and in major cities such as New York. Though next to nothing has been written about Nana Dinizulu's life as Gus Edwards, we can imagine, with some certainty, that he and perhaps his parents were a part of the first migratory wave to New York, since he established an organization called the *Ghanas* in 1947, when he was seventeen. The *Ghanas* conducted classes in African singing, dancing, history, and culture and became the vehicle through which his Dinizulu African Dancers, Drummers, and Singers were established in 1947. These developments, however amazing for a seventeen-year-old, were consistent with Dinizulu's own account and the scant literature. Nana Dinizulu, in *The Akan Priests in America*, wrote, "I have been worshipping the Gods and Ancestors of Africa since the early [1940s]. I became the first Akan priest and chief in America to worship the Gods and Ancestors of the Akan people of Ghana." The claim of being the "first Akan priest" in North America may be reasonable in a certain context, but it is largely an inflated one, for Akan spiritualists were undoubtedly transported to the Americas since at least the seventeenth century, and even Dinizulu himself wrote, "Many great priests and noblemen were forced to come here [North America] during slavery." Nonetheless, the constant interaction with anyone from African heads of states to those in the cultural, artistic world afforded Dinizulu (through his dance troupe) many opportunities to study and continue to propagate the cultures and dance traditions of Africa, particularly, though not exclusively, West Africa.

Nana Dinizulu became a part of Damballa Hwedo, the first recorded "religious" institution based upon Akan, Yorùbá-Fon, and Haitian (Vodun) traditions in North America and, in doing so became associated with Oseijeman Adefunmi, who is largely responsible for reestablishing the Yorùbá spiritual tradition in North America. Upon Adefunmi's return from his initiation into the "priesthood" of Ôbàtálá in the Matanzas region of Cuba in 1959, he founded the Order of Damballa Hwedo with a Haitian associate in 1960 and then the Shango and Yorùbá temples. The Order of Damballa Hwedo was established in Harlem—where Dinizulu's wife, Alice Brown (Afua Owusua Dinizulu), settled at the age of ten and later met her husband—during the historical confluence of the civil rights and black power era. The Order of Damballa Hwedo, however, disintegrated in a few years, and when Oseijeman Adefunmi left New York to establish Oyotunji Village (based on the Òrìsà-Vodun spiritual practices) in Beaufort County, South Carolina, Nana Dinizulu began forging the groundwork for the reestablishment of Akan spiritual practice through the Bosum Dzemawodzi organization based in Queens (Long Island City), New York. On Bosum Dzemawodzi (*dzemawodzi* is the Gã-Adangme synonym for the Akan *obosom*), Nana Kwabena Brown recalls the following:

> Interesting enough, at that time there were not any Akan deities, at the time that I arrive[d], but there were gods [*abosom*]. There was a [Gã] priest.... Almost 90 percent of the gods that were there were Yorùbá gods (Shango, Yemanya, etc.). The introduction of the Ghanaian gods was mostly Gã. It was not until Nana Yao Opare made his trip in 1969 (which probably was his second trip) that he met Nana Oparebea, and when he came back [to the United States] in late '69, that

is when the Akan gods came.... I think it was January 1970 Nana Oparebea [made] her first trip, and that was the full, full introduction of the Akan gods. Prior to that ... most of the services of Bosum Dzemawodzi were Yorùbá (Shango, Ogun, Yemanja, etc.). That is because he had a very strong orientation with Baba Oseijeman [Adefunmi], chief of the Yorùbá culture for African Americans.

By the 1960s, Nana Dinizulu had traveled to Ghana on several occasions. In 1965 a local official of the Ghanaian capital of Accra introduced Nana Dinizulu to Nana Akua Oparebea, *okomfohemaa* (head female *okomfo*, "spiritualist") of the Akonnedi Abena shrine in Larteh-Kubease, in the eastern region of Ghana. Larteh is approximately thirty-five miles north of Accra, on the Akwapem Ridge. Through consultations at the Akonnedi shrine, it was revealed that Nana Dinizulu was an ancestor of Nana Oparebea's family who had come to reunite the descendants of enslaved Africans with their people and culture in Ghana and elsewhere. Nana Dinizulu later wrote, "She [Nana Akua Oparebea] and I trace our ancestry to Nana Atwidan and Op[anin] Kwame Mensah of Nsaba, who are descendants from the Agona clan in [the] Ashanti [region of central Ghana]." With regard to ancestry, Nana Dinizulu also wrote, "The Akans and Ga were brought to the new world and were first settled in such places as South Carolina, Georgia, etc., and in Jamaica and other British-owned West Indian islands." As a child born in Georgia and to parents of African descent, he certainly had no reservations about the revelation of the Akonnedi consultation or his claim not only to Akan ancestry but also to the prerogatives of that claim.

Nana Dinizulu was given the titles *omanhene* (male leader of the nation) and *okomfohene* (head male *okomfo*) of the Akan, that is, diasporic Africans who joined the "Akan movement" rather than persons of Akan cultural origin who migrated to North America with or without an association with that movement or adherence to Akan spirituality as practiced in the homeland. He was initiated into specific dimensions of Akan culture and traditions, and upon his return to North America brought the shrines or *abosom* known as Asuo Gyebi, Esi Ketewa, and Adade

Kofi. One source indicates that "in the late 1960s Nana Yao [Dinizulu] founded the Bosum Dzemawodzi as a religious institution in America. He established the first temple in New York City [in 1967]. He established the first temple for traditional worship in Washington [D.C.] in 1971." Nana Oparebea first traveled to North America in 1971 to help Nana Dinizulu with labors associated with the shrines and the training of the *akɔmfoɔ* (sg. *okomfo*) in New York. On later visits, Nana Oparebea established centers for the practice of Akan spirituality in New York, Philadelphia, the District of Columbia, California, and Toronto. Nana Oparebea was well-known for having cured persons who suffered from spiritual complications, mental disorders, barrenness, impotence, epilepsy, stomach troubles, *abayi* ("witchcraft"), pregnancy problems, and difficulties during childbirth. In 1962 the Ghana Psychic and Traditional Healing Association was established through the efforts of both Nana Oparebea, who was unanimously elected its first president, and Ghana's first prime minister and president, Kwame Nkrumah. It so happened that a high-ranking academician suffered from strange headaches but remained uncured even after both local and foreign biomedical treatments; he then came to the Akonnedi shrine through a friend's recommendation, and Nana Oparebea diagnosed and cured his disease. Thereafter, the academician initiated research into herbal medicine, and with the support of Kwame Nkrumah, who consulted Nana Oparebea, the Ghana Psychic and Traditional Healing Association received full recognition from Nkrumah's government.

Nana Akua Oparebea was the *okomfohemmaa* for Nana Asuo Gyebi in Larteh-Kubease and the primary *okomfo* for Akonnedi Abena, who was the principal *obosom* of Larteh in particular and one of the best-known in Ghana. Akonnedi Abena, as the name suggests, was a feminine expression of divine origination "born" on a Tuesday, and Akonnedi trained only women to assume the role of *ɔkɔmfoɔ*; however, this policy was modified to allow diasporic African men to undergo training as well. Nana Oparebea was the primary spiritualist for and custodian of the shrine rather than its owner, since Akonnedi belonged to the Asona *abusua* (clan, family) of Larteh. As principal spiritualist, the power and prestige of Akonnedi rested squarely on Nana Oparebea, who inherited the position of custodian from Adwoa *okomfo* and *okomfo*

Amma Ansa. Nana Oparebea was born in 1900 as Akua Opare during the famous Yaa Asantewaa War against British incursion and reared at Anhuntem, near Ankwansu, near Adawso. Her father, Kwame Akuffo Mensa, was a prosperous farmer and *abusuapanin* (family/clan head) of Aboanum in Aburi. Nana Oparebea's mother, Aba Oyedi, was of the "royal" families of Amansore and Akantsane. Nana Oparebea followed in the footsteps of *okomfo* Ejo (first "priest" of Akonnedi, who died in 1800), *okomfo* Animah (Oparebea's grandmother), and *okomfo* Amma Ansa; she established her practice in her father's village of Nkumkrom (on the Aburi-Nsawam road) upon graduation as an *okomfo*.

In Nkumkrom Nana Oparebea rose to fame, and people from near and far came for consultations and healing. As principal medium for Akonnedi Abena, Nana Oparebea also possessed Nana Asuo Gyebi, the *obrafo* (shrine assistant) for Akonnedi; Nana Esi Ketewa, the *okyeame* (speech intermediary) for Akonnedi. In addition to that court structure of Akonnedi, she added Tigare and Adade Kofi, whom some regard as an offspring of Akonnedi. Her sacred stream remained the river Nsakye. This set of *abosom* reveals much about the composite strands that informed Akan spiritual practice in twentieth-century Larteh: Asuo Gyebi and Adade Kofi originated in the forested Asante region, Esi Ketewa was from the coastal Fante area, and Tigare emerged in northern Ghana. Originally of non-Akan import, Tigare went through a process of Akanization from a *suman* (talisman) to an *obosom* in the Takyiman area of central Ghana. Furthermore, Larteh was also a Guan- rather than an Akan-inhabited area, and when one combines this setting and the set of *abosom* that Nana Oparebea held and transmitted to North America, many who practice Akan spirituality on either side of the Atlantic Ocean may in fact adhere to a pan-Ghanaian or pan-African construct rather than one that is wholly Akan in constitution. As such, and granted the veneration of Akan *abosom* and Yorùbá *òrìsà* (e.g., Ṣàngó, Ogun) at Bosum Dzemawodzi, the claims that centered on an engagement in "authentic" Akan spirituality and culture by diasporic Africans, especially those associated with Larteh via Nana Oparebea and Nana Dinizulu, are indeed questionable.

Diaspora and Internal Dialogue

In the District of Columbia, a cross-section of diasporic Africans held a reception and grand performance in honor of Asantehene Osei Tutu II's visit to North America at Howard University, a well-reputed historically black college (HBCU). The performance ended and the diasporic community donated large sums of money to "development" in Asanteman (Asante nation), but there was no dialogue between that community and members of the Asantehene's entourage. Did the practice initiated by the likes of Chief Sam and Nana Amoah—where diasporic Africans are viewed as fiscal and "development" resources—receive new life during the Asantehene's visit to the an "elite" HBCU? Is there a need for dialogue and, if so, what kind of dialogue? The recent history of Ghana-diasporic African relations seems to suggest that the lack dialogue—at whatever level—serves the interests of neither party, for Ghana continues to market itself to diasporic Africans as the "gateway to Africa," but arriving and settled diasporic Africans continue to experience Ghana (and "Africa") as "strangers" and "foreigners" whose value lies in the foreign currency that accompanied them. Indeed, the Asantehene's visit underscored this state of affairs: Effective diasporic relations require an ongoing and meaningful internal dialogue.

The decade before the Asantehene's visit was punctuated by two significant yet unconnected transitions in the diasporic African and Ghanaian worlds, especially those of the latter now residing in Harlem—a historic place of meeting in an unfolding African diaspora. At a high school in Camden, New Jersey, Nana Dinizulu collapsed from a heart attack before a concert and made his transition to *asamando* (place where the ancestors dwell) in 1991. That same year, Otelia Oteng participated in her *bragoro* rite in Harlem, and this Akan ritual and ceremonial puberty rite signaled the transition from childhood to female adulthood. Although born in North America to parents from Ghana, Otelia tells those who inquire of her nationality, "I'm Ghanaian. That's my nationality." Otelia's claim to an identity that is "Ghanaian" appears at odds with her American citizenship (which she did not claim here), but its roots are both cultural (via her rites) and political, since Ghana grants dual citizenship to those born of Ghanaian parentage abroad.

Among the approximately 10,000 Akan from Ghana in New York City, "the coming-of-age ceremony is rarely performed [in New York or in Ghana]." One participant, a Ghanaian physician at Columbia Presbyterian Medical Center, commented, "This is not a pagan practice.... This is a folk practice incorporating much common-sense wisdom." Otelia and her family, including those in attendance at her *bragoro* rite, constitute a fraction of the 20,000 Asante people in North America and the 10,000 or more in the New York metropolitan area, all of whose concerns were attended to by Nana Opoku Asamoah, *Asantefohene* (surrogate leader of Asante people in the United States) from 1989 to 1992. The first *Asantefohene* was enstooled in 1982, and in that line of leadership, the forty-one-year-old Asamoah, who hails from a cocoa-farming family in Ghana, provides leadership to the Asanteman Association, which helps new Akan immigrants settle marital and legal challenges, those without kin create a sense of belonging, and Asante youth develop a full appreciation of their culture so as not to lose "sight of their culture in the melting pot of New York."

Unlike in Ghana, Nana Asamoah was chosen by way of an election in the association and ceremonially enstooled in May of 1989, with Ghanaians of distinct cultural groupings coming from Chicago, the District of Columbia, Los Angeles, and Canada to partake in the ceremony. Culture remained one of Nana Asamoah's top priorities, and to that effect, the association under his leadership envisioned the establishment of a school so that the children would learn to "dress properly" and "master the Ashanti language, our dances and drumming." Interestingly, that apparent attention to indigenous Akan culture and Otelia's rare *bragoro* rite did not involve or consider involving those diasporic Africans who engaged in Akan culture and its attendant spirituality. In the places where the Asanteman Association has branches one finds a number of Akan shrine houses or organizations that base their existence on the practice of "Akan religion" and culture, and these organizations are located largely on the East Coast from Florida to New York, as well as in California and Canada. However, there was no dialogue between two groups of people who claimed to engage in relatively the same cultural praxis. In fact, Onipa Abusia, "an Akan religious organization" based upon the founding philosophy of Nana Dinizulu and now led by

two women founders of Bosum Dzemawodzi, were not a part of ceremonies like Otelia's, and it is highly unlikely they would have been invited as guests. However, during Nana Dinizulu's leadership of Bosum
Dzemawodzi, quite a number of people from Jamaica, Puerto Rico,
Haiti, Cuba, Nigeria, Ghana, and Sierra Leone came to and participated
in Bosum Dzemawodzi activities and healing services, and some
became official members, while others of Akan cultural origin were
active in *akom* and other spiritual ceremonies in the 1970s and 1980s.
Most of these (diasporic) Africans felt their participation in those
activities and in the organization helped in the transition from their
homelands to North America and fostered a substantive sense of family
and community.

     In South Florida, each of two Jamaican-born women became, ac-
cording to one report, "a graduate Okomfo (priest) in the African religion of Akom" in 2007. The two women, Akua Bakofoa (Nyoka
Samuels) and Afua Fofie (Carol L. Miller), went through "three years
of intense study and sacrifice" and were trained by Nana Mena Yaa,
"chief priest for the Nana Adade Shrine in South Florida." One attendee
at the women's graduation ceremony was Abenaa Mensah, who commented that her family was "very religious" and that her "grandfather
was an Okomfo in Jamaica." In lieu of reports that say otherwise, we
are left to conclude that Akan persons who have settled in South Florida
and are perhaps one or two generations removed from Ghana did not
participate in the *akɔmfoɔ* graduation ceremony. Particularly when we
consider that the vocation of Akan spiritualists is premised upon service
to one's community, the questions raised are as follows: Whose community will these "representatives" serve? And is the culture that they
claim best served this way? The opportunity for dialogue was left to osmosis rather than seized by both diasporic Africans and Akan migrants.
Unfortunately, even scholars of the "new African diaspora" in North
America fail to grasp the significance of diasporic discourses structured
around Akan culture and spirituality rather than matters of chieftaincy.
For example, in a recent collection titled *The New African Diaspora in
North America*, one contributor who focused his discussion on the import of Asante chieftaincy in North America devoted less than a page
to the singular phenomenon of diasporic African enstoolment in Asante

communities in Ghana as "development chiefs and queen-mothers," with no attendant discussion of the latter's engagement with Akan spiritual practices or its larger cultural orbit. To be sure, the graduation ceremony of two Jamaican-born *akɔmfoɔ*, and that of Otelia's, demonstrates that the politics of cultural identity—and the claims that underpin it—is not simply a diasporic African preoccupation as scholars would lead us to believe, but rather such matters matter to Africans in Ghana, in North America and Canada, and in places populated by longstanding diasporic African communities and new arrivals.

Missed opportunities to engage such attendant matters at the personal, organizational, or academic level, however, are not simply a North American failing. Those who study the Akan in Canada suffer from a similar shortsightedness, especially in social climates where both diasporic Africans and Akan immigrant communities share experiences of institutionalized racism and occupy seemingly inflexible underclass positions. Again, this shortsightedness has its origins in the supposition that *only* diasporic Africans or "blacks" in the Americas are engrossed in identity politics and, specifically, issues of locating an "African" cultural identity and thus a "homeland" in which to anchor that identity. The Akan case, especially those abroad, contradicts that belief. As in North America, the 1980s witnessed waves of Ghanaian and specifically Akan immigrants forming associations in Canada that were similar to other forms of mutual aid associations among enslaved Africans during past centuries; these organizations were also in the tradition of rural–urban migrants in Ghana who formed associations, thereby creating "diasporas" in towns and urban centers. As was the case for Nana Opoku Asamoah of the Asanteman Association in North America, cultural concerns have been central to the existence of these Canadian-based associations. Those concerns include issues of socialization in a foreign land, language acquisition and maintenance, and the transmission of culture, traditions, and histories. Yet, it appears that "ethnic associations," which address those cultural concerns, wane as members become more economically mobile and seek partnership with the established order and its views and values. In turn, these seekers acquiesce to the European-based ethos of Canada and North America—in terms of language, religion, aspiration, and popular culture (among the youth)—

and find themselves grappling with the contested demands of an "African" cultural identity and that of Americanization—matters diasporic Africans know all too well.

In the early twenty-first century, more than three million Ghanaians were living abroad. Most emigrated on their own volition and remained within West Africa, and only fourteen and ten percent, respectively, made North America and Europe their destination. As of 2006, approximately 56,112 Ghanaian immigrants resided in Britain and 84,274 in North America, and these numbers formed the highest estimates of the Ghanaian-born population in non-African countries. In the places where Akan immigrant communities are located in North America and Britain, one also finds recent and longstanding diasporic African communities—some the descendants of Akan ancestors who populated the Americas since at least the seventeenth century. Unlike the internal dialogues amongst Akan and other Africans that created pathways for cultural continuity and transformation in the Americas, most efforts to enshrine and perpetuate Akan culture abroad have lacked a communicative process that includes diasporic Africa, even though both share the same cultural concerns and existential challenges. Indeed, a single, diasporic African identity never existed, but neither have there been nor is there is specific Akan identity, for the "Akan" were constituted by numerous and distinct clans (*mmusua*) who came to share a common language, spiritual and calendrical system, socio-political organization, and the like. Akan identity, like that of the diaspora, has been and remains a composite cultural identity forged through processes that identified "strangers" and assimilated "other" Africans into its communities, and assigned each a place in that composite web of belonging. In effect, the historic Akan in the West African forest and those who made the one-way crossing to the American diaspora formed identity and community through convergences and dialogue. Though the mechanisms of international enslavement facilitated the historic Akan diaspora in the Americas, recent Akan and diasporic African peoples continue to encounter each other in sites of memory, in neo-European nations that profited from enslavement, and in and around the "slave dungeons" that marked the departure from homelands.

Slave Castles and Claims to a Cultural Identity and Praxis

Akan spiritual culture and political leadership in the Americas have contributed decisively to a composite and unfolding African diaspora since
at least the seventeenth century. That contribution was facilitated by a
largely internal dialogue among distinct and kindred strands of African
cultural identities. Ironically, that conversation is recurring yet again,
but on different terms and with different meaning, as the "slave castles"
of Ghana become contested sites of encounter and reinterpretation.

Akan peoples in their homeland are becoming increasingly Christianized—claiming an "amputated" version of an Akan identity constituted by its spiritual culture—and they are leaving in appreciable
numbers. Yet, meanwhile, diasporic Africans are engaging in Akan cultural institutions and spiritual practices in their returns to Ghana. The
diasporic Africans who have entered Ghana as tourists, businesspersons,
teachers, Fulbright and study-abroad participants, and repatriates have
almost all found their way to the Elmina and Cape Coast castles at some
point during their stay. Most often, these diasporic Africans encounter
the Fante and other Twi-speaking peoples situated on the coast and
whose settlements surround an Elmina castle that embodies layered
identities—as a trading post, dungeon for the enslaved, military fortifi-
cation, colonial administrative center, prison, school, and office.

The Fante and other Ghanaians see diasporic Africans as tourists and
tourism as primarily a path to "development" and generally are uncon-
cerned with the so-called "slave trade" or slavery in their own historic
backyard. An acute silence suffocates the topic in public discourse. Perhaps that silence is linked to specific Fante and larger Akan roles in the
international enslavement enterprise. Diasporic Africans, however, view
"the castles as sacred ground not to be desecrated," and, for them, confronting the castles is confronting lived histories and memories embedded in collective experiences. It is, therefore, not surprising that many
break down and cry not out of performance or pity but rather out of an
equally real need to engage and embrace that history so painful—in
order to heal. The contestation between diasporic Africans and the Akan
over the meaning of the Elmina castle goes beyond a divide between
the two. It is rather about vested interests in the interpretation of the re-

stored castle and about whose story should be told: Dutch tourists are interested in the period when the castle was under Dutch rule, British tourists in British colonial rule, Asante persons in the room that housed Nana Agyeman Prempeh I, whom most Ghanaians see as a symbol of resistance to British colonialism, and diasporic Africans in all of these.

For many diasporic Africans who come to Ghana and are not unilaterally concerned about slavery or its implications, they all, at some point in their visit or residence, are referred to as "oburoni," a term that is generally used as a synonym for "European" or "white man." Although that rendering is far removed from the idea of "lagoon person" (*buro*, "lagoon"; -*ni*, suffix for "person") and the connotation of "foreigner" or "stranger" from beyond the southern extreme of the Akan world, it has assumed pejorative powers, especially when applied to diasporic Africans. "Oburoni" is applied unevenly to refer to some non-Ghanaians and even children and adults born in Ghana but of light complexion or with curly hair. Even the Maroons of Jamaica use the term for non-Maroon persons. In all this, one wonders about the intent and frequent use of the term for diasporic Africans in contradistinction to efforts like the Joseph Project, spearheaded by the Ghana Ministry of Tourism and Diaspora Relations. The Joseph Project is rooted in the biblical character of Joseph and, according to Jake Obetsebi Lamptey of the Ministry of Tourism and Diasporan Relations, involves a series of activities and events that encourage diasporic African investment and missionary work in Ghana, the country that purportedly serves as the gateway to an African homeland. At the same time, those who work with the Joshua Project—a Christian fundamentalist organization that is premised on spreading passion for "God" through Jesus Christ and that monitors and strongly encourages the proselytization of those "unsaved" peoples of the world—would certainly find much support for their efforts in the Joseph Project.

The Joseph Project and the efforts of the Ministry of Tourism and Diasporan Relations reveal that their efforts are not too dissimilar from those of Nana Amoah, Chief Alfred Sam, and others who sought the technical knowledge and skills of Western import through diasporic Africans. Ghana has translated few of its pan-African claims and calls from Marcus Garvey or W. E. B. Du Bois into the long-awaited dual citizenship for those from the diaspora; nor has it institutionally re-vamped its curricula, broken the silence on slavery in the public dis-course, or seriously engaged its own yoke of neocolonialism and evangelical fanaticism so that an internal dialogue among those con-cerned can occur. Recall that Chief Sam's movement in the early twen-tieth century, if nothing else, reveals that diasporic Africans in North America have provided a powerful lens with which to apprehend the deep contradictions of black life in white-controlled societies, including the quest for partnership with and full acceptance by the latter. In that context, the governing views and values of Ghana drive the country's quest for partnership and full acceptance in the global capitalist world, yet they ignore the global networks of racism and inequity—as well as how those networks extend into the commonly held views of ordinary Ghanaians, who employ "oburoni" without awareness of its implica-tions.

Diasporic Africans do, however, find two layers of racism in Ghana through multiple encounters, or even a single one: Certain Ghanaian proprietors will routinely serve or offer service to whites before dias-poric Africans and, in doing so, will call the latter and not the former "oburoni," though both might be "foreigners." This situation reflects an overt and an internalized racism that diasporic Africans know all too well, and this knowing is compounded by the payment of monthly fees, periodic stamping of passports, and other obligations diasporic Africans must fulfill in order to remain in Ghana, "the gateway to Africa." The diasporic African presence in Ghana also raises key issues of culture, for the enslavement experiences of both Akan and diasporic ancestors have become commodified as highly commercial spectacles for tourists, whose interest in indigenous culture may lead to the same among the local population, but that culture is largely performing arts and festivals, which disclose much of the deep-seated conflict between indigenous culture and Christianization. A number of "chiefs" and persons who benefit from these festivals in terms of exposure and some tourism rev-enue are Christians, and conflict arises when those who accrue and an-ticipate such benefits are required to engage in an indigenous culture of a non-Christian character—for example, pouring libations to the an-cestors and the *abosom* and completing attendant sacrifices. The predicament of these "chiefs" and others is no different from that faced by Westernized and Christianized intellectuals of the nineteenth- and twentieth-century Gold Coast, who sought to partner with the colonial order through traditional offices and institutions but without a commitment to the cultural outlook and values that underpinned those institutions and without contradicting too many of their Christian claims.

These issues of culture and commodification provide an important background against which to examine the Ghanaian government's encouragement of diasporic Africans to think of Africa in general and Ghana in particular as a "home" to visit, invest, and even retire. As such, it has marketed this idea to its target audience without a concurrent sensitizing of Ghanaians, who regard many of their diasporic compatriots as "rich tourists," "white foreigners," or both, in spite of official pronouncements to not treat them as "whites." The irony of this pronouncement is that Europeans or whites are not explicitly or publicly viewed in pejorative terms (e.g., *oburoni*) rooted in an internalized racism. In addition, beyond the diasporic Africans who visit Ghana as "tourists," there is an African American Association of Ghana and a Ghana-Caribbean Association, and thousands live in the country as neither "rich tourists" nor "white foreigners."

Perhaps the most recent outward display of Ghana's diaspora marketing occurred in 2007, when the country celebrated its fiftieth anniversary of political independence and the bicentennial of the British abolition of the "slave trade." Yearlong events, including rituals to ceremonially provide proper burial to millions of Africans who died during the international enslavement enterprise, marked a sort of euphoria for Ghana in 2007. These celebrations, designed and funded by the government and civic and business leaders, received their share of praise and criticism for how much of the national body was included and how distinct cultures were incorporated into the celebratory events, including the issue of ownership of "Independence Day." Few discussions or analyses, however, focused on how diasporic Africans in Ghana and in the American diaspora viewed the events and their meaning or the symbolism embedded in the literal "whitening" of the very "slave castles" that functioned as ports of nonconsensual departure and the seat of government. Here, restoring the Cape Coast Castle in the interests of tourism and diaspora marketing has meaning that is more than symbolic. Like Elmina Castle, its Cape Coast sibling had been repainted white in a restoration process that produced similar kinds of contested responses, as noted earlier in the Elmina case. Haile Gerima's film *Sankofa* is introduced and ends with pivotal scenes at Cape Coast Castle and features Akan, as well as diasporic African, actors in a journey of transformation, enslaved African rebellions, segmentation and hierarchy among enslaved African peoples, slavery as religiously sanctioned, intra-African violence sponsored by plantation owners and agents, rape of African women, and maroonage. In an interview, Gerima made the following statement:

> I, myself, have gone through an amazing spiritual transformation in doing this film. And most of the actors, too. To be sitting in the dungeon for hours to shoot a film and still smell the stench of the history of hundreds of years ago is not an easy experience.... I asked a Ghanian [*sic*] woman to pour libation [to help with problems associated with filming *Sankofa*], and this is something I had forgotten for years though we do it at home [in Ethiopia] ... throughout the shooting in Ghana, the drummer, who is a high priest, continued to pour libation, and I feel there was more power for that reason to finish the film.

For diasporic Africans, the castles and forts that line Ghana's coast bring to mind the composite of processes and experiences that a thematic part of the film *Sankofa* narrates and to which they and their ancestors were bound. Thus, as Obiagele Lake argues, "many diasporic peoples view themselves as parts of a larger African community in spite of and in resistance to political and cultural hegemony which represents these populations as bounded ethnic entities." Most expatriates view themselves as Africans and as diasporic Africans, while they remain clear about "cultural differences and the consequences of these differences in everyday encounters." In 1989 there were approximately 120 expatriates (mostly from North America and the Caribbean) living primarily in the Accra region and but also in Kumase, and some have been residents since the 1960s. Most have married indigenous spouses (with children integrated into both worlds), and the issue of their cultural acceptance (or lack thereof) is not especially dissimilar from that of other cultural groups in Ghana who do not originate in the American diaspora.

Diasporic Africans, such as Nana Dinizulu and others who root their cultural identity in an ancestral claim, are no less (or more) "African" than those who have been historically called or self-identified as African and whose claims associated with cultural identity often reference a longstanding ancestry that emerged in Africa. African studies as a field of inquiry has yet to deal adequately with the calculus of how cultural development processes that span thousands of years have shaped not only identities in specific locales and among kindred and differentiated African peoples, but also the meaning or supposed transmutation of those identities in their historically recent interactions with Europeans and the Americas. A number of scholars have built careers on the term "Africa(n)" as a linguistic import or an invention, but few have moved us beyond that frontier without resorting to nihilistic and postmodernist jargon that is unintelligible and difficult to digest. It was of little consequence or meaning if an African was a Stone Age or an Iron Age person, a hunter-gather or a pastoralist, Nilotic or Bantu, sub-Saharan or Congolese, or Hottentot or Pygmy during the greater part of a relatively mapped human history. These racialized constructs and academic conventions came to be once the greater part of Africa had more pervasive and largely disruptive encounters with Europeans and Asians and once Europe "invented" the historian, who, in turn, did much to reinvent the world and others in it.

Arguably, diasporic discourses have forced an urgent reexamination of the African cultures and cosmologies that continue to place a far-reaching emphasis—across artificial borders and colonial languages—on ancestry as a powerful basis for cultural identity, clan constitution, the rights and privileges thereof, the construction of lineages and genealogies, leadership and contestation of power, and the like. This is certainly the case for the Akan, whose very cosmology, spiritual values, and ethos have always been deeply anchored in a dialogue between its indigenous conceptions of a "Creator" and an ancient ancestress, which in fact remains the basis of Akan matrilineality and the construction of a composite spiritual-ideational-material culture in Akan societies. Thus, Nana Dinizulu could claim Gã, Akan, and another cultural group or its spiritual values, as part of an African identity that is largely a composite identity formed not the least out of the convergences of varied clans over the vast African landscape, across time, and via sophisticated trade routes and networks, roadways, and waterways. One of the biggest historical fallacies is that such convergences occurred because of the so-called slave trade, a process that supplanted all other processes of disaggregation and reconstitution and wherein distinct African groups were forced to find commonality and interact in ways unknown before. This could not be so far from the historical record and the cultural self-understandings of African societies, such as those of the Akan, as they have moved through their histories.

African movement is perhaps one of the most neglected dimensions of African history, and this is understandable by virtue of the very clear impediments that mitigate studying such movement in historical time-depth. Yet, we have sufficient evidence in the West African case of movements, interactions, convergences of lineages and spiritual practices, and the earlier formations of composite cultural identities that predate international enslavement and its aftermath. There is no reason, counter-study, or evidence to unequivocally state or suggest that these processes could not have taken place much earlier in time in ways that they did in later centuries and are continuing to do during the present epoch. The movement of proto-Akan and Akan peoples in the West African forest and in interactions with savanna- and forest-based peoples began much earlier than what scholars have been willing to concede, but, unlike the peoples of the West African savanna who were Islamized in varying degrees, and the Christianized peoples of the Kôngo kingdom and the nineteenth-century converts of the bights of Bénin and Biafra, the Akan came to the Americas (and remained in West Africa until the early twentieth century) with a distinctively un-Islamic and un-Christian spirituality rooted in a composite culture of indigenous origination. As such, the most enduring and constant element of Akan culture has been its spirituality as a proxy for the identity of that composite culture and its bearers. Since the mid-seventeenth century, key constituents of a composite Akan culture and spirituality have been archived in the Americas in the form of cosmologies, rituals, sacred and publicly transmitted knowledge, and attendant social practices. These elements exist in the lives of diasporic Africans whose ancestors preserved memories and materials that some diasporic Africans have renewed through a contemporary engagement with what they understand as Akan culture and spirituality.

Conclusion

Diasporic Africans possess archived and renewed layers of Akan culture, and some self-consciously continue to learn an Akan language, spirituality, and its composite culture in close approximation. They have, somewhat clumsily, embraced a history and engaged a culture worth preserving, while the homeland part of the equation might soon be on the endangered culture list. Most who are conversant with the contours of Ghanaian society in general and Akan peoples in particular cannot but notice the rapid erosion of the proverbial beauty of the Akan language to an elite-sanctioned Anglicization process, an evangelical and fundamentalist Christianity that assaults the spirituality of a host culture and fulfills its quota of souls and proselytized converts, and a parochial schooling system and missionary curriculum with far-reaching tentacles. Further, we find a host of contradictions between high personal hygiene and ecological degradation, the loss of voluminous indigenous medicinal knowledge and healers who are vilified for possessing this wisdom, the whitening of the "slave castles" and African women's skin, and the selling of Ghana to foreign interests while marketing Ghana as the *gateway* for diasporic Africans to Africa. These exigencies have everything to do with the diasporic African, for, if nothing else and in spite of some of their own contradictions, they raise the necessity of another level of internal dialogue between diasporic versions of African or Akan culture and the incomplete cultural narrative of Akan peoples lodged between the Komoé and Volta rivers in West Africa. That dialogue is a cultural one that has to be historically situated and free of the performance or pretenses that characterize how African ministries of culture define culture, and tempered by a critical understanding of spiritual culture in the matrix of one's cultural identity.

John D. Y. Peel once posed a critical question for the study of African spirituality, specifically, of Yorùbá spirituality and its historically situated interactions with religions and cultures external to Africa. He wrote, "Concretely, the [question] is whether 'Yorùbá religion' is to be regarded as whatever religion(s) the Yorùbá people choose to practice or as religious practices of distinctively Yorùbá origin and character, wherever or by whomever they are practiced. In the former case the defining unit of analysis is Yorùbá society, in the latter it is certain given forms of Yorùbá culture." If we substituted "Akan" for "Yorùbá" the question would be no less valid. In West Africa, the identity of Akan culture and its spirituality was defined by distinctiveness, and though it shared some of the views and values of other African societies, it became Akan not out of sameness. The conclusion here is that Akan cultural identity was a composite in its early formation in the West Africa forest and in its interaction with other Africans who were assimilated into the Akan social order and gene pool through clan arrangements, thereby engendering a localized "diaspora" in the Akan homeland. That cultural identity was largely birthed by its spiritual culture as a "parent" to its ideational and material dimensions, and those Akan persons who made that one-way crossing of the Atlantic into the Americas disembarked with their spiritual and ideational culture and engaged in an "internal dialogue" with other Africans and the exigencies of their environments. That dialogue framed and still continues to shape an unfolding African diaspora in the Americas and around the globe. The ocean that facilitated the Akan encounter with Western Europe in the fifteenth century and the American diaspora thereafter is now a path that both diasporic Africans and their continental counterparts cannot avoid, but must traverse while engaging in a new dialogue on fully disclosed terms.

Asante History:
A Personal Impression of Forty Years

T.C. MCCASKIE

Thomas McCaskie is Professor of African History at the School of Oriental and African Studies (SOAS), University of London. He has written extensively on the history of As-ante over the past four decades and is the author of State and Society in Pre-Colonial Asante *(1995) and* Asante Identities *(2000).*

Imagination is not, as is sometimes thought, the ability to invent: it is the ability to disclose that which exists.
—John Berger

I.

[I was] invited me to write a short memoir of my forty years of involvement with Asante history, and to record my impressions of where we have got to now and where we might go in the future. This is by no means an easy thing to do. I have imposed two conditions on what I have to say. First, my own experience is central to what follows, as it must be, and I use that as a basis for broader commentary and speculation. Second, I have taken the decision not to write a bibliographical essay, which would hardly be comprehensive but would certainly be indigestible. Instead, I have refrained from writing this piece until I was physically removed from my own study and all it contains. I am writing this in the Tarn in south-west France, and there is nothing in the house that relates to the Asante past.

What follows, then, is a series of impressions, reflections on a people, place and past that have dominated my entire career as a historian. There are no footnotes. However, it is worth noting here that any such battery of references would have shown how far the study of Asante history has advanced over the past four decades. In 1972, as a postgraduate student, I published an essay on Asante in *Comparative Studies in Society and History*. I wrote this in the university library in Cambridge, and to this day remember my ambition was to read everything that was available and relevant to the argument. Youthful hubris? Perhaps. But the point is that then it was possible to entertain such a thought. This is no longer the case. Few of my PhD students now work on Asante. They say it would take their allotted three years of research time just to master the secondary literature. This may be true, but it is also a matter for regret. Asante historiography is richer, fuller and deeper than that pertaining to any other African culture, but there is much, much more to do.

This, then, is a work of memory. I bounce thoughts off my own experience. It is proverbial that memory is selective, incomplete and marshaled by shifting orderings of the self. I plead guilty along with everyone else. What I have tried to do here is to summon up those episodes and insights from my experience that still seem to be-at least today, and for now-relevant to thinking about the past and future of Asante history. There is no particular ordering to these observations beyond their status as a trace of how I think now about issues I have thought about on and off for years. A final view is impossible in its own right, and anyway it would leave me with a sense of wounded superannuation. My present research has turned away from Asante, for the first time but I think only momentarily, and it is perhaps the unusual liberation of distance that has coaxed forth the thoughts that follow.

II.

It is an overcast day in 1990. Baffour Osei Akoto and I face each other across the kitchen table in the old Manhyia palace in Kumasi. The table is heaped up with plastic shopping bags. These are filled with banknotes. This is payment from two foreign TV companies for the right to film when the Asantehene next displays the Golden Stool to his peo-ple. We work in companionable silence, emptying the bags, sorting the cash and counting it. In late afternoon the skies darken. Crashing thun-der announces a cloudburst. The rain falls in sheets. The kitchen is now unbearably humid. The banknotes are damply plastered together. We give up and go and sit on the porch outside. Brandy is produced. We drink and talk.

We have been talking on and off since 1968 when Akoto was sixty-four and a nationally famous politician and I was twenty-two and a stu-dent. When I met him he was much amused by my youth. He asked constantly what I was doing in Asante and what I hoped to learn about it. I felt that I was not being taken seriously, or at least as seriously as I wished to be. This rankled. I learned to suffer in silence over the years whenever he laughed and repeated the same question. It became a joke between us, a routinised exchange, but I found it patronizing. Now, as we sit drinking, he asks me yet again what it is I am trying to find out. Pent up irritation, alcohol or the weather—an opaque deluge rent by lightning—makes me want to end this game once and for all. But there is more to it than that. I want to justify to Akoto and to myself why it is that I keep returning to Asante.

I ask if he knows anything about Homer. He says he does, but I am not to be deflected and go on talking. I say the first word in the *Iliad*, and hence the first word in all western literature, is *mēnis*. It is used to describe the feeling(s), the mood of an insulted Achilles after a decade of war. But what does it mean? How is it to be translated? What are the ideas it encodes and the meaning(s) it implies? This has been argued over since the days of Bentley and Jowett. It is variously rendered into languages other than ancient Greek as anger, rage, wrath or fury, but every such translation is qualified by explanatory footnotes. Prudent in-tellectuals—Weil, Bespaloff, Carson—speak only of "force." This is because *mēnis* is the property of an alien, now vanished historical cul-ture. It lacks transparency in any other linguistic and cultural scheme. There can be no direct translation, for in its own cultural world the word encodes and implies elements of the supernatural, of the gift, welcome or otherwise, of the gods, of an enduring, all consuming blank rage, of a lethal energy, of a drive to kill that is both unwilled and narcissistic.

I tell Akoto that this is what I keep coming for—the historical under-standings that have shaped action within his own culture. He is silent. The rain has stopped. It is late and there is no time to tell Akoto how I came to this view of what I thought I was doing—or at least in 1990.

III.

I arrived in Ghana in 1967 as a Junior Research Fellow in the depart-ment of History at Legon. I had little intention of becoming an academic let alone an Africanist. It seemed an adventure, almost time out, and I was well paid by the British government. I thought my time in West Africa would sit well if or when I came home to take the Foreign Office examinations. Anyway, the idea was that I would lecture on medieval European history, of all things, so I talked about Bloch and Pirenne to what in hindsight were tolerant students. My other task was to research and write the History department's first M.A. by thesis. I did this over my allotted two years with the guidance of Kwame Daaku, Isaac Tu-fuoh, and, above all, Adu Boahen. Looking back, I can see that I was hugely privileged. My Ghanaian colleagues were tactful with and sup-portive of a very young man who really had no idea of what he wanted to do with his life. Two people proved crucial to my future plans.

The first was that Adu Boahen, beginning research on his sadly un-completed book on Juaben, took me off to Kumasi with him as a sort of informal research assistant, companion and "gofer." In truth it was not remotely love at first sight. After Accra, back then an aspirant and self-consciously "modem" postcolonial capital, the chaotic energy and sheer vibrant confidence of Kumasi took some getting used to. Accra talked; Kumasi shouted. Asante people were voluble in the extreme and noisily opinionated. Frankly, and unlike Accra, they expected you to be interested in them, and to adjust yourself to their lives. I coped—with Adu's help. I came to realize that Asante people's *élan* was grounded in, and indeed shot through with, an obsessive pride in and willing de-sire to talk about themselves, their culture and their history.

This was my first and only useful research methodology course. Long into the night every night, and often all night, with Adu and an ever changing cast of his friends, acquaintances and total strangers, listening to and trying to take in what was being discussed. Adu presided over a local version f a Plutonic symposium in Boateng's Bar near the Adom roundabout convenient for both the palace and Kejetia market. Anybody and everybody came in to talk, and in the days before Pentecostal Christianity, this involved prodigious amounts of alcohol. Two memories will suffice. One night two royal servants (*nhenkwaa*) reduced a packed room to tears by intoning what I had to be told was a dirge. On another occasion all talk was stilled by a duet of bellowing voices. Oaths were exchanged between the two protagonists and the police arrived. I was told that the matter at dispute concerned land ownership and first arose in the reign of Asantehene Kwaku Dua Panin (1834-67). I understood barely a word, but can see now that my nights in Kumasi with Adu were one of the formative influences of my life. It seemed to me that this was history as electricity.

The second key person was identified through my new appetite, acquired in Kumasi, to read about Asante. This was Ivor Wilks, who had left Legon for Cambridge the year before I arrived in Ghana. His justly celebrated essay on the "northern factor" in Asante history had a large impact on me, but the piece of his that really impressed was the chapter on Asante government that he had contributed to a volume on *West African kingdoms* (1967), co-edited by Daryll Forde and Phyllis Kaberry. To put matters plainly, this was a written vindication of the project of African history, and was immediately recognized as such by the book's reviewers. In it, Ivor combined archival and oral materials to furnish forth a grounded historical account of government in precolonial Asante. This was diachronic history in a continent still dominated by synchronic ethnography. It gave the lie to those many in the academy who still doubted the possibility of a truly African history. It was the real thing. I was hooked.

IV.

I did a Ph.D. with Ivor, starting in Cambridge, continuing in Chicago, and then finishing in London. It was on the life and times of the Asan-

tehene Kwaku Dua Panin (1834-67), a period I have since often returned. It was examined and passed in Cambridge in1974, and Ivor's
Asante in the nineteenth century was published in 1975, winning the
ASA-USA's Herskovits Prize. While all this was going on we talked
about where we might take research on the Asante past. It was a new
field and much needed to be done. It was clear that the structural and
institutional history of Asante politics—enshrined and commemorated
in stool or office histories, and in the many oral traditions and written
documents about their individual occupants—was a historical resource
without parallel in sub-Saharan Africa. So, with the support of a generous grant from the NEH in Washington, we set out to construct a proso-
pography—in the manner of late Roman and Byzantine historiography
—of Asante office holders and political actors from the seventeenth
century to the present. The tool used was blank 8x5-inch file cards, for
this was the era just before personal computers. We carded data on
named individuals from every oral and written source we could obtain.
This was the ACBP (Asante Collective Biography Project). It ran for
six years (1973-1979), published eleven issues of a bulletin on its research findings, and amassed some thirty-five thousand file cards.

The ACBP had purposes other than the core one just described. We
felt then—and I still do—that at one level the six years that we spent in
single-minded harrowing of the sources put into place an unequalled
instrument for studying and restudying the political dynamics of an
African polity. More importantly, at least to me, the ACBP was a fundamental learning process. In fleshing out the horizontal and vertical
links between individuals and cohorts our research took us far away
from the political elite into every stratum and aspect of the Asante past.
I had intuited in Boateng's Bar, and now fully understood, that the crucial articulation in Asante society was the exercise of power (*tumi*) in
all its diverse combinations of imposition and benefaction. Like it or
not, more a question for ethicists than historians, unequal reciprocities
lie at the core of Asante culture. Power is both oppressive and supportive, but all Asante people are aware that in their own culture there is
little usable oxygen outside of its workings. Here I am hazarding a
guess, but I believe the web forged by three centuries of *tumi* and all of
its ramified manifestations still defines, structures, and binds Asante

culture. "Joining power" remains a sure path to self-realization and success in Asante society, and the door to the career open to talent—best smoothed, of course, by connections—has been held ajar, but carefully policed, throughout Asante history. One commanding reason why chieftainship continues to survive is that so many people want to join its ranks, or otherwise associate themselves with its status and influence.

People today seldom do sustained research over decades in the same place. Funds have vanished, of course, and younger scholars now face hard career choices, constraints and directives undreamed of forty years ago. This is to be regretted. In my own experience it is the asking of new questions that makes research, and new questions evolve out of older ones. Continuity of research, I think, still offers the richest materials and best insights. It also nourishes the researcher through the contacts and friendships made over decades of visits to a given culture. Perhaps this is one reason why I am often stumped for an answer when younger colleagues ask me about how I went about "doing my research." The truth is I began in a world before academic plans and projects. I literally just looked at what seemed to me to be interesting or important and over time this became a self-reinforcing habit. One thing has led to another in an "organic evolution." I have been spared the business of defining topics and designing projects to frame questions to which answers must be supplied. Of course temperament plays a part here. I like to work and write on my own.

V.

In 1975 I was appointed to a post at the Centre of West African Studies at the University of Birmingham. I was to remain there until 2006. In due course, the university offered me a professorship of African history. I asked that my Chair be in Asante not African history. The reason will be plain to anyone who has read this far. I worked on a historical culture called Asante and not on Africa, and my colleagues and peers in ancient Greek or modem French history did not occupy generic Chairs of European history. So, I duly became the world's first Professor of Asante history. This was a small but gratifying victory over outdated prejudices, and hailed as such in Kumasi.

At CWAS my view of the kind of history I might attempt shifted. My colleagues there, and especially Cohn Flight (whom I had known at Legon), Paulo Farias, and, later but importantly, Karin Barber, played their parts in this shift. All were interested in culture history broadly construed in the aftermath of the "linguistic turn." All were interested in *mentalités* and in what de Certeau taught us to call the social history of everyday cultural practices. Other straws in the wind were Italian *microstoria* and German *Alltagsgeschichte*. Importing the insights of a historically renewed ethnography (and philosophy) into writing about the past chimed with my own temperament. As a student I was much more interested in the Annales, and especially its cohort of classical scholars—Gernet, Vidal-Naquet, Vernant, Detienne, Loraux, Veyne—and the medievalist Duby, than I was in the dominant but tired British materialist "school" of E. P. Thompson and his ilk. Among other things the *annalistes* (remotely echoing Michelet) seemed to suggest that the production of history was a quest for how to write as much as what to write about.

From the mid-1980s on my writing sought to push the envelope with regard to subject matter, approach and style. A piece I wrote in 1986 on Komfo Anokye drew an unusually large (in those days) postbag. I was praised for attempting to "open up" African history, and condemned for doing the same thing. "Guild" historians are, I think, conservative in relation to their discipline. Among other things, they seldom interrogate the fact that how they write history is in itself a historical construct, rooted originally in nineteenth-century German practice. I must admit that I was taken aback by the degree of hostility to experiment that was evident even in African history, a subject that barely existed when I was a boy.

I thought my own writing was becoming sharper and more questing. However, others disagreed, and most painfully for me Ivor Wilks. We had an infamous quarrel in print over a number of years, with extremely blunt language used on both sides. I accused Ivor of positivism; he accused me of postmodernism. We were both wrong, but I must shoulder the lion's share of the blame for this falling out for I initiated matters. Why? Leaving aside the callow Freudianism that declares one must overcome one's "academic father" in order to flourish, I think now—

as I explained then, but was not heeded—that I disassembled all of Ivor's work just because it was so powerfully modeled. It seemed to me at the time that, just as I was trying to open things up, here was a body of work whose whole architecture was about finality and closure.

Looking back I think I now agree with Elisabeth Isichei and others: Ivor and I were embarked on diverging trajectories, but over the long run these were complementary rather than mutually exclusive. My most lasting regret is that my writing at that time more or less self-excluded me from contributing to Ivor's *Festschrift*. Happily, however, reconciliation was eventually achieved and the two of us worked in tandem as part of the team that brought Asantehene Agyeman Prempeh I's *History of Ashanti Kings* to publication in 2003. I should add that it was the editors at the journal *Ghana Studies* that contributed much to the restoration of relations. Both Ivor and I contributed extensively to the first few issues, and both of us understood from these writings that we could still learn from each other.

VI.

In my quest to "make it new" I drew inspiration from the old. I have described elsewhere the impact made upon my thinking and writing by Isaiah Berlin. It is harder to characterize the equally important impact made upon me by Meyer Fortes. I knew Meyer only slightly in the later 1960s in Cambridge, where he was William Wyse Professor of Social Anthropology. I thought then that we had little in common, for wasn't social anthropology the author of that timeless customary present that infant African history was seeking to displace? Then, in 1979, family circumstance made me a commuter, teaching in Birmingham but again living in Cambridge. This time around I came to know Meyer well and to value him. I think that in his heart of hearts Meyer thought African history to be a quixotic subject at best. However, one might in Meyer's Grantchester house, my fellow guest Isaac Schapera suggested, in great good humor, that "the boy" (me) might be able to make use of "all that stuff you collected m Asante." I was puzzled, for I knew that the data from Meyer's Ashanti Social Survey of 1945-1946 had been donated to Cambridge University, catalogued by its African Studies Centre, and deposited in the university library. I knew this because I had read the materials on deposit. But I was misinformed. Meyer's donation had been made so that one of his postgraduate students might be paid to do the work of cataloguing. So he had given over only the materials that he had been able to sort. There was still a mass of boxed but unsorted ASS data in his home. And not only that, but Meyer's ASS co-investigator Robert Steele still had more than half of the project's data in his garage in Swansea, where he was Vice-Chancellor of the University of Wales. To cut a long—but to me very exciting—story short, I was in due course able to read through all this material. This was an ethnographic bonanza and it formed the core of my second book. I handed over copies I made of the Kumasi Market Survey files compiled by the ASS, a detailed inquiry into commodities, to Gracia Clark as an acknowledged expert in this area. I am sure she will make good use of this material.

Meyer was trained first as a psychologist and he carried this perspective over into his work among the Asante and Tallensi. In talking with me, he was able to impart a strong sense of the emotional grounding and shaping of personal lives among the Asante in the contexts of their kinship and jural domains. He talked, I questioned, and I learned a great deal from this dialogue. If the piece I wrote on *konnurokusem*—the Kumasi dynastic infighting of the 1840s to 1960s—succeeded in individualizing structural antagonisms, then it was Meyer who assisted me to these insights. He also underlined something I learned earlier from Ivor in an entirely different context. That is, the longer one works in and on a given culture like Asante, the more one develops a—what?—a "nose" for what is plausible and implausible. History is an art not a science, and hunches rooted in experiential knowledge are as often to be trusted as not. I still try to tell this to skeptical postgraduate students.

VII.

I have put off writing about Asante and its people for long enough in this short memoir. The place certainly would not suit everybody. To this

348 AKAN PEOPLES IN AFRICA AND THE DIASPORA

day Asante is a notably hierarchical society, avid for I money and every-thing else that supports status. It is an unequal, striving, noisy, and even bombastic culture with strong investments in its own sense of virtue. I have lost count of all the times I have been told what a misfortune it is for me that I was not born Asante. Putting all that to one side, and pace everyone who simply recoils from Kumasi's "in your face" style, I con-fess that for me its exciting fascination is as magnetic now as it was four decades ago.

Why is this? I can only answer by summarizing my own preoccupa-tions. Like Syme on late republican Rome, my chief interest is the fil-aments of power that move a culture through time. This is not at all an elitist perspective, for the possession of power or exclusion from it—to coin a phrase—affects all the people all the time. We may wish it oth-erwise, and well meaning academics generally do, but the wish is not the deed. I think that the Asante, like myself, are of the school of Thucy-dides; none, of whatever class or condition, would fail to recognize what is being said in the Melian Dialogue.

From Asante, then, to Asante people. I have spoken with hundreds of them in every walk of life, from three successive occupants of the Golden Stool to—a particularly memorable example—a naked "mad-man" who used to wander the grounds of Kumasi's National Cultural Centre. And yes, he too voiced views of the Asante past. Some individ-uals—Akyempemhene Boakye Dankwa II, I. K. Agyeman, [and] suc-cessive Manwerehenes—I spoke with for years or decades. Of all the very many Asante I have relied and depended upon, two very different individuals are, at least for my purposes here, representative.

For whatever reason I did not meet Nana Arhin Brempong (Kwame Arhin) until the early 1980s. He was then Director of the Institute of African Studies at the University at Legon and was soon to become a Minister of State as Chairman of the Cultural Committee under Presi-dent Rawlings. He was also, of course, a prolific writer on Asante. I learned an enormous amount from Kwame, some of it properly "acad-emic," but most valuably he provided countless insights into Asante lives and mores. His knowing asides could pin a character or dissect a family, never maliciously, but with an engaging weariness about the foibles of his fellow men and women.

A revelation came when he was enstooled as Nifahene of his natal village of Bare Kese. In truth this was a relatively minor office, but Kwame's pride in it told me more about the enduring significance of chiefship than any book has ever done. Kwame believed very strongly in the Asante maxim that "a man is made at the cannon's mouth;" that is, one must stand up and be counted. That is why, one day in the 1990s, I found myself going with him to a house in Kumasi's Mbrom quarter. We were paying a courtesy call on Peggy Appiah—the widow of Joe Appiah and mother of Kwame Anthony Appiah. At the time this was not the most popular thing to do. The Appiahs had been ostracized because of Kwame Anthony's disobliging portrait of the Asantehene Opoku Ware II's wife Victoria in his *In My Father's House*. The house was locked up and its residents nervous. I think it meant a lot to Peggy that we had publicly come to see her. Kwame was magnificent. Kindness itself, and he meant it. I asked later why he had insisted we paid this call. He said, "Tom, as you know, this is a society in which to be excluded is a kind of death."

I cannot leave the subject of Kwame without recounting our failed efforts to convince Baffour Osei Akoto to leave his papers to the Manhyia Record Office in Kumasi. This episode said so very much about Asante. We wheedled, we coaxed, [and] we offered Baffour a brass plate naming him as a donor on the door to the archive. But to no avail. Kwame was philosophical, saying that Asante dignitaries like Baffour had to think of their posthumous reputations and did not want "spies" fossicking about in their papers. Later, Baffour put the same point to me privately. He threw up his hands and said, "Look, Tom, you know what this place is like. I do not want people building themselves up by tearing me down. If I make my papers public I will certainly lose something." In the event, Baffour did make a selection of his papers available to Drs. Britwum and Donkoh of the university in Kumasi. The result was a biography that in no way challenged Baffour's views of himself.

The other person I want to mention is Nana Abass, founder of the Black and White shrine at Medoma in north Kumasi. In 2008 I published a paper about him and his work. What I want to say here is more personal. Nana Abass, a formidable exponent of self-help, incarnates something that runs powerfully throughout Asante history. This is what might be termed the *nkwankwaa* ethic of "self help," in which men without position or resources unite into a company or *kuo* to advance themselves. The political aspirations of *nkwankwaa* have been studied. What has not yet been analyzed is the impulse to generalized betterment or improvement that characterizes the lives of such men. Here is a rich subject for researchers, the drive to self-help—and self-expression—of a person like Nana Abass. The pioneering study here is Miescher's work on the *krakye* Boakye Yiadom of Kwawu, not Asante, for the matters I am describing are disseminated throughout the Akan world. Detailed biographical studies—or subjectivities, their creation and representation—is a promising way ahead for historians and others in Asante.

People are one side of my experience of Asante. The other, inevitably, is the archive. This is immensely rich, and during the decades I have worked with it its organization and ease of use has improved beyond all recognition. In the earlier 1970s, I obtained permission to work in the collections that eventually became the Manhyia Record Office. At the time these papers were stored in a dusty and neglected building within the Kumasi palace complex. Some of the records were shelved, if in no especial order, but masses of documents were simply piled up vertiginously against the rear wall of the building. Pulling paper out of this unstable ziggurat was a double adventure: one never knew what might be revealed, and one watched to see if the act of dislodgement might cause an avalanche. True, there was an air-conditioner, but it was broken and was home to a nest of irritable hornets. This is not the situation now. Funds raised by Legon's Institute of African Studies have wrought a miracle of order and access. Here I must mention the sterling efforts of the excellent archivist Tommy Aning, who turned Kumasi's branch of the National Archives and then the Manhyia Record Office into true scholarly havens.

Finally, here, photocopying machines. When I first worked in Kumasi the city contained precisely one such machine. It belonged to the manager of Barclays Bank DCO, and it was jealously guarded. At one stage I even played nine holes of golf with the bank manager just to get a few pages copied on his cumbrous and impossibly slow pride and joy. In those days notes were taken by hand. I think there was value in this, for one actually read the document at hand rather than just piling up hundreds of pages of unread photocopies. But perhaps such nostalgia is misplaced, for Kumasi is now a city of photocopying machines. I know, for I once had to buy a nice man in Bantama a new one as my overuse of his old one simply burnt out his machine. Photocopying now dominates the archival landscape of research. Mobile phones now perform a similar function in arranging meetings and talk. Here the improvement is very welcome indeed. I will leave for another day the tale of my month long battle in the 1980s to secure a landline for a Kumasi friend. Unbelievably I won, but then it turned out the new line could not be connected to the failing telephone system.

VIII.

... I said at the start that these brief notes were an impressionistic memoir. I am certain if I had written this in my study at home it would have turned out differently. I am equally certain that the outcome would be different if I had written it last week or next. But no matter. I have spent forty years of my professional life working on Asante, and I think there is some value in pausing to take stock. The conversation I had with Baffour Osei Akoto in 1990 is as close as I can come in a compressed space to describing why I still work in and on Asante. In recent years, however, there has been a reorientation in that work. I have reached a stage where I feel confidence in ranging over the whole temporal record of Asante history, from the seventeenth- to the twenty-first century. I have, for example, written about Kumasi's Kufuor dynasty, a story that starts with mid-seventeenth marriages and concludes in the Presidency of Ghana's Fourth Republic. I feel increasingly drawn to this sort of exposition, in which the Geertzian "thick description" of the workings of the past in the present, and vice versa, supply historical density and ethnographic nuance to argument. I think this is as near as I can come to embracing the current cult of "relevance." Surely, nothing can be more to the point than holding past and present up to each other and delineating the filigrees that bind them and the ruptures that separate them.

I am a wide, a very wide, reader of history, among many other things. This is an exercise in perspective and comparison. I have spent this summer reading my friend Chris Wickham's two massive recent volumes on early medieval Europe. Chris, now Chichele Professor of Medieval History at Oxford, is sure and compelling in his judgments and narrative. But what is most striking to an Africanist in these books is how very thin the documentary record is for long stretches of Europe's early Middle Ages. Medievalists have had to look—and look very hard—at evidence other than the written: archaeology, numismatics, topography, linguistics, material culture, and the rest. Now, the suite of such things that might prove useful to students of Asante will vary from those of the European medievalists. But, and this is the point I want to make, the history of Africa is a markedly—or even preposterously—youthful discipline. The study of medieval Europe is hundreds of years old and has more practitioners than Africa can presently count. However, the problem and challenges evident in the two fields remain remarkably, even intractably, similar. It might be said that African history over the past forty years has exhilaratingly learned to run. Now is the time when it must learn to walk.

I said at the outset that this would in no way be a bibliographical essay. But man, *homo historicus* included, is not an island. So I want to end by pointing to some of the writers on Asante who have recently made an impact upon me. This is not a beauty parade of the included and excluded, but quite simply a few notes on what I have read recently. Firstly, Gareth Austin's long awaited book on the cocoa economy in Asante was well worth the wait: it belongs, one senses, in that category of research whose effects will be slow-burning and profound. Secondly, the challenges set down by the work of Jean Allman and Richard Rathbone on Asante in the 1950s need taking up, again by those two authors and anew by others. Thirdly, Sara Berry has recently arrived from her distinguished research career in Nigeria to enlighten us about the vital matter of land ownership and use in modem Asante. Fourthly, and very importantly, a cohort of young scholars—Karen Lauterbach, Kate Skinner, Janine Ubink, Marlene de Witte, and others—are addressing new issues. Finally, and here I grant myself a wish, it would be wonderful if both Emmanuel Akyeampong of Harvard and Takyiwaa Manuh of Legon would turn to writing about their own culture.

Suggestions for Further Readings

Adjaye, Joseph K. *Diplomacy and Diplomats in Nineteenth Century Asante*. New York: University Press of America, 1984.

Allman, Jean. *The Quills of the Porcupine: Asante Nationalism in an Emergent Ghana*. Madison: University of Wisconsin Press, 1993.

Allman, Jean, and Victoria B. Tashjian. *I Will Not Eat Stone: A Women's History of Colonial Asante*. Oxford: James Currey, 2000.

Anquandah, James. *Rediscovering Ghana's Past*. Accra: Sedco Publishing Limited, 1982.

Antubam, Kofi. *Ghana's Heritage and Culture*. Leipzig: Koehler and Amelnag, 1963.

Arthur, G. F. Kojo. *Cloth as Metaphor: Rereading the Adinkra Cloth Symbols of the Akan of Ghana*. Legon, Ghana: Centre for Indigenous Knowledge Systems, 2001.

Austin, Gareth. *Labour, Land and Capital in Ghana: From Slavery to Free Labour in Asante, 1807-1956*. Rochester, NY: University of Rochester Press, 2009.

Boahen, A. Adu. *The Ghanaian Sphinx: Reflections on the Contemporary History of Ghana, 1972-1987*. New York: Ghana Democratic Movement, 1989.

Boahen, A. Adu et al., eds. *The History of Ashanti Kings and the Whole Country Itself and Other Writings by Otumfuo Nana Agyeman Prempeh I*. New York: Oxford University Press for the British Academy, 2008.

Brempong, Owusu. *Akan Highlife in Ghana: Songs of Cultural Transition*. Ph.D. diss., Indiana University, Bloomington, 1986.

DeCorse, Christopher R. *An Archaeology of Elmina: Africans and Europeans on the Gold Coast*. Washington and London: Smithsonian Institution Press, 2001.

Effah Gyamfi, Kwaku. *Bono Manso: An Archaeological Investigation into Early Akan Urbanism*. Calgary: Department of Archaeology, the University of Calgary Press, 1985.

Ephirim-Donkor, Anthony. *African Spirituality: On Becoming Ancestors*. Trenton, NJ: Africa World Press, 1997.

Farrar, Tarikhu. *Building Technology and Settlement Planning in a West African Civilization: Precolonial Akan Cities and Towns*. Lewiston, NY: Edwin Mellen Press, 1996.

Garrard, Timothy. *Akan Goldweights and the Gold Trade*. London: Longman, 1980.

Gyekye, Kwame. *An Essay on African Philosophical Thought: The Akan Conceptual Scheme*. Philadelphia: Temple University Press, 1995.

Hunwick, John, and Nancy Lawler, eds. *A Cloth of Many Colored Silks: Papers on History and Society Ghanaian and Islamic in Honor of Ivor Wilks*. Evanston, IL: Northwestern University Press, 1996.

Kea, Ray A. *Settlements, Trade, and Polities in the Seventeenth Century Gold Coast*. Baltimore and London: The Johns Hopkins University Press, 1982.

Konadu, Kwasi. *The Akan Diaspora in the Americas*. New York: Oxford University Press, 2010.

Kwame, Safro, ed. *Readings in African Philosophy: An Akan Collection*. Lanham: University Press of America, 1995.

Kyei, Thomas E. *Our Days Dwindle: Memories of My Childhood Days in Asante*, ed. Jean Allman. Portsmouth, NH: Heinemann, 2001.

McCaskie, T. C. *State and Society in Precolonial Asante*. Cambridge: Cambridge University Press, 1995.

McCaskie, T. C. *Asante Identities: History and Modernity in an African village, 1850-1950*. London: Edinburgh University Press, 2000.

McLeod, M. D. *The Asante*. London: British Museum Publications, 1981.

Niangoran-Bouah, Georges. *L'univers Akan des Poids à Peser l'or* [*The Akan World of Gold Weights*], vols. 1-3. Abidjan: Nouvelles Editions Africaines, 1984.

Owusu-Ansah, David. *Islamization Reconsidered: An Examination of Asante Responses to Muslim Influence in the 18th and 19th Centuries*. Washington, D.C.: African Studies Association, 1982.

Owusu-Ansah, David, and Daniel M. McFarland. *Historical Dictionary of Ghana*. Metuchen, NJ: Scarecrow Press, 1995.

Rathbone, Richard. *Nkrumah and the Chiefs*. Oxford: James Currey, 2000.

Ross, Doran. *Wrapped in Pride: Ghanaian Kente and African American Identity*. Los Angeles: UCLA Fowler Museum of Cultural History, 1998.

Ross, Doran H., and Timothy F. Garrard, eds. *Akan Transformations: Problems in Ghanaian Art History*. Los Angeles: Regents of the University of California, 1983.

Schildkrout, Enid, ed. *Golden Stool: Studies of the Asante Center and Periphery*. New York: American Museum of Natural History, 1987.

Valsecchi, Pierluigi, and Fabio Viti, eds. *Mondes Akan: Identité et Pouvoir en Afrique Occidentale* [*Akan Worlds: Identity and Power in West Africa*]. Paris: Harmattan, 1999.

Wilks, Ivor. *Asante in the Nineteenth Century. The Structure and Evolution of a Political Order*. Cambridge: Cambridge University Press, 1975/1989.

Wilks, Ivor. *Forests of Gold: Essays on the Akan and the Kingdom of Asante*. Athens: Ohio University Press, 1993.

Wiredu, Kwasi. *The Akan Worldview*. Washington, D.C.: Woodrow Wilson International Center for Scholars, 1985.

Yankah, Kwesi. *Speaking for the Chief: Okyeame and the Politics of Akan Royal Oratory*. Bloomington: Indiana University Press, 1995.

Yankah, Kwesi. *The Proverb in the Context of Akan Rhetoric*. New York: Diasporic Africa Press, 2012.

Yarak, Larry W. *Asante and the Dutch*. Oxford: Clarendon Press, 1990.

Acknowledgment of Copyrights

A. Adu Boahen, "The Origins of the Akan," Ghana Notes and Queries 7 (1966): 3-10. Reprinted by permission of the Historical Society of Ghana.

David Kiyaga-Mulindwa, "The 'Akan' Problem," *Current Anthropology* 21, no. 4 (1980): 503-6. Reprinted by permission of the University of Chicago Press.

A. Norman Klein, "Slavery and Akan Origins?" *Ethnohistory* 41, no. 4 (1994): 627-56. Reprinted by permission of Duke University Press.

Ivor Wilks, "'Slavery and Akan Origins?' A Reply," *Ethnohistory* 41, no. 4 (1994): 657-65. Reprinted by permission of Duke University Press.

A. Norman Klein, "Reply to Wilks's Commentary on 'Slavery and Akan Origins?'" *Ethnohistory* 41, no. 4 (1994): 666-67. Reprinted by permission of Duke University Press.

Sam Spiers, "From European Contact to the Komenda Wars: The Eguafo Kingdom during the Height of the Gold Trade" (a revised chapter drawn from his unpublished dissertation, "The Eguafo Kingdom: Investigating Complexity in Southern Ghana," Syracuse University, 2007). Used by permission of the author.

Ray A. Kea, "Zones of Exchange and World History: Akani Captaincies on the Seventeenth Century West African Gold Coast" (revised unpublished conference paper). Used by permission of the author.

Stefano Boni, "A Precolonial Political History of the Sefwi Wiawso *Oman*," *Ghana Studies* 4 (2001): 139-68. Reprinted by permission of the author and the editors of the journal.

Pierluigi Valsecchi, "Formation des etats et alliances intercommunautaires dans la Côte d'Or (XVIIe-XVIIIe siècles)," *Journal des Africanistes* 75, no. 1 (2005): 77-100. Reprinted by permission of the author and the journal, and translated from French by the editor as "State Formation and Intercommunal Alliances in the Gold Coast (17th to 18th Centuries)."

James Sanders, "The Expansion of the Fante and the Emergence of Asante in the Eighteenth Century," *Journal of African History* 20, no. 3 (1979): 349-64. Reprinted by permission of Cambridge University Press.

Ivor Wilks, "Asante at the End of the Nineteenth Century: Setting the Record Straight," *Ghana Studies* 3 (2000): 13-59. Reprinted by permission of the author and the editors of the journal.

Kwabena Opare Akurang-Parry, "Slavery and Abolition in the Gold Coast: Colonial Modes of Emancipation and African Initiatives," *Ghana Studies* 1 (1998): 11-34. Reprinted by permission of the author and the editors of the journal.

Adam Jones, "'My Arse for Okou': A Wartime Ritual of Women on the Nineteenth-Century Gold Coast," *Cahiers d'études Africaines* 33, no. 132 (1993): 545-66. Reprinted by permission of the author and the editors of the journal.

Jean Allman, "Archival Fragments: *Ntamoba* and the Political Economy of Child-Rearing in Asante" (originally entitled "Fathering, Mothering and Making Sense of Ntamoba: Reflections on the Economy of Child-Rearing in Colonial Asante," *Africa* 67, no. 2 (1997): 296-320). Reprinted (with some revision) by permission of the author and Cambridge University Press.

Susan Benson, "Connecting with the Past, Building the Future: African Americans and Chieftaincy in Southern Ghana," *Ghana Studies* 6 (2003): 109-33. Reprinted by permission of the editors of the journal.

Lynda R. Day, "What's Tourism Got to Do With It? The Yaa Asantewa Legacy and Development in Asanteman," *Africa Today* 51, no. 1 (2004): 99-113. Reprinted by permission of the author and Indiana University Press.

Kwasi Konadu, "Diaspora Discourses," an abbreviated and revised version of chapter 6 in *The Akan Diaspora in the Americas* (New York: Oxford University Press, 2010). Reprinted by permission of the author.

T. C. McCaskie, "Asante History: A Personal Impression of Forty Years," *Ghana Studies* 10 (2007): 145-61. Reprinted by permission of the author and the editors of the journal.

www.ingramcontent.com/pod-product-compliance
Lightning Source LLC
Chambersburg PA
CBHW030810280326

41926CB00085B/160